THE
PATENT GUIDE
SECOND EDITION

THE
PATENT GUIDE

SECOND EDITION

*How You Can Protect and
Profit from Patents*

CARL W. BATTLE, ESQ.

Registered US Patent Attorney

ANDREA D. SMALL, ESQ.

Registered US Patent Attorney

ALLWORTH PRESS
NEW YORK

Allworth Press books may be purchased in bulk at special discounts for sales promotion, corporate gifts, fund-raising, or educational purposes. Special editions can also be created to specifications. For details, contact the Special Sales Department, Allworth Press, 307 West 36th Street, 11th Floor, New York, NY 10018 or info@skyhorsepublishing.com.

22 21 20 19 18   5 4 3 2 1

Published by Allworth Press, an imprint of Skyhorse Publishing, Inc., 307 West 36th Street, 11th Floor, New York, NY 10018. Allworth Press® is a registered trademark of Skyhorse Publishing, Inc.®, a Delaware corporation.

www.allworth.com

Cover design by Mary Belibasakis

Library of Congress Cataloging-in-Publication Data

Names: Battle, Carl W., author. | Small, Andrea D., author.
Title: The patent guide: a friendly guide to protecting and profiting from patents / Carl W. Battle, Esq., Registered US Patent Attorney; Andrea D. Small, Esq., Registered US Patent Attorney.
Description: Second edition. | New York, New York: Allworth Press, [2018] | Includes bibliographical references and index.
Identifiers: LCCN 2017052418 (print) | LCCN 2017056881 (ebook) | ISBN 9781621536277 (e-book) | ISBN 9781621536260 (pbk.: alk. paper)
Subjects: LCSH: Patent laws and legislation—United States—Popular works.
Classification: LCC KF3114.85 (ebook) | LCC KF3114.85 .B38 2018 (print) | DDC 346.7304/86—dc23
LC record available at https://lccn.loc.gov/2017052418

Hardcover ISBN: 978-1-62153-626-0
eBook ISBN: 978-1-62153-627-7

Printed in the United States of America

Contents

Preface

The world has seen a lot of creative people. From the late Apple cofounder Steve Jobs to the conventional garage or basement inventor, people like you are coming up with great ideas for products every day. These innovative ideas are essential to business and economic progress.

Have you had an idea for an invention or an innovative way of doing something that could improve productivity, create jobs, solve some long-standing problem, and make a lot of money for you and your supporters? Although coming up with a great idea or invention is often the biggest step, it is still only the first step. Several things remain to be done before you can expect to realize financial gain from your idea or invention. Many great ideas fail because the inventors do not take appropriate steps to protect, promote, and profit from their ideas.

First, you need to find out if your idea is original, or if someone has already produced it; there are many places you can check. Check stores and catalogs if your idea is for a consumer product. Check trade associations and trade publications in the field related to your idea or invention and visit relevant trade shows. Next, if your idea or invention can be patented, conduct a patent search and consider filing a patent application to protect the invention.

The chances that you are the first or only person to think of a particular idea or invention may be small. Even if you are the first to produce "the better mouse trap," nobody is going to beat a path to your door for the product. You must devote the required time, effort, and money to make your idea or invention successful.

The Patent Guide, Second Edition, provides basic and comprehensive information on making your ideas and inventions a success. This book includes easy-to-follow instructions, and advice on how to obtain a US patent on your idea or invention, information and guidance on using patent attorneys and agents, and methods for commercializing your invention. Additional topics are also included, such as dealing with invention brokers and promotion firms, maintaining confidentiality of your ideas, obtaining foreign patent rights, enforcing your patent against infringement, licensing opportunities, and many others.

The easy-to-use forms and step-by-step instructions allow you to handle patenting and commercializing your invention without hiring a patent attorney or invention broker. Depending on the complexity of the invention and your own skills, you may need the advice of a patent attorney or agent or marketing specialists. *The Patent Guide, Second Edition,* provides information that can assist in the selection of an attorney or agent and can help you get involved and monitor the patent and marketing process. Many expense-saving techniques are provided to help you minimize costs and maximize profits from your ideas and inventions.

Acknowledgments

To my wife, Charmaine, for all of your love and inspiration.
—Carl W. Battle

A special note of thanks to Lindette Hassan, friend and counsel at Fox Rothschild, LLP in Philadelphia for her support and contributions toward the completion of this project. Your support means a lot to me.

Finally, to my beloved husband, Shaun, I could not complete this or any other project without your unyielding support, encouragement, guidance, and good humor. Your partnership in managing our life and family has been tremendous. My achievements, both professionally and personally, could never have happened without you.

—Andrea D. Small

Introduction

New concepts and ideas come in many forms: a new book, product name, machine, chemical composition, manufacturing process, medical treatment, or ornamental design. All of these are considered "intellectual property," or "property of the mind," and you can buy, sell, license, and otherwise exploit intellectual property for value in the same way that you can other personal property and real estate. How you can protect and profit from your idea depends on the type of idea it is, the kind of legal protection that is available, how concrete and developed your idea is, and how effectively you promote and market your idea.

A bare idea is usually not protected by patents, copyrights, trademarks, or any other form of intellectual property. A concept is difficult to protect, license, or market, unless it is in a tangible form. An invention must be reduced to practice before it can be patented. An idea must be created via some medium, such as a book, a videotape, or a sound recording, before it can be protected by copyright. Trademark rights ultimately require use of the mark with some good or service. Thus, an idea merely carried in your head is useful to no one.

Some people occasionally confuse patents, copyrights, and trademarks. Although the rights of patents, copyrights, and trademarks resemble each other, they are different and serve different purposes. The differences between each of these rights are explained below.

A US patent for an invention is a grant of a property right by the government, acting through the US Patent and Trademark Office (USPTO), to the inventor, or to his or her heirs or assigns. The term of a patent is i) seventeen years from the date on which the patent was granted if the application was filed before June 8, 1995, or ii) twenty years from the date of first filing for an application filed on or *after* June 8, 1995. The term of the patent is subject to the payment of periodic maintenance fees. The right conferred by the patent grant extends throughout the United States and its territories and possessions, and is, in the language of the statute and of the grant itself, "the right to exclude others from making, using, or selling" the invention. A patent does not grant the owner the rights to make, use, or sell the invention; it only grants the right to exclude others from making, using, or selling the invention. Because the essence of the right granted by a US patent is the right to exclude others from commercial use of the invention, the patent owner is the only one who may make, use, or sell his or her invention. Others cannot do so without authorization from the patent owner. Thus, a patent owner can choose to manufacture and sell the invention or can license others to do so. Detailed information on patents is presented in chapters 8 through 12 of this book.

A copyright protects writings and other artistic creations of an author against copying. Literary, dramatic, musical, and artistic works are included within the protection of the copyright law, which in some instances also confers performing and recording rights. The copyright protects the form of expression rather than the subject matter of the writing. A description of a machine could be copyrighted as a written work, but this would only prevent others from copying the description. The copyright would not prevent others from writing a description of their own or from making and using the machine. Copyrights are registered in the US Copyright Office in the Library of Congress and additional information concerning copyrights can be obtained from the Register of Copyrights, Library of Congress, Washington, DC, 20559 (telephone 202-707-3000). Detailed information on copyrights can also be found in chapter 2 of this book.

A trademark relates to a use in trade of any word, name, symbol, or device that identifies the source of goods. The trademark indicates the source or origin of the goods and distinguishes the goods from the goods of others. Trademark rights can prevent others from using a confusingly similar mark but do not prevent others from making the same goods or from selling the goods under a nonconfusing mark. Similar rights can be acquired in service marks, which are used in the sale or advertising of services. Trademarks and service marks, which are used in interstate or foreign commerce, can be registered in the USPTO. Basic information on trademarks is provided in chapter 2. Before introducing the basics of patenting your invention, *The Patent Guide, Second Edition*, provides a requisite overview of how to make your ideas and inventions a success. The first thought of many inventors is to present their ideas to a big national company. If you do approach a company or anyone else about your idea, ask that party to sign a confidentiality agreement. The confidentiality agreement obligates the other party to maintain your idea in confidence and to not use or disclose it without your permission. If the other party refuses to sign a nondisclosure agreement, file a patent application for your invention before disclosing it. Present written terms to the other party, nevertheless, that any disclosures you make are in confidence and that you expect compensation if your invention is used. Important information on how to maintain the confidentiality of your idea or invention is provided in chapter 3.

You may be able to produce your idea or invention yourself. Working from your home and selling items on the internet or via mail order is a good way to get started. If you can start (or already have started) your own company, you will usually be better off, because selling your company may be easier than promoting an idea or patent to a larger company, even if your company is losing money. Starting a business to market your invention is discussed in chapter 16. Between the extremes of starting your own company and selling your company to a big business is taking your idea to small- and medium-sized businesses. Such firms may be happy to produce an item that sells in amounts too small to interest large companies. Thus, a small firm may be a better choice and more interested in trying to make your idea a reality.

Once you have looked at issues such as originality, production, distribution, and marketability, it's time to consider protecting your idea. If you do have a patentable idea, look into protecting it under the patent laws. To document your invention, ask a close friend (under a confidentiality agreement) who understands your invention to sign his or her name on a dated diagram or written description of it, or file a disclosure document or a provisional patent application with the USPTO. Taking one of these measures will provide evidence of the time you came up with your invention in case of a dispute with other inventors over who conceived the idea first. Filing a disclosure document with the USPTO does not give you patent protection, but it does provide evidence of your invention. Sending a registered letter to yourself describing the invention is useless as evidence.

Make a patent search to find out if the invention has already been patented. Chapter 8 provides information on determining the patentability of your invention. Search on a computerized database of patents, such as LEXIS, or at the USPTO in Alexandria, Virginia. The staff at the USPTO will assist in conducting patent searches and in using the facilities of the office. If your invention is complex or involves complicated issues, you may need the help of a patent agent or patent attorney to review the search results to determine whether your invention is patentable. Chapter 8 explains the details of using patent agents and attorneys.

If the invention has not already been patented or publicly known, you can prepare a patent application and file it with the USPTO. Specific information on preparing and filing a simple US patent application is presented in chapter 9. A US utility patent can be obtained on a new, useful, and unobvious process; machine; article of manufacture; or composition of matter; or a new and useful improvement of any of these.

The basic rule is that an invention is not "new" if the invention was patented or described in a printed publication, or in public use, on sale, or otherwise available to the public before the effective filing date of the patent application. There is an exception for public disclosures made by the inventor or his assignor (or by someone who obtained the information from the inventor or his assignor), where a one-year grace period is provided.

If you can show that your invention performs a function, it will easily meet the usefulness test. An invention can be useful even if it is destructive. For example, a gun or explosive is patentable even though its primary purpose is to kill or destroy. Typically, the most difficult requirement in establishing patentability is whether the invention is obvious. You cannot obtain a patent on your invention if it is obvious in view of earlier patents, publications or products (referred to as "prior art"). So, even if the invention is not identically disclosed or described in the prior art, it will be considered obvious if the differences between the invention and the prior art are such that the subject matter as a whole would have been apparent and perceivable, at the time the invention was made, to a person having ordinary skill in the art to which the subject matter pertains. Even if the subject matter sought to be patented is not exactly shown by the prior art and involves one or more differences over the most similar thing already known, a patent may still be refused if the differences would be obvious. The subject matter sought to be patented must be sufficiently different from what has been used or described before so that it may be said to amount to invention over the prior art. Small advances that would be obvious to a person having ordinary skill in the art are not considered inventions capable of being patented. For example, the substitution of one material for another, or changes in size, are ordinarily not patentable.

If an inventor is merely utilizing the teachings or suggestions of the published literature or prior art to solve a problem and no unexpected results are obtained, it is doubtful that the invention will overcome the obviousness test. The invention must be evaluated on the basis of how it relates to a problem, how it creates a solution, how it differs from prior art, and how commercially successful it might be.

Policy can prevent certain inventions from being patentable. Inventions suitable solely for the use of special nuclear material or atomic energy for atomic weapons are excluded from patent protection by the Atomic Energy Act. Remember that a patent cannot be obtained on a mere idea or suggestion; rather, a complete description and reduction to practice of the invention is required.

In addition to the utility patent discussed above, a design or plant patent can be obtained. A design patent can be granted to a person who has invented any new, original, and ornamental design for an article of manufacture. The design patent is effective for fourteen years and protects the appearance of an article but not features of structure or utility. A plant patent can be granted to anyone who has invented or discovered and asexually reproduced any distinct and new variety of plant. This includes cultivated sports, mutants, hybrids, and newly found seedlings, other than a plant found in an uncultivated state or a tuber-propagated plant such as the Irish potato.

Specific review and helpful advice on all issues regarding the patenting process are presented in Chapters 8 through 12. This includes information such as how to obtain foreign patent rights, how to enforce your patent against infringers, and what the licensing opportunities are for your patents and inventions.

While you probably still have to invest considerable time, money, and effort in your invention, you can get help from a number of sources. Patent attorneys and agents can help you make a patent search and file and prosecute a patent application, if you cannot do this yourself. Invention promoters are firms that offer—for a fee—to take on the whole job of protecting and promoting your idea. Invention brokers work for a portion of the profits from an invention. Invention brokers may help inventors raise capital and form companies to produce and market their inventions, and they often provide sophisticated management advice.

Other sources of help include invention and entrepreneurial centers located at university campuses. The National Science Foundation funds some centers and provides assistance for inventors and innovators. The Small Business Administration's (SBA) Small Business Institutes (SBI) are located at several hundred colleges and universities around the country, and they may provide the market research, feasibility analysis, and business planning necessary to make an invention successful. The Office of Energy-Related Inventions in the US Department of Commerce's National Bureau of Standards sometimes evaluates, free of charge, non-nuclear energy–related inventions and ideas for devices, materials, and procedures.

Inventor's clubs, associations, and societies are useful sources for networking, gathering information about patenting, and promoting your ideas and inventions. Such organizations might be located in your area. Talking with other inventors is probably the most helpful thing you can do. Don't forget that a big part of being successful with your ideas and inventions will involve being informed, learning from experience, and networking with others for advice and assistance.

The Appendix of this book provides helpful information on various sources of information, including publications, addresses, telephone numbers, internet sites, and other contacts that are useful to you in protecting and profiting from your ideas and inventions, as well as important patent laws and regulations.

CHAPTER 1

How to Profit from Your Ideas and Inventions

Do you have an idea to improve something that you know could be made better? Do you want to champion it, but don't know how? Keep reading. . . . There are several ways in which you can profit from your idea or invention. Realize that there is no magic formula for success with any idea and no certainty that any approach will guarantee your expectations of success. What's important is that you review and analyze all available options and take steps toward your goal. Your main objective is to realize a financial gain from your idea or invention, not to merely patent, copyright, or trademark it. Keep in mind, however, that protecting your idea or invention can be extremely important to your ability to profit from it.

Don't fall into the trap of thinking that because you are the first to think of an idea or the first to patent it, you will be guaranteed fame and fortune. Nothing could be further from the truth. Less than 5 percent of all patented inventions make money, and the percentage is even lower for small, independent inventors. Big corporations can spend millions of dollars on research and development before finding a commercial success, whereas the small inventor typically cannot afford to do so.

In order to profit from your invention, you need to develop a plan, be open to changing circumstances, and execute. This is no time for linear thinking, because there is no guaranteed route to success. Therefore, you need to be aware of available avenues to profit from an invention or idea. Look at the merits of manufacturing and marketing the invention yourself, selling or licensing the invention to a large company, or working with a small- or medium-sized company to produce your product, or a combination of all of them.

Once you have decided on which of the options you want to primarily focus on, you will need to consider the following:

- Have you documented your idea?
- Will your invention be profitable?
- What steps should you take to secure legal rights to your idea or invention?
- What are the ways to market and monetize your idea or invention?

Remember to be open to change, because you will encounter unexpected issues that will require you to change your plans. Some of these changes may include people who make other suggestions and/or offers to monetize your invention, changes in the technical field of your invention, changes in the law may either increase or decrease the value of your invention, changes in the market, such as an introduction of new disruptive technology that renders your idea or invention defunct, etc. You need to be nimble enough to change your plan or broaden it to accommodate a changing landscape.

DOCUMENTING YOUR IDEA OR INVENTION

Documentation of your idea or invention is important in protecting your rights. For example, thorough documentation of your invention can be helpful in proving theft of your invention and in avoiding disputes over ownership of the invention. If someone steals your invention, convincing documentary evidence will be the key in showing that you made the invention first and that the other party stole or derived it from you. An inventor often makes an invention while working for a company or is employed by a company after making an invention. In many cases, the company requires the employee to sign an employment agreement giving the company rights to any inventions made during the employment. Even without an employment agreement, a company typically has the right to freely use inventions made by employees on company time or with company resources. Again, proper documentation will be crucial in such cases in proving that the employee made the invention before starting his or her employment or without using company time or resources.

Documenting your idea can be as simple as getting the idea on paper and having it witnessed or as complicated as filing a patent application. You can start simple. Write a description and create a drawing (if applicable) of your idea or invention as soon as you have conceived your idea. Sign and date this documentation and also have it read, signed, and dated by one or more witnesses, who have signed a confidentiality agreement and also did not contribute to the conception of the invention. This documentation can be crucial to prove inventorship and the date thereof, in case of a dispute over who invented the item first. Look to chapter 4 for more details on this topic.

Another way to document your invention and gain some time to evaluate and test it is to file a provisional patent application with the USPTO. A provisional patent application is an abbreviated version of a regular patent application and is useful in establishing an early filing date for a subsequent regular patent application. Filing a provisional patent application is about one-fifth of the cost of a regular application and can save you money upfront. This type of application can be as simple as a power-point presentation describing your invention, along with how to make and how to use your invention. Additional information on filing a provisional application is detailed in chapter 9.

DETERMINE WHETHER YOUR IDEA OR INVENTION IS PROFITABLE

There are several approaches for evaluating the commercial potential of your invention. Evaluating the marketability and commercial potential of your idea or invention is important. Although this commercial evaluation is a continuous and ongoing process, the process should start before you invest time and money in an idea that may not be salvageable. All too often people spend countless hours and thousands of dollars on ideas that are not commercially feasible. The world may not want your "better mouse trap" if it is too expensive to build and maintain, or if there are not many mice to catch.

You can start by searching the internet, checking trade publications and trade shows in fields that relate to your invention. Learn what other inventors have tried and whether their attempts failed or succeeded. Visit the library and search catalogs and product directories for information about inventions similar to yours. Contact inventors' clubs and organizations, and talk to other inventors about problems and solutions in the field of your invention. Attend workshops and classes at universities and community colleges covering the subject matter of your invention, and talk to instructors about consumer and business needs for inventions such as yours. Consult with buyers and sales personnel in stores and shops that carry articles and devices that are similar or related to your invention. Talk to technical people, scientists, and engineers who work in relevant fields to determine if there is a real need for your invention.

Be careful about discussing or disclosing your invention to others without taking proper precautions to protect its confidentiality and proprietary nature. Before discussing or showing your invention to others, ask them to sign a confidentiality agreement wherein they agree to keep your invention a secret and not use the invention without your permission. This confidentiality agreement is extremely important to protect your ability to obtain foreign patents on your invention, because any public disclosure, sale, or use of your invention before filing a patent application will preclude you from patenting the invention. See chapter 3 for sample confidentiality agreements.

Never disclose your unpatented invention to any person or company that you do not trust. Rather, always try to deal with ethical and reputable organizations in discussing, evaluating, and testing your invention. Even reputable organizations may refuse to sign a confidentiality agreement before reviewing your invention. Despite this, it may be necessary for you to disclose your invention to these firms to exploit the invention commercially. If you are unable to get the other party to sign a confidentiality agreement, you should still indicate in your initial contact and in a follow-up letter that your invention was disclosed in confidence, and you expect that it will not be used without your permission and compensation. Refer to chapter 3 for further details on maintaining the confidentiality of your invention.

SECURING PROTECTION FOR YOUR IDEA OR INVENTION

Once you have determined that you can prepare a credible market value case and that there is profit to be generated from your idea or invention, you should consider securing your rights to the idea or invention. Assuming your idea involves a new invention, the mechanism to secure such rights is through a patent application. If on the other hand, your idea involves an artistic, literary, software, or other creative work, consider a copyright. If you have an idea to brand something to increase marketability, consider filing a trademark. Chapter 2 provides you with more details on the different protections offered and Chapters 8–12 provide you with detailed guidance on preparing and filing a patent application.

MARKETING AND MONETIZING THE RIGHTS YOU HAVE SECURED

If you decide that you wish to start your own business making and selling a product or service covered by your idea or invention, remember that prospective buyers are likely to understand a business much better than they would the technical details of your invention. Many business people are likely to believe that they have better business and marketing skills than you do as an inventor and can make the product profitable, if you have a good product. Also, many of them typically assume that when they purchase a business, some customers already exist and most of the bugs have been worked out of the product.

In resolving the issues above, there are a number of related factors that must be considered. Based on information from the Small Business Administration (SBA), the following list of areas is provided that might need to be evaluated for each new idea or invention:

- Potential market
- Length of time the product is useful
- Learning how to use the product
- How the product looks
- How the product functions
- How the product will be produced

- Investment costs
- Is there a need or demand for the product?
- How will the product be promoted?
- What are the potential sales of the product?
- How long can you maintain your market position?

This list is not intended to discourage you with your invention but to highlight the myriad of variables that may have to be considered before your invention can be successfully commercialized.

You can also consider selling or licensing your invention to a major company. After all, a big company usually has the funds, manufacturing capability, and marketing expertise to commercialize the invention and make it profitable. Most major companies, however, are usually not interested in unsolicited ideas from people outside of the company. In fact, many companies do not accept or consider outside ideas. First, they believe that their own research and development staff can do a better job at inventing than an independent inventor working out of a basement or garage can. Second, they are afraid that outside ideas or inventions will conflict with their own in-house research efforts. Many companies have become involved in expensive lawsuits with outside inventors to prove that the companies were already developing the disputed invention. Third, many ideas and inventions from outside inventors are simply too small in potential sales to interest large corporations. For example, your niche market of $1 million in potential sales is typically not appealing to a big company that is looking for tens or hundreds of millions of dollars in sales. Thus, trying to interest a large company in your invention will be extremely difficult.

Invention brokers or invention promotion firms with a proven track record may be helpful in getting your idea considered by a big company. These firms may already have established relationships with large corporations, investment capitalists, or other organizations interested in new ideas. Be careful when using invention promotion firms because many of them are a sham. Federal Trade Commission (FTC) investigations found that several invention promotion firms, charging fees of several thousand dollars, had more than 30,000 clients, but fewer than a dozen of these clients made money on their inventions. See chapter 6 for more information about invention brokers and invention promotion firms.

Besides selling your business to a big company, you should consider taking your invention to a small- or medium-sized company. These firms may be easier to approach than a big corporation, and they would be more likely to market a product with smaller sales volumes. Smaller companies may not be as sophisticated with marketing and distribution, but they can still successfully commercialize your invention and make it profitable.

Keep in mind that you need to be more than an idea person to be successful with your inventions. You need to be an entrepreneur, one who invents a product, finds backers for the product, and gets the product on the market. You need to be good at communication, negotiation, publicity, and networking. Most of all, you need to have persistence and good business sense.

CHAPTER 2

How to Protect Your Ideas

As we learned in the last chapter, once you have come up with an idea, no matter how simple it is or what type it is, you should always look at ways to protect it. Your ideas and creations are valuable property that you can protect, defend, sell, license, mortgage, or otherwise transfer for economic benefit. Here is where the value proposition of your idea comes into play. Just as you can build a fence or install an alarm system to protect your home, you can protect intellectual property rights to your ideas by means of patents, trademarks, copyrights, and/or trade secrets.

The term "intellectual property" refers to any creation or product of the mind. This includes ideas, inventions, methods of doing business, industrial processes, artistic works, writings, product names, distinctive packaging, chemical formulas, and anything else that is created by mental processes. The type of intellectual property you have created will determine what type of protection you can obtain for it. The five basic forms of protection for intellectual property are patents, copyrights, trademarks, trade secrets, and protection from unfair trade practices. These forms of protection for intellectual property are not mutually exclusive and often overlap.

People typically confuse the types of intellectual property protection without realizing that each is distinct and protects specific subject matter. A preliminary introduction to patents, copyrights, and trademarks was provided earlier in this book. A detailed review of the forms of protection for intellectual property follows. This review will help you develop methodologies for assessing your ideas and inventions and for seeking the maximum protection for your intellectual property.

WHAT ARE PATENTS AND HOW CAN YOU PROTECT YOUR IDEAS WITH THEM?

Perhaps the best form of intellectual property protection for your invention is a patent. A patent gives the patent owner the legally enforceable right to exclude others from making, using, selling, and importing the patented invention. A patent owner enjoys this right for the life of the patent.

Anyone who makes an invention can apply for a patent, no matter his or her age, national origin, mental capacity, or other traits. The inventor can file for a patent whether or not he or she is represented by a patent attorney or agent. Patents, once properly obtained, are usually given great deference by industry and the courts.

The patent is issued by the government through the USPTO. An official printed copy of the patent with specification, drawing, and claims is provided to the patentee. The patent confers the right to exclude others from making, using, or selling the invention throughout the United States and its territories and possessions for the term of the patent, subject to the payment of maintenance fees as provided by law.

The exact nature of the right conferred is the right to exclude. The patent does not grant the right to make, use, or sell the invention; it only grants the exclusive nature of the right. The patent only grants the right to exclude *others* from making, using, or selling the invention. Because the patent does not grant the affirmative right to make, use, or sell the invention, the patentee's own right to do so is dependent on the rights of others and any general laws that might be applicable.

A patentee, merely because he or she has received a patent for an invention, is not thereby authorized to make, use, or sell the invention if doing so would violate any law. An inventor of a new automobile who has obtained a patent thereon would not be entitled to use the patented automobile in violation of state laws requiring a license to operate the automobile, nor may a patentee sell an article whose sale may be forbidden by a law, merely because a patent has been obtained. A patentee may not make, use, or sell his or her own invention if doing so would infringe the patent rights of others. A patentee, by virtue of having a patent, may not violate the pure food and drug laws or federal antitrust laws through resale price agreements or restraints of trade. Otherwise, there is nothing that prohibits a patentee from making, using, or selling his or her own invention.

Because the essence of the right granted by a patent is the right to exclude others from commercial exploitation of the invention, the patentee is the only one who can commercially exploit it. Others may not commercially exploit the invention without authorization from the patentee. The patentee may manufacture and sell the invention or may license or otherwise permit others to do so as long as the patentee is not violating the patent rights of another party or other areas of the law.

According to the law, only the inventor may apply for a patent, although there are some exceptions. If a person who is not the inventor applied for a patent, any patent obtained would be invalid. The person applying in such a case, who falsely states that he or she is the inventor, would be subject to criminal penalties. If the inventor is dead, the application for patent may be made by legal representatives, such as the administrator or executor of the estate. If the inventor is insane, the application for patent may be made by a guardian. If an inventor refuses to apply for a patent or cannot be found, a joint inventor or a person having a proprietary interest in the invention may apply on behalf of the missing inventor.

If two or more persons make an invention, they apply for a patent as joint inventors. A person who makes a financial contribution is not a joint inventor and cannot be listed in the application as an inventor. An innocent mistake in erroneously omitting an inventor or in erroneously naming a person as an inventor can be corrected on the application.

The patent law specifies the subject matter that can be patented and the conditions under which a patent may be obtained. The law provides that any person who invents or discovers any new and useful process, machine, article of manufacture, or composition of matter, or any new and useful improvements thereof, may obtain a patent, subject to the conditions and requirements of the law. A process is defined as a process, method, or set of steps. A machine is a device or equipment for performing physical functions. Articles of manufacture are goods and products that are made, and includes all manufactured articles. Compositions of matter are chemical compositions and may include mixtures of ingredients, as well as new chemical compounds. These classes of subject matter include practically everything made by man and the processes for making them.

A patent cannot be granted for mixtures of ingredients, such as medicines, unless there is more to the mixture than the known effect of its components. The mixture must have synergy or some unexpected advantage to be patentable. Remember, a patent cannot be obtained for a mere idea or suggestion. A complete description of the actual machine or other subject matter sought to be patented is required.

The three types of patents that you may be able to obtain on an invention are a utility patent, design patent, and a plant patent. The most common type of patent is a utility patent, which covers the utilitarian features of an invention. Utility patents include patents on the functional characteristics of machines, apparatuses, electronic devices, manufacturing processes, chemical compounds and compositions, medical treatments, manufactured articles, and the like. If other requirements for patentability are met, consider obtaining a utility patent on the functional and operational features of your invention.

The utility patent is perhaps the most difficult type of patent to obtain. To receive a utility patent on your invention, you have to file a patent application that includes a detailed description (including best mode of practicing the invention) of how to make and use the invention, claims that define the specific elements to be protected, drawings of the invention where necessary to help understand it, an abstract, a formal inventor's declaration, and the required filing fee. A utility patent protects the claimed invention from infringing items that literally tread on the patent claims, as well as others that are substantially similar under the "doctrine of equivalents." A sample utility patent is shown at the end of this chapter.

A design patent protects the shape or ornamental or artistic features of an article. Unlike a utility patent, a design patent does not protect the functional elements of an invention. If a design has functionality, it cannot be protected by a design patent, even if the design is also ornamental. Some examples of designs that can be patented are unique bottle shapes, a computer screen display, an artistic lamp, an ornamental pin, a watch design, and the grill of an automobile.

A design patent has a fourteen-year term and protects against any design that is substantially similar to the patented design. A design patent is relatively easy to obtain if the design is new and nonfunctional. A design patent application is also simple to prepare and should include a preamble, a specification that explains the design, a single claim, one or more drawings, a formal inventor's declaration, and the filing fee. A sample design patent is presented at the end of this chapter.

You can file for a design patent and a utility patent on the same article. The design patent would be directed to the exterior appearance of the article, whereas the utility patent would be directed to the function of the article. You can also copyright your unique design, in addition to obtaining a patent on it. Thus, one form of patent or intellectual property coverage does not preclude another. Be sure to consider all the available options for protecting your invention.

The law also provides for the granting of a patent to anyone who has invented or discovered and asexually reproduced any distinct and new variety of plant, including cultivated sports, mutants, hybrids, and newly found seedlings, other than a tuber-propagated plant or a plant found in an uncultivated state. Asexually propagated plants are those that reproduced by means other than from seeds, such as by the rooting of cuttings, layering, budding, grafting, inarching, and so on.

With reference to tuber-propagated plants, for which a plant patent cannot be obtained, the term "tuber" is used in its narrow, horticultural sense as meaning a short, thickened portion of an underground branch. The only plants covered by the term "tuber-propagated" are the Irish potato and the Jerusalem artichoke.

An application for a plant patent consists of the same parts as a utility patent application, as discussed earlier.

WHAT IS A COPYRIGHT AND HOW CAN YOU PROTECT YOUR CREATIONS WITH IT?

Obtaining a copyright is another way to protect your artistic, literary, software, or other creative works. Unlike a patent that covers the idea, a copyright covers only your particular form of expression of the idea.

A copyright gives you the sole right to control the reproduction and distribution of your copyrighted work. You have the right to prevent others from reproducing the work without your permission.

Copyright does not prevent others from using the ideas or information revealed by your work. Copyright protects only the literary, musical, artistic, or graphic form in which you express your work. Anyone is free to use your concepts and create his or her own expression of the same concepts as long as he or she does not copy your form of expression. Copyright protection does not extend to names, titles, and slogans. These can be appropriately protected by trademark.

Always review your creative works to see if they can be protected by copyright. The federal copyright law permits copyright protection for the following seven types of original works of authorship:

- literary works
- musical works, including any accompanying words
- dramatic works, including any accompanying music
- pantomimes and choreographic works
- pictorial, graphic, and sculptural works
- motion pictures and other audiovisual works
- sound recordings

Literary works are works, other than audiovisual works, that are expressed in words, numbers, or other verbal or numerical symbols, such as books, magazines, manuscripts, directories, catalogs, cards, and computer programs. Musical works include written musical arrangements, lyrics, and songs. Dramatic works include written plays and any written music that is a part thereof.

Pantomimes and choreographic works include physical expressions and dance. Pictorial, graphic, and sculptural works include two- and three-dimensional works of art, photographs, paintings, sketches, prints, maps, globes, charts, designs, technical drawings, diagrams, and models. Motion picture and audiovisual works include films, movies, and video recordings.

Sound recordings, such as discs, tapes, and phonorecords, are works that result from fixation of a series of musical, spoken, or other sounds but do not include the sounds accompanying a motion picture or other audiovisual work. Works not listed above may also be protected by copyright if they meet the definition of "original works of authorship."

Copyright protection is only available for original works of authorship. The originality requirement means that the work must be the independent creation of the person seeking copyright protection. The test for originality is met if the work owes its origin to the author and was independently created and not copied from other works. The mere fact that someone else has created something similar will not prevent you from obtaining copyright protection on your independent creation.

The works of authorship must be fixed in a tangible form to qualify for federal copyright protection. The work must be in a form that can be reproduced or otherwise communicated. Thus, a mere idea or other abstract and imaginary creations cannot be protected by copyright.

A copyright originates automatically when the work is created, and registration is not required for copyright to exist. Your rights to enforce copyright, however, are maximized if the copyright is registered with the US Copyright Office.

You can register your copyright by filing an application with the Copyright Office. This involves filing the appropriate application form along with the required fee and deposit of your work. Detailed instructions for completing the copyright application and a copy of Form TX, which is used for registering nondramatic literary works, are provided in chapter 13. The instructions are also useful for Forms PA, SR, and VA, which are applicable for works of performing arts, sound recording, and visual arts, respectively.

A copyright is good for fifty years after the life of the author. For a work-made-for-hire via employment or contract, the copyright is good for the lesser of seventy-five years after publication or one hundred years after creation.

Some areas where copyrights and patents overlap include the shapes and designs of containers, devices, and apparatuses; toys and games; and computer software. Remember that an artistic bottle shape, for example, can be protected by a copyright and a design patent. A board game can be covered by a utility patent; the ornamental game board can be covered by a design patent and a copyright; and the rules, instructions, and packaging can be covered by copyright. Computer software can be protected by copyright, or it can be patented in conjunction with a process or some physical article, device, or apparatus. Now you see how copyrights and patents interface, and why you should consider them in protecting creative works.

Additional information on copyrights can be obtained from the US Copyright Office.

PROTECTING TRADEMARKS AND TRADE DRESS

Trademarks are probably the most commonly known type of intellectual property because we encounter them every day. Popular trademarks, such as Apple*, Xerox*, Coca Cola*, Listerine*, Plexiglas*, and GE*, are part of life in our home, in the office, or in public. Trademarks have become powerful forms of intellectual property protection, with some marks worth hundreds of millions of dollars.

Trademarks may also be important in protecting certain aspects of your proprietary ideas and invention. Although trademarks will not protect the idea or invention itself, they can protect a proprietary name or symbol used with goods or services. Often the success of a product depends more on its name and packaging than on the product itself.

A trademark indicates the origin or source of goods or services; it symbolizes or guarantees the quality of the goods that bear the mark. A trademark is any word, name, symbol, device, or any combination thereof, adopted and used by a manufacturer or merchant to identify his or her goods and to distinguish them from those manufactured or sold by others. Rights in a trademark are acquired only by use of the trademark on particular goods. The right to use a trademark is a property interest that the trademark owner can assert to prevent others from using the mark, or from using one that is confusingly similar.

Federal registration of a trademark is not mandatory, but it does provide major benefits to the trademark owner. To be eligible for federal registration, a trademark must actually be used in commerce or the owner must have a bona fide intent to use the trademark in commerce. The intent to use the trademark can be extended for periods of six months up to a maximum of two years: Intent-to-use is a good way of reserving a trademark with the USPTO. A trademark is deemed to be used in commerce when it is placed in any manner on goods or on containers, tags, or labels affixed thereto, and the goods are sold or transported in interstate commerce.

Federal registration of a trademark protects the exclusive right of the trademark owner to use the mark nationwide. Federal registration also gives the trademark owner the right to use the registration symbol, ˚, which may deter others from using the mark. Additionally, the trademark owner has the right to sue unauthorized users of the trademark for an injunction, damages, or recovery of profits. If the trademark has not been registered, you should use the symbol Ô to protect your trademark rights under state law.

The US trademark laws provide for the registration of trademarks on two types of registers: the Principal Register and the Supplemental Register. Trademarks that are created, arbitrary, or fanciful can, if otherwise qualified, be registered on the Principal Register. A trademark that does not qualify for registration on the Principal Register can be registered on the Supplemental Register, provided that the applicant shows that the mark is capable of distinguishing the applicant's goods and has been used in commerce for at least one year.

If all other requirements are satisfied, a trademark may be registered on the Principal Register, unless it consists of a mark that (1) when applied to the applicant's goods or services is merely descriptive or deceptively misdescriptive of them, (2) when applied to the applicant's goods or services is primarily geographically descriptive or deceptively misdescriptive, or (3) is primarily a surname.

As an exception to the general rules, marks may be registered on the Principal Register if they have become distinctive as applied to the applicant's goods in commerce. This usually requires proof by the applicant of exclusive and continuous use of the mark in commerce for the prior five years.

The owner of a trademark that is used, or is intended to be used, in commerce may register the mark by filing an application for registration with the USPTO. The application must be filed in the name of the trademark owner and comprise a written application, a drawing of the mark, three specimens or facsimiles of the mark, and the filing fee (as of

March 19, 2013, the fee was $375 for filing a paper trademark application and $325 for filing an electronic trademark application). A sample trademark application is provided in chapter 13.

The USPTO will allow registration of your trademark if all application requirements have been met and if your mark is not confusingly similar to other marks. If your application indicated a bona fide intent to use the mark, you must normally file a statement of actual use (along with dates of actual use, three specimens, and the required fee) within six months after receiving a notice of allowance from the USPTO. The mark is published for opposition after allowance is granted and, if no opposition is filed, the mark is registered.

Distinctive packaging or trade dress, in addition to unique advertising slogans, colors, jingles, architecture, or business designs, can also provide proprietary rights related to your product. Your use of these can give you offensive rights to stop others from using similar techniques that are likely to cause confusion with your products or services in the marketplace.

When creating a new product or service, always try to make the product name, packaging, and trade dress as unique and distinctive as possible. This uniqueness gives these features secondary meaning that is important in acquiring and enforcing trademark and unfair competition rights.

MAINTAINING TRADE SECRET RIGHTS

Keeping your idea or invention a trade secret may be another means of protecting valuable proprietary rights.

A trade secret is generally defined by many court decisions as follows:

> A trade secret may consist of any formula, pattern, device, or compilation of information which is or can be used in one's business, and which gives one an opportunity to obtain an advantage over competitors who do not know or use it, and which the law protects from misappropriation by others.

The subject matter covered by trade secret protection is broad. Almost any information or method used in business can be a trade secret if it is not generally known and if proper precautions are taken to maintain secrecy. For example, trade secrets can be applied to a formula, pattern, compilation, program, device, technique, process, customer list, business plan, method of doing business, and more.

The subject matter of a trade secret must be secret. Matters of public knowledge or of general knowledge in an industry cannot be appropriated as a trade secret. Matters that are disclosed by the goods that one markets cannot be a trade secret.

There are no precise rules for determining the existence of a trade secret. Rather, there are a number of factors that courts consider in deciding to recognize a trade secret. Usually, a trade secret must be novel and not generally known outside the holder of the trade secret. Courts generally do not require absolute secrecy, but a substantial element of secrecy must exist so that the information is not in the public domain.

Courts require the possessor of a trade secret to take reasonable measures to protect the secret. If reasonable and appropriate precautions are not taken to prevent disclosure or observation of a trade secret, trade secret protection may be lost.

Trade secrets are recognized even when the information has been disclosed to contractors, suppliers, and others dealing with the holder of the trade secret, provided that the information is disclosed under a secrecy agreement or other confidential relationship.

Information that has no commercial value generally cannot be the subject of trade secret protection. Information has value if it gives the owner an opportunity to obtain an advantage over competitors who do not know or use it. A trade secret can have value even if it is not currently being used, so long as it has a potential use.

The amount of effort or money expended by the holder of a trade secret in developing the secret is a factor in determining whether a trade secret exists. The larger the expenditures, the more likely a court is to uphold trade secret protection.

Courts typically require that trade secret information be marked confidential, or in some similar fashion, and be kept under lock and key. Additionally, trade secret processes and equipment should be isolated (where possible) in a restricted area. If the information is readily ascertainable from sources available to others, or if it can be analyzed or reverse-engineered from products on the market, it is generally not considered a trade secret.

1. Sample Utility Patent (see page 21)
2. Sample Design Patent (see page 27)
3. Copyright Application Form TX (from the US Copyright Office), see section on Forms and Templates in chapter 13
4. Trademark/Service Mark Application (from US Patent and Trademark Office) can be filed online at https://teas.uspto .gov/forms/bas/ or presented in a written application. See section on Forms and Templates in chapter 13

United States Patent [19]

Nick et al.

[11]   **Patent Number:**   **4,699,792**

[45]   **Date of Patent:**   **Oct. 13, 1987**

[54]   **SELF-ADHESIVE PLASTER CONTAINING MEDICATION**

[75]   Inventors: Erích Nick, Pinneberg; Günter Guse, Hamburg; Bodo Asmussen, Ammerbek, all of Fed. Rep. of Germany

[73]   Assignee: Beiersdorf AG, Hamburg, Fed. Rep. of Germany

[21]   Appl. No.:   **745,169**

[22]   Filed: **Jun. 17, 1985**

[30]   **Foreign Application Priority Data**

Jun. 23, 1984 [DE]   Fed. Rep. of Germany 3423328

[51]   Int. Cl.⁴ **A61F 13/02; A61L 15/03; A61L 15/06**

[52]   U.S. Cl. 424/446; 424/449; 604/896; 604/897; 604/307; 128/156; 428/355

[58]   Field of Search 424/16, 19, 20, 21, 424/26, 27, 28, 78, 83, 443, 446, 449; 604/897, 896, 304, 307; 128/156; 156/327, 332, 334; 428/354, 355, 356

[56]   **References Cited**

U.S. PATENT DOCUMENTS

4,390,027   6/1983   Alani et al. 604/307

FOREIGN PATENT DOCUMENTS

2743979   4/1979   Fed. Rep. of Germany .
3202775   3/1983   Fed. Rep. of Germany 424/28

Primary Examiner—John Kight
Assistant Examiner—Nathan M. Nutter
Attorney, Agent, or Firm—John C. Smith, Jr.

[57]   **ABSTRACT**

A self-adhesive medicinal plaster comprises a plurality of adhesive elements spaced from each other on a surface of a carrier web and a plurality of active ingredient elements, containing a medication, spaced from each other and from the active ingredient elements on the surface of the carrier web whereby the medicinal active ingredient composition is isolated from the adhesive composition.

21 Claims, 2 Drawing Figures

THIS IS TO CERTIFY that this is a true copy from the records of the U.S. Patents and Trademark Office of the first page of the above identified patent:

Certifying Officer   Date

U.S. Patent   Oct. 13, 1987   4,699,792

FIG. 1

FIG. 2

4,699,792

1

SELF-ADHESIVE PLASTER CONTAINING MEDICATION

FIELD OF THE INVENTION

This invention relates to a self-adhesive plaster with medicinal active ingredient elements and adhesive elements spaced from each other on a carrier for transdermal application.

BACKGROUND OF THE INVENTION

Plasters for transdermal application of medicinal active ingredients are known. Transdermal plasters are commercially available and are described in a large number of publications and patents.

In one type of transdermal plaster the medicinal active ingredients are arranged in a reservoir which is shielded from the skin with a control membrane which releases a controlled amount of active ingredient onto the skin through this membrane. A disadvantage of this arrangement is that the active ingredient, reservoir constituents and membrane must be carefully matched with one another, and consequently this system cannot be employed for all medicinal active ingredients. In addition, the production of such a plaster is expensive due to the complicated assembly of the parts.

In another type of transdermal plaster the medicinal active ingredient is incorporated into the adhesive composition of the plaster. In this case also, it is necessary for the active ingredient and adhesive composition to be carefully matched with one another. Although these systems are simpler and more economical to produce, they unavoidably result in interactions between the active ingredient and adhesive especially since as a general rule adhesives do not consist of defined individual constituents but are diverse mixtures.

German Offenlegungsschrift No. 3,202,775 describes an adhesive plaster for transdermal application of an active ingredient in which the active ingredient is printed onto the adhesive surface of the plaster in the form of separate spaced elements. Although such a plaster is economical to produce it has serious disadvantages and has not found acceptance in practice. In particular, the interactions between the active ingredient and adhesive composition impair uniform long-term release of the active ingredient through the skin because of migration, either of the active ingredient into the adhesive composition or the plasticizer or plasticizer-like substance into the active ingredient element, depending on external influences such as temperature and moisture. Such a plaster cannot fulfill the strict regulations of governmental registration as a drug especially in respect of the required storage stability under possibly adverse conditions during which migration phenomena may take place over a prolonged period.

An object of the present invention is, accordingly, to provide a medicated self-adhesive plaster for transdermal application which does not have, or has only to a substantially lesser degree, the above-mentioned disadvantages of the prior art. In particular, a plaster is provided which on the one hand can be produced economically and on the other hand is free from problems of migration of adhesives into the medicinal active ingredient and vice versa, and in addition, as far as possible, avoids any type of interaction between the two components.

2

SUMMARY OF THE INVENTION

The invention, accordingly, relates to a self-adhesive plaster with separate active ingredient elements on a carrier for transdermal application which is characterized in that adhesive elements are arranged spatially separate from the active ingredient elements on the carrier, the adhesive elements consisting of adhesive systems which can be processed as a dispersion, plastisol or organisol, and both the adhesive elements and the active ingredient elements being approximately cap-shaped and adhering to the carrier by their base.

It is particularly advantageous for the apex of the medicinal active ingredient and adhesive elements to have about the same height in relation to the carrier. A uniformly good contact of both types of elements to the surface of the skin is thereby achieved.

The plaster, according to the invention, is thus free from interaction between the medicated active ingredient and adhesive. The resulting advantages are, in particular, that adhesives of the dispersion-type and the like, which are known per se, can be used as the adhesive and that, on the other hand, the medicated active ingredient can be processed with suitable pharmaceutical auxiliaries which are used for fixing to the carrier, according to the invention, and for optimum diffusion of the active ingredient into the skin. It is therefore no longer necessary to develop a formulation of the adhesive to suit the particular medicinal active ingredient or, conversely, a formulation of the active ingredient to suit the adhesive. Rather, an exceptionally variable system results with which medicinal active ingredients of the most diverse types may be used for transdermal application.

Advantageously, both the adhesive elements and the medicinal active ingredient elements are each applied from dispersions with a high solids content by a printing process. Suitable printing processes are gravure printing processes and, in particular, screen printing processes which are distinguished by single handling and exceptional economy with precise arrangement of the elements on the carrier web.

The adhesive elements and the medicinal active ingredient elements are preferably arranged in a regular pattern due to the geometry of the screen printing devices. The caps preferably have a base diameter of up to about 5000 μm, in particular 200–500 μm. If desired, however, it is possible to produce larger caps.

Because of the spatial separation of the active ingredient and adhesive the adhesive can be any adhesive which is known per se and which does not irritate the skin and which can be processed as described above. Suitable adhesives are, inter alia, rubber, polyacrylic acid esters and polyisobutylene, if appropriate, together with tackifying resins. These adhesives are advantageously processed from aqueous, concentrated, thixotropic dispersions of adhesives, the solids content preferably being 55–65% by weight. Suitable examples are adhesives based on methyl acrylic acid esters with alkyl radicals of 4–18 carbon atoms, such as butyl acrylate, ethylhexyl acrylate or stearyl acrylate, cross-linked or noncross-linked, it being possible to effect cross-linking, if appropriate, by electron beam radiation.

The rotary screen printing process uses a rotating weldless, drum-shaped and perforated rotary screen. In the inner jacket, a mechanically or magnetically held round-edged or square doctor blade forces the dispersion into the drum through the perforations of the

4,699,792

3

screen wall onto the carrier web. The carrier web passes the drum at a speed corresponding to the peripheral speed of the rotating screen drum driven by a backpressure roller against the outer cover of the screen drum. To produce the plasters according to the invention, two synchronously running screen printing units connected in series, which place the adhesive elements and then the active ingredient elements exactly alongside one another in accordance with the whole geometry of the screens, are used in a suitable manner. The size and dosage of the microsize areas of adhesive and active ingredient which form as caps can be accurately determined by the diameter of the screen perforations and the wall thicknss of the screen. The number of possibilities of the arrangement is unlimited, and the arrangement can be selected as desired. There is thus the additional economic advantage that the adhesive formulation and active ingredient formulation can be applied to the carrier web in a production line with a high dosage accuracy.

The dispersions should be gelatinous to paste-like and, after drying, form an elastic film, for example, by addition of polvinyl alcohol, polyvinyl pyrrolidone, water-soluble cellulose derivatives or other more or less water-soluble film-forming agents. Microencapsulated substances can also be processed via the dispersion.

It is furthermore possible to apply membrane-forming substances separately in the production line, to accurately match the active ingredient, by including another screen printing unit without interfering with the adhesive.

If electron-beam cross-linking is to be carried out, this is advantageously effected after application of the adhesive and before application of the medicated active ingredient without interrupting the production line.

The coating is then advantageously dried in a hot-air canal or by infrared or high-frequency radiation.

Possible carrier webs are, in particular, diffusion-tight films. Particularly suitable carriers are those to which the adhesive and active ingredient formulation adhere without auxiliary materials. If appropriate, the surface of the carrier can also be additionally treated, for example, by corona discharge or coating with an adhesion promoter which, as a primer, effects anchoring of the active ingredient and adhesive elements.

A large number of medicinal active ingredients which are suitable for transdermal application are known. Thus, European Published Specification No. 72,251 describes a large number of such active ingredients. The following are examples:

Antihypertensive agents
Antihypotensive agents
Vasodilators
β-Blockers
Calcium antagonists
Antiemetic agents
Antitussive agents
Sedatives
Analgesics
Psychotropic agents
Antiasthmatic agents
Antirheumatic agents
Antiarythmic agents
Antihistamines
Hormones
Antibiotics
Cytostatics.

4

BRIEF DESCRIPTION OF THE DRAWINGS

The features and advantages of the present invention will become more clearly appreciated from the following description taken in conjunction with the accompanying drawings in which:

FIG. 1 is a perspective view of one embodiment of the plaster of the present invention, and

FIG. 2 is a cross-sectional view of a second embodiment of the plaster of the present invention.

DETAILED DESCRIPTION OF THE PREFERRED EMBODIMENTS

In FIG. 1, cap-shaped adhesive elements 2 and medicinal active ingredient elements 3 are located on a surface of a carrier web 1. A releasable cover 4 extends over the active ingredient and adhesive elements and is releasably retained by the adhesive elements. The cover 4 preferably has an adhesive-repellent finish on the side facing the adhesive elements 2 and active ingredient elements 3, if the cover 4 is not itself already adhesive-repellent.

FIG. 2 shows a variant of the FIG. 1 embodiment with the carrier web 1, adhesive composition elements 2 and active ingredient elements 3 embedded in an adhesive promoter 6 and covered with a releasable cover 4. On the underside of the carrier 1 is a covering lacquer 5 which can consist of a lacquer coating or a metal layer produced by vapor deposition.

The following is an example of a specific embodiment of the present invention:

EXAMPLE

A.

Preparation of a medicated active ingredient formulation

27.35 parts by weight of hydroxypropylmethylcellulose (Pharmacoat 603) are stirred into a cold mixture of 30 parts by weight of isopropanol, 30 parts by weight of water and 8.20 parts by weight of 1,2-propylene glycol. The mixture is warmed to 50° C., with continuous stirring, until a clear solution has formed. 4.45 parts by weight of micronized 2-methyl-4-chloro-6-methoxy-5-(2-imidazoline-2-yl)-amino-pyrimidine   (Moxonidin) are carefully mixed into said solution.

B.

Preparation of an adhesive formulation

100 parts by weight of a commercially available aqueous polymer dispersion based on acrylic acid ester (Acronal 80 D) are thickened to a viscosity of about 200 Pas by addition of 4 parts by weight of a 16% strength ammoniacal-aqueous solution of a polyacrylic acid (Collacral P).

C.

Printing Operation

A polyethylene terephthalate (Hostaphan RN 15) film 15 μm thick, which on one side is aluminized and lacquered the color of skin, is coated with the medicinal active ingredient formulation by a first rotating screen printing unit at a web speed of 20 m/minute. A perforated cylinder which produces rows of medicinal active ingredient elements in the longitudinal direction of the web is used. Each element has a base diameter of about 400 μm; the distance between the elements being about

5

100 μm in the longitudinal direction of the web and about 600 μm in the transverse direction. The amount applied is regulated via adjustment of the doctor blade so that cap-shaped elements are formed which, in the dried state, have a height of about 160 μm. This corresponds to about 25 g of medicated active ingredient formulation per m² of the carrier web. Drying is carried out at about 70° C. in a warm-air canal 6 m in length.

A second rotating screen printing unit of the same type then prints rows of elements of the adhesive formulation on the carrier web between the dried rows of elements containing the medicinal active ingredient. Thus, the amount of active ingredient formulation applied to a predetermined area of the carrier web is controlled by the element size and height. The second printing is followed by another drying zone of the type described above. The carrier web with the adhesive and medicated active ingredient elements is then passed through a laminating unit in which the web is covered with a releasable protective film, for example, a polyethylene terephthalate film 100 μm thick (Hostaphan RN 100), which is aluminized and siliconized on one side.

D.

Fabrication

The dried and covered web which has been printed twice is now divided into individual plasters of any desired size, depending on the desired doses of medicinal active ingredient. If, for example, a size of 25 cm³ is chosen, this has in each case about 5000 elements of medicinal active ingredient and adhesive, the active ingredient content being about 7 mg of 2-methyl-4-chloro-6-methoxy-5-(2-imidazolin-2-yl)-amino-pyramidine (Moxonidin). These plasters are sealed individually in a diffusion-tight primary packing material, for example, a flat bag of polyethylene/aluminum/paper laminated material.

It will be appreciated that various arrangements of the above-disclosed arrangement are possible without departing from the spirit of the present invention.

What is claimed is:

1. A self-adhesive transdermal medicinal plaster in which the medication is isolated from the adhesive, comprising:
(a) an impermeable carrier web;
(b) a plurality of adhesive elements spaced from each other at predetermined locations on a surface of said carrier web; and
(c) a plurality of active ingredient elements, containing at least one transdermal medication, spaced from each other and from said active ingredient elements at predetermined locations on said surface of said carrier web;
(d) said active ingredient elements being disposed between a plurality of said adhesive elements and said adhesive elements being disposed between a plurality of said active ingredient elements on said surface of said carrier web, and the height of said active ingredient elements and the height of said adhesive elements on said carrier web being about the same to assure, when said plaster is applied to the skin, uniformly good contact of both said active ingredient and adhesive elements with the surface of the skin.

2. A self-adhesive medicinal plaster according to claim 5 wherein each of said adhesive elements and each of said medicinal active ingredient elements are

6

approximately cap-shaped and adhere at its base to said surface of said carrier web.

3. A self-adhesive medicinal plaster according to claim 2 wherein the apexes of said medicinal active ingredient elements and said adhesive elements are approximately the same height relative to said surface of said carrier web.

4. A self-adhesive medicinal plaster according to claim 5 wherein each of said medicinal active ingredient elements is surrounded by a plurality of said adhesive elements and each of said adhesive elements is surrounded by a plurality of said medicinal active ingredient elements.

5. A self-adhesive medicinal plaster according to claim 4 wherein said medicinal active ingredient elements and adhesive elements have a base dimension of up to about 5000 μm.

6. A self-adhesive medicinal plaster according to claim 5 wherein the base dimension of said medicinal active ingredient elements and said adhesive elements is between 200 and 1500 μm.

7. A self-adhesive medicinal plaster according to claim 5 wherein the adhesive of said adhesive elements is selected from the group consisting of rubber, a polyacrylic acid ester, polyisobutylene and mixtures thereof with tackifying resins.

8. A self-adhesive medicinal plaster according to claim 5 wherein said medicinal active ingredient further comprises at least one pharmaceutical auxiliary or excipient.

9. A self-adhesive medicinal plaster according to claim 5 further comprising an adhesion promoter coating on said surface of said carrier web for promoting adhesion of said medicinal active ingredient elements and said adhesive elements to said carrier web.

10. A self-adhesive medicinal plaster according to claim 5 further comprising a film covering the surface of said carrier web opposite said surface supporting said medicinal active ingredient and adhesive elements, said film being selected from the group consisting of lacquer and metal.

11. A self-adhesive medicinal plaster according to claim 5 wherein said active ingredient elements comprise 2-methyl-4-chloro-6-methoxy-5-(2-imidazolin-2-yl)-amino-pyramidine.

12. A self-adhesive medicinal plaster according to claim 5 wherein a portion of said active ingredient elements comprise one type of medicinal composition and the remainder of said active ingredient elements comprise a different medicinal composition.

13. A self-adhesive medicinal plaster according to claim 5 further comprising a releasable cover web covering said surface of said carrier web including said medicinal active ingredient and adhesive elements.

14. A method of making a self-adhesive transdermal medicinal plaster in which the medication is isolated from the adhesive, comprising applying, by gravure printing processes, a dispersion, plastisol or organisol of an adhesive having a high solids content and a dispersion of at least one transdermal medication having a high solids content at spaced locations on one surface of an impermeable carrier web and drying said adhesive and said medication to form a plurality of adhesive elements and a plurality of transdermal medicinal active ingredient elements spaced from each other at predetermined locations on said surface of said carrier web, said elements being arranged such that each of said medici-

4,699,792

7

8

nal active ingredient elements is disposed between a plurality of said adhesive elements and each of said adhesive elements is disposed between a plurality of said medicinal active ingredient elements, the amount of dispersion, plastisol or organisol of said adhesive and the amount of said dispersion of at least one medication applied to said carrier web being such that the height of the resultant adhesive elements and the height of the resultant active ingredient elements on said carrier web are about the same to assure, when said plaster is applied to skin, uniformly good contact of both said adhesive and active ingredient elements with the surface of the skin.

15. A method of making a self-adhesive plaster according to claim 19 wherein said gravure printing processes are screen printing processes.

16. A method of making a self-adhesive plaster according to claim 19 wherein said adhesive applied to said carrier web is an aqueous, thixotropic dispersion of adhesive with a solids content of 55–65% by weight.

17. A method of making a self-adhesive plaster according to claim 19 comprising first applying said adhesive to said carrier web, drying said adhesive to form said plurality of adhesive elements, and cross-linking the composition of said adhesive elements and then applying said medication to form said medicinal active ingredient elements and drying said medicated active ingredient elements.

18. A method of making a self-adhesive plaster according to claim 17 wherein said cross-linking of said

adhesive elements is by means of electron beam radiation.

19. A method of making a self-adhesive plaster according to claim 14 wherein the amount of dispersion, plastisol or organisol of said adhesive and the amount of said dispersion of at least one medication applied by said gravure printing processes, respectively, provides adhesive elements and medicinal active ingredient elements respectively having a maximum base dimension of about 5000 μm.

20. A method of making a self-adhesive plaster according to claim 19 wherein said dispersion, plastisol or organisol of an adhesive having a high solids content is first applied by said gravure printing process to said surface of said carrier web and said adhesive is dried to form said plurality of adhesive elements on said carrier web and then said dispersion of at least one medication having a high solids content is applied by a further gravure printing process at spaced locations and spaced from said adhesive elements on said surface of said carrier web and said adhesive is dried to form said plurality of adhesive elements.

21. A method of making a self-adhesive plaster according to claim 19 wherein the amount of dispersion, plastisol or organisol of said adhesive and the amount of said dispersion of at least one medication applied by said gravure printing processes, respectively, provides adhesive elements and medicinal active ingredient elements respectively having a base dimension between 200 and 1500 μm.

* * * * *

35

40

45

50

55

60

65

United States Patent [19]

Edstrom et al.

[11] Patent Number: **Des. 316,225**

[45] Date of Patent: ** **Apr. 16, 1991**

[54] **BOTTLE**

[75] Inventors: Richard C. Edstrom, New York, N.Y.; Richard N. Hirst, Teaneck; Richard B. Gerstman, Tenafly, both of N.J.; David O. Pressler, Fairfield, Conn.

[73] Assignee: Warner-Lambert Company, Morris Plains, N.J.

[**] Term: 14 Years

[21] Appl. No.: 326,959

[22] Filed: Mar. 22, 1989

[52] U.S. Cl. D9/404

[58] Field of Search .... D9/403–413, D9/370; 215/1 R, 1 C

[56] **References Cited**

U.S. PATENT DOCUMENTS

D. 38,385 12/1906 Kohn D9/404
D. 94,157 12/1934 Marcus D9/404

D. 255,987 7/1980 Gentili D9/404
D. 262,778 1/1982 Britt et al. D9/404
D. 294,121 2/1988 Cramer D9/404

Primary Examiner—Melvin B. Feifer
Assistant Examiner—Lucy Lieberman
Attorney, Agent, or Firm—Charles A. Gaglia, Jr.

[57] **CLAIM**

The ornamental design for a bottle, as shown and described.

DESCRIPTION

FIG. 1 is a perspective view of a bottle showing our new design;
FIG. 2 is a top plan view thereof;
FIG. 3 is a side elevational view with the opposite side being identical;
FIG. 4 is a front elevational view with the rear elevation being identical; and
FIG. 5 is a bottom plan view.
The broken line showing of a bottle cap is for illustrative purposes only and forms no part of the claimed design.

THIS IS TO CERTIFY that this is a true copy from the records of the U.S. Patents and Trademark Office of the first page of the above identified patent:

Certifying Officer

7/30/97
Date

U.S. Patent   Apr. 16, 1991   Sheet 1 of 2   **Des. 316,225**

FIG-1

U.S. Patent   Apr. 16, 1991   Sheet 2 of 2   **Des. 316,225**

FIG-2

FIG-3   FIG-4

FIG-5

CHAPTER 3

How to Maintain Confidentiality of Your Ideas

There are several reasons for maintaining the secrecy of an idea or invention and restricting or preventing its disclosure to others. You may want to keep your idea confidential to prevent someone else from stealing it before you can obtain legal protection for it. You may also want to maintain the confidentiality of your idea to retain your ability to file for a patent in the United States or foreign countries. Most countries, including the United States, require that there be no public use, sale, or disclosure of the invention before the date on which a patent application covering the invention is filed (the so-called "absolute novelty" requirement). Thus, initially maintaining confidentiality of your idea or invention allows you to protect it later for optimum commercial exploitation. It is wise to maintain the confidentiality of your idea or invention until the patent application has been published. Patent applications are held in secret by the USPTO until they are published eighteen months after filing of the application.

DISCLOSING YOUR IDEAS TO OTHERS IN CONFIDENCE

To protect and exploit your ideas and inventions from a practical standpoint, you will need to disclose the nature of the ideas and inventions to outside parties, such as witnesses to the invention, model makers, employees, draftsmen, patent attorneys, invention promoters, consultants, and manufacturers. Otherwise, you will not be able to have the invention tested, patented, licensed, manufactured, or sold. Minimize disclosure of your ideas or inventions to those who have a need to know to help you protect or exploit your ideas or inventions. Disclose your ideas and inventions only after outside parties agree in writing to keep the information confidential.

When someone reviews the invention or a description of it and signs the invention documentation as a witness, he or she has an implied obligation to keep the details of the invention in confidence. Rather than rely on this implied confidentiality obligation, ask the witness to sign a written confidentiality agreement.

Likewise, your employees, agents, and consultants may be under an implied obligation of confidentiality, however, ask each of them to sign an appropriate written confidentiality agreement. Include provisions prohibiting your employees and consultants from stealing your ideas or inventions for the purpose of competing with you, and, furthermore, require them to assign to you any improvements they make on your inventions. These types of provisions are standard in most employment and consultant agreements.

When submitting your ideas to companies for their review and evaluation, state the purpose and advantages of your invention in one brief paragraph, and require the company to sign a confidentiality agreement before they obtain more detailed information. A sample confidentiality agreement is provided at the end of this chapter for use in situations where you will be disclosing your ideas or inventions to companies and others. Make sure that the person signing on behalf of the company is, or represents himself or herself to be, in a position to bind the company to the agreement. Language to that effect has been included in the sample confidentiality agreement.

Many companies may refuse to sign a confidentiality agreement before reviewing the idea. If such a company is important to getting your idea to market, you may have to disclose your idea to them even if they are unwilling to enter into a confidentiality agreement. If the idea is patented or otherwise protected, there is less risk in disclosing it. However, when you disclose unprotected ideas without a confidentiality agreement, mark the copies as confidential and indicate in a letter to the company that the idea is submitted in confidence.

When you discuss your ideas and inventions with a patent attorney or patent agent, he or she is generally under a professional duty to maintain the confidentiality of your privileged information. If the attorney or agent violates this duty of confidentiality, he or she can face professional discipline and liability for damages caused to you by the unauthorized disclosure of your ideas. It is recommended that you enter into an Attorney Retainer Agreement that specifically obligates the patent attorney or agent to keep your ideas in confidence and not use or disclose them to others without your consent.

To protect the confidentiality of your ideas and to guard against theft when dealing with invention promoters and brokers, require them to sign a confidentiality agreement, as discussed earlier. If the broker steals your invention or idea, despite signing a confidentiality agreement, the broker may be "judgment proof"—that is, the broker may have no assets from which you can extract monetary damages for the theft. Therefore, require the broker to provide you with evidence of professional liability insurance or bonding, or both, before disclosing your ideas or inventions, so that you know the broker's compliance with the agreement is reasonably guaranteed.

HANDLING PROPRIETARY INFORMATION AS A BUSINESS OWNER

Whether you are a sole proprietor or a corporate business owner, the handling and transfer of confidential or proprietary information requires care and discretion. This is especially true when parties are dealing with intellectual property, such as invention disclosures, patent applications, and trade secrets, that can be extremely valuable to the success of a business.

Confidential trade secret information can include, without limitation, any formula, pattern, device, plan, process, or compilation of information that (1) is, or is designed to be, used in business; (2) is private or confidential in that it is not generally known or available to the public; and (3) gives the business an opportunity to obtain an advantage over competitors who do not know or use it. Take protective measures to maintain trade secrets, as discussed later in this chapter.

The research, technical, and marketing information of a business is usually confidential and proprietary information. Such information should not be disclosed outside of the business and should be kept confidential within the business (with certain exceptions). Employees of a business should not, without authority, either during the term of employment or thereafter (1) use or disclose any such confidential information outside the business; (2) publish any article with respect thereto; or (3) remove or aid in the removal from the premises of the business any such confidential information or any property or material which relates thereto.

Be concerned about safeguarding information that is critical to your business. The major factor to consider in assessing the criticality of information is what effect the loss or misuse might have on the competitive position, financial standing, employee relations, and so forth of your business. This information can have varying degrees of criticality, and you may want to classify this information accordingly.

For example, you may want to classify some information as "strictly confidential." This marking should be used to identify critically important information concerning technological breakthroughs, new product plans, acquisition plans, privileged financial data, and so on. Information that is strictly confidential must be rigidly controlled while plans are being formulated, until the information or process is protected by other means (patents, license agreements, etc.), or the information has lost its critical degree of importance.

The test to determine if information is strictly confidential is whether this information, if published, could cause you considerable material damage to the point of endangering, in whole or in part, the very existence of the business. If the answer is yes, the information should be classified strictly confidential. Examples of documents that are strictly confidential include long-range strategic plans, critical chemical formulas, merger and acquisition plans, operational plans, important patent applications, and research and technical reports.

Mark or stamp "Strictly Confidential" on the cover, at least, of all documents containing such information. The information should not be made available to anyone but those people on the distribution list. Such information should never be left unattended, and it should be kept under lock and key.

Documents marked strictly confidential should only be copied by the owner of the information. Copies should be numbered and should contain a distribution list, and their issue and distribution should be monitored. The transmission of strictly confidential information via telefax or electronic mail should be allowed only when the information is encrypted or when it is ensured at both the sending and receiving end that only authorized personnel are operating the machines. Only pass on information that is strictly confidential to third parties when it is in the best interest of your business and subject to a written confidentiality agreement. Shred and destruct documents that are strictly confidential when they are no longer needed, and document the destruction of such documents.

Moderately important information, such as comparatively short-range plans, financial reports that are not extremely sensitive, impending announcements of significant personnel or organizational changes, and manufacturing methods, should be considered confidential. Examples of other confidential documents include documents involving lawsuits, legal opinions, purchase contracts, trade agreements, certain customer correspondence, financial statements, budgets, forecasts, projections, and market share.

The word "Confidential" should be conspicuously marked on each document containing such information. Try not to over-mark documents as confidential if they are not truly in this category. If, because of content or necessarily broad distribution of a particular document, it is unlikely that the document can receive the protection prescribed for documents marked confidential, it should not be classified as such.

Employees should have their proposed speeches and articles reviewed and approved by appropriate company personnel to make sure that confidential information is not being inadvertently disclosed. Make sure that employees leave company documents behind when they leave the company. Remind departing employees during their exit interviews of their duty to maintain the confidentiality of the company's proprietary information.

Any program to protect a company's confidential information must be tailored to the nature of the information and the needs of the particular company. Certainly, in any event, a company should identify its confidential information, establish reasonable programs to protect them, and conduct periodic checks to make sure the programs are working.

PROTECTING THE CONFIDENTIALITY OF TRADE SECRETS

Confidential trade secret information may embrace customer lists, technical data, commercial plans, sources of raw materials, and a variety of other proprietary information. Public disclosure of this type of information destroys the trade secret, thereby permitting a competitor's use of it. Therefore, take affirmative steps to maintain the confidentiality of trade secrets.

The subject matter that qualifies for trade secret protection is broad. Almost any information or method used in business can be a trade secret if it is not generally known and proper precautions are taken to maintain its secrecy. Trade secrets can be applied to a formula, pattern, compilation, program, device, technique, or process. Thus, trade secrets may include chemical processes, key ingredients, process equipment, plant designs, raw material suppliers, customer lists, and other proprietary information. If reasonable and appropriate precautions are not taken to prevent disclosure of a trade secret to, or observation by, an outside party, trade secret protection may be lost.

Courts have found the measures taken to protect trade secrets to be adequate where the owner of the trade secret took precautions to protect the confidential nature of its production process and equipment. These precautions were established by building a fence around the facility, limiting access to the facility, employing security guards to monitor premises, distributing confidential information only to employees who needed to know the information, and requiring all employees to sign employment agreements that obligated them to safeguard confidential information. The courts have also found adequate measure where the owner of the trade secret marked all information relating to the secret as confidential and used coded symbols to represent process ingredients and conditions.

On the other hand, trade secrets have not been protected when employees were given no indication as to what specific subject matter was confidential, when no signs were posted in areas where the trade secrets were located, where there were no locked fences or watchman at the facility, when blueprints and drawings involving the trade secrets were left on the floor and in trash containers, when visitors were permitted to tour the facility without a confidentiality agreement, or when the trade secret was published in a magazine or the company's annual report.

SECURITY OF ELECTRONIC DATA

Treat electronic media containing confidential data with the same care and respect as confidential paper documents. Confidential data can reside on the file server, as well as on the workstation hard drive or other data storage devices. Take adequate security measures for this data. At a minimum, sensitive data that are kept locally should be locked (in a safe or equivalent, or in the case of the hard disk, by locking the computer with a power-on password) and backed up regularly, with the backup kept secure. Store storage devices in locked cabinets.

Electronic mail systems (email) provide easy access to many linked computers worldwide. It would be prudent to exercise some caution about assuming the confidentiality of email messages. Ultimately individual users must assess the appropriateness of email for sensitive messages. Consider the risk and the benefits of this method versus others. Generally, using email is more secure than sending documents to an unattended fax, and it provides confirmation of receipt. The security of email depends, however, on the computer system being protected by passwords and the email being encrypted.

USING THE SAMPLE CONFIDENTIALITY AGREEMENT

A sample confidentiality agreement is provided at the end of this chapter. The sample confidentiality agreement is adaptable for use in practically any situation where proprietary information and ideas are disclosed to others.

The first paragraph of the sample confidentiality agreement identifies parties to the agreement, their addresses, and the effective date of the agreement. Paragraphs two and three identify the purpose of the agreement and describe the nature of the information to be disclosed and protected. Paragraph four recites the obligations of the recipient to maintain the confidentiality of the information and states that the recipient not use the disclosed information except as provided. It also provides that the recipient is not given any rights to the information that is disclosed. Additional paragraphs determine the return or destruction of the information that is disclosed or provided, and identify the state law that is to be applied in case of disputes and other terms.

The duration of confidentiality in a confidentiality agreement is typically a negotiated term dependent on, among other things, the relative negotiating power of the parties and the relative importance of the confidential information. If one of the parties to the agreement is involved because of a special skill or indispensable expertise, that party can often influence the term of confidentiality in its favor. Also, if the confidential information represents a vitally important discovery or information that is fundamental to the success of a party, that party would likely require a relatively longer period of confidentiality. Typical time periods of confidentiality are three to ten years, although you should seek as long a period as possible (e.g., twenty years) when disclosing your confidential information.

Other terms and conditions may be added to the confidentiality agreement depending on the particular circumstances (e.g., broker situation). After full agreement on the terms and conditions, the agreement should be signed and dated by both the recipient and the discloser.

CONFIDENTIALITY AGREEMENT

1. This Agreement is made on this _____ day of _____,
    20___ ("Effective Date") by and between _____
    (Discloser's name) _____
    _____ (Discloser's address)
    and _____ (Recipient's name) _____
    _____ (Recipient's address).

    In consideration of the mutual covenants hereinafter set forth and other valuable consideration, the parties hereto agree to the following terms and conditions:

2. Discloser shall disclose to Recipient confidential and proprietary Information of Discloser relating to:
    (describe subject matter to be disclosed)

(Continued)

3. Recipient shall use said Information of Discloser only for the purpose of:
    (describe the reasons for Recipient to receive and review Discloser's Information)

4. Recipient shall maintain said Information of Discloser in confidence for a term of _____ years from disclosure hereof, and shall not disclose said Information to any party, and shall not use said Information in any way whatsoever, except as expressly provided herein. Nothing contained in this Agreement shall be deemed to give Recipient any rights whatsoever in and to said Information.

5. Upon the written request of Discloser, Recipient shall return all the Information of Discloser, or destroy such Information at the option of Discloser, except that one (1) copy of such Information may be retained by Recipient, solely for the purpose of monitoring its ongoing obligations hereunder.

6. The obligations of confidentiality and nonuse hereunder shall not apply to any Information which is or becomes publicly available through no fault of Recipient, or which was already known by Recipient before disclosure by Discloser as evidenced by written documents and records.

7. This Agreement shall be effective until _____ years after the Effective Date of this Agreement.

8. This Agreement shall be binding upon and shall inure to the benefit of the parties and their respective heirs, successors, assigns, and legal representatives.

9. This Agreement constitutes the entire agreement of the parties with respect to the subject matter hereof and shall not be amended orally, but only by an agreement in writing signed by both parties that states that it is an amendment to this Agreement.

10. This Agreement shall be governed by the laws of the State of
    _____.

(Continued)

11. Each person signing this Agreement as Discloser or Recipient hereby represents that he/she is authorized to sign on behalf of the party
represented by him/her.

AGREED TO AND ACCEPTED BY:

_____   _____
Discloser's signature   Recipient's signature

_____   _____
Date   Date

CHAPTER 4

How to Keep a Record of Your Invention

Preparing a record of your invention is important because the record can be treated as credible evidence of your conception of the invention. The record will also serve you well as evidence during any subsequent litigation with the patent. Such evidence may include, among others, that you were the first to come up with the idea and the first to determine how to make and how to use the idea or invention. The record will also serve you well in a situation where someone you spoke with about your invention and steals the invention and files a patent application on it. You can show from your record that the invention was derived from you, thus helping provide evidence to negate the other person's ability to patent your invention.

To properly keep a record of your invention, you may employ a simple record of invention document, keep an inventor's notebook, or file a provisional patent application.

RECORD OF INVENTION

A Record of Invention is the simplest form of evidence you can have about your invention. It is a few pages in length and is signed and dated by you and witnessed by a person who did not contribute to your invention. Make sure the witness is under a confidentiality agreement before they review and witness your record of invention. The record of invention can include the following:

(a) The name of the person preparing the document.

(b) The title of the invention.

(c) A general description of the invention. This can include drawings or photographs. Make sure the descriptions explain the best way you know to make and use the invention. Include any advantages the invention has over other similar products or services in the market. This will help distinguish your invention from what has come before. Identify the features that are new. Give details about the structure of the apparatus, formula, or processes included in your idea.

(d) Provide the date and place where you conceived your invention.

(e) Provide names and addresses of any others that might have contributed to your idea or invention.

(f) Provides names of companies or entities that may have funded or contracted you to develop the idea or invention.

(g) Describe on a timeline if you have discussed your invention with others. If so, identify the confidentiality agreement s/he signed. Include the date of such an agreement.

(h) If you have developed a prototype of your invention, identify the place and time you tested your prototype.

(i) Include any articles or publications (scientific or otherwise) that you believe are closest to your idea and invention. Include a statement as to why your idea is different from that described in the article of publication.

(j) Finally, sign your full name at the end of the record.

(k) Have a witness (under a confidentiality agreement), who did not contribute to your invention, sign and date the record as follows:

WITNESSED, READ and UNDERSTOOD

_____

Witness Name and Signature

_____

Date

The record of invention will not reserve your legal rights to the invention at the USPTO, it is merely a mechanism by which you can keep an accurate record of your invention. This record contains all the information about your invention, so you want to keep it safe. It is best to keep this signed record under lock and key, in a safety deposit box, or some other place where no one will have access to it until you are ready to act on it.

INVENTOR NOTEBOOK

An inventor's notebook is similar to a record of invention, except that it is a serial record of your invention over time as you develop it. The record of invention is a static picture in time, while the inventor notebook can act as several pictures showing the development of the idea or invention over time. There are electronic notebooks and hard paper notebooks. Both paper and electronic notebooks have to be relied upon for veracity and credibility, particularly from tampering. Large companies employ electronic notebooks and employ complicated software to ensure the notebooks can be relied on in court for evidence. These software systems and databases can be expensive to purchase and maintain. For most everyday inventors, I would recommend a hard paper notebook. They are inexpensive, easy to show they have not been tampered with, and are often used in court as credible evidence.

An inventor's notebook is a bound notebook with each page individually numbered. You can purchase one on Amazon.com, or other online vendor.

Each page should be used sequentially and blank pages should be crossed out. Each page should be dated and signed by you and witnessed by a witness as discussed before. The notebook can contain the same information as a record of invention; however, each date you work on the idea or invention, you can detail what you did in the notebook on that date.

If you have sketches or other drawings or photographs, print them and attach them by staple or glue to your notebook page. This will preserve the date on which you came up with the particular sketch or photograph.

You can also use the notebook as a place to record your discussions with other people. You should include a brief description of your discussion, the date, time, and place where you had the discussion. This will serve you well in determining who invented what, and providing evidence that someone derived or stole your invention.

You can use the notebook throughout the invention development phase. The notebook is your daily diary of how you came up with your idea or invention. It is personal to you and should be used as such.

The record of invention or inventor notebook will also save you money when hiring a patent attorney or agent to draft your patent application because all your data, history of development, and closest technology will already be sketched out in these documents.

PROVISIONAL PATENT APPLICATION

This is the ultimate record of your invention. It provides you with an official date for your invention. A provisional patent application is an abbreviated version of a regular patent application and is useful in establishing an early filing date for a subsequent regular patent application. Filing a provisional patent application is about one-fifth of the cost of a regular application and can save you money upfront. Additionally, filing a provisional patent application allows you time to review the commercial potential of your invention. A provisional patent application will not issue as a patent unless within one year you either convert it to a regular patent application or file a separate regular patent application claiming the benefit of the provisional application. The provisional patent application has minimum requirements. This type of application can be as simple as submitting a PowerPoint presentation describing your invention, along with how to make and how to use your invention. Additional information on filing a provisional application is detailed in chapter 9.

Now that you have established a way to properly record your invention, you can move to the next steps in your journey to profit from your idea or invention.

CHAPTER 5

Where to Find Help to Protect and Market Your Inventions

Protecting and profiting from your ideas and inventions is no easy exercise, as a considerable amount of time, money, effort, and networking is required. No matter what your skills and experience level, you will likely need assistance in making your ideas a success. Whether this source of assistance is from patent attorneys and agents, invention brokers and promotion firms, inventors clubs, or universities, please ensure that you are dealing with reputable people and organizations.

PATENT ATTORNEYS AND AGENTS

There are numerous resources to help you protect and market your ideas and inventions. Patent attorneys and agents have already been mentioned as sources of assistance in conducting patent searches and filing and prosecuting patent applications. Patent attorneys can also be helpful in licensing your invention and in enforcing your intellectual property rights.

The USPTO has geographical and alphabetical listings of patent attorneys and agents, but it does not make recommendations or assume responsibility for your selection from the lists. You can find a listing of patent attorneys and agents on the USPTO website at https://oedci.uspto.gov/oedci/practitionersearch.jsp.

Typical attorney's fees for preparing and filing a patent application for a simple idea or invention range from about $5,000 to $10,000. Fees for prosecuting simple applications in the USPTO usually range from approximately $5,000 to $15,000. Chapter 7 of this book provides additional information on using patent attorneys and agents.

INVENTION PROMOTERS AND BROKERS

Invention promotion firms are another resource to help you protect and profit from your ideas and inventions. These firms will take on a part of the job or the entire job of protecting, developing, and marketing your idea. The can be found by searching the internet. Some firms are also advertised on late-night television.

Always exercise caution when doing business with invention promotion firms. These firms typically charge fees from $1,000 to $10,000, and they may not have a proven track record of success. In fact, many firms are sham operations that prey on unsuspecting inventors. These unethical invention promoters will typically glorify all ideas, charge a large up-front fee, and do little or nothing with the ideas. Several firms have been fined and penalized by state and federal governments and have been the subject of congressional hearings.

If you elect to use an invention promotion firm, choose one that (1) can provide solid evidence of its track record—not just a few flashy success stories, but verifiable statistics on the number of clients it has had and the number who have actually made money; (2) does not collect the entire fee in advance; and (3) will provide samples of its promotional materials and lists of companies to whom it has sent these materials (then verify that exchange with those companies yourself). Check the promotion firm's reputation with its state attorney general, the Better Business Bureau, the Chamber of Commerce, a patent attorney, local inventors or innovators clubs, or former clients of the firm.

Invention brokers can also be helpful in making your invention a success. Invention brokers typically work for a portion of the profits from the invention, and their initial fees are relatively small.

Invention brokers may help raise money and form companies or strategic alliances to produce and market your inventions. They often provide management research and development advice. In general, brokers are interested in relatively complex technology with a fairly large sales potential.

Here are some good sources of help for inventors:

Edison Nation at www.edisonnation.com is a platform to help everyday inventors turn their product ideas into real products on retail shelves worldwide by reviewing and evaluating idea submissions at any stage of development.

TeleBrands at www.telebrands.com operates an open call to would-be inventors, or anyone with a great idea, and reviews a number of products each year for potential infomercial testing.

Allstar at www.allstarmg.com is a consumer products company that uses direct response advertising to maximize the potential of innovative, quality products and sustainable brands.

Shark Tank at www.abc.go.com/shows/shark-tank/apply is an acclaimed reality show that has inspired people with good ideas to pitch them to a critical team of potential investors.

Etsy at www.etsy.com could be a resource to help inventors sell their products by using the Sell on Etsy App to manage orders, edit listings, and respond to buyers instantly, from anywhere.

Building your business, whatever your role or industry, requires a comprehensive understanding of the relevant markets and companies that best meet your target criteria.

Only do business with reputable firms and make sure you investigate the firms and fully understand i) what services are provided and ii) what financial obligations are required of you. Be certain that all of the terms are stated in a written agreement.

Some additional noted firms that work with promising inventors and small companies across the country are as follows:

The Battelle Memorial Institute
Invention Administrator
505 King Avenue
Columbus, OH 43201
(800) 201-2011
www.battelle.com

Arthur D. Little Enterprises
One Federal Street, Suite 2810
Boston, MA 02110
(627) 532-9503
www.adlittle.com

Refer to chapter 6 of this book for additional information on using invention brokers and promotion firms.

INVENTORS CLUBS, ASSOCIATIONS, AND SOCIETIES

Inventors clubs, associations, and societies may be located in your region. Opportunities for professional, business, and social networking are often provided by inventors organizations. These centers of innovation can be valuable sources of information and services. For their locations contact the following organizations:

United Inventors Association of the United States of America
(UIA-USA)
1025 Connecticut Avenue, Suite 1000
Washington, DC 20036
(stamped, self-addressed envelope required)
Email: www.uiausa.org

National Congress of Inventor Organizations (NCIO)
727 North 600 West
Logan, UT 84321
(801) 753-0888

Inventors Awareness Group, Inc.
1533 East Mountain Rd, Suite B,
Westfield, MA 01085-1458
(413) 568-5561

The Minnesota Inventors Congress
PO Box 71
Redwood, MN 56283
(800) 468-3681

Contact the inventors organizations in your area. Talking with other inventors can be very helpful. Find another inventor who has already filed a patent, applied research and development, and experienced the stages of financing. It does not matter if that person's end result was a financial success or failure. Getting the nuts and bolts of the process can be helpful to you.

Bounce your ideas off other inventors, but be sure to have them sign a confidentiality agreement before you disclose your ideas. Welcome their criticism, and do not be afraid to ask for their assistance in finding ways to perfect, patent, and market your ideas.

UNIVERSITY INVENTION AND ENTREPRENEURIAL CENTERS

Invention and entrepreneurial centers operated by universities and the National Science Foundation can be valuable sources of help with your ideas and inventions. The University of Oregon's Experimental Center for the Advancement of Invention and Innovation, for example, evaluates ideas for a modest fee.

Invention and entrepreneurial centers can help inventors weed out bad ideas to avoid further wasting time and money. The centers can also identify trouble spots that require special attention in planning the development or commercialization of a potential new product. If an idea shows it has merit and is commercially feasible, the centers try to link the inventor with established companies or refer him or her to sources of funds. Similar programs may be available at colleges and universities in your area.

THE SMALL BUSINESS ADMINISTRATION

The Small Business Administration (SBA) operates Small Business Institutes (SBI) located at several hundred colleges and universities throughout the country. Currently few SBI centers can provide much help with the technical research and development aspects of innovations, although they may be able to provide the necessary assistance in market research, feasibility analysis, and business planning to make an invention successful.

Small Business Administration field offices (listed in your local telephone directory under the heading US Government) can provide information about the SBI program. You may find other management assistance programs offered at the field offices that can be helpful in developing your idea as well. Publications containing information on patenting and marketing inventions are available by writing to the Small Business Administration, at 1441 L Street, NW, Washington, DC 20416 (800-827-5722).

NATIONAL BUREAU OF STANDARDS

The Office of Energy-Related Inventions in the US Department of Commerce's National Bureau of Standards sometimes evaluates, free of charge, nonnuclear energy–related inventions and ideas for devices, materials, and procedures. If the office finds that the invention or idea has merit, it can recommend further study by the Department of Energy, which may provide support for the invention if they believe it shows promise.

This process can take up to a year, but it could be fruitful for energy-related inventions. For further information on this program, write to the US Department of Commerce, Office of Energy-Related Inventions, Washington, DC 20230, or the US Department of Energy, Office of Technical and Financial Assistance, Washington, DC 20585.

MANUFACTURERS AND DISTRIBUTORS

Often you can go directly to prospective manufacturers and distributors, particularly small- to medium-sized firms, for assistance in commercializing your ideas. Be certain to take the required steps described earlier in the book to protect your idea by a patent, copyright, trademark, confidentiality agreement, or otherwise. Check the telephone directory and the library for listings of potential manufacturers. Compile a list of local, national, and international manufacturers who might be interested in manufacturing and distributing your product.

Check local and national trade publications in the field of your invention, as well as sources such as Moody's, Standard & Poor's, the Dun & Bradstreet Million Dollar Directory, and the Thomas Register. Some retailers, such as Kmart, J.C. Penney, Hammacher Schlemmer, Sharper Image, and others, may welcome new ideas and may assist in developing and marketing them. Most large companies, however, are not favorable to outside ideas for fear of litigation.

Some companies will require that you sign a waiver before they accept submission of your idea. This waiver typically provides that the company has no obligations to maintain your idea in confidence or to compensate you if they use your idea. If your idea is patented, or will be patented or otherwise protected by intellectual property rights, this waiver is less of a concern. Nevertheless, avoid signing such a waiver if possible. Rather, ask the companies to sign your confidentiality agreement. If you have friends or contacts at these companies, use them to your advantage in making introductions to key decision-makers.

Prepare a professional model or portfolio of your idea. If you work with a model maker or other artisan, enter into a contract for services that acknowledges your ownership of the idea and any improvements and that obligates the contractor to confidentiality. Demonstrate your model or show the portfolio of your idea to prospective manufacturers and distributors. Keep your presentation simple, yet professional.

Be prepared to explain the function, operation, benefits, and perceived market of your invention and understand the anticipated costs, competition, and business risks. Show how your idea fits with the manufacturer's existing or future line of products and services.

Talk to a number of manufacturers at the same time. See if you can generate interest at several companies, then go with the company that offers the greatest potential. Evaluate the companies just as they are evaluating you and your idea. Ask to see their new product catalogs and bulletins. Check the reputations of the companies with the Better Business Bureau and consumer affairs agencies.

Try to deal directly with the people who are in a position to make decisions regarding your idea. Focus your efforts on the presidents of the companies, directors of research and development, and others in charge of intellectual property or invention submissions.

Be willing to discuss what you want out of the deal. Do you want to sell the invention or license it? Are you interested in being involved in the manufacturing or marketing of your invention? What would be an acceptable sales price or royalty rate for your invention?

After you have reached an agreement with a manufacturer or distributor, present the terms in a written contract and have it signed by you and an authorized representative of the company. You should probably have a patent or licensing attorney assist you in the negotiations or review the agreement before you sign it. Additional information on licensing your inventions is provided in chapter 15.

CHAPTER 6

How to Deal with Invention Brokers and Promotion Firms

Many inventors turn to invention brokers or invention promotion firms for help in commercializing their inventions. Some of the reputable firms with a proven track record may help you get your idea or invention into the marketplace. Inventors anxious to get their products to market, however, are routinely taken advantage of by unscrupulous invention promotion firms that steal their ideas or neglect to promote the invention after collecting large fees from the inventors.

Distinguishing between a fraudulent invention promotion firm and a legitimate one is often difficult. Unscrupulous and honest firms use similar advertising and sales techniques, market evaluations, and contract strategies. You need to know how to spot common signs of trouble, how to protect yourself, and what to do if you become a victim.

EVALUATING INVENTION PROMOTERS

There are legitimate invention promotion firms as well as many disreputable ones. As an aspiring inventor, you need to be able to tell the good firms from the bad firms. Investigating and evaluating the reputation and track record of each firm is the first step in protecting yourself.

Many government agencies and private organizations offer information and assistance to independent inventors in dealing with invention marketing and promotion firms. These agencies and organizations include the USPTO, the SBA, the FTC, and inventors clubs and associations. The FTC is particularly aggressive in monitoring and policing the activities of invention promoters and offers helpful pointers in comparing legitimate versus illegitimate firms.

Examine the advertising and sales techniques of each firm for false, misleading, and impractical claims. Some invention promotion firms advertise in classified ads in newspapers and magazines and through television and radio. They target independent inventors and frequently offer free information to help patent and market inventions. These firms may also advertise a toll-free "800" telephone number that inventors can call for written information. The information, however, usually consists only of brochures about the promoter.

If you respond to the ads, a salesperson may contact you and will likely request information about you, your idea, and a sketch of the invention. As an inducement, the firm may offer a free preliminary review of your invention.

Some invention promotion firms may claim to know or have special access to manufacturers who are likely to be interested in licensing your invention. These kinds of claims often can be false or exaggerated. Before signing a contract with an invention promotion firm that claims special relationships with particular manufacturers, always ask for proof to support their claims, and be cautious if the firm refuses to document such claims.

After a preliminary review of your invention, a firm might request a market evaluation on your idea, which may cost several hundred dollars. Such evaluations from questionable firms often make vague and general statements and provide no hard evidence that there is a market for your invention. Reputable companies report specific information. Before you pay for a report on your idea, ask what specific information you will receive and demand that it be put in writing.

CHECKLIST FOR USING INVENTION PROMOTERS

If you are interested in working with an invention promotion firm, follow the checklist below before you sign a contract and pay significant amounts of money.

☐ Early in your discussions with a promotion firm, ask what the total cost of its services will be. Be warned if the salesperson hesitates to answer.

☐ Be careful of an invention promotion firm that offers to review or evaluate your invention but refuses to disclose details concerning its criteria, system of review, and qualifications of company evaluators. Without this information, you cannot assess the competence of the firm or make meaningful comparisons with other firms. Reputable firms should provide an objective evaluation of the merit, technical feasibility, and commercial viability of your invention.

☐ Require the firm to check existing invention patents. Because unscrupulous firms are willing to promote virtually any idea or invention with no regard to its patentability, they may unwittingly promote an idea for which someone already has a valid, unexpired patent. This means that even if the promotional efforts of your invention are successful, you may find yourself the subject of a patent infringement lawsuit. If you have not filed a patent application covering your idea, seek advice from a patent professional before authorizing the public disclosure of your idea.

☐ Be wary of an invention promotion firm that will not disclose its rates of success and rejection. Success rates show the number of clients who made more money from their invention than they paid to the firm. Rejection rates reflect the percentage of all ideas or inventions that were found unacceptable by the invention promotion company. Check with your state and local consumer protection officials to learn whether invention promotion firms are required to disclose their rates of success and rejection in your locality.

Keep in mind that few inventions make it to the marketplace, and still fewer become commercial successes. According to some experts used in FTC cases, an invention promotion firm that does not reject most of the inventions it reviews may be unduly optimistic, if not dishonest, in its evaluations.

☐ Be wary of a firm that claims to have special access to manufacturers looking for new products but refuses to document such claims. Legitimate invention promotion firms substantiate their claims.

☐ Be skeptical of claims and assurances that your invention will make money. No one can guarantee the success of your invention.

☐ Avoid being taken in solely on a firm's promotional brochures and affiliations with organizations that appear impressive. Beware of high-pressure sales tactics.

☐ Investigate the company before making any commitments. Call the Better Business Bureau, consumer protection agency, and attorney general in your state and in the state where the company is located to learn if they know of any unresolved consumer complaints about the firm.

☐ Make sure your contract contains all agreed-upon terms, written and verbal, before you sign. The contract should specify that the invention promoter will perform significant services, such as identifying prospective manufacturers, preparing an invention presentation or demonstration, building and testing the invention, and negotiating a license or sales agreement for you. Make sure the agreement sets a time limit for the invention promoter to succeed. If possible, have an attorney review the agreement before you sign it.

☐ If you do not get satisfactory answers to all of your questions with an invention promotion firm, consider whether you want to sign a contract. Once a dishonest company has your money, it is unlikely your money will be returned.

☐ If you believe you are a victim of a fraudulent invention promotion firm, contact the firm immediately and ask for your money back. If the firm does not return your money, report your problem to the Better Business Bureau, local consumer protection agency, and the attorney general in your state and in the state where the company is located. Your information may help an ongoing investigation or demonstrate the need for one.

You also may file a complaint by writing to the FTC. The FTC generally does not intervene in individual disputes; however, the information you provide may indicate a pattern of possible law violations.

The addresses and telephone numbers for the national and regional offices of the FTC are listed below:

FTC Headquarters
6th & Pennsylvania Avenue, NW
Washington, DC 20580
(202) 326-2222

FTC Regional Offices
1718 Peachtree Street, NW, Suite 1000
Atlanta, GA 30367
(404) 347-4836

101 Merrimac Street, Suite 810
Boston, MA 02114-4719
(617) 424-5960

55 East Monroe Street, Suite 1437
Chicago, IL 60603
(312) 353-4423

668 Euclid Avenue, Suite 520-A
Cleveland, OH 44114
(216) 522-4207

100 N. Central Expressway, Suite 500
Dallas, TX 75201
(214) 767-5501

1504 Curtis Street, Suite 2900
Denver, CO 80202-2393
(303) 844-2271

11000 Wilshire Boulevard, Suite 13209
Los Angeles, CA 90024
(310) 575-7575

150 William Street, Suite 1300
New York, NY 10038
(212) 264-1207

901 Market Street, Suite 570
San Francisco, CA 94103
(415) 744-7920

2806 Federal Building,
915 Second Avenue
Seattle, WA 98174
(206) 220-6363

CHAPTER 7

How to Use Patent Attorneys and Patent Agents

If an invention is to receive patent protection in the United States, a patent application must be written to describe and claim the invention and must be filed, processed, and examined by the USPTO, and only after meeting all of the requirements for patenting will it be granted as a patent. Although many inventors have successfully drafted their own patent applications, many others have hired either a patent agent or a patent attorney to draft and prosecute the application. This chapter provides guidance on how to select a patent agent or a patent attorney and how to work most efficiently and effectively with your agent or attorney to obtain the best possible patent protection at a reasonable cost. Remember that patent attorneys and patent agents can also provide assistance in conducting literature searches and reviewing the prior art to determine if your invention is patentable. Patent attorneys can help in licensing your invention and enforcing your patent against infringers.

WHO CAN REPRESENT YOU IN PATENT MATTERS

An inventor can be represented before the USPTO by himself or herself or a registered patent agent or patent attorney. There are advantages and disadvantages to representing yourself or using a patent attorney or patent agent. Many factors should be considered in deciding your representation.

Preparing an application for patent and conducting the proceedings in the USPTO to obtain the patent is an undertaking that requires knowledge of patent law and practices of the USPTO. Knowledge of the scientific or technical matters involved in the particular invention are also required. Inventors may prepare their own applications, file them in the USPTO, and conduct the proceedings, but they may face considerable difficulty unless they are familiar with these matters or study them in detail. While a patent may be obtained, in many cases, by persons not skilled in this work, there would be no assurance that the obtained patent would adequately protect the invention.

On the other hand, the inventor who originated the idea for which patent protection is sought knows the idea better than anyone else. Drafting a patent application based on that idea is usually within the grasp of an inventor who is comfortable with drafting technical papers. Many inventors write their own patent applications, although caution is advised. Patent laws are complex, and knowledge of them can mean the difference between obtaining a patent that adequately protects the invention and failing to receive any patent protection at all. Thus, even if the inventor writes the application, it makes good sense to retain a patent agent or patent attorney to review the draft. Instructions for writing a patent application are provided in chapter 9.

Many inventors employ the services of registered patent attorneys or patent agents. By law the USPTO has the power to make rules and regulations that govern the conduct of patent attorneys and agents and recognize attorneys and agents who are qualified to practice before the USPTO. People who are not recognized for this practice are not permitted by law to represent inventors before the USPTO. The USPTO maintains a register of attorneys and agents. To be admitted to this register, a person must comply with the regulations prescribed by the office, which require showing that the person is of good moral character and good repute and that he or she has the legal, scientific, and technical qualifications necessary to render a valuable service to patent applicants. These qualifications must be demonstrated by passing an examination.

Admission to practice in and represent clients before the USPTO has been granted to two classes of people: patent agents and patent attorneys. The basic qualifications of both classes are the same. The prospective agent or attorney must have sufficient technical knowledge to understand the ideas brought to them by inventors and to describe and discuss those ideas adequately. Possession of a Bachelor of Science degree in the engineering disciplines, such as electrical engineering, mechanical engineering, or chemical engineering, or in the sciences, such as physics, chemistry, or biology, is sufficient technical background. For applicants who do not have a degree in these or similar areas, the USPTO evaluates the applicant's technical course work to determine if the applicant can successfully represent clients.

The major difference between patent agents and patent attorneys is that agents usually do not have a law degree and are, consequently, not lawyers. Although agents have the basic minimum knowledge of the patent law required by the USPTO, they are not trained in general legal matters and cannot represent an inventor in a court or jurisdiction other than the USPTO. Insofar as preparing an application for patent and conducting the prosecution in the USPTO, patent agents are usually just as well qualified as patent attorneys. Patent agents cannot conduct patent litigation in the courts or perform various services that the local jurisdiction considers as practicing law. For example, a patent agent could not draw up a contract relating to a patent, such as an assignment or a license, if the state in which he or she resides considers drawing contracts as practicing law.

You can find a list of qualified patent attorneys or agents on the USPTO website (oedci.uspto.gov/oedci/practitionersearch.jsp). A general myth in the field of patent law is that a qualified registered patent attorney or agent is required to file an application at the USPTO. This is untrue; one of the rules of the USPTO outlines that an applicant for patent may file and prosecute his or her own case, or he or she may give a power of attorney so as to be represented by one or more patent practitioners or joint inventors. An applicant may represent himself or herself by simply signing the oath and/or declaration when filing by mail (see section on oath and declaration in chapter 9) or designating himself or herself as the "pro se inventor" on the Certificate Action Form when subscribing to file electronically (see the section on electronic filing in chapter 9).

In addition, the USPTO has several resources to help inventors file and prepare patent applications at the Inventors Assistance Center (IAC), which provides patent information and services to the public and is staffed by former supervisory patent Examiners and experienced primary Examiners who answer general questions concerning patent examining policy and procedure. You may reach the IAC at 800-786-9199 or 571-272-1000.

The **America Invents Act** enables the USPTO to "work with and support intellectual property law associations across the country in the establishment of pro bono programs designed to assist financially under-resourced independent inventors and small businesses" www.uspto .gov/inventors/proseprobono/. The USPTO in conjunction with IP law associations is working to establish programs to provide such assistance. The first such program was launched in June 2011 with the Minnesota pilot program. An additional five programs were slated to begin in 2012. A national pro bono task force has been formed by the USPTO in collaboration with major IP law associations, the federal circuit judiciary, and others. As indicated by the USPTO, the overall goal of the USPTO and the Task Force is to have the entire country covered by pro bono assistance for financially under-resourced inventors so that no worthy invention is left undiscovered. More information on the Task Force can be found at www.uspto.gov/sites/default/files/docuemnts/ProBono-McDowell _Final_LawReview_Web_Publication.pdf.

The USPTO cannot recommend any particular attorney or agent, or aid in the selection of an attorney or agent, as by stating, in response to inquiry, that a named patent attorney, agent, or firm is "reliable" or "capable." There is a directory published by the USPTO that lists all registered patent attorneys and agents who have indicated availability to accept new clients. The directory is arranged by states, cities, and countries, and can be purchased from the US Government Printing Office (GPO). (You can reach the GPO online at www.gpo.gov.)

The classified section or yellow pages in telephone directories of most large cities, as well as online information sites, have a heading for patent attorneys, under which the attorneys in that area are listed. Many large cities also have associations of patent attorneys, which may be helpful in finding an appropriate patent attorney or agent.

In employing a patent attorney or agent, the inventor executes a power of attorney or authorization to the agent. The power of attorney is usually part of the application papers and is filed in the USPTO. When an attorney has been appointed, the USPTO does not communicate with the inventor directly but conducts correspondence with the attorney who is acting for the inventor. The inventor is free to contact the USPTO concerning the status of his or her application. The inventor may remove the attorney or agent by revoking the power of attorney at any time.

CHOOSING BETWEEN PATENT AGENTS AND PATENT ATTORNEYS

If the inventor has decided not to draft a patent application on his or her own, he or she must choose between retaining a patent agent or a patent attorney. The choice is not clear-cut, and either option may be perfectly acceptable in a given situation. Several factors should be considered in making the decision.

By far the most important factor from the inventor's point of view is the ability of the prospective agent or attorney to understand the invention, to describe it well in a patent application, and to prosecute it to allowance with the USPTO.

The level of technical expertise required from the patent agent or attorney can vary widely. Simple mechanical or electrical inventions may be readily understood by anyone with a minimal amount of technical knowledge. Innovative computer architectures and new monoclonal antibodies may require a PhD in electrical engineering or biochemistry, respectively. The inventor should exercise a great deal of self-honesty in evaluating the invention and appraising the amount of technical knowledge needed to understand it. Although even the simplest invention can be incredibly useful and profitable, hiring a patent agent or attorney with technical qualifications greater than necessary will undoubtedly cost the inventor more money in legal fees. Whether an agent or attorney, a person with a PhD will likely charge more than one with a Bachelor of Science would. By honestly appraising the technical complexity of one's own invention and by hiring an agent or attorney with an adequate technical knowledge necessary to understand the invention, the inventor can obtain more cost-effective representation.

The technical complexity of the invention can also affect the potential legal complexity of the case, and this is another factor to consider in choosing between an agent and an attorney. Although patent agents have much experience in drafting and prosecuting patent applications on highly complex technology, they typically do not have any experience in negotiating and drafting patent licenses or in patent litigation, except perhaps as an advisor. In general, you will pay significantly less in legal fees if you use a patent agent instead of a patent attorney. Once again, you can save money by honestly appraising the legal complexity of the invention and by hiring a patent agent or attorney based on your needs. If commercialization is a possibility for your invention, and if there is a high likelihood of copying by third parties and potential litigation, it may be beneficial to hire a patent attorney with litigation experience to draft and prosecute the application, as opposed to an agent with no such experience.

In selecting a patent agent or attorney, the inventor should conduct a background evaluation. Make sure that the agent or attorney is registered with the USPTO. Ask each potential agent or attorney to provide samples of granted US patents that he or she has drafted and prosecuted, preferably in the field of your idea. Read these patents carefully and determine whether the agent or attorney can write clearly about the relevant technology. The patents should be clear, complete, and easy to understand. Although the claims section of every patent must be written in a precise and legally proscribed manner, a good set of claims should still be understandable, even to a relatively inexperienced inventor. If the patents seem unnecessarily long or difficult to read, discuss this with the agent or attorney and consider this a factor in making a selection.

Every patent agent or attorney should be willing to provide a list of references who can be called to discuss their experiences in working with the agent or attorney. Ask the agent or attorney for a list of references, and call several of the references to investigate the agent's or attorney's reputation. Appropriate questions to ask include the following: Did the agent/attorney take a reasonable amount of time to understand the invention? Did the agent/attorney set a schedule for completing the application, and was that schedule kept? Did the agent/attorney communicate well at all stages of the preparation and prosecution of the application? When investigating an attorney, the inventor should also contact the state bar to which the attorney is admitted to determine whether the attorney has previous or pending disciplinary actions against him or her. There are simply too many qualified patent agents and attorneys available to retain one whom others have found difficult to work with or who is of questionable character.

Other factors that should be considered in selecting an agent or attorney are location, access, and convenience. All other things being equal, a local agent or attorney with whom face-to-face meetings are easy to arrange and attend is preferable to an attorney or agent located far away. Location used to be a greater problem, when finding patent agents and attorneys outside of Washington, DC, and other major urban areas was difficult. However, finding competent local patent agents and attorneys is no longer difficult in most parts of the country.

Another factor in choosing between a patent agent and attorney is the marketability of the invention. The more assistance the inventor believes he or she will need to market or license the invention, the more attention should be paid to the business experience of the patent agent or attorney. Even if an attorney does not have an extensive business law practice, he or she will probably have seen many more patent licenses and confidential disclosure agreements than an agent would have.

Always remember that you are not locked into any one form of representation. It is easy to imagine circumstances where a patent agent is selected to draft the patent application and prosecute it, but a patent attorney is later retained when the prosecution becomes more complex than originally anticipated. Similarly, the agent may bring the invention through the entire patent application process, at which point a patent attorney is retained to help license and market the invention.

SELECTING COST-EFFECTIVE REPRESENTATION

Patent agents and attorneys operate under a variety of arrangements and fee schedules, and you should always select the ones that will provide the most cost-effective representation. Although patent agents can share office space, they cannot form professional corporations. Even though some agents are employed by law firms, the choice of hiring an agent will be based on the personal qualifications of the individual patent agent. Patent attorneys, on the other hand, may practice alone or in professional corporations or in law firms consisting of any number of attorneys.

Within a firm, there are typically two classes of attorneys: partners, who actually own shares of the professional corporation, and associates, who are employees of the firm but not shareholders. The first choice for an inventor is often whether to retain an attorney or agent practicing on his or her own or to retain a law firm; there are no fixed rules for making this choice.

Many competent patent attorneys have found the legal practice within a firm unacceptable and have decided to pursue their careers as solo practitioners. They are usually free to work whatever hours they choose; do not have a yearly minimum billable hours requirement, as associates and partners in firms typically have; and are free to establish any type of fee relationship with their clients that they wish, based on their individual financial situations. A few years ago, establishing a solo practice was an expensive proposition. An office was typically rented, secretarial help and bookkeeping assistance hired, and a professional library purchased or leased. Even with the development of shared office arrangements, wherein several solo practitioners shared the aforementioned services and facilities, the fixed costs were relatively high and were reflected in the charge structure that solo practitioners offered.

Because of the development of powerful and relatively inexpensive computers, with affordable and effective software for word processing, accounting, and docketing, along with Internet access to various legal databases and research services, the costs of establishing a solo patent practice are now relatively small. With these developments, many talented patent agents and attorneys have established solo practices with highly competitive rates. Thus, an inventor who retains a solo practitioner can often get a more personal and cost-effective service than an inventor who retains the services of a large law firm.

There are a few disadvantages to retaining a solo practitioner. Most important, if the solo agent or attorney experiences an illness, accident, or emergency, he or she may suddenly be unavailable. Although many attorneys have arrangements for such emergency situations, a situation can still occur where the carefully chosen attorney is suddenly not available, and an unknown attorney provides the service instead.

The solo patent attorney also may not be able to readily consult with another patent attorney, should the preparation of the application involve a technology that is unfamiliar to the attorney, or should the prosecution of the application generate a new and unforeseen legal twist that the attorney has not handled before. The informal consultation and exchange of ideas that occurs in law firms often adds a great deal of value, even if it occurs in a manner unseen by most clients.

Patent law firms can range from two to more than one hundred attorneys, with larger law firms frequently having satellite offices in other cities and, in some cases, other countries. While there are many firms that specialize in only the practice of patent and intellectual property law, other law firms consist of attorneys who practice in many different legal areas, such as corporate law, antitrust, mergers, and acquisitions, with only a few patent attorneys within the firm forming a "patent boutique." These patent boutiques may share some of the disadvantages of solo practice, wherein the patent attorney does not necessarily have colleagues to discuss patent issues with. Further, patent boutiques may also share some of the disadvantages of practice in a large firm, such as high overhead costs and resultant high hourly rates.

Choosing among the array of patent agents, patent attorneys, and law firms is not a simple task. Consequently, insist on meeting both the billing partner as well as the associate who will draft the case. The factors that were mentioned earlier in choosing between a patent agent and a patent attorney (i.e., technical competence, legal experience, costs, and personal rapport) should also be considered when making a choice between a solo attorney and a law firm.

Regardless of the level of complexity of the invention, expect that the attorney with whom you will be working will have a good general knowledge of the relevant area of technology. Although you will have to explain the details of the invention to the attorney, you should not have to pay for a technical review course for the attorney. Remember that competence in subject matter can be established in several ways, such as the educational background of the attorney and previous patent experience in the particular technology as evidenced by issued patents on similar matters.

The legal fee is perhaps the most difficult issue discussed with the prospective attorney. Discuss this issue fully and obtain a written fee arrangement before beginning any substantive work. Many types of fee arrangements are possible, and they should all be explored before a final fee agreement is reached. Exercise great care in this area, as misunderstanding and disagreement about fees result in unnecessary and undesirable litigation between clients and their former attorneys.

In patent law practice, the two primary fee structures are an hourly rate and a set fee for a designated service. Historically, attorney services have been billed by the hour, and this practice remains common today. But, increasingly, small independent inventors and solo practitioners are using the set-fee-for-service arrangement. With the set-fee arrangement, the inventor and attorney generally review the case, then the attorney proposes a single fee for handling the matter.

Both fee structures may be workable, but the most cost-effective arrangement should be pursued. If a fixed fee is used, the agreement might contain a provision that permits an additional sum if more time and work by the attorney is needed than initially anticipated by the inventor and the attorney. If an hourly rate is used, an estimate of the time to complete the patent application or other work should be obtained from the attorney. The inventor should be contacted for approval if more time is required than what was documented in the estimate. Again, no work should be started until both the inventor and the attorney have reached an acceptable fee arrangement and have put that fee arrangement into a written agreement.

When working with a law firm, understand that the partners and associates typically have different hourly rates. If an associate is going to handle a patent matter, ensure that only a reasonable amount of additional time is spent by the partner to review the associate's work. Know the billing rate of each attorney who might work on your case before they begin.

It is difficult to state which patent agent, attorney, or law firm will provide the best rate for preparing and prosecuting a patent application or handling other patent work. Because the fixed costs of a solo patent agent or solo attorney are somewhat lower than most firms', the individual agent or attorney can frequently perform patent work at a very competitive rate. Solo practitioners are typically more willing to perform work, such as drafting a patent application, for a fixed fee than are many law firms. However, some law firms see patent prosecution as a "loss leader" and are willing to provide patent preparation and prosecution services at a rate well below their normal fees to gain a position for the client's future licensing and litigation work.

Ask for a listing of all likely additional charges, such as copying costs, telephone charges, travel expenses, and so forth. Fees from the USPTO should also be factored into the final cost estimate. As with any other good or service, shopping around for legal services is the best way to determine their relative cost-effectiveness.

THE INITIAL MEETING BETWEEN INVENTOR AND PATENT ATTORNEY

Once you have retained a patent agent or attorney, he or she can review the invention for patentability and prepare and prosecute a US patent application. The process usually starts with an initial meeting between the inventor and the agent or attorney to review the merits of the invention. Careful planning for the initial meeting can expedite the preparation of a good patent application and lay the groundwork for an expeditious prosecution and allowance of the application. At the initial meeting with the patent attorney or agent, bring all the information and materials necessary to give him or her a clear understanding of your invention.

Determining whether the invention is patentable requires a review of what inventions already exist in the relevant technical field. Conducting a prior art search is the best way to learn about earlier patents and publications. Although it is possible to prepare and file a patent application without conducting a prior art search, this generally results in an unfocused application, as the invention will not be presented in the context of related existing technology. This could also result in a situation wherein the USPTO rejects the application based on a number of references having every feature of the invention. It is also quite possible that the prior art search conducted by the USPTO as part of the patent application examination process will not find the most relevant prior art to the invention; this could result in a patent that is easily invalidated. The risks of not performing any prior art search before drafting and filing the patent application outweigh the relatively small, incremental cost of having the attorney or agent perform at least a basic prior art search.

Provide the attorney or agent with copies of all relevant prior art that you are aware of. This will aid him or her with the patentability review, preparation of the patent application, and compliance with the duty to disclose to the USPTO all relevant prior art that is known by you, the inventor, and those assisting with the patent application.

Provide the patent agent or attorney with all drawings and figures, including flow charts, that aid in understanding the assembly or operation of your invention. At some point during the prosecution of the application, the drawings must be revised to meet requirements of the USPTO. Informal drawings may be submitted if they fulfill the minimal requirement of allowing the reader of the application to re-create the invention and show all features for which the inventor is claiming patent protection. By filing the application with informal drawings, it is possible to delay the expense of creating formal drawings until the USPTO decides to allow the application.

Having received an explanation of the invention and all relevant material, the attorney or agent will carefully review the materials for complete understanding of how the invention operates. The results of the prior art search will also be reviewed so that both the inventor and attorney or agent can determine differences between the prior art references and the invention.

USING THE SAMPLE ATTORNEY RETAINER AGREEMENT

A sample Attorney Retainer Agreement is provided at the end of this chapter for use when hiring a patent agent or patent attorney. Any time you hire an agent or attorney, a written agreement should be entered into that clearly spells out the rights and responsibilities of each party.

The sample agreement includes the date, the name and address of the client, and the name and office address of the attorney or agent. The agreement should describe, as completely as possible, the transaction or matter for which legal representation is sought, including a complete list of the duties and services the attorney is to perform. The agreement can be used as a checklist for gauging the performance of the attorney or agent.

The Attorney Retainer Agreement should document the manner in which you will pay the attorney or agent for legal services. This should include amounts, payment dates, and all other terms and conditions regarding payment of legal fees.

The Attorney Retainer Agreement provides that you can terminate your agreement at any time and for any reason. Your attorney or agent can also terminate the agreement for valid cause, such as your noncooperation or nonpayment or with your consent. The agreement also provides for the immediate refund of the money paid to your attorney or agent if the agreement is terminated, except to deduct payment for time, costs, and expenses from your refund or credit.

The agreement obligates your attorney or agent to maintain your information in confidence and to give you or any new attorney or agent a copy of all documents in your file at your request. Any additional terms that you or your attorney or agent may have can be added to the agreement.

Both you and your attorney or agent should sign the agreement. Keep a copy of the fully signed agreement for your records.

Attorney Retainer Agreement

1. This is an Agreement made as of the _____ day of _____, 20___, between
   (Client's name) _____
   (Client's address) _____
   (hereinafter referred to as the "Client") and
   (Attorney's name) _____
   (Attorney's address)_____
   (hereinafter referred to as the "Attorney"), which defines the terms and conditions under which Client has retained Attorney to provide legal counsel and services relating to the following matter:
   (describe the subject matter of the invention, patent, license or other legal issues of the Client)

   _____

   _____

   (hereinafter referred to as "Client's Case").

2. Attorney agrees to provide competent legal counsel and services to Client in connection with Client's Case and to perform the services provided below:

(Continued)

(i.e., conduct prior art search, review patentability of invention, prepare US patent application, prepare license agreement, handle patent litigation, etc.)

_____

_____

3. In consideration of the legal counsel and services performed by Attorney, Client agrees to make payment to Attorney as follows: (i.e., hourly rate, fixed fee, time period for payment, etc.)

    _____

    _____

4. a) Client agrees to pay all reasonable costs and expenses incurred by Attorney in connection with Client's Case. Attorney estimates in good faith that these costs are as follows:

    _____

    _____

    _____

    b) Attorney agrees to obtain Client's prior approval before incurring any costs and any other expenses on behalf of Client in an amount greater than $ _____.

5. Client has the right to terminate this Agreement at any time at Client's discretion. Attorney may terminate this agreement for valid cause upon Client's consent, provided that Client's Case is not prejudiced or harmed thereby.

6. Upon termination of this Agreement by either Client or Attorney, Client shall be entitled to the immediate refund or credit of all amounts paid or due, except as provided below:

    _____

    _____

    _____

(Continued)

7. After termination of this Agreement, Attorney agrees to provide to any new attorney or to Client, upon Client's request, a copy of all documents which Attorney has possession of relating to Client's Case.

8. Attorney shall maintain information regarding Client's Case in confidence and shall not disclose or use said information except for the benefit of Client as provided herein.

9. Additional terms and conditions:

    _____

    _____

    _____

Client and Attorney, intending to be legally bound, have signed this Agreement on the date first indicated above.

_____   _____

Client's signature   Attorney's signature

CHAPTER 8

Is Your Invention Patentable?

Knowing as soon as possible whether your invention is patentable is important if you will be spending significant amounts of time and money on patenting and commercializing it. Patentability depends on a number of factors, such as the type, utility, and novelty of the invention, as well as its unobviousness in view of the known prior art. You can always file a patent application on an invention and let the USPTO review and determine whether it is patentable. It is preferable to search and review the relevant prior art before spending a lot of effort and resources on an unpatentable and otherwise unprotectable invention.

Unfortunately, not everyone who creates or develops something has a patentable invention within the laws and regulations of the USPTO. There are a number of criteria that must be met and a number of traps and pitfalls that can render an otherwise patentable invention unpatentable. Even though you may be able to evaluate the patentability of the invention yourself, it may be prudent to seek out the help of a patent attorney or agent.

WHAT IS A PATENTABLE INVENTION?

Over the years Congress, through legislation, and the courts, through case law in this area, have created rules and guidelines that provide a basis for determining which inventions are entitled to patent protection. An inventor must evaluate his or her invention against the required criteria, and if these criteria are met, there is a strong likelihood patent protection of some degree will be available.

Remember that before you can have a patentable invention, there must first be conception and reduction to practice. Conception is the mental formulation of the invention in sufficient detail that someone familiar with the subject matter to which the invention relates could make and use the invention. Reduction to practice is generally making or constructing the invention (i.e., preparing a model or composition) and testing it to demonstrate its usefulness for its conceived purpose.

Your invention must fall within the required statutory classes for patentable invention to qualify for a US utility patent. These classes include processes, machines, articles of manufacture, compositions of matter, or any improvements thereon. Statutory classes will be discussed in greater detail later in this chapter.

In order for an invention to be patentable in the United States, it must be new or novel, useful, and unobvious.

Basically, for an invention to be new or novel, as required by the US patent laws, the invention must not have been previously known by others. For example, you generally cannot obtain a patent if your invention has been described in a printed publication anywhere, or if it has been available to the public, in public use, or on sale anywhere before you filed your patent application.

A patent cannot be obtained even though the invention is new, if the difference between the subject matter sought to be patented and the prior art are such that the subject matter "as a whole" would have been "obvious," at the time the invention was made, to a person having "ordinary skill in the art" to which the subject matter pertains. The standard for obviousness was amended by the American Invents Act effective March 16, 2013, to require that the invention must not be obvious at the time of the effective filing date of the patent application claiming the invention. Obviousness will now be determined at the time of filing rather than the time of invention. The determination of obviousness of an invention is a legal issue based on rules from court decisions.

For an invention to be unobvious, the invention need not have been the result of some flash of genius, nor require a synergistic result. If an invention merely utilizes the teachings or suggestions of the prior art to solve a problem and no unexpected results are obtained, it is doubtful that the invention overcomes the obviousness test. The invention must be evaluated on the basis of how it relates to the problem faced, the need for a solution, how the it differs from the prior art, what features are not taught or suggested from the prior art, and its prospects of commercial success.

The usefulness requirement can be easily met by showing any kind of utility for the invention. Where a special utility is being claimed for the invention (i.e., a cure for cancer), it will have to be demonstrated by appropriate testing.

THE STATUTORY CLASSES OF PATENTABLE INVENTIONS

The US patent laws provide that in order for a utility invention to be patentable, it must fall within one of five classes:

- Compositions of matter
- Processes or procedures
- Articles of manufacture
- Machine
- A new and useful improvement on any of the above

A single patent may include more than one type of invention, as long as each type is properly related to the other. These classes of patentable subject matter need not be specifically referred to in a patent, although the invention must fit into one or more of these classes.

Composition of Matter

A compound that refers to a new chemical entity, wherein the invention resides in the absolute novelty of the compound, is a composition of matter. Compound inventions are rare in certain research areas, while in other areas, such as pharmaceutical and agricultural chemicals, they are often the result of the discovery of a new compound having a medicinal or agricultural use. The new compound is not patentable solely because it is novel unless a use (utility) can be established.

A chemical composition refers to a combination of two or more compounds (i.e., a mixture). The invention resides in the utility and combination of the composition. The combination must provide some i) new use or ii) an improvement over the individual components of the composition for the same use, if any component present in the composition is known to be effective for that use.

Anyone other than the patentee who makes, uses, or sells a patented composition without the patentee's permission will infringe the composition of matter claim. Composition of matter claims, therefore, can provide strong patent protection. To obtain patent protection for composition of matter, a compound or composition must be thoroughly analyzed and described in terms of its chemical structure (as in the case of a new compound), and/or its physical and chemical properties, or by its method of preparation. If the compound or composition is prepared by only one technique, claims to the product according to the process of its preparation may be included in the patent. The patent protection for a compound or composition that can only be defined by the process of its preparation (product-by-process) is generally not considered as strong as protection for composition of matter, per se.

Process

A process or method invention is the operation or series of steps that lead to a useful result. The synthesis of a new compound or composition or a new method for making a known product may be a patentable process invention. Process inventions may be made by those who discover the need for a new step or the need to select certain process parameters for some improved result, such as a better product or a higher yield.

A process that uses a computer program or mathematical formula to produce a physical result, such as the computer control of a process for producing a product, may be patentable. The mathematical formula or method of calculation is not patentable.

A use invention is closely related to a process invention and is commonly referred to as a process or method of use. The new use of an old product or process may be patentable.

Article of Manufacture

Any item that does not fulfill the composition of matter, compound, process, or device categories will likely fall in the category of an article of manufacture. Articles of manufacture include nearly every man-made object, from a paper clip to a skyscraper.

Machine

Any mechanical or electrical apparatus or device is considered a machine, including a camera, a bicycle, a computer, an airplane, and the like.

Improvements

Any new, useful, and unobvious improvement on a composition of matter, process, article of manufacture, or machine can be protected by patent. For example, the discovery of a new use for any of the first four statutory classes is also patentable, such as when the use of a drug that is administered to cure one disease is discovered to be beneficial in the treatment of an entirely different disease or condition. Changes to a known composition, machine, article of manufacture, or process to achieve a better or different result may be patentable inventions. Even improvements on already patented inventions can be patentable.

UTILITY

As mentioned earlier, one requirement that must be met for an invention to be patentable, as dictated by 35 United States Code Section 101, is that the invention be useful, otherwise known as having utility. Generally, any known utility will suffice, and the only caveat to keep in mind is that the utility must be functional and not merely aesthetic. Aesthetic features are more suitable for design patent or copyright protection as discussed in chapter 2. Although nearly any invention can have utility, or "usefulness," in one way or another, some otherwise inventive ideas could be denied patent protection by falling in one of the "not useful as a matter of law" statutory classes. These include illegal inventions and products, unproved and unsafe new drugs, whimsical inventions, immoral inventions, non-operable inventions, and the like.

There must be some good derived from the use of the invention in order for it to be patentable. The good so derived need not be of any great degree or extent but need merely confer a benefit to the user in a defined manner. Thus, inventions that are considered destructive by their nature can still be useful and patentable such as a gun, explosive, nerve gas, or electric chair. If the invention provides any benefit to society, no matter how small or unusual, it will likely pass the utility test for obtaining a US patent.

In many cases a mere allegation of utility and operability by the inventor in a patent application is sufficient to meet the test, particularly if the allegation is apparent from the description of the invention. Utility and operability may have to be demonstrated in some cases where they are not inherent from a review of the invention, such as cancer treatments, cures for baldness, and perpetual motion machines.

NOVELTY AND ANTICIPATION

One requirement for patentability of an invention in the United States is that the invention be new or novel and not merely a copy or repetition of those of the past. The specific statutory requirements for novelty are provided by the patent laws in 35 United States Code Section 102.

For US patent applications filed prior to March 16, 2013, to satisfy the novelty requirement, the invention must:

1. Not have been known, published, or used publicly anywhere by others before the invention was made by the patent applicant;

2. Not have been patented or described by anyone in a printed publication anywhere, or on sale in the United States more than one year prior to the date of filing the US patent application;

3. Not have been abandoned by the patent applicant;

4. Not have been first patented in a foreign country prior to the date of the patent application based on an application filed more than twelve months before the filing of the US application;

5. Not have been described in a patent granted to another where the other patent application was filed in the United States before the invention by the patent applicant; and

6. Not have been made in the United States by another before the invention by the patent applicant.

For a US patent application filed on or after March 16, 2013, to meet the requirements of novelty,

1. The invention must not have been patented, or described in a printed publication, or in public use, on sale, or otherwise available to the public before the effective filing date of said patent application; and

2. The invention must not be claimed or described i) in a patent, or ii) in a published patent application, which names another inventor and which was effectively filed before the effective filing date of said invention.

The effective filing date is defined as either the actual filing date of the patent or published application, or the date on which the patent or published application is entitled to claim a right of priority.

The failure of the invention to meet any one of the above criteria means the invention is not novel, but is anticipated by the prior art and bars the right to a US patent.

There are specific exceptions to the above criteria that protect the inventor from his or her own public disclosures. These exceptions include the following:

1. A one-year grace period where disclosures made by the inventor or joint inventor or another who obtained the subject matter directly or indirectly from the inventor or joint inventor will not be considered prior art.

2. Any disclosures that appear in a patent application or patent that names another inventor and was filed before the effective filing date of the application for patent will not considered prior art if (a) the subject matter was either obtained directly or indirectly from the inventor or a joint inventor; (b) the subject matter had been publicly disclosed by the inventor or a joint inventor or another who

obtained the subject matter from the inventor or a joint inventor prior to the effective filing date of the application; or (c) the subject matter disclosed was owned by the same person or subject to be assigned to the same person.

Common ownership is where (1) the subject matter disclosed was developed and the claimed invention was made by, or on behalf of, one or more parties to a joint research agreement that was in effect on or before the effective filing date of the claimed invention; (2) the claimed invention was made as a result of activities undertaken within the scope of the joint research agreement; and (3) the application for patent for the claimed invention discloses or is amended to disclose the names of the parties to the joint research agreement.

Most foreign countries are not as compassionate toward inventors as the United States is. Whereas the US patent laws grant a one-year grace period for filing an application from an inventor's own public disclosures, most foreign countries regard such acts of disclosure as absolute bars to patentability. That is, any act of a public disclosure of the invention prior to the filing of a patent application is an immediate bar to any patent rights in most countries. In such a case, there is no grace period in most of the world, including Europe, the Pacific Rim, and South America, and your rights to a patent on the invention in these countries will be forever lost.

One issue that arises with respect to the effect of prior art, on what is and what is not patentable, is a concept known as anticipation. This bar to patentability is essentially the situation where each and every element of the invention can be found disclosed or described in a single prior art reference or source. For example, if you as an inventor combine elements A + B + C + D to yield E and there is a patent, scientific journal, or other publication that by itself teaches A + B + C + D yields E, your invention is anticipated and will not be patentable.

In order for a single prior art reference to anticipate your invention, however, all the elements must be arranged in substantially the same way to achieve the same result as your invention. If for example, the prior art reference teaches that the elements must be arranged B + D + C + A to yield E, your invention of A + B + C + D yields E will not likely be anticipated and patent protection for your invention may be available. Further, if all of your elements are not described (i.e., the patent or article teaches that A + B + C yields E), again there is no anticipation because each and every element of your invention must be found within the teachings of that reference, and here D is lacking.

A prior art reference may still anticipate your invention if one or more of the elements of your invention are inherently disclosed within that reference. In other words, an anticipatory reference need not duplicate word for word the elements of a claimed invention, but it is enough if some of the elements of the invention are inherent or otherwise implicitly described in that reference. For example, this time you've discovered that E possesses some feature or characteristic never before described or realized in the prior art. If a prior art reference discloses E without specifically describing that feature or property of E, your invention may still be anticipated by the reference if that feature is an inherent property of E. E possesses that property or characteristic regardless of whether or not that property was described in the reference.

Even if there is no existing prior art that may render your invention obvious or anticipated, you as the inventor can unfortunately take actions that, by themselves, can defeat your right to a patent. These bars to patentability involve the premature disclosure, sale, or foreign patenting of your invention more than one year prior to filing a patent application in the United States or some other country covered by the Patent Cooperation Treaty (PCT).

The disclosure or sale of your invention, which will result in a bar to patentability, can happen in a number of ways. This may consist of the sale or mere offer of sale of the invention to others; advertising the invention or any other written publication thereof; audio and video disclosure of the invention; and any disclosure of the invention in a speech, journal article, or promotional literature. Any of these acts by you or by others whereby your invention is disclosed to the public before filing an appropriate patent application may constitute a bar to a patent for that invention.

There is the judicially created doctrine known as experimental use that makes an exception to the public use and disclosure bar. Although narrowly construed, certain inventions need to be tested by the inventor in order to determine if they are workable. An example of experimental use is an old court case to decide whether the inventors discovered an improved asphalt for making roads. At the time, the only way the inventors could test whether or not the asphalt lasted longer, with less wear and tear, was to use it in a roadway. Although patentability was initially denied, the US Supreme Court later concluded that, because public use was the only way the invention could be tested, disclosure of the composition through its incorporation in a public road was not a bar under the patent laws.

OBVIOUSNESS

The obviousness test is usually the toughest requirement to pass in obtaining a US patent on your invention. Even if the invention is new and useful, it is not patentable unless there is some unobvious and unexpected result.

The obviousness test in practical effect prevents an inventor from getting a patent when all of the elements of the invention are not found within a single prior art reference, but all the elements can be found when two or more references are combined. Again, you have invented A + B + C + D = E. One reference teaches the elements A + B. Another reference teaches the elements C + D. Your invention would likely be considered obvious because of these references if there is a basis for combining the references.

It is important for the obviousness test that the prior art references must in fact be combinative in order to lead one skilled in the art to the invention at issue. In essence, the references must in one way or another be related or at least concerned with the same field of endeavor to suggest to one skilled in the art the benefits of the combination. The USPTO, once knowing your invention, cannot use hindsight and review the plethora of prior art references and selectively pick and choose the elements of your invention from various isolated and unrelated references that deal with different fields of study or inventive purpose.

For example, you've combined A + B + C + D to obtain E, which is a low-calorie fat replacer compound for use in foods. Suppose elements A and B are known thickeners in food products. And suppose element C is disclosed in reference #1 as an emulsifier in paints, while D is disclosed in reference #2 as a component in shampoos. Here, one skilled in the art (i.e., a food scientist) would not be motivated to take something used in making paints and combine it with something used in shampoos to produce a food product. These references are not combinative to show obviousness, because they do not suggest the use of elements C and D in anything even remotely similar to an edible food product. A similar situation exists where the prior art reference specifically teaches that one of the elements, C or D, cannot be used in food due to its bad taste or smell. This would not motivate one to combine it as an ingredient so as to come up with your invention.

Obviousness is a fairly gray area and not as clear-cut as the anticipation bar to patentability. Anticipation under 35 United States Code Section 102 is fairly black-and-white. Either all of the elements of your invention are specifically or inherently disclosed within the four corners of a prior art reference or they are not. Obviousness, on the other hand, often depends on whether combining the references involved would be logical and reasonable, and, even if so, whether all the elements of the invention are taught or suggested in the manner and for the purpose as the invention.

Many times, references used in rejecting an invention for obviousness teach more than the elements of the invention itself and may suggest that the elements can be used for other unrelated purposes. Whether partially unrelated references can be combined is always debatable, and even if the references are combinative; whether your invention would be the logical end result of the combination would also be an issue.

Show that your invention provides surprising and unexpected results to prove that it is not obvious. You can do this by conducting comparative tests between your invention and the prior art to demonstrate the unexpected advantage of your invention.

Fortunately for inventors, the courts have interpreted the patent laws to allow other intangible aspects of inventions to be considered in determining patentability. Known as "secondary considerations" of nonobviousness, these aspects are factual or evidentiary features of the invention that may be used to show the invention is novel, useful, and nonobvious. Taken together, these secondary considerations are not all controlling or dispositive of the issue, but they will go a long way in proving the invention is worthy of patent protection.

The secondary considerations are as follows:

- Proof that the invention cures a need or solves a problem where others have often tried yet failed
- Proof that the invention solves a problem that always existed but was never before recognized or, if recognized, thought to be unsolvable
- Proof that the invention satisfies a long-felt, unfulfilled need
- Proof that the invention has already attained commercial success on its own merit
- Proof that the invention achieves a desired purpose or result in a manner contrary to the beliefs or teachings of the prior art

MAXIMIZING THE PATENTABILITY OF YOUR INVENTION

Before creating your invention, define the problem you are faced with or the objective you are trying to reach, and record this information and these ideas. Review prior art to help generate potential solutions and to determine what ideas or inventions are new and patentable. These are some of the steps you should take to keep from reinventing the wheel and to enhance your chances of creating a patentable invention.

The following checklist will assist you in maximizing the likelihood of patent protection for your invention.

Define the Problem or Objective

☐ Describe the technical area related to the problem or objective, or describe areas that are closely related.

☐ Describe the problem in detail, as well as the possible cause of the problem or the objective, including the economic and technical concerns. Alternately, describe the parameters and analytical techniques that may determine whether or not you have met your objective or solved the problem. Outline the steps you will have to take to ensure success.

☐ Describe all conventional products or processes known that have been tried to solve the problem or meet your objective, list their technical and economic successes or failures and limitations, and explain how your proposed idea differs from each of the prior techniques.

Conduct a Literature Search

☐ Conduct a literature search and compile publications related to the problem, its cause, or your proposed solution, prior to conducting any experimental work. The literature search will inform you as to what others have proposed as solutions and may help you avoid wasting time on rediscovering known inventions.

☐ Frame a search request and strategy for conducting a literature search to find all published articles, patents, and published patent applications relating to your problem and your possible solution. Make a list of key words that generally define the problem and your conception of its solution. Precise definitions of the best key words will be important in conducting effective literature searches. A patent attorney or patent search services (e.g., www.delphion.com, www.thomsoninnovation.com, and www.landon-ip.com) can assist in uncovering patents in the areas related to your problem. Patent searchers or information retrieval specialists are usually trained to conduct searches not only of published patents but also of journal articles and other documents published worldwide. They use a variety of computer databases, such as Derwent, Chemical Abstracts, and Lexis.

☐ Review the search results carefully, and obtain copies of all the relevant publications and patents. Digest all the references, and analyze which approaches have been taken in the past, as well as which approaches have not been taken and why. This information will help you determine whether you should proceed to making your invention and will maximize your chances of getting a patent.

☐ Formulate a research strategy to make your invention after your initial analysis of the literature search is complete. Write a concise statement of your idea when you get an idea of how to solve your problem. This statement should include all the parameters you believe are necessary for solving the problem and as many individual features, elements, compounds, compositions, or processes that might be necessary for your idea to work. Then, describe how you plan to proceed to prove whether your idea actually is the answer to solving the problems you defined earlier.

☐ Explore all the variables of your invention; this includes materials of construction, ranges for each component in a composition, substituents on a structure, molecular weights, temperatures, pressures, and so on. Also explore the outer limits of your invention to obtain the broadest patent coverage needed for the invention. An invention is not completely defined until you know how to change each of the variables to determine when the invention works and when it does not. This type of experimentation is the only true way to define the scope of the invention, the preferred embodiment(s) of the invention, and the best products or methods to practice your invention.

☐ Describe your invention fully after testing the limits of it in a systematic way. This description will help you and your attorney or agent draft a patent application covering everything that works (and is not disclosed or suggested in prior publications), while eliminating things that do not work. An overly broad patent that claims items that do not work is to be avoided, just as an unduly narrow patent is, because overly broad patent claims can be challenged as invalid. By employing this systematic approach to testing, you will not leave holes in the patent protection or provide avenues for others to avoid your patent by working around the invention you have defined.

CHAPTER 9

How to Prepare and File a US Patent Application

After reviewing the prior art and determining that your invention is patentable and economically viable, you should file for patent protection on the invention. If you are a US inventor, the easiest process is to file a nonprovisional or provisional patent application with the USPTO. The process for filing these applications will be discussed later in this chapter.

This chapter provides step-by-step instructions on how to prepare and file a simple US patent application. These instructions will take you through the preparatory steps to writing the specification and claims, preparation of drawings, and completion of all other formalities and requirements for filing the patent application. By following the process outlined in this chapter, you will be able to prepare a patent application that should successfully withstand the scrutiny of the USPTO, licensees and assignees, and the federal courts. Approach the task with confidence and optimism that comes from being a patent-knowledgeable inventor and the best person to describe your invention, and you will have little or no difficulty handling the preparation and filing of your patent application.

UNDERSTANDING THE TYPES OF PATENT APPLICATIONS

There are three categories of patent applications you can file. The requirements for each category of patent applications are different, and you as the inventor need to ascertain which type of patent application you are filing. The three categories are as follows:

(a) **Plant patent:** This category of patent application covers new varieties of asexually produced plants.
(b) **Design patent:** This category of patent application covers ornamental characteristics embodied in an article of manufacture.
(c) **Utility patent (most common application):** This category of patent application covers a new and useful process, machine, article of manufacture, and composition of matter or any improvement on these.

This chapter will concentrate on the preparation and filing of utility patents, as they are the most common type of patent application.

There are two types of patent applications that you can file initially, a provisional patent application or a nonprovisional patent application. A provisional application offers inventors the option of filing a patent application that provides a low-cost first patent filing in the United States. The provisional patent application is not examined by the USPTO and acts merely to establish a filing date for your invention; therefore, the formal requirements for a provisional patent application filing are less than those required for a nonprovisional application. By filing a provisional application first, and then a nonprovisional within the twelve-month provisional application period, a patent term may be extended by as much as twelve months.

To establish a filing date with a provisional patent application, the application must be in English and include

- A written description of the invention; and
- Any drawings necessary to understand the invention.

A provisional application must also include

- A filing fee as set forth in 37 Code of Federal Regulation ("CFR") 1.16(d), which is regularly $260 and $130 for a small entity, and $65 for a micro entity as of April 27, 2017; and
- A cover sheet identifying the following (see USPTO form UPTO/SB/16):

- The application as a provisional application for patent;
- The name(s) of all inventors;
- Inventor residence(s);
- Title of the invention;
- Name and registration number of attorney or agent and docket number (if applicable);
- Correspondence address; and
- Any US Government agency that has a property interest in the application.

When filing a provisional application, you do not have to include a formal patent claim, an oath or declaration, or an information disclosure statement. The provisional application acts as an inexpensive placeholder to establish a filing date for your invention and allows for a twelve-month period to include other formal requirements for a full, nonprovisional patent application. A provisional application for patent exists for twelve months from the date it is filed. The twelve-month pendency period cannot be extended. Therefore, you must file a nonprovisional application corresponding to the provisional application during the twelve-month period after the filing of the provisional patent application to benefit from the earlier filing date of the provisional application.

A nonprovisional patent application is a complete US patent application, which the examiner at the USPTO will scrutinize and review for patentability. Therefore, this type of patent application has more formal requirements and higher fees than a provisional patent application does.

A nonprovisional utility patent application must be in English or include a translation in English and a statement certifying that the translation is accurate. The application must also include the appropriate filing fee. As of April 27, 2017, the basic filing fee for a US utility patent application was $280 plus $400 if filed as a paper application, $70 (if filed electronically or $140 plus $200 if filed as a paper application for a small entity, or $70 for a micro entity plus $200 if filed as a paper application). If the application is in a language other than English and does not include a translation, statement, or fee, the USPTO will provide notice and time for submission of these missing items.

UNDERSTANDING THE FORMAT OF A US PATENT APPLICATION

A complete US patent application has several components, some of which are mandatory and some of which are optional. The mandatory components of a US patent application include (1) a specification with a description of the invention and one or more claims; (2) drawings, if necessary to describe or disclose the invention; (3) the names of the inventors, usually included on an oath or declaration; (4) the required declaration of inventorship; and (5) the requisite filing fee.

The specification is the written description of the invention, which should include a description of how to make and how to use the invention and should conclude with at least one claim to the invention. The claim to the invention must begin on a new page. The specification must be in clear, full, concise, and exact terms so as to allow a person skilled in the art or science to make and use the invention.

The specification, claims, and drawings in a patent application become a part of the granted and published patent and normally follow a specific format. A specification with claims, necessary drawings, and names of all inventors must be included in the patent application for it to be given a filing date. A declaration and filing fee are also mandatory for an application to be complete, but these can be submitted within two months of filing the application, with the payment of a surcharge, without losing the original filing date.

In addition to the above mandatory items, the following optional items should also accompany a completed application: an Application Transmittal Letter, an Information Disclosure Statement, a Verified Statement of Small Entity Status (if applicable), an Assignment (if applicable), and a self-addressed return postcard to acknowledge receipt of the application by the USPTO (if you decide to mail the application to the USPTO).

The Specification

The specification should consist of the following parts, which may be ordered as separate headings:

1. Title of the Invention

2. Cross-Reference to Any Related Application(s) (if any)
3. Statement Regarding US Government-Sponsored Research (if applicable)
4. If applicable, Incorporate by Reference to a compact disc appendix containing i) an Amino Acid or Nucleotide Sequence Listing, ii) a Table, or iii) a Computer Program Listing
5. Background of the Invention
6. Brief Summary of the Invention
7. Brief Description of Drawings (if any)
8. Detailed Description of the Invention
9. One or More Claims
10. Abstract
11. Drawings (if applicable)
12. Amino Acid or Nucleotide Sequence Listing (if applicable)

The specification is the core of a completed patent application. Before you begin drafting the specification, it is a good idea to do the following preliminary work to prepare to write the specification:

1. Become familiar with the patent regulations. There are three sets of statutes or regulations that govern all patent matters. The first two are the Patent Statute, 35 US Code, and the Patent Rules, 37 Code of Federal Regulations, a more detailed set of regulations based on the Patent Statute. All of the requirements for drafting an application can be found in the Patent Statute and the Patent Rules. The USPTO website is a great resource for information on drafting and filing patent applications (www.uspto.gov/patents/law/index.jsp). The third set of rules governing patent procurement is the Manual of Patent Examiner's Procedures (MPEP), which is followed by the patent examiners in reviewing applications. You probably do not need this large and detailed manual to draft a patent application, but it could be useful in prosecuting the application, particularly sections 700 and 2100. The MPEP is available online on the USPTO website at www.uspto.gov/web/offices/pac/mpep/index.html.

2. Write a brief description of the invention. Here is a list of questions you should be able to answer and information you need to prepare that will help you organize your thoughts and write a sufficient description of your invention:

    a) Give some background about your invention. For example, what is the problem the invention solves?

        i) Are there existing products or processes that solve the same problem? What are they, and how do they differ from your invention?

    b) What are some of the unique attributes of your invention?

        i) Make a list of the features or attributes of your invention that make it different from the other inventions in the same technology area.

        ii) List the advantages of your invention over known products or processes, particularly those advantages that are surprising or unexpected.

    c) Prepare a more detailed description of your invention:

        i) Describe how to make and use your invention, generally and specifically.

        ii) Prepare sketches of your invention if drawings are the best way to depict your invention.

        iii) List some of the variations on your invention that you would like to include in your description.

    d) Prepare a list of actual uses of your invention and other likely uses for your invention.

3. Review all relevant prior art you have located. You can locate prior art in your technology area by searching the standard databases following the discussion on conducting a literature search in chapter 8 of this book. You may also be able to purchase a literature search from various vendors who provide these searches for a fee. They include services such as Delphion, Thomson Innovation, and Landon IP. You can use this art to generate terminology to describe your invention and to see how similar inventions are described and drawn. Refer to this prior art in the background section of the specification. Finally,

submit copies of the prior art to the USPTO with an Information Disclosure Statement. The details of the Information Disclosure Statement will be discussed later, in chapter 8.

4. Draft a sample claim, one sentence, to describe the invention and the necessary elements of the invention. A claim is a formalized, precise description of the invention. For further explanation, see the discussion on drafting claims later in this chapter.

5. Review other US patents in the field of your invention to help you decide how to organize your application. You can search the USPTO database with keywords to find other US patents in the field of your invention by visiting this link: patft.uspto .gov/. The advanced search option provides you with the ability to use keywords, date ranges, and so forth to narrow your search to a reasonable number of patents. Because US patents are not protected by copyright law, sections of text from these patents can be copied and included in your application.

After you have completed these preliminary steps, you should have a good understanding of what your invention is and what unique elements you will be able to claim. When you are satisfied that you know your invention, and you can describe it in words and drawings, you are ready to begin drafting the specification.

DRAFTING THE PATENT SPECIFICATION

The specification, along with the drawings and claims, is published in the granted patent. At the end of the specification are one or more claims that specifically define the invention and all the required elements. Because the claims are such a unique and important part of the specification, they are discussed in greater detail later in this chapter. The specification is a detailed description of the invention that must fully disclose everything one needs to know, as well as the inventor's best mode, to practice the invention.

The full disclosure requirement for patent applications is mandated by 35 United States Code, Section 112(a), of the Patent Statute, which states,

> The specification shall contain a written description of the invention, and of the manner and process of making and using it, in such full, clear, concise, and exact terms as to enable any person skilled in the art to which it pertains, or with which it is most nearly connected, to make, and use the same, and shall set forth the best mode contemplated by the inventor or joint inventor of carrying out the invention.

It is critically important that your patent specification meet the requirements of the first paragraph of Section 112. These requirements basically mean that (1) the specification must adequately describe the invention; (2) the specification must teach or enable someone else who has skill in the technical area of the invention to make and use the invention; and, (3) the specification must present the best way known by the inventor for practicing the invention.

There are a number of reasons why it is imperative that your application meet the requirements of the patent statute when you file the application. First, failure to meet these requirements can result in a rejection of your application by the USPTO or in a subsequent finding of patent invalidity should the granted patent ever be litigated. Second, after the patent application has been filed, you are not allowed to add new information (called "new matter") without re-filing the application. Third, everything you claim as your invention must be in the specification.

Other requirements for the specification are that it be on sheets of paper of the same size, typed on either letter-size (8.5 x 11 inches), legal-size (8.5 x 13–14 inches), or A4-size (21 x 29.7 centimeters) paper. The paper should be in portrait orientation and written only on one side. Spacing between lines should be set at 1.5 or double. Use the following margins for letter- and legal-size paper: at least 0.75 inch at the top and bottom, and at least 1 inch on the left and at least 0.75 inch on the right. Number each page of the specification, preferably at the bottom. Text should be written in a nonscript type of font (e.g., Arial, Times Roman, or Courier, preferably at a font size of 12), with the lettering style having capital letters at least 0.3175 centimeters (0.125 inch) high, but no smaller than 0.21 centimeters (0.08 inch) high (e.g., a font size of 6). Each page of the specification should include only a single column of text. Finally, the specification, claims, and abstract should each begin on a new page.

Many foreign patent offices require that the application be filed on A4-size paper. The margin requirements for this size of paper are slightly different: Top, left, and right margins must be at least 2 centimeters; the bottom margin must be at least 2.5 centimeters. If you are planning to also file your application outside the United States, it may be easier if you use A4-size paper and margin requirements for both the United States and foreign patent applications.

Let's review the parts of the specification.

1. Title of the Invention

Sometimes the most difficult part of drafting a patent application is putting the first words on paper or into your word processor. Put a title at the top of the first page to help you get started. The title should be descriptive and state, in just a few words, the essence of your invention. It is acceptable to use laudatory words in the title such as "An Improved Cleaning Solution" or "A Novel Can Opener." Remember that the title is a required item of the application, so writing it down will help you get one step closer to completing the application. The title of the invention should be placed at the top of the first page of the specification. The title of the invention should be two to seven words. It may not contain more than 500 characters.

2. Cross-References to Related Applications

If you have previously filed any applications for the same or one or more related inventions, reference those applications at the beginning of the patent specification. For example, you should use language such as, "This application is a [continuation/continuation-in-part/divisional] of application Serial No. _____, filed on _____, titled "_____."

Omit this item if there are no related applications.

3. Statement Regarding Federally Sponsored Research (if any)

This section should contain a statement of whether or not the inventions are made under federally sponsored research and development.

4. Incorporation by Reference to a Genetic Sequence Listing, a Table, or a Computer Program Listing Compact Disc Appendix (if applicable)

This section incorporates by reference any material submitted separately on a compact disc that must be incorporated by reference in the specification. The only materials accepted on compact disc are computer program listings, gene sequence listings, and tables of information.

5. Background of the Invention

The background of the invention is made up of two parts:

(a) Field of the Invention, which includes a statement describing the field of technology to which your invention pertains.

(b) Description of the Related Art, which includes information disclosed on your information disclosure statement. For this section, you should discuss the prior art and how your invention is distinguishable from it. Explain the objectives and advantages of your invention.

For example, you can make a statement such as, "One objective of this invention is to provide a can opener that can be operated with one hand. A further objective of this invention is to provide a foldable can opener that can be operated with one hand." Stating the objectives in this manner is a way to try to persuade a patent examiner that your invention is unique and patentable.

6. Brief Summary of the Invention

Include a brief synopsis of the invention and its benefits. Begin by summarizing the objectives identified earlier. Then the subject matter of the invention should be described in one or more clear, concise sentences or paragraphs. In many cases, the summary of the invention can simply be a recitation of the main claim in the application and a brief explanation of the elements of the invention.

7. Brief Description of the Drawings (if any)

If the application includes drawings, provide a brief description of all the figures by number in the specification. This part of the application typically begins with a sentence, such as, "The accompanying drawings further describe the invention." After that introduction, in separate paragraphs, write only one or two sentences describing the drawings, such as, "Figure 1 is a perspective view of the gear shift constructed in accordance with the invention."

8. Detailed Description of the Invention

The detailed description is the most comprehensive item in the specification. In this section of the specification, describe the invention fully, clearly, concisely, and exactly to enable a technically skilled person to make and use the invention without extensive experimentation. Disclose the best mode known by you for practicing the invention, and disclose every element of your invention that you plan to claim. Prepare an outline of the detailed description of the invention before you begin to write it.

A sample outline could start out with a description of the invention and possible embodiments of the invention. Then include a detailed description of figures, if any. Next, include a section on the definition of terms that are particular to your invention and that further elaborate on the meaning of your claim terms. Finally, include any examples of practicing your invention and label each example by number. You may include the best mode in your preferred embodiment description or in your specific examples.

Make certain you have sketched all the drawings you plan to use and have labeled and numbered all elements. Name and describe each numbered element in the detailed description.

In a typical patent application, the first paragraphs of the detailed description introduce the invention by describing it in broad terms. With this broad description as a beginning, you can then describe the invention in greater and greater detail. The beginning of the detailed description should be like the base of a pyramid or the trunk of a tree from which the rest of the description will emerge.

As you write the specification, name all elements of the invention that you plan to claim. Finding the appropriate name for an element is important and can be tricky. Here are a few suggestions to help in defining elements of your invention. Keep in mind that a patent applicant can be his or her own lexicographer in choosing words to describe the invention. In other words, you define the elements and terms of your invention. For example, if the invention is a novel antiseptic composition, you could state, "In this invention, *antiseptic* means a composition that kills microorganisms or prevents or inhibits their growth and reproduction." Use a thesaurus, dictionary, or glossary of technical terms for assistance. Avoid using nonspecific terms such as gadget, thing, or widget. After you have selected a name for an element, use that name consistently throughout the specification, and do not use different names interchangeably. It is important to remember that when defining terms that are different from their ordinary and customary meaning, you should ensure the definition is not diametrically opposite to the term's ordinary meaning. For example, *right* cannot mean *left* and vice versa.

After describing the invention in broad terms and defining all of its important elements, describe each element of the invention as specifically as possible. For example, if the invention is a one-handed, foldable can opener that includes the elements of a handle and a cutting edge, describe for each element the shape, size, and materials that it could be made of, and any other relevant characteristics. If the invention is a new composition, the elements are the ingredients in the composition. Identify every ingredient and all possible examples of each ingredient. If the invention is a process, the elements are the steps of the process such as mixing, heating, or drying. Describe each step in complete detail, stating mixing time, heating temperature, and drying conditions. Err on the side of being overly inclusive. Keep in mind that new matter cannot be added to the application once it has been filed.

Make sure you have identified and described, in detail, each element of the invention. Keep in mind the requirements of 35 United States Code, Section 112(a) (e.g., fully disclose, enable, and teach the best mode). This portion of the application might include several pages if the invention has many elements, ingredients, or steps. On the other hand, if there are only one or two elements in the invention, this description will be much shorter. Whether it is long or short, however, the description must completely describe and disclose the invention.

Identify the "preferred" and "most preferred" embodiments of the invention in the detailed description. If a component can be made of several different materials, identify these by stating, "Preferred materials for the handle of the can opener of this invention are aluminum, tin, and stainless steel." You can then narrow the description even more by stating, "The most preferred material for the handle is stainless steel." You will then have a basis in the claims for drafting increasingly more specific or narrower claims directed to the preferred and most preferred materials.

Because specificity is critical in an application, the use of trademarks instead of generic names for components or ingredients should be avoided, unless the mark is necessary for full identification. Use generic names when possible; for example, instead of "Velcro®," use "hook-and-loop fastener," and instead of "Scotch Tape®," say "plastic tape."

It is optional whether to include any examples of making, using, or testing the invention in the detailed description. Examples are not required in a US patent application, but they can be useful in describing the invention and demonstrating patentability to the examiner. In a US patent application, you can even use prophetic or hypothetical examples (provided you show them as such, e.g., "The invention could be made by . . ." or "If the invention were made by . . ."). These hypothetical examples should be in present or future tense. But actual examples may be needed for filing in some foreign countries with stricter requirements. If you have created one or more working models of the invention, you should describe them in the detailed description under a subpart titled "Examples." If you have experimented with the invention, you should include the experimental results in the examples. If the invention includes drawings, correlate the elements in the drawings and their description in the specification. When you refer to an element of the invention in the specification, you should name it and refer to it by its drawing number. For example, "the handle 12" or "a hinge 13." Refer to the elements in the drawings in numerical order. You could start by assigning only even reference numbers (e.g., 2, 4, . . .) to the elements. That way, as you complete the description, you can add new elements and reference numbers without upsetting the numerical order of the description.

Your US patent application must include the best mode contemplated by you or any co-inventors for practicing the invention. Thus, you cannot keep important parts of your invention secret and obtain a US patent on it. You can describe the best mode for carrying out the invention in the detailed description or include it in the examples. However, you do not have to refer to the best mode as such, or otherwise highlight it, as long as it is included within the patent application.

Every element or feature included in the patent claims must find support in the patent specification. Again, identify and describe every critical and claimed feature of your invention in the detailed description. Copy the wording of the claims into the detailed description to make certain that all elements in the claims have an antecedent basis in the description.

Briefly summarize the invention and its benefits and advantages at the end of the detailed description. There is a good deal of repetition in a patent application, but this repetition can help you sell the invention and its patentability.

You want your patent application to be interpreted as broadly as legally possible and do not want to restrict the scope of the invention unless absolutely necessary. To help ensure a broad interpretation, a short statement such as the following is useful:

> The above description and examples should be not construed as limitations on the scope of the invention. Many other variations are possible. Accordingly, the scope of the invention is determined by the claims and their legal equivalents.

A patent examiner is not given sufficient time to read through your specification in great detail and will use your specification as a guide to interpreting the scope of the claims and the meaning of terms and whether you have taught an ordinary, skilled artisan reading your patent how to make and use the invention. Therefore, break up paragraphs so as to alert the examiner to key claim terms, be precise in your examples, do not employ hypertechnical language to explain your invention, and employ good comparative technique to distinguish your invention from those in the prior art.

9. One or More Claims

The claim defines the invention you are trying to protect. In concept it defines the boundary lines of your property; therefore, great care and attention to detail should be taken when writing and later possibly amending your claims. The examiner determines whether your patent will be granted largely on the way you have defined your invention in the claims.

A nonprovisional application for a utility patent must contain at least one claim. A more detailed discussion on writing claims appears later in this chapter.

10. Abstract

The abstract is presented on a separate sheet of paper at the end of the specification, after the claims. When the patent is published, the abstract will appear on the first page. The abstract should be no more than a 150-word summary of the invention and generally limited to a single paragraph. The purpose of the abstract is to disclose the novel elements of the invention and to help the examiner and the public quickly determine the nature of the technical disclosure. Writing the abstract should be relatively simple after you have completed the rest of the specification, and, for simplicity, it could be a summary of the main patent claim.

11. Drawings (if any)

If drawings are necessary to understand the subject matter to be patented, the patent application must include them. The drawings should include every feature of the invention as described in the claims. If drawings are required, omitting them may cause the application to be considered incomplete, and you may not receive a filing date for your application.

12. Amino Acid or Nucleotide Sequence Listing (if any)

In certain applications, an amino acid and/or nucleotide sequence may be necessary to properly describe the invention and/or the claims. For such applications to be complete, an amino acid and/or nucleotide sequence should be included in the application complying with 37 CFR §1.821 through 37 CFR §1.825 and may be in paper or electronic form.

THE CLAIMS

The claims are the last part of the specification and are perhaps the most important part of the patent application. Claims are numbered sentences that define the patentable invention. The patent statute provides that the specification shall conclude with one or more claims particularly pointing out and distinctly claiming the subject matter that the applicant regards as his or her invention. For a more detailed discussion on writing claims, see the section on drafting claims later in this chapter.

The claims must describe the invention clearly enough so that anyone reading them knows the scope, or the metes and bounds, of the invention.

It is a good technique to draft the claims from an outline of the important elements of the invention—even before you start to write the detailed description. Drafting patent claims takes practice, and you may spend a good deal of time completing this portion of the patent application. You may want a skilled patent agent or attorney to review the claims and the rest of the application before you file to make sure the application is formatted correctly. The examiner in the USPTO can help you draft allowable claims after you have filed an application with at least one claim.

Keep in mind Sections 102, 103, and 112, paragraphs two through six, of the patent statute when drafting claims of your invention. Under Section 102, a patent will be granted only if the claimed invention is novel. Thus, be sure to recite the novel features of your invention in the claims. Claims to inventions that are not novel, under Section 102, are rejected by the USPTO on the grounds of "anticipation" by the prior art. Under Section 103, claims in a patent application will be rejected if the USPTO finds that the claimed invention is "obvious" in view of the prior art. The claims should be as broad as possible, yet narrow enough so that the claimed invention is both novel and nonobvious. Good claim drafting requires balancing these conflicting considerations, while at the same time claiming your invention as broadly as reasonable.

In addition, 35 United States Code, Section 121 provides that each application must be for one "independent and distinct" invention. In other words, you cannot claim two unrelated inventions in the same application. The meaning of independent and distinct, however, is murky. Should you be uncertain whether you are claiming more than one invention, err on the side of being overly broad or inclusive. The USPTO may require that you restrict the application to one invention, and you can make an election then.

As you may have observed from reading granted patents, the form and language of claims are highly stylized.

Some basic requirements of claims include the following:

(a) The claims section begins with the statement, "What is claimed is . . ."; "I (or We) claim . . ."; or "The invention claimed is . . ."

(b) Each claim begins with a capital letter and ends with a period.

(c) Each claim should be numbered sequentially in Arabic numerals.

(d) When a claim sets forth a number of elements or steps, each element or step of the claim should be separated by a line indentation.

(e) Claims should preferably be arranged in order of scope so that the first claim presented is the broadest and the least restrictive. The least restrictive claim should be presented as claim number 1, and all dependent claims should be grouped together with the claim or claims to which they refer. More on independent and dependent claims follows this section.

(f) Each claim is one, and only one, sentence. Each sentence, in turn, has three components: a preamble, a transition, and a body. Let's review each component and the format of a patent claim.

1. Preamble of the Claim

The preamble is a brief introductory statement that summarizes, describes, or defines the basic nature or class of the invention and precedes the body of the claim. The preamble can be general or specific depending on the character of the invention and the prior art. Typical preambles to claims are, "A composition . . ." or "A composition for preventing oral malodor . . ." or "An apparatus . . ." or "An apparatus for opening metal containers . . ."

Usually, the preamble of a claim is given little or no weight in determining patentability of the claim. For this reason, it is important that all the critical elements of the invention be included in the body of the claim and not in the preamble.

2. Transitional Phrase

Following the preamble is a transitional word or phrase connecting the preamble to the body of the claim. The transition phrase affects the scope of your claim and, consequently, the search and art applied to your claim by the examiner. There are three transitional phrases: "comprising," "consisting of," and "consisting essentially of."

The broadest transitional words are "comprising" or "that comprises." These are called open transitional words. A claim with "comprising" or "that comprises" as a transition encompasses additional elements that are not specifically recited in the claim. For example, if what is claimed is "a composition comprising A, B, and C," one who makes a composition with A, B, C, and D would still be infringing the claim. In other words, any other composition with A, B, and C in it, even if it contained numerous other ingredients, would be an infringing composition. Therefore, it is preferable to use open transitional words to obtain the broadest possible patent coverage.

The narrowest transitional words are "consisting" or "consisting of." These are called closed transitional words. These words limit the claim only to those elements specifically recited in the claim. For example, if what is claimed is "a composition consisting of A, B, and C," the only infringing compositions would be those with only components A, B, and C; no more, and no less. Use these closed transitional words only if the claims must be narrowed to overcome the prior art.

Between open and closed transitional words are partially closed transitional words, the best example of which is "consisting essentially of." In general, partially closed transitional words are used to overcome the prior art, yet they allow the claimed invention to encompass certain unrecited elements, provided these elements are not essential to define the novel and nonobvious aspects of the claimed invention. For example, if what is claimed is "a composition consisting essentially of A, B, and C," a composition made of A, B, C, and D, wherein D is not an essential component of the composition (e.g., it merely changes the color), would still infringe this claim.

3. Body of the Claim

The body of the claim contains (1) a statement of the elements of the invention and (2) a description of how these elements related to each other to make the invention. The elements of the invention are the structural components of an article of manufacture or a machine, the ingredients of a composition of matter, or the steps of a process. These are the same elements you include in the detailed description of the invention.

The fundamental principle of drafting claims is to include all the critical elements, regardless of the class of the invention. For example, if the invention is a machine for sorting bottles, the elements would consist of the parts of the machine. Similarly, if the invention is a new method for manufacturing plastic, the elements would include the steps of the new method or process. If the invention is a new laundry detergent, the elements would consist of the ingredients that comprise the detergent. Make sure the names of the elements in the claims are consistent throughout the specification.

The first time a new element is named in the claims it is preceded by the article "a" or "an." Thereafter, in the same claim or in a subsequent dependent claim (more on dependent claims below), the element is referred to as "said" element or "the" element. "Said" has a specific meaning in claim language that might make it easier for a potential infringer or patent attorney to understand. On the other hand, "the" is less formal and may be easier for a judge or jury to understand. Either is acceptable.

"Means for" may also be used to identify elements. For example, ". . . comprising a means for connecting . . ." is called a means-plus-function claim. Another variation of "means for" language could be, for example, ". . . comprising a connecting means . . ." If you use such language, make sure it is clear and well described in the specification.

The relationship between the elements of the invention should be clearly disclosed. Words such as "surrounded by," "inserted into," or "connected to," describe the relationship between elements. When deciding the order in which to list the elements and the words used to describe their relationship, ask yourself whether, after reading the claim, one would be able to easily diagram or draw the invention.

List the elements in the most logical order. Because an invention may consist of several main elements, each in turn comprised of several sub-elements, organize a claim in an outline using numbers and letters.

4. Independent and Dependent Claims

Claims can be written in either "independent" or "dependent" form. An independent claim stands by itself and does not directly relate to any other claim or claims. Dependent claims, on the other hand, are specifically dependent on another claim. One or more claims may be presented in dependent form and refer back to and further narrow the claim from which they depend. Dependent claims are interpreted by the examiner as including all the elements of the claim from which they depend.

In the case of our one-handed can opener, for example, the first independent claim might be as follows: claim 1, "A one-handed can opener comprising a handle attached to (a) a turning means and (b) a cutting means." The first dependent claim might be as follows: claim 2, "Said one-handed can opener of claim 1, wherein said handle is shaped to conform to the human hand."

There are typically between one and three independent claims in a patent application. Additional fees are charged for more than three independent claims. Each independent claim in turn has several subordinate or dependent claims that refer to the independent claim. It is also acceptable, for the appropriate fee, to write multiple dependent claims, where one claim depends on more than one independent claim. For example, "Said one-handed can opener of claims 1, 5, or 9 wherein . . ." It is important to note, however, that a multiple dependent claim cannot depend on a claim that is also a multiple dependent claim.

Not only do independent claims stand alone, but, as you can see from the example of the can opener, they are also broader and more general than dependent claims. Claim 1 will likely be the broadest claim. The broadest claim should describe a generalized version of the invention.

After you have drafted the broadest independent claim, you can then narrow the scope of the invention by drafting several dependent claims, each of which further narrows and more specifically describes the invention.

For example, suppose your invention is a new laundry detergent. One element in the broadest independent claim could be an element C. A typical set of patent claims could look like the following:

> **Claim 1.** A laundry detergent comprising element A, B, and C.
> **Claim 2.** The laundry detergent of claim 1, wherein element C is a long-chain polymer.
> **Claim 3.** The laundry detergent of claim 2, wherein the long-chain polymer consists of twenty carbons.

As you can see, each successive dependent claim can be further narrowed from the broader claim. So, claim 2 is narrower than claim 1, and claim 3 in turn is narrower than claim 2.

You can also achieve a similar narrowing in dependent claims by using narrowing transitional phrases. For example:

> **Claim 1.** A laundry detergent comprising A, B, and C.
> **Claim 2.** The laundry detergent of claim 1, consisting essentially of A, B, and C.
> **Claim 3.** The laundry detergent of claim 1 or 2, consisting of A, B, and C.

The advantage of writing a series of claims that are increasingly narrow and more specific is that, should the broadest claim be found to be unpatentable or invalid due to prior art, there is still valuable patent protection due to the language used to describe the narrower dependent claim.

Once you understand and are comfortable with the basic principles of drafting claims, you should find it relatively easy to draft the broadest independent claim, followed by several dependent claims. Again, you may want to retain a patent attorney or agent to prepare or review the patent application to make sure it is drafted adequately.

RULES FOR DRAFTING PATENT CLAIMS

Follow the rules listed below when drafting patent claims:

1. Make sure all claims are supported by the specification. All claimed elements must be described in the specification exactly the same way they appear in the claims. For example, if you want to recite in the claim that "one element of the invention is a steel rod connecting two pistons," you must include that in the specification. Review the specification to make sure that all claims are supported. If you find that a particular claim term and/or phrase is not defined in the specification, go back to the section in the specification where you have defined terms and include a definition for the claim term.

2. Use only one sentence per claim. This seems self-explanatory, but it cannot be ignored. It is okay to use commas (usually employed when separating embodiments of a claimed element), semi-colons (usually used to separate elements within a claim), and colons (usually used after a transitional term or phrase) within the claim; however, make sure the only period in the claim is at the very end.

   The example below illustrates the usage of these types of punctuation within a claim:

   Claim 1. A composition comprising an active agent selected from X, Y, and Z; a binder selected from L, M, and O; and a pharmaceutically acceptable carrier.

3. Make sure an element has been named in the claim before modifying or qualifying it. Failure to follow this rule will result in the rejection of the claim for "lack of antecedent basis." More specifically, introduce an element for the first time in a claim by referring to it with "a" or "an." For example, "a rod" or "an insignia." After this first use, you may refer to the element as "said" or "the."

For example, "said rod" or "the insignia." This format must be followed within a claim as well as in dependent claims.

4. Make sure the elements of the claimed invention logically inter-relate. A claim must recite an operative combination of elements, not a mere aggregation of elements. The interrelationship between the parts may be structural or functional. Structural relationships between elements are described by words such as "connected to," "secured to," "near," "adjacent to," "attached to," or "mixed with." For example, "Wherein A is connected to B, D is adjacent to C, or E is mixed with F." Functional relationships between elements are described by words such as "to support," "in order to," and "so that it moves." Functional relations between elements could be stated as, "Wherein A is positioned to support B . . ."

5. Use Markush groups if appropriate. A *Markush group* is defined as an artificial or generic group. A Markush group recites alternatives in a format, such as, "selected from the group consisting of A, B, and C." Members of a Markush group belong to a recognized physical or chemical class or to an art-recognized class. Technology areas where Markush groups are often employed include chemistry, metallurgy, refractory, ceramics, pharmacology, pharmacy, and biology. There are times when an element of the invention could be made of a number of different materials. These different materials, however, may not neatly fit into a single generic group such as metals or liquids. For example, the handle of the can opener could be made of metal, plastic, or wood. But the USPTO generally does not accept claims of "plastic or wood or metal." In such instances, you can create a Markush group. The operative phrase for a Markush group is "selected from the group consisting of." The following example uses a Markush group: "Said can opener, wherein said handle is made from material selected from the group consisting of metal, plastic, or wood."

6. If appropriate, use relative terms such as "about" and "essentially." These terms are acceptable in claims to indicate that a particular number is not absolutely specific, and it helps in obtaining a broader interpretation of the claim. For example, the phrases

"comprising about 2 percent water," "heating said liquid for about twenty-five minutes," or "a circumference of no more than about three feet" effectively use the term "about" in the claim. This type of term may be defined in your specification to give more clarity to the claim. For example, you may define "about" to be + or − 10 percent. Relative terms that are unacceptable and have been found to be indefinite include "similar," "type," "comparable," "superior," and "like material"; these should be avoided in the claims.

7. Avoid overly precise numbers. The corollary to using the term "about" is that overly precise numbers should be avoided. For example, instead of saying, "mixing said composition for thirty minutes," say, "mixing said composition sufficiently long enough that said particles are evenly dispersed." Being overly precise in your terms enhances the possibility of someone employing a slight change to your process or composition to avoid coverage by your patent claims.

8. Use functional language when appropriate. Sometimes an element in a claim can best be broadly defined by what it does (e.g., its function). For example, a "means for attaching" could include screws, nails, and adhesives.

9. Be consistent in your use of terms. Once you have used a term in a claim to identify a particular element, use that same term consistently throughout the claims. Define the term as broadly as possible in the description.

10. Avoid unnecessary wordiness or "prolixity." Under Section 112(b), a claim must be specific enough to particularly point out and distinctly claim the subject matter of your invention. Draft your claims with this rule in mind, and you will likely avoid a rejection of "prolixity" by the USPTO. Also, do not recite in the claims any elements unless they are critical to practicing the invention.

11. Claim what you plan to sell or license. As obvious as this rule may seem, it is not always followed. When drafting the claims, make sure at least some claims encompass all possible marketable versions, including the version you plan to commercialize. For

example, if your invention can be made of any material, be careful not to limit the material from which it can be made in the claims. Try to imagine what other variations your invention might take during its development, and do not preclude those variations by writing claims that are too narrow.

12. Do not hesitate to seek advice or help. No matter how sophisticated you are as an inventor, you may still need help in preparing your patent application. You may want a patent practitioner to review the application before you file it with the USPTO. Also, remember that after the application is filed, you can ask the examiner assigned to your case for assistance.

PREPARING DRAWINGS

As recommended earlier, prepare, or have a draftsman prepare, sketches of the invention even before you begin drafting the specification. These sketches can be submitted as part of the original filing to meet the drawings requirement of the USPTO, with the understanding that they will be revised and resubmitted as final drawings to comply with USPTO formalities. These sketches are called "informal" drawings because they may not meet the requirements for "formal" patent drawings.

The USPTO has many formalities that must be met for formal drawings. Formal drawings must be on a certain size and type of paper; margins must be a certain width; shading and hatching must be applied using certain methods; and rules for using symbols, legends, and arrows must be followed. These rules are listed in 37 CFR, Sections 1.81 through 1.85. See also the USPTO's website, at www.uspto.gov/web/patents/pubs/pdg0602 .zip and www.USPTO.gov/patents/resources/general_info_concerning _patents.jsp#heading-18. Unless you are a skilled draftsperson, it is recommended that you hire a professional to make the final, formal drawings.

In addition to drawings to illustrate articles of manufacture, apparatus, or manufacturing equipment, flow charts can also be submitted to illustrate electronic, chemical, or mechanical processes. Flow charts should consist of separate blocks illustrating each step in the process.

The USPTO will accept photographs if they are the only practicable medium for illustrating the invention. Some examples of instances where photographs are accepted include electrophoresis gels, immunological blots, stained and unstained cell cultures, auto-radiographs, histological tissue cross-sections, animals, plants, in vivo imaging, chromatography plates, and crystalline structures. Color photographs are acceptable only if they are submitted in triplicate with an additional fee and a petition requesting their acceptance.

FILING OPTIONS

A provisional or nonprovisional patent application can be filed with the USPTO through the Office's electronic filing system called EFS-Web, delivery by US mail, or hand delivery to the Office in Alexandria, Virginia. Any regular nonprovisional application filed by mail or hand-delivered will require payment of an additional $400 fee, called the "nonelectronic filing fee," which is reduced by 50 percent to $200 for applicants that qualify for small entity status or micro entity status. **The only way to avoid paying the additional $400 nonelectronic filing fee is by filing the nonprovisional utility application via EFS-Web.** The nonelectronic filing fee does not apply to provisional, reissue, design, or plant applications. EFS-Web is a web-based patent application and document submission system in which anyone with a web-enabled computer can file patent applications without downloading special software or changing document preparation tools and processes. More information is available at www.uspto.gov/patents-applicaiton-process/applying-online /about-efs-web.

Full technical support for EFS-Web is available through the Patent Electronic Business Center (EBC) by calling 866-217-9197 from 6:00 a.m. to 12:00 a.m. Eastern Standard Time (EST), Monday through Friday, except federal holidays. You may also send an e-mail to ebc@uspto .gov.

To become a registered user of USPTO's Electronic Filing System (EFS-Web) and Patent Application Information Retrieval (PAIR) system, you will have to provide some information to the USPTO to ensure that you and only you have access to your data.

(a) Obtain a Customer Number

A customer number allows you to easily associate your filing and correspondence with a single mailing address, eliminating typographical errors or variations in addresses that can make it difficult to correspond with the USPTO. This customer number will also ensure that only you can access your patent application information. To obtain a customer number, fill in USPTO Form USPTO/SB/125A (see chapter 13) and fax it to the Electronic Business Center at 571-273-0177, or mail the form to Mail Stop: CN, Commissioner of Patent, PO Box 1450, Alexandria, VA 22313-1450.

(b) Obtain a Digital Certificate

A digital certificate provides a mechanism to uniquely identify you and allow secure access to your patent data. You can obtain a digital certificate by submitting USPTO Form 2042 (USPTO-2042), the Certificate Action Form, to USPTO's Electronic Business Center at Mail Stop: EBC, Commissioner of Patents, PO Box 1450, Alexandria, VA 22313-1450 (Find this at: https://www.uspto.gov/patents-application-process/applying-online/getting-started-new-users#heading-2). Once the form is submitted, the USPTO will then issue a digital certificate that authenticates your identity. If you are filing the application yourself, you should check the box that is marked "Pro Se Inventor" on the form.

After the USPTO has received the form and has verified your identity, you will receive two codes, an authorization code and a reference number. The authorization code will be sent via email and the reference number via US mail. Once you have both codes, you will be able to access Private PAIR (efs.USPTO.gov/authenticate/AuthenticateUser LocalEPF.html) and file your application electronically.

EFS-Web accepts electronic documents formatted in Portable Document Format (PDF). The specification (description and claims) can be created using a word processing program and then converted into a PDF format that can be included as an attachment when filing the application via EFS-Web. Other application documents, such as drawings and a hand-signed declaration, may have to be scanned as a PDF file for filing via EFS-Web.

Each document to be created in a PDF format for filing via EFS-Web must have a top margin of at least 2.0 centimeters (3/4 inch), a left-side margin of at least 2.5 centimeters (1 inch), a right-side margin of at least 2.0 centimeters (3/4 inch), and a bottom margin of at least 2.0 centimeters (3/4 inch). The application pages must be numbered consecutively (centrally located above or below the text), starting with page one. In addition, the PDF document size should be 8.5 by 11 inches (standard size) or 21 by 29.7 centimeters (DIN size A4). The specification, including the abstract and claims, must have lines that are 1.5 or double-spaced in a single column of text. The text must be a nonscript font (e.g., Arial, Times Roman, or Courier), preferably with a font size of 12. Handwritten text scanned into PDF format is not acceptable.

When submitting the application electronically, remember that the specification is considered to have multiple documents (those items in the specification begin on a separate sheet, i.e., Specification, Claims, and Abstract), and you will have to specify the page numbers in the PDF document that houses each of the sections. For example, if the application as uploaded contains thirty pages, twenty-five of which comprise the specification, four of which comprise the claims, and one of which comprises the abstract, you should check the box that says "yes" to the PDF containing multiple documents and then use the drop-down menu to identify each section and identify its page numbers. For example, select "specification" and type in "pages 1 to 25," next select "claims" and type in "pages 26 to 29," and finally select "abstract" and type in "pages 30 to 30."

A complete nonprovisional utility patent application should contain the elements listed below, arranged in the order shown. Description of these elements is provided in the following sections:

- Utility Patent Application Transmittal Form or Transmittal Letter (Form USPTO/AIA/15)
- Appropriate Fees using a Fee Transmittal Form (Form USPTO/SB/17)
- Application Data Sheet (see 37 CFR §1.76) (Form USPTO/AIA/14)
- Specification (with at least one claim)

- Drawings (when necessary)
- Executed Oath or Declaration (Form USPTO/AIA/08)
- Nucleotide and/or Amino Acid Sequence Listing (if applicable)
- Large Tables or Computer Listings (if applicable)
- Verified Statement of Small Entity Status (if applicable) (check box on Form USPTO/AIA/15)
- Assignment (if applicable) (see Notice of Recordation Form USPTO-1595)
- Information Disclosure Statement (if applicable) (Forms USPTO/SB/08a and USPTO/SB/08b)
- Self-addressed Return Postcard (if mailing application to the USPTO)

Note that all the forms identified above may be accessed and filled out online by visiting the USPTO website at www.uspto.gov/patent/patents -forms.

Utility Patent Application Transmittal Form or Transmittal Letter

A Utility Patent Application Transmittal Form (Form USPTO/AIA/15) or a transmittal letter should be filed with the application. The form or letter identifies the items being filed (e.g., specification, claims, drawings, declaration, information disclosure statement, etc.). The form should identify the applicant(s), the type of application, the title of the invention, the contents of the application, and any additional enclosures. See the forms in chapter 13 for the example of the Application Transmittal Form.

Appropriate Fees

You can submit the required fees using a credit card or electronic funds transfer. You should pay these fees online when filing the application via EFS-Web, rather than later, because if the filing fees are paid on a date later than the patent application filing date (or if you file the required oath or declaration on a date later than the application filing date), you are required to pay a late surcharge of $140 ($70 for small entity applicants, and $35 for a micro entity). As discussed earlier, if you file your nonprovisional utility application in paper by mail or by hand-delivery, you will be charged an additional nonelectronic filing fee of $400 ($200 for small entities and micro entities) on top of the regular filing fees. If you file in paper anyway, use the Fee Transmittal Form (Form USPTO/SB/17) to calculate the required filing fees, any excess claim fees or application size fee, and indicate the method of payment (by check, money order, deposit account, or credit card).

If you pay the fees later by check or money order, make the check or money order payable to the "Director of the United States Patent and Trademark Office." If you file an application without the fees, the USPTO will notify you, and you will be required to submit the fees plus the late surcharge within the time period set in the notice.

A nonprovisional application will be charged certain excess filing fees under certain circumstances—for example, an application filed via EFS-Web that includes pages in excess of 133 (specification and drawings), or an application filed in paper that includes pages in excess of 100 (specification and drawings). Also, an application that has more than three independent claims or more than twenty total claims will be charged an excess claim fee. Always refer to the current fee schedule at the USPTO before filing the application, as fees are subject to change. USPTO fee information can be obtained via the following link: www.uspto.gov/learning-and-resources/fees-and-payment/uspto-fee-schedule#PatentFees.

There are two sets of fees: one set for large entities, one set for small entities, and one set for micro entities. The small entity fees are reduced fees as compared to those paid by large entities. If you qualify as a small entity, you may check the box on the transmittal form USPTO/AIA/15. You should only pay small entity fees after ensuring that you qualify for small entity status. You can claim small entity status if:

- You are an individual (or individuals) who has not assigned, granted, conveyed, or licensed any rights in the invention (and is under no contractual or legal obligation to do so).
- You are the owner of a "small business concern" pursuant to the US Small Business Association (SBA) regulations; wherein the owner, including affiliates, has fewer than

500 employees and the owner has not assigned, granted, conveyed, or licensed any rights in the invention (and is under no contractual or legal obligation to do so).

- You are a non-profit organization (regardless of size), including institutions of higher education who has not assigned, granted, conveyed, or licensed any rights in the invention (and is under no contractual or legal obligation to do so).
- You have transferred or licensed rights, or are under obligation to do so, so long as each party to whom rights have been transferred or licensed meets the requirements for "small entity status."
  - The micro entity fees are also reduced fees as compared to those paid by large entities. If you qualify as a micro entity, you may check the box on the transmittal form USPTO/AIA/15. You should only pay micro entity fees after ensuring that you qualify for micro entity status.
  - You can qualify for micro entity status if:
    - You qualify as a small entity;
    - You have not been named as the inventor or joint inventor on more than four previously filed patent applications, other than applications filed in another country, provisional application, or international applications for which the national fee was not paid;
    - You, in the calendar year preceeding the calendar year in which the applicable fee is being paid, did not have a gross income as defined in section 61(a) of the Internal Revenue Code of 1986 (26 U.S.C. 61(a)) exceeding three times the median household income for the preceding calendar year, as most recently reported by the Bureau of the Census; and
    - You have not assigned, granted, or conceived, nor are under an obligation by contract or law to assign, grant, or convey, a license or other ownership interest in the application concerned to an entity

that, in the calendar year preceeding the calendar year in which the applicable fee is being paid, had a gross income, as defined in section 61(a) of the Internal Revenue Code of 1986, exceeding three times the median household income for that preceding calendar year, as most recently reported by the Bureau of the Census.

You can also claim micro entity if:

- You qualify as a small entity; and
- Your employer is an institution of higher education; or
- You have assigned, granted, conveyed or are under an obligation by contract to assign, grant, or convey, a license or other ownership interest in the particular application to such an institution of higher education.

Application Data Sheet

The application data sheet or sheets are forms that provide certain bibliographic data, such as the applicant information, correspondence information, application information, representation information, domestic priority information, foreign priority information, and assignment information. The submission of this sheet or sheets is voluntary. You may access a guide on the Application Data Sheet by visiting www .USPTO.gov/web/offices/pac/dapp/sir/doc/adsguidelines.pdf.

Executed Oath or Declaration

An oath or declaration is required for applicants filing design, plant, or utility patent applications. The application must be accompanied by a declaration signed by all the inventors. The oath or declaration certifies that each named inventor believes himself or herself to be the original and first inventor of the subject matter of the application. The oath or declaration also acts as a certification that the inventors acknowledge that they have a duty to disclose information of which they are aware that is material to the examination of the application. This information includes (1) all prior art of which they are aware at the time the application is filed or of which they become aware during the prosecution of the application and (2) any other information believed to be relevant to a thorough review of the application by the examiner. A sample declaration form is provided in chapter 13.

Do not execute the declaration until the application is completed and reviewed by the inventor(s). Sign the declaration only after the final changes have been made and you have read the final draft of the application.

The oath must be sworn to by the inventor before a notary public or other officer authorized to administer oaths. A declaration, on the other hand, does not require any witness or a person to verify the signing. The oath or declaration must be signed by the inventor in person or by a person entitled to sign on the inventor's behalf. See Form USPTO/AIA/08 for a sample oath and declaration.

If you have more than one inventor listed, ensure that all inventors have signed the oath and/or declaration.

Verified Statement of Small Entity Status (if applicable)

In order to establish small entity status for the purpose of paying a maintenance fee, a written assertion of entitlement to small entity status must be filed prior to or with the maintenance fee paid as a small entity. A written assertion is only required to be filed once and will remain effective until changed. A sample form is included in chapter 13.

Generally, fees charged to small entities will be reduced by 50 percent with respect to their application to any small business concern as defined under section 3 of the Small Business Act, and to any independent inventor or nonprofit organization.

Verified Statement of Micro Entity Status (if applicable)

In order to establish micro entity status for the purpose of paying a maintenance fee, a written assertion of entitlement to micro entity status must be filed prior to or with the maintenance fee paid as a micro entity. A written assertion is only required to be filed once and will remain effective until changed.

Assignment

A patent is personal property and may be bought, sold, or licensed for valuable consideration. The patent law provides for the transfer of a patent application by means of a formal Assignment. If you are an individual inventor, chances are you will be looking for a company to make and market your invention. If a company wanted to purchase your patent, you would execute an assignment to transfer ownership. If, at the time the application is filed, you have already agreed to assign the patent to another individual or a company, you can file an Assignment. Have the Assignment notarized to authenticate the document. After filing the Assignment, the USPTO will officially record it for a small fee. Sample Assignment and Recordation Forms are included in chapter 13.

All assignments are processed through a management system called the Patent and Trademark Assignment System (PTAS).

- Paper documents are manually scanned into the PTAS. Documents received electronically through EFS are electronically scanned into the PTAS system.
- This bibliographic data is entered into the USPTO Assignment Historical Database. The data submitted is reviewed for completeness, and the USPTO will determine if the documents are recordable or not.
- The images of the cover sheet and the document are assigned reel and frame numbers by the PTAS and put on searchable media (microfilm and CD-ROM).
- The PTAS generates a "Notice of Recordation," which is mailed to the correspondence address provided on the cover sheet.

Assignments that are submitted but are determined to be non-recordable are returned to you with a "Notice of Non-Recordation" citing the reason for non-recordation.

Beyond these ministerial duties, the office simply puts the information on the public record and does not verify the validity of the information. The USPTO does not make a determination with regard to the legality of the transaction nor the right of the submitting party to record the assignment. This recordation with the USPTO serves as notice to the public as to the ownership of the patent.

You may contact the Assignment Recordation Branch's customer service desk at 571-272-3350 from 8:30 a.m. to 5:00 p.m. Eastern Time if you have questions about assignments and recordation of assignments.

Information Disclosure Statement

An applicant for a patent has a legal obligation to disclose to the USPTO any information that is material to the patentability of the invention. To meet this full disclosure requirement, file an Information Disclosure Statement when you file the application. Technically, the Information Disclosure Statement can be filed without a fee up to three months after the application is filed, or before the emailing of a first Office Action on the merits. For ease in dealing with the USPTO and while everything is fresh in your mind, you should prepare and file the statement when filing the patent application.

The Information Disclosure Statement typically consists of two parts. The first is a form on which all material information is listed. This includes relevant material identified during the prior art search including patents, journal articles and other publications, references cited in related patents, and any commercial activity relating to the invention which the inventor or anyone involved in preparing the application is aware. Even documents that are not in English should be submitted if they are material to the patentability of the invention. In addition, a transmittal letter should accompany the form stating that all documents relevant to the application are being submitted. If any documents are not in English, they should briefly be summarized in this transmittal letter. See the forms in chapter 13 for a sample Information Disclosure Statement (USPTO/SB/08A and USPTO/SB/08B) and sample Transmittal Letter. As a second part of the Information Disclosure Statement, one copy of each reference cited on the form should be submitted. However, you do not have to submit copies of US patent applications or US patents that you have cited on your Information Disclosure Statement.

Deciding what information to disclose to the USPTO requires reasoned judgment. There is no need to submit irrelevant or cumulative information, although information that is relevant to patentability must be disclosed. It is best to be overly inclusive. Remember, "When in doubt, do *not* leave it out."

The duty of candor with the USPTO is ongoing. If you uncover a piece of prior art after you have filed the application, or if you discover that one embodiment of the invention does not work, you must advise the office before the patent issues. Otherwise, if your patent is granted and it is determined that you withheld material information from the USPTO, a court can find your patent unenforceable.

Petition to Make Special

The USPTO will expedite the review of an application under special circumstances. If you want your application to be put at the front of the line, and you can justify this request, you might want to file a Petition to Make Special. A Petition to Make Special may be granted for one of the following reasons:

- The applicant's age (age sixty-five or greater), or
- The applicant's health.

If you are claiming the reason of age above, you may file the petition electronically using Form USPTO/SB/130: www.USPTO.gov/ebc/portal/efs/petitionagesb130.pdf. If you are mailing the petition, it must include either a statement by one of the named inventors that he or she is sixty-five years of age or more, or a certification by a registered patent attorney or agent of evidence that one or more of the named inventors is sixty-five years of age or more. Such evidence may include a driver's license, passport, birth certificate, or other proof of age.

If you are claiming the reason of health, you have to file a sworn declaration and provide evidence showing that the health of the applicant is such that he or she might not be available to assist in the prosecution of the application if it were to be taken in turn. Evidence of such a state of health may be provided by a doctor's certification or a medical certification.

A Petition to Make Special for either the age or health of a named inventor does not require a fee to be processed.

RECEIPT OF CORRESPONDENCE

(a) Correspondence received by the USPTO will be stamped with the date of receipt (except in instances [b], [c], and [d] below), unless it is received by the USPTO on a Saturday, Sunday, or federal holiday within the District of Columbia, in which case the date stamped will be the next succeeding day that is not a Saturday, Sunday, or federal holiday within the District of Columbia.

(b) Applications filed employing the United States Express Mail postal service will be stamped with the date on the "Express Mail."

- Any correspondence received by the USPTO that was delivered by the "Express Mail Post Office to Addressee" service of the United States Postal Service (USPS) will be considered filed with the USPTO on the date of deposit with the USPS.
- The date of deposit with USPS is shown by the "date in" on the "Express Mail" label or other official USPS notation. If the USPS deposit date cannot be determined, the correspondence will be accorded the USPTO receipt date as the filing date.
- The paper(s) or fee(s) that constitute the correspondence should also include the "Express Mail" mailing label number.

Since December 1996, the USPTO no longer requires a "Certificate of Express Mailing," however, for the Express Mail "date in" to be effective for the filing date, the Express Mail number must be placed on each separate paper and each fee transmittal either directly on the document or by a separate paper firmly and securely attached thereto. In a situation where correspondence is filed with several papers at the same time (e.g., when submitting a new application that includes the specification, drawings, and declaration), the correspondence may be submitted with a cover or transmittal letter, which should itemize these papers. It is not necessary that the Express Mail number be placed on each page of a particular paper or fee transmittal. Merely placing the number in one prominent location on each separate paper or fee transmittal (or cover sheet or transmittal letter which should itemize the separate papers and fees) will be sufficient.

(c) Correspondence transmitted by facsimile (fax) to the Patent and Trademark Office will be stamped with the date on which the complete transmission is received in the Patent and Trademark Office, unless that date is a Saturday, Sunday, or federal holiday within the District of Columbia, in which case the date stamped will be the next succeeding day which is not a Saturday, Sunday, or federal holiday within the District of Columbia.

(d) Correspondence submitted using the USPTO electronic filing system will be accorded a receipt date, which is the date the correspondence is received at the USPTO.

Self-Addressed Postcard

If you decide to file the application by mail, enclose a self-addressed, postage-paid postcard with the patent application. The postcard will be returned to you in approximately two to four weeks with both the receipt date and application number. A postcard receipt will serve as *prima facie* evidence of receipt in the USPTO of all the items listed on the postcard on the date stamped by the USPTO. The identifying data on the postcard should include the following:

(a) Applicant's name(s);

(b) Title of invention;

(c) Number of pages of specification, claims (for nonprovisional applications), and sheets of drawing;

(d) Whether oath or declaration is included;

(e) A list of any additional forms included with the application (e.g., application transmittal form, application data sheet, fee transmittal form, and/or provisional application cover sheet); and

(f) Amount and manner of paying the fee.

A return postcard should be attached to *each* patent application for which a receipt is desired. It is important that the return postcard itemize all of the components of the application. If the postcard does not itemize each of the components of the application, it will not serve as evidence that any component which was not itemized was received by the USPTO.

If you have followed all of the above steps, your application should be ready to file with the USPTO. You have accomplished a big job, but do not file the application until you have double-checked it.

Set aside some time to carefully review the application before you file it. Refer to the patent application checklist at the end of this chapter to make sure you have properly prepared the application. Make sure all signatures are in place, no pages or drawings are missing, and all documents are in proper form.

After you have signed all appropriate documents, make a photocopy of everything to keep in your file. Unfortunately, papers can get lost at the USPTO. Your best safeguard against such a mishap is to keep copies of your entire application and forms in a secure place at your office or home.

If you have decided to mail your application to the USPTO, place the specification, all related papers, and the filing fee, unfolded, in a large envelope addressed to Commissioner for Patents, PO Box 1450, Alexandria, VA 22313-1450. The application can also be carried by hand to the USPTO.

Remember, if you are going to mail the application, you should use only US Express Mail, as your filing date will be the date the application is mailed. Furthermore, if you send the application via US Express Mail, the express mail receipt will provide proof of the date the application was sent. Otherwise, the filing date will be the date the application is received by the USPTO.

PREPARING AND MAILING A DESIGN PATENT APPLICATION

In addition to, or instead of, filing a utility patent application, you may want to file a design patent application. Unlike a utility patent, a design patent protects only the ornamental or aesthetic elements of an invention. Further, design patents do not protect any functional elements of an invention. Design patents can protect, for example, unique bottle shapes, an artistic lamp, an ornamental pin, a watch design, or the grill of a car.

The application for a design patent is much easier to prepare than that for a utility patent. Drawings are the heart of the design patent application, although a short preamble and one claim are also included. The drawings must fully disclose the ornamental features of the invention and should be drawn from a number of views in order to meet full disclosure.

A complete design patent must also include a declaration and the filing fee (effective March 19, 2013. the basic filing fee for a design patent application was $180, or $90 for a small entity, or $45 for a micro entity). You should also file an Information Disclosure Statement and an Application Transmittal Letter identifying everything that you are submitting. Remember, you can file the Information Disclosure Statement within three months of filing the application without penalty. If applicable, file a Verification Statement of Small Entity Status and a Petition to Make Special.

Submit all these papers just as you would for an application for a utility patent. Remember to include a self-addressed, stamped postcard, and send the application by US Express Mail, with a Certificate of Express Mail included in the application.

ACCESSING YOUR PATENT APPLICATION AFTER FILING

After you have filed your application and received a filing receipt, you may access your application immediately by becoming a registered user of Patent Application Information Retrieval (PAIR) system as described above. Once you have become a registered user, you will have access to Private PAIR and be able to access your application at any time. If, however, you do not wish to register, you will only be able to view your application online through the Public PAIR system after your application has published (approximately eighteen months after you have filed your application).

PATENT APPLICATION CHECKLIST

☐ A US Patent Application Transmittal Form identifying every paper being submitted with the application and an Express Mail label number (if you decide to mail the application) on the documents being submitted.

☐ The Specification is complete and has the following components:

    (a) Title of the Invention

    (b) Cross-Reference to Any Related Application (if any)

    (c) Statement Regarding Sponsored Research (if applicable)

    (d) Incorporation by Reference to Sequence Listing, a Table, or a Computer Program Listing Compact Disc Appendix (if applicable)

    (e) Background of the Invention

    (f) Brief Summary of the Invention

    (g) Brief Description of Drawings (if any)

    (h) Detailed Description of the Invention

    (i) One or More Claims

    (j) Abstract

    (k) Drawings (if applicable)

    (l) Sequence Listing (if applicable)

☐ All drawings are present, and each sheet of drawings is given a figure number. Your name and address are on the top back of each sheet of formal drawings, if mailing the application.

☐ The Declaration is completed, signed, and dated in ink by all inventors after they review the specification.

☐ The Fee Transmittal Sheet is enclosed, including a check or money order (if this is the method of payment selected) payable to the Director of the United States Patent and Trademark Office for the correct filing fee.

☐ If applicable, the Verified Statement of Small Entity Status form is completed, signed, and dated in ink or checked in the box on the Transmittal Form.

☐ If applicable, an Assignment is completed, signed, and dated in ink by all inventors and notarized. When filing the Assignment electronically, you will have to provide a separate cover sheet if you are filing the assignment with your application; otherwise, you can submit it separately through the assignment section of the USPTO.

☐ An Information Disclosure Statement and Form PTO/SB/08a and 08b are completed. Copies of all cited references are attached.

(Continued)

□ If applicable, a Petition to Make Special is completed, signed, and dated in ink.

□ A self-addressed, postage-paid postcard, with your name, the mailing date, the title of the invention, and all documents enclosed written on the back (if you decide to mail your application).

□ A large envelope addressed to

Commissioner of Patents

PO Box 1450

Alexandria, VA 22313-1450

□ If you are submitting the application electronically, remember that the Specification is considered to have multiple documents (those items in the Specification begin on a separate sheet, i.e., Specification, Claims, and Abstract), and you will have to specify the page numbers in the PDF document that contains each of the sections.

IN THE UNITED STATES PATENT AND TRADEMARK OFFICE

Applicant: _____   Examiner: _____

Serial No.: _____   Art Unit: _____

Filing Date: _____

Title: _____

INFORMATION DISCLOSURE STATEMENT
UNDER 37 CFR § 1.97

Commissioner of Patents and Trademarks
PO Box 1450
Alexandria, VA 22313-1450

Sir:

Please find, pursuant to 37 CFR § 1.98(a)(1), the enclosed Form USPTO-1449, which contains a list of all patents, publications, or other items that have come to the attention of one or more of the individuals designated in 37 CFR § 1.56(c). While no representation is made that any of these references may be "prior art" within the meaning of that term under 35 U.S.C. §§ 102 or 103, the enclosed list of references is disclosed so as to fully comply with the duty of disclosure set forth in 37 CFR § 1.56.

Moreover, while no representation is made that a specific search of office files or patent office records has been conducted or that no better art exists, the undersigned believes that the enclosed art is the closest to the claimed invention (taken in its entirety) of which the undersigned is presently aware, and no art that is closer to the claimed invention (taken in its entirety) has been knowingly withheld.

In accordance with 37 CFR §§ 1.97 and 1.98, a copy of each of the listed references or relevant portion thereof is also enclosed.

In accordance with 37 CFR § 1.98(c), all English translations within the possession, custody, control, or availability of anyone designated in 37 CFR § 1.56(c) of each non-English reference, if any, are also enclosed.

(Continued)

(if applicable)
Statement of Relevance of References Listed
Unaccompanied by English Translation

Under 37 CFR § 1.98(a)(3)

In accordance with 37 CFR § 1.98(a)(3), the following concise explanation of the relevance of each listed reference that is either not in the English language or unaccompanied by a translation into English is provided.

Because all listed references are either in the English language or are accompanied by a translation into English, no concise explanation of relevance is required under 37 CFR § 1.98(a)(3).

(if applicable)
Statement of Cumulative References
Under 37 CFR § 1.98(c)

The following listed references are not enclosed because, under 37 CFR § 1.98(c), they are substantially cumulative of the reference.

(if applicable)
Statement of References Previously Disclosed
Under 37 CFR § 1.98(d)

The following listed references are not enclosed because, under 37 CFR § 1.98(d), they were previously cited by or submitted to the Office in the prior application, which is relied upon for an earlier filing date under 35 U.S.C. § 120.

Respectfully submitted,

Date: _____   _____

Direct communications to:

CHAPTER 10

About Foreign Patent Rights

Once you have filed a patent application in the United States, consider whether or not you as the inventor (or the assignee if the invention has been assigned to some other entity) wish to pursue patent protection for the invention in countries other than the United States. Keep in mind that the rights and privileges afforded by your US patent gives you the ability to prevent others from using, making, or selling your invention in the United States as defined by the claims in your patent. If similar applications are not filed in other countries, there is nothing to prevent someone in a foreign jurisdiction from copying your invention and making, using, or selling it.

This chapter will provide a review of the basic rules and requirements for filing a foreign patent application when you have a properly filed US patent application covering an invention. Patent laws and regulations vary among countries, and the specific requirements of each country are not covered in this book.

FILING YOUR PATENT ABROAD

US patents provide protection only within the boundaries of the United States and its territories—they have no effect on activities outside the Unites States. An exception, however, are process patents, which can enable you to prevent the importation of infringing goods made overseas using the patented process. Also, a US patent might be influential in getting corresponding patents allowed in some foreign countries. For all practical purposes, however, a US patent protects only the market in the United States against infringing products.

Patent protection is granted on a country-by-country basis. It is therefore necessary to obtain a patent in each country where the inventor wants the right to stop others from making, using, or selling the invention.

Every inventor probably would like to patent his or her invention around the world and gain as extensive a monopoly as possible for the invention. A major factor to consider, however, is that obtaining patents in foreign countries is generally very expensive. Because of the expense and other important issues, the countries in which a patent will be pursued should be carefully selected. An inventor, before applying for foreign patents, should be satisfied that he or she could make some profit or satisfy some particular reason for obtaining them.

Expenses, such as legal fees, translation costs, filing fees, and periodic maintenance fees, must be taken into account when deciding where to file foreign patent applications. Select countries where a significant market exists for your invention and where there are realistic manufacturing, marketing, or licensing opportunities for you. Avoid countries that have weak patent laws or difficult procedures for enforcing patents against infringers.

Remember that the patent laws of many countries differ from those of the United States. Publication of the invention before the date of filing the patent application will bar the right to a patent in most foreign countries. Maintenance fees are required in most foreign countries. Many countries require that the patented invention be manufactured in that country within a certain period, usually three years. The patent can be void in some countries if there is no manufacture within this period, although in most the patent can be subject to the grant of compulsory licenses to any person who may apply for a license.

After you have decided to seek foreign patent protection and have selected the countries of interest, file a national patent application in each country or file a central Patent Cooperation Treaty (PCT) application or European patent application. The foreign application is usually filed in a central clearing house, such as the European Patent Office (EPO) or in the USPTO, under the PCT. When filing with the EPO or via PCT, the applicant designates the countries in which patent protection is sought. The EPO and PCT applications are first examined and prosecuted in a central filing office. The applications subsequently enter what is called "the National Phase," where they are filed in each of the designated countries.

As already discussed, this process can cost a considerable amount of money. For example, there are filing fees for the initial filing of the application in the PCT receiving office or the EPO, and legal fees will certainly be incurred during the prosecution of the application. Once the application enters the national phase, additional application fees are required for each respective country, and translations may also be required if the country is non-English speaking. A foreign patent agent or attorney will likely be hired in each country to handle most of the paperwork and ensure that all the local rules are followed and that the formal papers are properly executed and filed. Miscellaneous filing fees are often incurred, and maintenance fees are required in most countries after the patent issues in order to keep it valid and enforceable.

Before incurring the costs of filing patent applications in foreign countries, determine whether or not the invention will be manufactured or sold outside the United States, and, if so, the likelihood of its commercial success. It is not worth going through the effort and expense of filing a patent application in a foreign country unless the invention will likely be of substantial commercial value in that country. When considering the commercial value of your invention, determine whether it will be marketed and/or sold by you or your affiliate, or whether it will have licensing potential in the foreign countries. Keep in mind that, although you may not have the ability or the desire to manufacture, market, or sell your invention overseas, others may be interested in doing so if the invention is likely to become a commercial success.

If foreign patent rights are obtained, others who wish to practice your invention in the respective countries will have to take a license under the foreign patents, which can generate royalty income for you. Foreign patents can also be beneficial if someone wants to obtain a license to make and sell your patented invention in the United States as well as abroad.

You must obtain a foreign filing license from the USPTO before you file a foreign patent application or otherwise transmit information concerning your invention abroad. You can request a foreign filing license from the USPTO, but one is routinely granted within six months of filing a US patent application. You can proceed with foreign filing even if you have not received a foreign filing license if six months or more have passed since filing your US patent application.

Remember that to protect your ability to obtain foreign patents, it is important to make sure your invention is not publicly disclosed prior to the effective filing date of your foreign patent application. As discussed earlier, any publication, sale, or public disclosure of the invention in any form prior to filing an application is an automatic bar to patentability in most foreign countries. Only in the United States and a few foreign countries, such as Canada, is there a grace period from the date of such disclosure to when the application must be filed in order to preserve the right to a patent.

Even if you are able to handle filing and prosecuting your US patent application, seek the advice of foreign patent attorneys or agents to ensure all necessary requirements are met when filing in another country. Foreign patent attorneys and agents in various countries are listed in the Martindale Hubbell Law Directory, which is available at most libraries. Foreign patent attorneys and agents can also be found through organizations such as the American Intellectual Property Law Association. Additionally, there are attorneys and law firms in the United States that specialize in filing and prosecuting patent applications abroad.

There are several important treaties and international rules governing patents and patent applications. These treaties and rules have been adopted by most industrial countries in an attempt to harmonize the various patent systems around the world. One of the earliest treaties is the International Convention for the Protection of Industrial Property entered into in Paris in 1883 (referred to as the Paris Convention). The Paris Convention allows a patent applicant to claim the benefit of the earlier filing date of the first-filed patent application for foreign applications filed within one year thereof. The European Patent Convention forms a central EPO where a single patent application can be filed that covers most of Europe. Another important treaty is the PCT, under which a single patent application can be filed designating nearly one hundred countries.

A list of the countries and their memberships in the various patent treaties is provided at the end of this chapter.

EARLIER FILING DATES UNDER THE PARIS CONVENTION

The most important aspect of the Paris Convention is that any application initially filed within one member country may be filed in any other member country within one year, and the patent application in the other country will receive the same earlier filing date as the first-filed application. For example, if you file a patent application for your new invention on January 1, 2018, in a Paris Convention country, you have until December 31, 2018, to file in any other member country under the treaty. Hence, prior art or acts between the first patent filing and the later foreign filings that might otherwise present a bar or obstacle to patentability will have no effect under the Paris Convention, because the later foreign-filed applications are given the earlier effective filing date. This allows an inventor to file a patent application in one country, such as the United States, and delay other filings for nearly one year while the invention is being marketed or evaluated. You can still file a foreign patent application after the one-year period has passed under the Paris Convention, but the filing date of these applications will be the actual date the application is filed in each respective country. These applications could become granted patents, provided that no sale or publication of the invention has taken place that would destroy patentability.

As mentioned earlier, the one-year grace period for filing abroad is quite beneficial because once the first patent application has been filed, the inventor can market or otherwise exploit his or her invention and get an idea of the commercial potential of the invention. If the invention enjoys considerable success from the beginning, the inventor may want to file in more countries to get greater control of the worldwide market. On the other hand, if the invention is a relative flop during the year preceding foreign filing, the applicant may find it prudent to file in just a few countries, if any at all, and thereby save considerable time and money.

THE EUROPEAN PATENT OFFICE

The countries from the European Economic Community entered into an agreement in 1978 known as the European Patent Convention, which establishes a central filing depository for filing a patent application. This depository is known as the EPO and is located in Munich, Germany. Filing a patent application in the EPO is tantamount to filing in all the specific enumerated countries that are members of the European Patent Convention. The EPO examines the patent application for all the selected countries, and once the patent is issued, it can be registered for granting in each of the selected member countries.

Any application filed in the EPO that is based on a previously filed US counterpart application can receive the earlier filing date with the USPTO, provided that the application is filed within one year from the US filing date. If this European application matures into a European patent, it can issue as a patent in each of the designated countries, and these national patents will have the same effective filing date as the US parent patent application.

The prosecution of a European patent application differs in many respects from prosecuting a patent application in the United States. All patent applications filed in the USPTO are subjected to an *ex parte* examination (the only parties involved are the applicant and the patent examiner), which is carried out in secrecy. However, in the EPO all applications are published six months after they have been filed in the office. This publication is essentially an invitation to the world to comment on the patentability of the invention described therein. While the patent examiner in the EPO conducts his or her own prior art search, the published application may cause someone to submit any relevant prior art or to prepare to file an opposition to the grant of a European patent.

Filing a patent application in the EPO offers several advantages, such as the ability to file and prosecute the application in English, a single prosecution that includes all the EPO countries, a thorough examination of the application, reduced costs where patents will be pursued in a large number of countries, and a quicker grant or issuance of relatively strong patents. Some disadvantages are increased costs in filing in only a small number of countries, a fairly rigid application format, and a possible loss of essentially all European patent rights if the European patent application is rejected or successfully opposed.

If a European patent is granted, it issues in each of the respective designated countries and will be effective for twenty years from the date of filing. Keep in mind that maintenance fees must be paid in each of these countries during the life of the patent and in the EPO during prosecution.

THE PATENT COOPERATION TREATY

Filing a patent application under the PCT is rapidly becoming the most popular and cost-effective method for filing abroad. The PCT provides a centralized filing and searching system for a single international patent application. The PCT application process is intended to simplify filing a patent application in foreign countries, eliminate the need to duplicate patent filing and searching, and reduce the costs of filing for patents around the world.

Filing through the PCT involves filing a PCT patent application in any member country, such as the United States, and designating the countries where the filing is to be effective. Separate translated national applications must be filed in each country of interest under the PCT within the required time after the filing date of the PCT application.

For a United States inventor, the PCT application is typically filed in the United States either initially as a PCT application or within one year of, and claiming the benefit of, an earlier regular or provisional US patent application. Generally, eight months after the filing date of the PCT application or twenty months after the filing date of the initial US patent application, the national filings of the PCT application is made in each designated country. If an election to proceed under chapter II of the PCT is made before nineteen months after filing an initial US patent application, the separate national filings can be delayed for thirty months after the US filing date.

Hence, under the PCT, a US patent applicant can take either twenty or thirty months from the original filing date of the US Patent application to decide where to file abroad. This grace period can be extremely beneficial in that it gives the applicant a considerable amount of time to determine to what degree his or her invention is a commercial success in the United States and to what scope of claim coverage can be expected from the US patent once it is granted. This insight can be of great benefit in deciding the likelihood of patent protection in the other countries as well as the extent of foreign filings and the cost versus benefit therefrom.

There are important advantages in filing a patent application under the PCT. As mentioned already, the PCT application allows time to evaluate the commercial potential and patentability of the invention before having to make a final decision on foreign filing. Other advantages are that the payment of national fees and translation costs are postponed, foreign applications under the PCT can be filed later than those not filed via PCT, and a stronger patent may be issued in some countries. The disadvantages of filing a PCT application are the relatively complex procedures, additional paperwork, and longer delays in obtaining a patent.

Remember that an inventor can always file for foreign patents without following the procedures of the PCT, EPO, or Paris Convention. Instead, the inventor would file a nonconvention national application in each country of interest. Be sure to obtain a foreign filing license from the USPTO or wait until six months or more after the US filing date of your application before filing any patent application outside the United States, or you will lose your right to obtain a US patent.

FILING IN NON-PCT COUNTRIES: THE EFFECT OF THE GENERAL AGREEMENT ON TARIFFS AND TRADE ON PATENTS (GATT)

The GATT was entered into by most industrialized countries and has had a major impact on patents. Any in-depth discussion of the ramifications of GATT would require far more space than is available in this book, because the agreement is extensive and covers more than intellectual property issues. The important thing to remember is that the GATT agreement went a long way in harmonizing the patent laws of the United States with those of most other countries of the world.

Prior to June 7, 1995, for example, the term of a patent in the United States was seventeen years from the date the patent issued. Patent terms in most industrialized countries lasted twenty years from the earliest filing date of the patent application. Now, under GATT, for applications filed in the United States before June 7, 1995, the term is either seventeen years from the date of issue or twenty years from the earliest filing date, whichever is longer. The patent term for US patent applications filed on or after June 7, 1995, is twenty years from the earliest filing date in the United States.

LIST OF COUNTRIES AND MEMBERSHIPS IN PATENT TREATIES

Two-Letter Code	Name of State	Date on Which State Became Bound by the PCT[1]
AE	United Arab Emirates	10 March 1999
AG	Antigua and Barbuda	17 March 2000
AL	Albania	4 October 1995
AM	Armenia[2]	25 December 1991
AO	Angola	27 December 2007
AT	Austria	23 April 1979
AU	Australia	31 March 1980
AZ	Azerbaijan	25 December 1995
BA	Bosnia and Herzegovina	7 September 1996
BB	Barbados	12 March 1985
BE	Belgium	14 December 1981
BF	Burkina Faso	21 March 1989
BG	Bulgaria	21 May 1984
BH	Bahrain[2]	18 March 2007
BJ	Benin	26 February 1987
BN	Brunei Darussalam	24 July 2012
BR	Brazil	9 April 1978
BW	Botswana	30 October 2003
BY	Belarus[2]	25 December 1991
BZ	Belize	17 June 2000
CA	Canada	2 January 1990
CF	Central African Republic	24 January 1978
CG	Congo	24 January 1978
CH	Switzerland	24 January 1978
CI	Côte d'Ivoire	30 April 1991
CL	Chile[2]	2 June 2009
CM	Cameroon	24 January 1978
CN	China[3, 4]	1 January 1994
CO	Colombia	28 February 2001
CR	Costa Rica	3 August 1999
CU	Cuba[2]	16 July 1996
CY	Cyprus	1 April 1998
CZ	Czechia	1 January 1993
DE	Germany	24 January 1978
DJ	Djibouti	23 September 2016

DK	Denmark	1 December 1978
DM	Dominica	7 August 1999
DO	Dominican Republic	28 May 2007
DZ	Algeria[2]	8 March 2000
EC	Ecuador	7 May 2001
EE	Estonia	24 August 1994
EG	Egypt	6 September 2003
ES	Spain	16 November 1989
FI	Finland[5]	1 October 1980
FR	France[2, 6]	25 February 1978
GA	Gabon	24 January 1978
GB	United Kingdom[7]	24 January 1978
GD	Grenada	22 September 1998
GE	Georgia[2]	25 December 1991
GH	Ghana	26 February 1997
GM	Gambia	9 December 1997
GN	Guinea	27 May 1991
GQ	Equatorial Guinea	17 July 2001
GR	Greece	9 October 1990
GT	Guatemala	14 October 2006
GW	Guinea-Bissau	12 December 1997
HN	Honduras	20 June 2006
HR	Croatia	1 July 1998
HU	Hungary[2]	27 June 1980
ID	Indonesia[2]	5 September 1997
IE	Ireland	1 August 1992
IL	Israel	1 June 1996
IN	India[2]	7 December 1998
IR	Iran (Islamic Republic of)	4 October 2013
IS	Iceland	23 March 1995
IT	Italy	28 March 1985
JO	Jordan	9 June 2017
JP	Japan	1 October 1978
KE	Kenya	8 June 1994
KG	Kyrgyzstan[2]	25 December 1991
KH	Cambodia	8 December 2016
KM	Comoros	3 April 2005
KN	Saint Kitts and Nevis	27 October 2005
KP	Democratic People's Republic of Korea	8 July 1980

KR	Republic of Korea	10 August 1984
KW	Kuwait	9 September 2016
KZ	Kazakhstan[2]	25 December 1991
LA	Lao People's Democratic Republic[2]	14 June 2006
LC	Saint Lucia[2]	30 August 1996
LI	Liechtenstein	19 March 1980
LK	Sri Lanka	26 February 1982
LR	Liberia	27 August 1994
LS	Lesotho	21 October 1995
LT	Lithuania	5 July 1994
LU	Luxembourg	30 April 1978
LV	Latvia	7 September 1993
LY	Libya	15 September 2005
MA	Morocco	8 October 1999
MC	Monaco	22 June 1979
MD	Republic of Moldova[2]	25 December 1991
ME	Montenegro	3 June 2006
MG	Madagascar	24 January 1978
MK	The former Yugoslav Republic of Macedonia	10 August 1995
ML	Mali	19 October 1984
MN	Mongolia	27 May 1991
MR	Mauritania	13 April 1983
MT	Malta[2]	1 March 2007
MW	Malawi	24 January 1978
MX	Mexico	1 January 1995
MY	Malaysia[2]	16 August 2006
MZ	Mozambique[2]	18 May 2000
NA	Namibia	1 January 2004
NE	Niger	21 March 1993
NG	Nigeria	8 May 2005
NI	Nicaragua	6 March 2003
NL	Netherlands[8]	10 July 1979
NO	Norway[5]	1 January 1980
NZ	New Zealand	1 December 1992
OM	Oman[2]	26 October 2001
PA	Panama	7 September 2012
PE	Peru	6 June 2009
PG	Papua New Guinea	14 June 2003

PH	Philippines	17 August 2001
PL	Poland[5]	25 December 1990
PT	Portugal	24 November 1992
QA	Qatar[2]	3 August 2011
RO	Romania[2]	23 July 1979
RS	Serbia[9]	1 February 1997
RU	Russian Federation[2]	29 March 1978[10]
RW	Rwanda	31 August 2011
SA	Saudi Arabia	3 August 2013
SC	Seychelles	7 November 2002
SD	Sudan	16 April 1984
SE	Sweden[5]	17 May 1978
SG	Singapore	23 February 1995
SI	Slovenia	1 March 1994
SK	Slovakia	1 January 1993
SL	Sierra Leone	17 June 1997
SM	San Marino	14 December 2004
SN	Senegal	24 January 1978
ST	Sao Tome and Principe	3 July 2008
SV	El Salvador	17 August 2006
SY	Syrian Arab Republic	26 June 2003
SZ	Swaziland	20 September 1994
TD	Chad	24 January 1978
TG	Togo	24 January 1978
TH	Thailand[2]	24 December 2009
TJ	Tajikistan[2]	25 December 1991
TM	Turkmenistan[2]	25 December 1991
TN	Tunisia[2]	10 December 2001
TR	Turkey	1 January 1996
TT	Trinidad and Tobago	10 March 1994
TZ	United Republic of Tanzania	14 September 1999
UA	Ukraine[2]	25 December 1991
UG	Uganda	9 February 1995
US	United States of America[11, 12]	24 January 1978
UZ	Uzbekistan[2]	25 December 1991
VC	Saint Vincent and the Grenadines[2]	6 August 2002
VN	Viet Nam	10 March 1993
ZA	South Africa[2]	16 March 1999
ZM	Zambia	15 November 2001
ZW	Zimbabwe	11 June 1997

Notes

1. All PCT Contracting States are bound by Chapter II of the PCT relating to the international preliminary examination.
2. With the declaration provided for in PCT Article 64(5).
3. Applies also to Hong Kong, China with effect from 1 July 1997.
4. Not applicable to Macau, China.
5. With the declaration provided for in PCT Article 64(2)(a)(ii).
6. Including all Overseas Departments and Territories.
7. The United Kingdom extended the application of the PCT to the Isle of Man with effect from 29 October 1983.
8. Ratification for the Kingdom in Europe, the Netherlands Antilles, and Aruba. The Netherlands Antilles ceased to exist on 10 October 2010. As from that date, the PCT continues to apply to Curaçao and Sint Maarten. The PCT also continues to apply to the islands of Bonaire, Sint Eustatius and Saba which, with effect from 10 October 2010, have become part of the territory of the Kingdom of the Netherlands in Europe.
9. Serbia is the continuing State from Serbia and Montenegro as from 3 June 2006.
10. Date of ratification of the Soviet Union, continued by the Russian Federation as from 25 December 1991.
11. With the declarations provided for in PCT Articles 64(3)(a) and 64(4)(a).
12. Extends to all areas for which the United States of America has international responsibility.

For more information, visit: www.wipo.int/pct/en/pct_contracting_states .html

CHAPTER 11

How to Prepare and File an International Patent Application

Now that you have a general understanding of foreign patent rights, we can discuss how to prepare and file an application through the PCT.

Once you have filed an application as outlined in Chapters 8–10, you can determine if you need to file an application internationally. The most economical way to apply for a patent in several different countries is through the PCT (as discussed in Chapters 10–11). The PCT filing is broken into two parts or phases. Phase 1 consists of the filing of the international application and phase 2 consists of the national filings in the specific countries you want to file in. Phase 1 is often referred to as the international phase and phase 2 is often referred to as the national phase.

Phase 1 includes the filing of the international application by the applicant via the international bureau of WIPO or via a receiving office, the establishment of the international search report and written opinion by one of the International Searching Authorities, and the publication of the international application together with the international search report. The last component of phase 1 is the communication of the international application and corresponding search report by the International Bureau to the designated countries in the national phase. There are two additional components that are optional; they include a supplemental international search report and the establishment of the international preliminary report on patentability by one of the International Preliminary Examining Authorities.

Once phase 1 is complete, the applicant has to select the countries in which they wish to file the international application leading to phase 2 (the national phase). For phase 2 to proceed, the applicant has to select the country, pay the fees that the particular regional office requires, provide translations of the filings and appoint a representative in the country selected. The regional or national patent offices will then examine the application based on its national laws, relying part on the international search report.

You have one (1) year or twelve (12) months from the date you file your first application for an invention to file a PCT with the PCT directly or through a receiving office. The USPTO, EPO, and JPO are some common receiving offices. The PCT application is then examined by the relevant searching authority. A search report is issued outlining the opinion of the examiner at the searching authority. The opinion will indicate whether your invention is novel, unobvious (contains an inventive step is the language used in the PCT), and meets the other criteria necessary for patenting. The PCT application will then publish eighteen (18) months after the first filing date of your application. Thirty (30) months from the first filing date of your application, the application will enter the national phase, where you have the choice to file your application in over 150 different countries. See chapter 10 for the list of countries. The countries that you select to enter into will rely on the opinion of the examiner at the receiving office, sometimes wholly or with some deference to determine whether your invention should be patented in the relevant country you select.

Following is a depiction of the overall PCT system as provided in the MPEP.[1]

If you have an interest in obtaining patent protection in foreign countries, below we will discuss the process of filing a PCT and entering national phase.

The PCT may be filed either directly through the PCT via the international bureau of the WIPO or via a competent national or regional receiving office. The USPTO is deemed a competent national receiving office. In this chapter, we will discuss primarily how to file a PCT via the International Bureau of the WIPO and the USPTO as a national receiving office.

---

1   To learn more, visit: www.uspto.gov/web/offices/pac/mpep/s1842.html.

The PCT system

Any national or resident of a PCT Contracting State (see current list in chapter 10) may file the application.

In order to be accepted, an international application in phase 1 must contain the following at the time of filing:

(a) a request for international filing. The form to be used depends on the avenue you employ to file, i.e., the IB or a receiving office

(b) a description of your invention (this can be the same as which you use your first filing)

(c) a claim or claims

(d) an abstract

(e) one or more drawings (where drawings are necessary)

(f) sequence listing (if any)

(g) fees (fees are not required at the time of filing for the application to be accepted, but may be filed within one month of filing, or later with the payment of a late fee)

These elements must be arranged in the following order: request, description, claim(s), abstract, drawing(s) (if any), and sequence listing (if any). All sheets constituting the international application must be numbered in consecutive Arabic numerals with three or four separate series of numbers. The first number may apply to the request, the second to the description, claims and abstract, the third to the drawings (if any), and the fourth to the sequence listing (if any).

The international application maybe filed in any language; however, the request has to be filed in one of the ten languages under the PCT: Arabic, Chinese, English, French, German, Japanese, Korean, Portuguese, Russian, or Spanish. You may have to furnish a translation if you use an international searching authority that does not use the aforementioned languages.

There are specific requirements and forms for each part of the application; the discussion below will include the forms and formatting you need to prepare for your international filing. Most of the forms discussed below may be downloaded from www.wipo.int/pct/en/forms/.

(a) The Request

The request form for the PCT international filing is Form PCT/RO/101. See chapter 13 for a copy of the form.

This form is a standard form that is used to meet the requirements in PCT. The form will contain the title of the invention, the identity of the applicant and the agent (if any), a claim to priority to the earliest filed application in any jurisdiction (for example, if you filed a provisional application in the United States and file a PCT 12 months later, you have to claim priority to the US application on the request form), and an indication of the applicant's choice of competent International Searching Authority. The request must be signed.

The capital letters of all text matter must not be less than 0.21 cm high. There are several parts of the form. They include:

- Box I, refers to the title of the invention. The title of the invention must be short (preferably two to seven words, when in English or translated to English) and precise. The box I title should match the title on the first line of the description.

- Box II and III, refer to who may file the application. Any resident or national of a Contracting State may file an international application. The applicant must be identified by the indicator of his or her name and address and checking the appropriate box, inventor only, inventor and applicant, or applicant only. The name should appear with the family name followed by the given name.
- Box III, refers to the status of the applicant vis-à-vis the designated office.
- Box IV, refers to the representative you choose to file your application.
- Box V, refers to jurisdictions where you can opt out of filing an international application.
- Box VI, refers to the priority claim. The priority claim should be an Arabic number of the date, the name of the month, and the Arabic number of the year, in that order. For example, 17 February 2016 (17.02.2016 or 17/02/2016 or 17-02-2017).
- Box VII, refers to the selection of the international searching authority you wish to search your invention.
- Box VIII, refers to the declarations to be made on the form.
- Box IX, refers to the checklist to allow for the receiving office to verify the completeness of the documents in the filing.
- Box X, refers to the signature of the applicant or agent.
- The fee calculation sheet, refers to the calculation of fees.

(b) Description

The description must start with the title of the invention as appearing in Box 1 of the Request. The remainder of the description should be in the following order: "Technical Field," "Background Art," "Disclosure of Invention," "Brief Description of Drawings," "Best Mode for Carrying Out the Invention," "Industrial Applicability," and where applicable, "Sequence Listing" and "Sequence Listing Free Text." You may follow the same detailed guidelines in Chapters 8–10 on patent drafting to fulfill the requirements of each of the aforementioned sections.

The description must be on A4-size paper, white and durable. The minimum margins must be 2 cm at the top, the bottom, and the right side of the sheet, and 2.5 cm on the left side of the sheet. The margins should not exceed 3 cm on the bottom and the right side of the sheet and 4 cm on the top and the left side of the sheet. The margins must be completely blank, except that a file reference not exceeding 12 characters in length may be placed by the applicant in the left hand corner of the top margin within 1.5 cm from the top of the sheet. The capital letters of the text matter must be a minimum 0.28 cm high. The page number must be centered at the top or bottom of the sheet, but not in the 2-cm margin. The description must be typewritten or printed. The typing must be 1.5 spaced and in dark indelible color.

(c) Claim or Claims

The claims must define the matter for which protection is sought. They must be clear and concise.

(d) Abstract

The abstract must consist of a summary of the disclosure as contained in the description, claims, and drawings. The abstract must be as concise as the disclosure permits.

(e) Drawings (if any)

The international application must contain drawings when they are necessary for the understanding of the invention. Moreover where (without drawings being actually necessary for the understanding of the invention) the nature of the invention admits of illustration by drawings, the applicant may include such drawings and any designated Office may require the applicant to file such drawings during the national phase.

(f) Sequence Listing (if any)

Where the international application contains disclosure of a nucleotide and/or amino acid sequence, the description must contain a listing of the sequence which is presented as a separate part of the description and which complies with the standards under the PCT.

(g) Fees

There are three types of fees to be paid. They include the transmittal fee, the search fee, and the international filing fee. The required fee may be made at the time of application or in response to an invitation to pay in any of the following manners:

- Electronically via the fee payment screens
- On the Request fee calculation sheet annex, including an authorization to charge a deposit account which is included in Form PCT/RO/101
- By uploading a document giving authorization to charge a deposit account.

FILING A PCT WITH THE INTERNATIONAL BUREAU (IB)

You may file a PCT with the IB in a variety of ways. They include:

- Electronic filing via ePCT or PCT-SAFE or EPO Online Filing. You may access each of these electronic mechanisms here: www.wipo.int/pct-safe/en/
- Facsimile filing to (41-22) 910 06 10 (or 41-22) 338 70 60; however, you must also provide an original of the faxed document to the IB within fourteen days from the date of the fax transmittal
- Mail your filing to:
  International Bureau of WIPO
  PCT Receiving Office Section
  34, Chemin des Colombettes
  1211 Geneva 20
  Switzerland
- Hand deliver the application to the same address identified above.

These applications may be filed up to midnight Geneva time and receive the date of the day it was received.

Additional Forms

Additional, non-mandatory forms may be included with the international application. For example, Form PCT/RO/198, may be used when filing applications and other documents. This form is accessible via the WIPO website and is included in the section on forms in chapter 13. The form will provide all the information the IB will need, such as number of pages and nature of documents filed. The form will be used to ensure all the documents received are as expected.

After the international application has been filed, the applicant will receive Form PCT/RO/199 as an acknowledgment receipt of the international application.

Choosing an International Searching Authority for Examination by the IB

Your choice of searching authority must be included in the request and the choice of International Preliminary Examining Authority must be indicated in the demand.

How to Pay Fees

- Credit card
- Debit account established at the WIPO in Swiss francs only
- Bank transfer in either Swiss francs, US dollars or euros
- Transfer to WIPO's postal account in Swiss francs only

FILING A PCT WITH THE USPTO AS THE RECEIVING OFFICE

You may file a PCT with the USPTO in a variety of ways. They include:

- Electronic filing via the EFS-Web.
    - In order to submit an application via EFS-web, make sure the following formatting requirements are met.
        - All PDF documents must have a minimum resolution of 300 DPI.
        - The required page size filed in PDF format is A4.
        - The electronic signature by an agent or attorney should be an S-signature consisting of an alpha-

numeric string between forward slash marks. The signer's name should be printed or typed immediately below or adjacent to the S-signature, and the attorney or agent's registration number as part of the signature or immediately below or adjacent to the S-signature.

- Mail filings to:
  Mail Stop PCT
  Commissioner of Patents
  PO Box 1450
  Alexandria, VA 22313-1450
- Hand delivery of filing:
  United States Patent and Trademark Office
  Customer Service Window, Mail Stop PCT
  Randolph Building
  401 Dulany Street
  Alexandria, VA 22314

Additional Forms

There are additional documents you can file with the USPTO as your receiving office. For example:

- Transmittal letter, see chapter 13 for a copy of Form PTO-1382 (which serves as a cover sheet to itemize the documents submitted and requested actions).

How to Pay Fees

The patent applicant can pay fees to the USPTO by any of the following methods:

- Credit card
- Deposit account established at the USPTO
- Electronic Funds Transfer
- Check or Money order, make payable to the "Director of the USPTO"
- Cash in person
- Wire payment

Other Steps Required of Patent Applicants

Once you have obtained an international search of your application, you have up to thirty (30) months from the time you filed your first application to enter national phase (phase 2). Once these countries are designated for national filing, the international application and the international search report are forwarded by the IB to the national patent offices. Once there, the applicant is responsible for submitting the requisite translations, adhering to the national requirements for entry, and paying the national examination fees. Once the national patent offices accept the international applications for examination, there will not be any more interaction with the IB of the WIPO. If no steps have been taken by the applicant within the thirty months to move the international application to the national offices, the international application ceases and you may forego your opportunity to secure patent rights in international jurisdictions.

Remember the international application is just that, an application. It does not confer any patent rights anywhere around the world. It is merely a streamlined process for you to file for a patent to your invention in several jurisdictions around the world.

How to Prosecute a Patent Application at the US Patent and Trademark Office

In chapter 9 you learned how to draft and file an application for a US patent. Chapter 12 explains the steps involved in the application review and examination process. This review and examination process is typically referred to as "patent prosecution." The complete process, from filing the application to the granting of a patent, takes about three to four years (also known in patent jargon as the "pendency" of your application). This time is broken into two phases. The first phase is the dormant phase of prosecution, which includes the time elapsed between the filing of the application and the time the examiner issues a first substantive Office Action (also known as First Action Pendency). The dormant phase is usually anywhere from one-and-a-half to two years. The second phase is the active prosecution phase, where the examiner and you will be engaged in the review of the application to identify allowable subject matter to issue as a patent. This phase takes another one to two years.

STRUCTURE OF THE USPTO

The USPTO patent examining core is organized by technology centers. Each technology center handles a broad area of technology. The technology centers cover the following areas:

- 1600—Biotechnology and Organic Chemistry

- 1700—Chemical and Materials Engineering
- 2100—Computer Architecture, Software, and Information Security
- 2400—Computer Networks, Multiplex Communication, Video Distribution, and Security
- 2600—Communications
- 2800—Semiconductors, Electrical and Optical Systems, and Components
- 2900—Designs
- 3600—Transportation, Construction, Electronic Commerce, Agriculture, National Security, and License & Review
- 3700—Mechanical Engineering, Manufacturing, and Products

Within each technology center are several art units, and within each art unit reside approximately fifteen examiners.

When you file an application in a particular area of technology, the application is first classified based on the technical focus of your patent applications into classes and subclasses as defined by the US Patent Classification System (available at www.uspto.gov/web/patents /classification/). The classification of your application determines which examiner within the USPTO examines your application. For example, if you have filed a patent application for a drug product classified in class 546, subclass 210, the patent application will be assigned to Technology Center 1600; it will be assigned to art unit 1626, the art unit that handles organic molecules in class 546; and it will be assigned to an examiner who handles organic molecules in class 546 and subclasses 1 through 500 (which includes subclass 210). Knowing the class and subclass of your patent application will also be helpful in determining the First Action Pendency for your particular patent application. See the statistics maintained at the USPTO website at this link: www.uspto.gov/about /stratplan/ar/2011/oai_05_wlt_04.html.

PROCESSING THE APPLICATION

When a patent application arrives at the USPTO, the Office of Patent Application Processing (OPAP) examines the papers to make sure the required parts of the application have been submitted. The application is then assigned a filing date and a serial number and forwarded to an art unit within the USPTO. The application serial number and confirmation number is stamped on the self-addressed postcard you sent the patent office when you mailed in your application and returned to you. If you electronically filed your application, you will receive an electronic filing receipt of the same. A formal filing receipt will be prepared and mailed to you.

A filing receipt is a document from the USPTO that officially acknowledges that the application has met the minimal filing requirements. The filing receipt includes the application number, filing date, a confirmation number, a suggested class in the US Patent Classification System, and the number of an art unit where the application is likely to be examined. The filing receipt also includes other information about the application as applicable, such as continuing data, foreign filing license data (assuming the invention is not a classified military secret), entity status information, and the date the USPTO anticipates publishing the application (which is eighteen months from your filing date).

The filing receipt represents the official assignment by the USPTO of a specific application number and confirmation number to a particular application. The confirmation number is a four-digit number that is assigned to each newly filed application. The confirmation number, in combination with the application number, is used to verify the accuracy of the application number placed on correspondence filed with the USPTO. The confirmation number may be found in the upper left-hand corner of the filing receipt. The confirmation number will also be available through the Patent Application Information Retrieval (PAIR) system. The confirmation number must be used on all correspondence submitted to the USPTO concerning the application.

When you receive the filing receipt, check it for accuracy. Make sure that the filing date is the date you electronically filed, express-mailed, or hand-delivered the application, that all the names are spelled correctly, and that there are no typographical errors. If the filing receipt has errors, you should file for a Request for Corrected Filing Receipt and explain the error and request for a correction. A new filing receipt will be mailed to you upon the correction of the error. A sample Request for Corrected Filing Receipt can be found in chapter 13.

During processing at OPAP, the USPTO will determine whether all the required parts of the application are included in your filing; if the patent application does not include all required parts, you will be sent a Notice of Missing Parts.

This paper identifies material that is necessary for a complete application, such as the signed Declaration or the filing fee. Although the incomplete application will be given a filing date and a serial number, the missing parts must be sent to the USPTO within the time specified on the notice (generally two months, but extensions of time can be obtained for a fee). Remember to include a self-addressed, postage-paid postcard and the appropriate Certificate of Mailing (see Form USPTO/SB/92 in chapter 13), if you are mailing the response, or a certificate of transmission (see Form USPTO/SB/92 in chapter 13) for all other modes of transmission.

After all the required parts of the patent application have been received by the USPTO, the filing receipt discussed earlier will be issued, and the application will be examined in due course.

PROSECUTION WITH THE USPTO

After the application is processed by the OPAP, it is forwarded to the appropriate art unit and assigned to a patent examiner. The patent application will sit on the examiner's docket until such time as the examiner takes up the case in turn (when checking on status, PAIR will describe the status as Docketed New Case—Ready for Examination). This is the dormant phase of your application filing, and you will likely not hear from the USPTO again for another fourteen to eighteen months.

Once the examiner picks up your application for examination, the examiner will review the application for compliance with USPTO formalities and the patent statute and regulations. This review includes grouping subject matter by the claims, determining a classification of the claims to ensure the patent application has been assigned to the correct examining group, and a determination of whether a Restriction Requirement should be made.

RESTRICTION REQUIREMENT

Even before you receive the first substantive Office Action, the examiner may issue a Restriction Requirement and/or a Request for an Election of Species. The examiner will issue a Restriction Requirement if he or she believes that more than one invention is claimed in the application. For example, if you have claimed two different compositions of matter, for example, a new plastic and a new steel, the examiner may issue a Restriction Requirement stating that the application is to be restricted to a single invention. You must then choose between the claims directed to plastic or the claims directed to steel and advise the examiner which set of claims you wish to continue to prosecute. The rest of the claims can be prosecuted in a divisional application at a later date without losing your original filing date. The examiner may also initiate a restriction requirement by trying to get you to elect the invention you want examined over the phone. Under such circumstances, the details of the restriction requirement will be included in the first substantive Office Action you receive that also details the examination findings in view of the prior art.

Try to convince the examiner that the Restriction Requirement is not reasonable, that all claims are directed to a single unitary invention, and that the search would not be unduly burdensome. It is not likely you will successfully overcome a restriction requirement, but stating that you are electing certain claims "with traverse" will allow you to challenge the Restriction Requirement and document in the record that you do not necessarily agree with the examiner.

A Request for an Election of Species will be issued if various species in a generic invention are claimed. This is often the case in an application relating to a composition that discloses various Markush groups of components. For example, you may have a claim for a composition comprising "component C, wherein C is selected from the group consisting of X, Y, and Z." Because the examiner will only examine a limited number of species, he or she may require you to elect only one species, that is, either X, Y, or Z, from the group for examination.

The examiner will not begin a substantive review of the application and issue the first substantive Office Action until your response to the Restriction Requirement and/or the Request for an Election of Species is received either by telephone or in writing. Therefore, respond to these requests as soon as possible in order to begin substantive prosecution of the application. A Restriction Requirement is usually given a shortened statutory response period of one month, and you may pay an extension fee for up to an additional five months, if necessary. A sample response to a restriction requirement can be found at the end of this chapter.

OFFICE ACTIONS

Once you have made your election, the substantive part of the examination will commence, whereby a prior art search will be conducted of earlier patents and publications to determine whether the elected claims are novel and unobvious.

The examiner will then prepare and mail a report called an "Office Action" setting forth his or her opinion of the application. The most common types of Office Actions you will receive are as follows:

(a) Non-final Office Action
(b) Final Office Action
(c) Advisory Action
(d) Notice of Allowance

All correspondence the USPTO sends to you is time sensitive and should be responded to within the time prescribed by the rules, or your application will be abandoned. Once you have received an Office Action from the USPTO, determine the type of Office Action you have received, determine the time period available for response, and set the task on your calendar to ensure that you do not miss the date for response.

CALCULATING THE RESPONSE DATE

When you receive the first Office Action, the date it was mailed will be typed near the top right. This date is important because it is the date from which the time period to respond to the Office Action is calculated. Failure to respond to an Office Action within the allotted time can result in the abandonment of the application.

This period of time specified in the Office Action for response is called the Shortened Statutory Period (SSP) and it is essentially the time period given to you to respond without the payment of a fee. If your response is filed after the SSP, but within the total extendable time period provided for in the rules for that type of Office Action, you will be required to pay a fee to have your response considered by the examiner, or your application will be abandoned.

Extensions of time from one, two, three, or four months can be obtained if requested by petition and by payment of the required fee. The maximum time to respond to most Office Action is six months from the mailing date of the action. This includes the three months from the mailing date plus up to three additional months after the payment of an extension fee. If the calculated date for responding falls on a weekend or a holiday, you can respond on the following business day. If you file your response by mail, the date of your response will be the date you deposit it with the US Postal Service, if you include the appropriate certificate of mailing with the response. Otherwise, the date of the response will be the date it is received by the USPTO.

If you respond after the third month but before the sixth month, you must submit a Petition for Extension of Time before or at the time you submit your response. This petition is typically a short form requesting a one-, two-, or three-month extension—whichever is applicable (see Form USPTO/AIA/22 in chapter 13). You must also submit an extension fee with the petition. For example: The date the Office Action was mailed was June 1, 2012, with a SSP of three months. Your due date for response without an extension of time is September 1, 2012. If you respond to the Office Action on November 2, 2012, the Office Action response must be accompanied by a petition for a three-month extension of time along with the three-month extension fee. Check the fee schedule with the USPTO for changes. A Petition for Extension of Time is always granted provided it is timely filed, properly completed, and accompanied by the correct fee.

Carefully check each paper you receive from the USPTO to determine when it is due. Some papers, such as the Notice of Missing Parts, may require a SSP response period of two months instead of the usual three months.

NON-FINAL OFFICE ACTION

This is usually the first Office Action you will receive on the merits of your application. Such an Office Action usually comes with a three-month SSP, which is extendable another three months with the payment of a fee. This type of Office Action delineates all the objections and rejections that the examiner has determined apply to your patent application upon examination. The Office Action will include copies of the relevant prior art uncovered in the examiner's search (except no copies for US patents and patent applications are included, as these are available on the USPTO website by their patent or application serial numbers). The Office Action identifies which claims, if any, are acceptable or "allowed" and which are unacceptable or "rejected." The Office Action will provide the basis and reasons for the rejected claims. The Office Action also indicates whether there are any other problems with the application.

It is not unusual for the examiner to reject all the claims in the first Non-final Office Action; however, this is not the end of prosecution. Examiners are under pressure to review cases quickly. Therefore, they may reject all the claims in order to force you to more clearly explain the essence of your invention and its unique features and distinguish it from the prior art.

Although most Office Actions are self-explanatory, be sure you fully understand the reasons for the examiner's objections and rejections. If you are having trouble understanding an Office Action, reread it. Then, read it a third time if necessary. If you simply cannot figure out what the examiner means, call him or her for clarification. The examiner's contact information is included in the Office Action.

It is also possible, but not likely, that upon initial review the examiner will find that all the claims are patentable and the application is acceptable as submitted. If so, the examiner will issue a "Notice of Allowance" instead of an Office Action (see the section on Notice of Allowance for next steps).

PREPARING AN AMENDMENT AND RESPONSE

Before responding to an Office Action, review it carefully, including all of the prior art cited by the examiner. If you find you do not have all of the prior art or pages of the Office Action, contact the examiner and ask that the missing materials be sent to you as soon as possible. If you find that the citation of a reference is incorrect or an Office Action contains some other error that affects your ability to reply to the Office Action, you should notify the examiner within one month of the mail date of the action. The Office will restart the previously set period for reply to run from the date the error is corrected, if requested to do so. If the error is brought to the attention of the USPTO within the period for reply set in the Office Action but more than one month after the date of the Office Action, the USPTO will set a new period for reply, which is substantially equal to the time remaining in the reply period. For example, if the error is brought to the attention of the USPTO five weeks after mailing the action, then the USPTO would set a new two-month period for reply. The new period for reply must be at least one month and would run from the date the error is corrected. Where for any reason it becomes necessary to re-mail any Office Action, the Office Action will be re-dated, as it is the re-mailing date that establishes the beginning of the period for reply. A supplementary action after a rejection explaining the references more explicitly or giving the reasons more fully, even though no further references are cited, establishes a new date from which the statutory period runs. If the error in citation or other defective Office Action is called to the attention of the USPTO after the expiration of the period for reply, the period will not be restarted, and any appropriate extension fee will be required to render a reply timely. The Office letter correcting the error will note that the time period for reply remains as set forth in the previous Office Action. In the event that correspondence from the USPTO is received late (a) due to delays in the US Postal Service or (b) because the mail was delayed in leaving the USPTO (the postmark date is later than the mail date printed on the correspondence), applicants may petition to reset the period for reply.

Next, you should categorize the examiner's remarks. They should normally fit into the following categories: (1) objections based on formalities, such as misspellings, trademarks, and so on; (2) rejection of the specification under 35 U.S.C. §112, first paragraph; (3) rejection of claims in view of 35 U.S.C. §112, second paragraph; and (4) rejection of one or more claims based on prior art as listed under 35 U.S.C. §102 and/or §103. The rejection section may be followed with an objection section; this section objects to claims that are dependent on rejected claims in the aforementioned categories. If there are rejections based on other sections of the patent statute, put those in yet another category. Using this technique, it will be much easier to respond to what may at first appear to be an overwhelming number of objections and rejections. Decide how you will respond to each objection and rejection and prepare your response. Your response should be complete, accurate, and persuasive, as it is the key to showing the examiner that the invention is patentable.

When considering a response to the Office Action issued by the examiner, consider first arguments you can make to overcome the rejection. Consider whether the examiner is wrong with regard to the patent law, rule, or regulation, or whether the examiner is incorrect about the fact as discussed in the prior art or a combination of all of the above. If not, the best way to respond to the Office Action is to revise the specification and claims to overcome the examiner's objections and rejections, provided that the revised claims adequately cover your invention and are sufficient to overcome the objections and/or rejections. These revisions are called "amendments," and they will be submitted with your remarks in a document called an "Amendment and Response." See the sample "Amendment and Response" at the end of this chapter.

Start your response by making amendments to the specification as necessary to overcome any objections raised by the examiner such as formalities or typographical and spelling errors. The specification may also be amended to overcome any rejection by the examiner under 35 U.S.C. Section 112, first paragraph, requiring adequate description of the invention. Remember when making amendments to the specification or the claims, no new matter can be added to the application. Next, consider making appropriate amendments to the claims. Amending the claims may require narrowing them to overcome prior art or revising them to more clearly describe the claimed invention. A new element or component may be added to the claims to overcome an anticipation rejection under 35 U.S.C. Section 102. Other limitations (e.g., amounts, forms, use, mode of operation) may be added to the claims to get around an obviousness rejection based on 35 U.S.C. Section 103. Your goal should be to overcome the examiner's rejections without narrowing the claims any more than necessary. You may want to speak to a patent attorney or patent agent about the best way to amend the claims. You can also ask the examiner to assist you in amending the claims.

After you have amended the specification and claims, begin the "Remarks" section of the Amendment and Response on a new page. In this section, respond directly to all of the examiner's objections and rejections. The best way to do this is to identify each of the examiner's objections and rejections and repeat it by stating, "The examiner has objected to the specification under Section 112, first paragraph, because . . ." Then, respond to this objection or rejection by pointing out how the specification has been amended. If you have chosen not to offer an amendment in response to the objection, explain why an amendment is not needed. Repeat this process for every rejection and objection made by the examiner. Follow these guidelines in preparing the Amendment and Response:

- Type the response in English, preferably double-spaced, on letter-size, legal-size, or A4-size paper. Use the same margins required in the specification.
- Make sure you follow the format described above to amend the specification and claims.
- Always be polite, and do not get personal with the examiner. The Amendment and Response is addressed to the Commission for Patents and Trademarks, not specifically to the examiner. Do not say, "You said;" instead say, "The examiner has stated . . ." or "Claim 1 has been rejected because . . ." Similarly, always refer to yourself as "the applicant."
- Refer to the amendments when responding to a rejection, if appropriate. State, for example, "In response to the examiner's rejection, claim 1 has been amended to claim the anti-inflammatory ibuprofen."
- If you have to convince the examiner that your invention is not obvious in view of the prior art, try the following arguments where applicable:
    - Distinguish your claims from the teachings of the prior art;

- Determine whether all the elements of the claims are included in the prior art. If they are not included, identify the differences that are not included in the prior art and indicate why the differences are not obvious for any or all of the following reasons:
  - The prior art does not lead one to overcome the difference;
  - The results achieved by your invention are "unexpected";
  - Your invention has been highly commercially successful;
  - Those skilled in the art were never able to solve the problem solved by your invention; the invention meets a long-felt, previously unmet need;
  - The prior art references teach away from your invention, for example, they state or imply that your invention would not work;
  - While your invention may combine two known compounds, elements, or steps, the result achieved by your invention is "synergistic." In other words, the whole is greater than the sum of its parts;
  - The prior art reference is from a different field, and is "nonanalogous art";
  - The art cited by the examiner is inoperative; and
  - The invention has been recognized by others in the industry as evidenced by awards, attempts to license, and copying.
- Consider submitting an affidavit under 37 C.F.R. Section 1.132 providing factual support for your remarks. For example, an affidavit might be appropriate (1) to present facts relevant to the operability of your invention that might not be in the specification; (2) to present experimental results that

clarify the uniqueness of your invention; and (3) to present supporting evidence that your invention has had impressive commercial success.

Your remarks and arguments should be as clear and concise as possible. After you have provided remarks for each objection and rejection, conclude by stating, "For the foregoing reasons, Applicant respectfully submits that the claims (as amended) are drawn to novel subject matter, patentably distinct from the art of record, and allowable in form. Favorable reconsideration and a Notice of Allowance are respectfully requested."

Finally, close your response with "Respectfully submitted," and sign and date the response. Type your address and telephone number below your name, in case the examiner needs to contact you.

The amendments you choose to make to your specification, claims. or both in order to appropriately respond to the examiner's objections and rejections have to be done in a particular manner in order to be compliant with the patent rules for amendments. The discussion below will provide guidance on how to make those amendments properly.

MANNER OF MAKING AMENDMENTS IN THE AMENDMENT AND RESPONSE
Amendments to the Specification

Amendments to the specification must be made by adding, deleting, or replacing a paragraph, by replacing a section, or by a substitute specification, in the manner specified in this section.

1. Amendments to delete, replace, or add a paragraph must be made by submitting:
   (a) An instruction, which unambiguously identifies the location, to delete one or more paragraphs of the specification, replace a paragraph with one or more replacement paragraphs, or add one or more paragraphs;
   (b) The full text of any replacement paragraph with markings to show all the changes relative to the previous version of the

paragraph. The text of any added subject matter must be shown by underlining the added text. The text of any deleted matter must be shown by strikethrough, but double brackets placed before and after the deleted characters may be used to show deletion of five or fewer consecutive characters. The text of any deleted subject matter must be shown by being placed within double brackets if strikethrough cannot be easily perceived;

(c) The full text of any added paragraphs without any underlining; and

(d) The text of a paragraph to be deleted must not be presented with strikethrough or placed within double brackets. The instruction to delete may identify a paragraph by its paragraph number or include a few words from the beginning, and end, of the paragraph, if needed for paragraph identification purposes.

2. Amendments made by a replacement section, if the sections of the specification contain section headings as provided in Title of the Invention; Cross-Reference to Related Applications; Statement Regarding Federally Sponsored Research or Development; the Names of the Parties to a Joint Research Agreement; Reference to a "Sequence Listing," a Table, or a Computer Program Listing; Background of the Invention; Brief Summary of the Invention; Brief Description of the Several Views of the Drawing; Detailed Description of the Invention; Abstract of the Disclosure; or Sequence Listing. Such may be made by submitting:

(a) A reference to the section heading along with an instruction, which unambiguously identifies the location, to delete that section of the specification and to replace such deleted section with a replacement section; and

(b) A replacement section with markings to show all changes relative to the previous version of the section. The text of any added subject matter must be shown by underlining the added text. The text of any deleted matter must be shown by strikethrough, but double brackets placed before and after the deleted characters may be used to show deletion of five or fewer consecutive characters. The text of any deleted subject matter must be shown by being placed within double brackets if strikethrough cannot be easily perceived.

3. Amendments made by substitute specification are made by submitting:

   (a) An instruction to replace the specification; and

   (b) A substitute specification.

4. Amendments to reinstate a previously deleted paragraph or section may be made by a subsequent amendment adding the previously deleted paragraph or section.

Examples of Amendment to the Specifications

In the body of the Amendment and Response, under the heading "Amendment to the Specification," your instruction would be as follows:

Sample Instruction to Replace a Paragraph:
Please replace paragraph [0033] with the following amended paragraph:

[0033] When preparing a composition comprising A, B, and C, combine A with B in the presence of heat [[can]] between 120 and 200 degrees centigrade and then combine the resulting slurry mixture with C.

Sample Instruction to Add a Paragraph:
Please add the following new paragraph after paragraph [0050]:

[0050.1] D is an optional ingredient that can be added to the composition comprising A, B, and C.

Sample Instruction to Delete a Paragraph:
Please delete the paragraph beginning on page 4, line 7, which starts with "The prior art describes . . ."

Amendment to the Claims

Amendments to a claim must be made by rewriting the entire claim with all changes (e.g., additions and deletions) as indicated, except when the claim is being canceled. Each amendment document that includes a change to an existing claim, cancellation of an existing claim, or addition of a new claim, must include a complete listing of all claims ever presented, including the text of all pending and withdrawn claims, in the application. In the claim listing, the status of every claim must be indicated after its claim number by using one of the following identifiers in a parenthetical expression: (Original), (Currently amended), (Canceled), (Withdrawn), (Previously presented), (New), and (Not entered).

1. All of the claims should be presented in ascending numerical order. Consecutive claims having the same status of "canceled" or "not entered" can be aggregated into one statement (e.g., Claims 1–5 (Canceled)). The claim should begin on a separate sheet of the amendment document.

2. All claims being currently amended in an amendment paper should be included in the claim listing, with the status of "currently amended," and should be submitted with markings to indicate the changes that have been made relative to the immediate prior version of the claims. When adding subject matter, you should underline the added text. When deleting subject matter, you should use strikethrough, but double brackets should be placed before and after the deleted characters for five or fewer consecutive characters. The text of any deleted subject matter should be placed within double brackets if strikethrough cannot be easily perceived. If you are amending a withdrawn claim, use the status identifier of "withdrawn—currently amended."

3. The text of all pending claims not currently amended should be included in the claim listing in clean version, that is, without any markings in the presentation of text. An unamended claim should have the status identifier of "original," "withdrawn," or "previously presented," which will constitute an assertion that it has not been changed relative to the immediate prior version. Any new claim added by amendment must be indicated with the status of "new" and presented in clean version, that is, without any underlining.

4. In order to cancel a claim, you should omit any claim text and should include the status identifier "canceled" or "not entered."

Example of Amendment to the Claims

In the body of the Amendment and Response, under the heading "Amendment to the Claims," your claims will be recited as follows:

> Claims 1–3 (Canceled).
> Claim 4 (Previously presented). A composition consisting essentially of A, B, and C.
> Claim 5 (Withdrawn). A composition comprising L, M, and O.
> Claim 6 (Currently amended). A composition consisting essentially of A, B, and C.
> Claim 7 (Original). A composition of claim 6, wherein A is selected from calcium, potassium, or sodium.
> Claim 8 (New). A composition of claim 7, wherein C is selected from water or saline.

The Amendment and Response can be sent to the USPTO by US regular mail, by facsimile, or by filing electronically. Prepare a cover Transmittal Form (for all forms of transmission except by mail) or certificate of mailing (if you mail your response to the USPTO) to send to the USPTO mail stop Amendment, Commission for Patents, PO Box 1450, Alexandria, VA 22313-1450, along with any documents you are submitting. A sample Certificate of Mailing and Transmittal Form is in chapter 13. If you use US mail, include a self-addressed, postage-paid postcard. The typical documents you would file with an amendment and response include the Certificate of Transmission or Mailing (USPTO/SB/92), a Fee Transmittal Form (USPTO/SB/17), Extension of Time Petition (if necessary, USPTO/SB/22) and the Amendment and Response separated by the cover sheet identifying the sections of the response and the page on which each section appears; separately, the amendment to the specification (if applicable), the amendment to the claims (if applicable), and the remarks (if necessary). See the sample Amendment and Response at the end of this chapter.

Amending the Drawings

The Office Action may also include objections to the drawings, especially if you submitted informal drawings when you filed the application. Drawing amendments are submitted as a separate document and routed to the USPTO draftsman for review and approval. However, acknowledge the drawing rejections to the examiner in the Remarks section, stating that the objections are noted and will be corrected separately. Frequently, drawings are not corrected and filed as formal drawings until after a Notice of Allowance has been received. At that time, make sure you submit drawings promptly to allow time for further corrections if necessary.

The drawings should be amended in the following manner:

> Any changes to an application drawing must be submitted on a replacement sheet of drawings as an attachment and in the top margin, labeled "Replacement Sheet." Any replacement sheet of drawings shall include all of the figures appearing on the immediate prior version of the sheet, even if only one figure is amended. Any new sheet of drawings containing an additional figure must be labeled in the top margin as "New Sheet." All changes to the drawings shall be explained, in detail, in either the drawing amendment or remarks section of the amendment paper. A marked-up copy of any amended drawing figure, including annotations indicating the changes made, may be included. The marked-up copy must be clearly labeled as "Annotated Sheet" and must be presented in the amendment or remarks section that explains the change to the drawings.

Example of Amendment to the Drawings

In the body of the Amendment and Response, under the heading "Amendment to the Drawings," your instruction would be as follows:

> The attached sheet of drawings includes changes to Fig. 5. The sheet, which includes Fig. 1 and 2, replaces the original sheet including Fig. 1, 2, and 3. In Fig. 1, a previously omitted element 15 has been added.
>
> Attachments:
> Replacement Sheet
> Annotated Sheet Showing Changes

INTERVIEWING THE EXAMINER

After you receive the first Office Action, it may also be helpful to call the examiner to arrange a face-to-face meeting, technically called an interview. Interviews normally occur in the examiner's office at the USPTO in Alexandria, Virginia. Interviews with the examiner can also be conducted over the telephone, but in-person interviews are usually more effective in getting claims allowed. If you decide to interview the examiner, make your request by telephoning the examiner. The examiner's phone number should be at the end of the Office Action.

Interviews are highly recommended, because trading paper with the examiner does not necessarily further the merits of your application; it often causes both parties to remain entrenched in their positions and unwilling to see the points the other party is making. During your interview you will be able to ascertain if the examiner is interpreting your claims incorrectly and, if so, the reason for it. The examiner may also be able to visualize the invention better when explained by the applicant in person using body language and props. The interview will give you a chance to explain and perhaps demonstrate your invention, and it will give the examiner a chance to meet and personally interact with you. Meeting with an examiner in an open and nonadversarial way allows you to establish a personal rapport with the examiner and can go a long way in getting a patent granted.

Come to the interview fully prepared. The examiner is taking time to discuss your invention with you; do not waste the opportunity by being ill-prepared. Be familiar with the examiner's objections and rejections and be prepared to discuss them. Draft proposed amendments to the claims for the examiner's review, which you can offer to send to the examiner before you meet. If appropriate, bring the invention with you for demonstration purposes.

The examiner may also take the opportunity to discuss the type of arguments and amendments that will get the application allowed. This information is extremely useful and will reduce the time spent in prosecution as well as ineffective arguments that may be held against you in litigation once the patent is allowed.

FINAL OFFICE ACTION

After the examiner has reviewed your Amendment and Response, he or she will allow all, some, or none of the claims. The examiner will issue a Notice of Allowance if all of the claims are allowed. If not all of the claims are allowed, another Office Action will be issued.

The second Office Action is usually a Final Office Action, and will be indicated on the document. There are several ways you can respond to a Final Office Action, such as (1) amending the claims and filing an Amendment and Response after Final Rejection and trying to convince the examiner to allow the claims; (2) filing a Response after Final Rejection and trying to convince the examiner to allow the claims without amending them; (3) appealing the examiner's rejections to the Board of Patent Appeals and Interferences or petitioning the Commission for Patents and Trademarks, whichever applies; (4) refiling the application as a continuing application anew; (5) filing a Request for Continued Examination (RCE) (see the section later in this chapter on refiling options for further discussion); or, (6) calling it quits and deciding to abandon the application. You can also elect to first respond and then, depending on the outcome of the response, exercise options two, three, four, five, or six.

AMENDMENT AFTER FINAL REJECTION

An amendment and/or response after final rejection should have a heading of, for example, "Amendment and Response under 37 C.F.R. §1.116" or "Response after Final Rejection under 37 C.F.R. §1.116."

The first sentence of the document might state, "In response to the Office Action dated _____, Applicant respectfully requests entry of this Amendment and Response pursuant to 37 C.F.R. §1.116." The rest of the document is prepared the same way you prepared the previous Amendment and Response.

Amend the specification and claims as needed to overcome the rejections of the examiner. In the Remarks, respond to every objection and rejection the examiner has made. Try to convince the examiner that his or her conclusions are erroneous and that you have shown a *prima facie* case of patentability of your invention.

When you are "under final rejection," the clock is ticking. You have only six months to submit an Amendment after Final Rejection, wait for a response from the examiner, and, if necessary, begin the appeal process or refile the application.

After the examiner has reviewed these documents, you will be notified by an Advisory Action or a Notice of Allowance. If the examiner has, at last, decided to allow the claims, you will receive a Notice of Allowance as described below. If the case is not allowed, you will receive an Advisory Action and should still have time to either file an Appeal or a Petition or file for a RCE. And, of course, you could give up on patenting the invention and abandon the application.

Which option you exercise depends on your answers to the following questions. In view of the prior art, is the invention patentable? Does the examiner understand the claimed invention? Are the examiner's rejections reasonable? Has the examiner incorrectly applied the patent statute in rejecting the claims? How important is the patent? If you file for a RCE or refile the application, is it likely the claims will eventually be allowed without going through the appeal process? How likely is it that you will prevail on appeal? Is it cost-effective to continue prosecution by filing a RCE, refiling, or appealing? If you appeal, are you willing to wait two years or more for a decision?

Advisory Action

An Advisory Action Before the Filing of an Appeal Brief is an Action sent by the examiner to indicate that the Response filed after final rejection has not placed the application in condition for allowance. This Action will advise you of the disposition of the proposed amendments to the claims and of the effect of any argument or affidavit that did not place the application in condition for allowance.

APPEALS AND PETITIONS

Rejection of claims for substantive reasons (e.g., rejection under 35 U.S.C. §102 and/or 103) are appealable to the Patent Trial & Appeal Board (PTAB). You must file a Notice of Appeal within the prescribed or extended time period to start the appeal process. A Notice of Appeal must be filed within six months of receiving a Final Office Action. An Appeal Brief must then be filed within two months after filing the Notice of Appeal, but this period can be extended to a maximum of six months. A sample Notice of Appeal (Form USPTO/AIA/31) appears in chapter 12 and the blank form appears in chapter 13.

An Appeal Brief must comply with certain formalities. The required sections of an Appeal Brief, itemized in 37 C.F.R. §41.37(c), are (1) a statement of real party in interest, (2) a statement of related appeals and interferences, (3) a statement of the status of the claims, (4) a statement of the status of the amendments, (5) a summary of the invention, (6) issues for review, (7) a grouping of claims, (8) an argument, (9) a conclusion, (10) your signature, and (11) a copy of the claims under appeal attached as an appendix. The examiner will review the Appeal Brief and file an answer called the examiner's Answer. You may then file a Reply Brief in response to the examiner's Answer.

Eventually, the PTAB will review your case. You may request an oral hearing, at which you will be given an opportunity to argue your case. You may use Form USPTO/AIA/32 to request an oral hearing. See chapter 13 for a copy of this form. If the board disagrees with the examiner, it will issue a written decision, which should eventually result in an allowance of the case. If the board upholds the examiner's rejection(s), you will also be so advised in a written decision.

The PTAB is not the "court of last resort." If the application is important enough, you can appeal to the Court of Appeals for the Federal Circuit or the Federal District Court for the District of Columbia, and up to the US Supreme Court if there is a legal basis. This is an expensive and time-consuming process that will almost certainly require the assistance of legal counsel.

Objections to applications based on noncompliance with formalities are petitionable to the commissioner for patents. Generally, petitionable matters are those relating to practice and procedure of the USPTO. Petition the commissioner as soon as possible after the occurrence of the petitionable event. Make sure the petition sets forth all the relevant facts and, if necessary, is accompanied by one or more declarations setting forth supporting evidence.

The chart below (based on data from the USPTO) will give you some perspective on the likelihood of success at the PTAB when appealing an examiner's rejections:

Disposition	Percent Decisions (Fiscal Year 2013)
Affirmed	57.4 percent
Affirmed-in-part	12.9 percent
Reversed	28.6 percent
Dismissed	0.8 percent

The PTAB of Appeals and Interferences statistics:www.uspto.gov /patents-application-process/patent-trial-and-appeal-board/statistics

REFILING THE APPLICATION

An alternative to appealing the examiner's rejections to the Board is to continue prosecution either by filing a Request for Continued Examination or by refiling the case anew. A continuation application retains the original application filing date and is prosecuted in much the same way as the original application. An advantage of refiling is that you may have two more chances to overcome the examiner's rejections by further amending the application and/or presenting arguments to the examiner as to why the claims should be allowed. A disadvantage of refiling is that you must pay another filing fee, and prosecution of the application is then extended.

Note that, in addition to refiling an application in order to overcome rejections, patent applications can be refiled for other reasons. The first case that is filed in a series of applications is called the "parent" application. Your original parent application, however, may have several generations of offspring. For example, if your original application was subject to a restriction requirement because it claimed two different inventions, you have the right to refile the claims you did not originally elect by filing a second application. This second application is called a "divisional" application. Even though you file the divisional application after filing the original application, it is still entitled to the original filing date.

Or perhaps after filing the parent application you have discovered a way to improve the invention by adding a new element. Remember, you cannot add new matter to an application after it has been filed. What you can do, however, is file a "continuation-in-part application." As its name implies, part of this second application is identical to and can claim priority on the first application, while the remainder of the application contains the new matter added after the parent application was filed.

REQUEST FOR CONTINUED EXAMINATION (RCE)

An RCE is a type of continuing application. The advantage of such a filing is that the prosecution continues from where you left off; the application retains the same serial number and gives you two more chances to overcome the rejections cited by the examiner without having to file the entire application anew.

The RCE request is fairly simple. The request includes filing a RCE request form, a qualifying submission, and a fee (see Form USPTO/SB/30). A qualifying submission depends on when you file for an RCE. If you file for an RCE after you have received a Final Office Action, you must submit an Amendment and Response or a Response to the outstanding rejections made by the examiner in the Final Office Action as your qualifying submission. If, however, you file an RCE because you received a Notice of Allowance, but just learned of some new prior art that is relevant to your application and want to have it considered by the examiner, filing an Information Disclosure Statement will be considered a qualifying submission.

NOTICE OF ALLOWANCE

When the examiner is satisfied that the claims are in allowable form, he or she will issue a Notice of Allowance. When you receive a Notice of Allowance, make any required corrections to the drawings, specification, and claims, and then carefully review them to make sure everything is correct. If you notice any errors in the application, you can correct them provided that they do not alter the substance of the application.

To correct errors, submit an Amendment Pursuant to 37 C.F.R. §1.312. The Amendment should begin with a statement such as, "Applicant submits this Amendment Pursuant to 37 C.F.R. §1.312. Applicant respectfully requests the above application be amended as follows: . . ." Then amend the specification and claims as described earlier. Finally, state in your remarks that the amendments do not alter the substance of the application. Sign and date the amendment and include your telephone number and address at the bottom of the amendment.

The Notice of Allowance will state that you have three months to respond and pay the issue fee. The three-month time period for paying the issue fee is nonextendable. The amount of the issue fee will be indicated on the Notice of Allowance and is $720 ($360 for a small entity, $180 for a micro entity), as of April 27, 2017.

Approximately six to eight weeks after you pay the issue fee, you will receive an Issue Notification Form, stating the serial number assigned to your patent and the date it will issue. The formal Letters Patent, a bond paper copy of the patent grant, is ribboned, sealed, and mailed by the Office of Patent Publication to you on that date.

Sample Request for Corrected Filing Receipt

IN THE UNITED STATES PATENT AND TRADEMARK OFFICE

Application No.: _____   Confirmation No.: _____

Applicant: _____

Filed: _____

Art Unit: _____

Examiner: _____

Docket No.: _____

Customer No.: _____

Commissioner for Patents
PO Box 1450
Alexandria, VA 22313-1450

REQUEST FOR CORRECTED FILING RECEIPT

Sir/Madam:

Enclosed is a copy of the filing receipt received in connection with the aforementioned application. The filing receipt spells the first named inventor's name as "Jon W. How," however, the name should be spelled "John W. How."

Accordingly, Applicant requests the United States Patent and Trademark Office issue a corrected filing receipt with the first named inventor identified as "John W. How." Because this error was made by the United States Patent and Trademark Office, no fee is due.

Respectfully submitted,

_____

Sample Response to Restriction Requirement

IN THE UNITED STATES PATENT AND TRADEMARK OFFICE

Application No.: _____   Confirmation No.: _____

Applicant: _____

Filed: _____

Art Unit: _____

Examiner: _____

Docket No.: _____

Customer No.: _____

MS Amendment
Commissioner for Patents
PO Box 1450
Alexandria, VA 22313-1450

RESPONSE TO RESTRICTION REQUIREMENT

Sir/Madam:

This communication is in response to the Restriction Requirement dated
_____. The due date for response is _____;
accordingly, this response is timely filed and no fees are due. Applicant
respectfully requests entry of the response.

Remarks begin on page 2

(Continued)

REMARKS

Status of the Claims:

Claims _____ to _____ are pending. No claims have been amended, added, or deleted.

Restriction Requirement:

The Examiner has required a restriction between _____ groups of claims:

Group I, claims _____ to _____, drawn to _____;

Group II, claims _____ to _____, drawn to _____;

Further, an election of species requirement was made within each group.

While not agreeing with the propriety of the Examiner's Restriction Requirement and solely to advance prosecution, the Applicant elects Group I, claims _____ to _____ and the species of _____ with traverse.

The traversal is on the grounds that . . .

Applicant requests rejoinder of Group II with Group I, should the Examiner find Group I allowable.

CONCLUSION

Applicant believes the application is in condition for allowance. If it is determined that a telephone conference would expedite the prosecution of this application, the Examiner is invited to telephone the undersigned at the number provided.

Respectfully submitted,

_____

Sample Amendment and Response

IN THE UNITED STATES PATENT AND TRADEMARK OFFICE

Application No.: _____   Confirmation No.: _____

Applicant: _____

Filed: _____

Art Unit: _____

Examiner: _____

Docket No.: _____

Customer No.: _____

MS Amendment
Commissioner for Patents
PO Box 1450
Alexandria, VA 22313-1450

AMENDMENT AND RESPONSE

Dear Sir/Madam:

This Amendment and Response is submitted in response to the Examiner's Office Action dated _____. Please amend the above identified application as follows:

Amendment to the specification begins on page _____

Amendment to the claims begins on page _____

Amendment to the drawings begins on page _____

Remarks begin on page _____

(Continued)

Appl. No. _____

Amendment dated _____

Reply to Office Action dated _____

Amendment to the Specification

(a) Please replace paragraph [0033] with the following amended
    paragraph:

> [0033] When preparing a composition comprising A, B,
> and C, combine A with B in the presence of heat [[can]]
> between 120 and 200 degrees centigrade and then
> combine the resulting slurry mixture with C.

(b) Please add the following new paragraph after paragraph [0050]:

> [0050.1] D is an optional ingredient that can be added to
> the composition comprising A, B, and C.

(c) Please delete the paragraph beginning on page 4, line 7, which starts
    with "The prior art describes . . ."

(Continued)

Appl. No. _____

Amendment dated _____

Reply to Office Action dated _____

Amendment to the Claims:

This listing of claims will replace all prior versions, and listings, of claims in the application:

Listing of Claims:

Claims 1–3 (Canceled).

Claim 4 (Previously presented). A composition consisting essentially of A, B, and C.

Claim 5 (Withdrawn). A composition comprising L, M, and O.

Claim 6 (Currently amended). A composition consisting essentially of A, B, and C.

Claim 7 (Original). A composition of claim 6, wherein A is selected from calcium, potassium, or sodium.

Claim 8 (New). A composition of claim 7, wherein C is selected from water or saline.

(Continued)

Appl. No. _____

Amendment dated _____

Reply to Office Action dated _____

Amendments to the Drawings:

The attached sheet of drawings includes changes to Fig. 5. The sheet, which includes Fig. 1 and 2, replaces the original sheet including Fig. 1, 2, and 3. In Fig. 1, a previously omitted element 15 has been added.

Attachments:
    Replace Sheet
    Annotated Sheet Showing Changes

(Continued)

Appl. No. _____

Amendment dated _____

Reply to Office Action dated _____

REMARKS

In the specification, the paragraphs [0033] and [0050] have been amended to correct minor editorial problems. The new paragraph [0050.1] has been added after paragraph [0050]. No new matter has been introduced into the application.

Claims 4 through 8 are currently pending. Claims 1 through 3 have been canceled, claim 5 is withdrawn, claim 6 is currently amended, and claim 8 is newly added. No new matter has been introduced into the application by way of amendment.

In amended Figure 5, the previously omitted element numeral 15 has been added.

Rejection under 35 USC 112, second paragraph:
The Examiner rejected claims 1 through 3 as being indefinite. The Applicant has canceled claims 1 through 3, rendering the Examiner's rejection moot. Therefore, withdrawal of the rejection is respectfully requested.

Rejection under 35 USC 103:
The Examiner rejected claim 6 as being obvious over Patel et al. in view of Hand et al. The Examiner states that Patel et al. teaches A, B, C, and D, and the Examiner also states that Hand et al. teaches that D will not affect compositions used in treating disease L. The Examiner further states that although the claimed invention recites a composition "consisting essentially of" A, B, and C, component D in Patel et al. will not change the basic and novel characteristics of the composition used to treat L disease as taught by Hand et al. Therefore, one of ordinary skill in the art would be motivated to make a composition of A, B, and C and remove component D to arrive at a composition that would treat disease L. Applicant respectfully traverses the rejection. The Examiner has failed to make a *prima facie* case of obviousness, because an ordinary skilled

(Continued)

artisan would not be motivated to remove component D from the composition. However, in order to further clarify the invention and advance prosecution, Applicant has amended claim 6 to "consisting of." Applicant believes the amendment is sufficient to overcome the Examiner's rejection. Withdrawal of the rejection is respectfully requested.

For the foregoing reasons, Applicant respectfully submits that the claims are drawn to novel subject matter, patentably distinct from the art of record, and allowable in form. Favorable reconsideration and a Notice of Allowance are respectfully requested.

Attachments

Respectfully submitted,

_____

Sample Notice of Appeal

IN THE UNITED STATES PATENT AND TRADEMARK OFFICE

Application No.: _____   Confirmation No.: _____
Applicant: _____
Filed: _____
Art Unit: _____
Examiner: _____
Docket No.: _____
Customer No.: _____

MS Amendment
Commissioner for Patents
PO Box 1450
Alexandria, VA 22313-1450

NOTICE OF APPEAL

Dear Sir/Madam:

In reply to the Office Action, mailed _____, Applicant(s) hereby appeal(s) to the Board of Appeals and Interferences from the decision of the Primary Examiner finally rejecting claims _____, in the above-identified application. In accordance with 37 C.F.R. § 1.17(e), enclosed is the fee for filing a Notice of Appeal in the amount of $_____.

Respectfully submitted,

_____

CHAPTER 13

The Latest USPTO and Copyright Office Forms and Templates

This chapter includes samples of the latest versions of the following official forms from the US Patent and Trademark Office and the US Copyright Office:[1]

Copyright Forms

Trademark Application Form

Patent Forms

---

1 Note: Full-size versions of these forms may be obtained from the following website: www.skyhorsesupplements.com/home/allworth-press

Form TX

Detach and read these instructions before completing this form.
Make sure all applicable spaces have been filled in before you return this form.

BASIC INFORMATION

When to Use This Form: Use Form TX for registration of published or unpublished nondramatic literary works, excluding periodicals or serial issues. This class includes a wide variety of works: fiction, nonfiction, poetry, textbooks, reference works, directories, catalogs, advertising copy, compilations of information, and computer programs. For periodicals and serials, use Form SE.

Deposit to Accompany Application: An application for copyright registration must be accompanied by a deposit consisting of copies or phonorecords representing the entire work for which registration is to be made. The following are the general deposit requirements as set forth in the statute:

Unpublished Work: Deposit one complete copy (or phonorecord).

Published Work: Deposit two complete copies (or one phonorecord) of the best edition.

Work First Published Outside the United States: Deposit one complete copy (or phonorecord) of the first foreign edition.

Contribution to a Collective Work: Deposit one complete copy (or phonorecord) of the best edition of the collective work.

The Copyright Notice: Before March 1, 1989, the use of copyright notice was mandatory on all published works, and any work first published

before that date should have carried a notice. For works first published on and after March 1, 1989, use of the copyright notice is optional. For more information about copyright notice, see Circular 3, *Copyright Notice.*

For Further Information: To speak to a Copyright Office staff member, call (202) 707-3000 or 1-877-476-0778 (toll free). Recorded information is available 24 hours a day. Order forms and other publications from the address in space 9 or call the Forms and Publications Hotline at (202) 707-9100. Access and download circulars, certain forms, and other information from the Copyright Office website at *www.copyright.gov.*

PRIVACY ACT ADVISORY STATEMENT Required by the Privacy Act of 1974 (P.L. 93-579)
The authority for requesting this information is title 17 U.S.C. §409 and §410. Furnishing the requested information is voluntary. But if the information is not furnished, it may be necessary to delay or refuse registration and you may not be entitled to certain relief, remedies, and benefits provided in chapters 4 and 5 of title 17 U.S.C.
The principal uses of the requested information are the establishment and maintenance of a public record and the examination of the application for compliance with the registration requirements of the copyright code.
Other routine uses include public inspection and copying, preparation of public indexes, preparation of public catalogs of copyright registrations, and preparation of search reports upon request.
NOTE: No other advisory statement will be given in connection with this application. Please keep this statement and refer to it if we communicate with you regarding this application.

LINE-BY-LINE INSTRUCTIONS

Please type or print using black ink. The form is used to produce the certificate.

SPACE 1: Title

Title of This Work: Every work submitted for copyright registration must be given a title to identify that particular work. If the copies or phonorecords of the work bear a title or an identifying phrase that could serve as a title, transcribe that wording *completely* and *exactly* on the application. Indexing of the registration and future identification of the work will depend on the information you give here.

Previous or Alternative Titles: Complete this space if there are any additional titles for the work under which someone searching for the registration might be likely to look or under which a document pertaining to the work might be recorded.

Publication as a Contribution: If the work being registered is a contribution to a periodical, serial, or collection, give the title of the contribution in the "Title of This Work" space. Then, in the line headed "Publication as a Contribution," give information about the collective work in which the contribution appeared.

SPACE 2: Author(s)

General Instructions: After reading these instructions, decide who are the "authors" of this work for copyright purposes. Then, unless the work is a "collective work," give the requested information about every "author" who contributed any appreciable amount of copyrightable matter to this version of the work. If you need further space, request Continuation Sheets. In the case of a collective work, such as an anthology, collection of essays, or encyclopedia, give information about the author of the collective work as a whole.

Name of Author: The fullest form of the author's name should be given. Unless the work was "made for hire," the individual who actually

created the work is its "author." In the case of a work made for hire, the statute provides that "the employer or other person for whom the work was prepared is considered the author."

What Is a "Work Made for Hire"? A "work made for hire" is defined as (1) "a work prepared by an employee within the scope of his or her employment"; or (2) "a work specially ordered or commissioned for use as a contribution to a collective work, as a part of a motion picture or other audiovisual work, as a translation, as a supplementary work, as a compilation, as an instructional text, as a test, as answer material for a test, or as an atlas, if the parties expressly agree in a written instrument signed by them that the works shall be considered a work made for hire." If you have checked "Yes" to indicate that the work was "made for hire," you must give the full legal name of the employer (or other person for whom the work was prepared). You may also include the name of the employee along with the name of the employer (for example: "Elster Publishing Co., employer for hire of John Ferguson").

"Anonymous" or "Pseudonymous" Work: An author's contribution to a work is "anonymous" if that author is not identified on the copies or phonorecords of the work. An author's contribution to a work is "pseudonymous" if that author is identified on the copies or phonorecords under a fictitious name. If the work is "anonymous" you may: (1) leave the line blank; or (2) state "anonymous" on the line; or (3) reveal the author's identity. If the work is "pseudonymous" you may: (1) leave the line blank; or (2) give the pseudonym and identify it as such (for example: "Huntley Haverstock, pseudonym"); or (3) reveal the author's name, making clear which is the real name and which is the pseudonym (for example, "Judith Barton, whose pseudonym is Madeline Elster"). However, the citizenship or domicile of the author *must* be given in all cases.

Dates of Birth and Death: If the author is dead, the statute requires that the year of death be included in the application unless the work is anonymous or pseudonymous. The author's birth date is optional but is useful as a form of identification. Leave this space blank if the author's contribution was a "work made for hire."

Author's Nationality or Domicile: Give the country of which the author is a citizen or the country in which the author is domiciled. Nationality or domicile *must* be given in all cases.

Nature of Authorship: After the words "Nature of Authorship," give a brief general statement of the nature of this particular author's contribution to the work. Examples: "Entire text"; "Coauthor of entire text"; "Computer program"; "Editorial revisions"; "Compilation and English translation"; "New text."

SPACE 3: Creation and Publication

General Instructions: Do not confuse "creation" with "publication." Every application for copyright registration must state "the year in which creation of the work was completed." Give the date and nation of first publication only if the work has been published.

Creation: Under the statute, a work is "created" when it is fixed in a copy or phonorecord for the first time. Where a work has been prepared over a period of time, the part of the work existing in fixed form on a particular date constitutes the created work on that date. The date you give here should be the year in which the author completed the particular version for which registration is now being sought, even if other versions exist or if further changes or additions are planned.

Publication: The statute defines "publication" as "the distribution of copies or phonorecords of a work to the public by sale or other transfer of ownership, or by rental, lease, or lending." A work is also "published" if there has been an "offering to distribute copies or phonorecords to a group of persons for purposes of further distribution, public performance, or public display." Give the full date (month, day, year) when, and the country where, publication first occurred. If first publication took place simultaneously in the United States and other countries, it is sufficient to state "U.S.A."

SPACE 4: Claimant(s)

Name(s) and Address(es) of Copyright Claimant(s): Give the name(s) and address(es) of the copyright claimant(s) in this work even if the claimant is the same as the author. Copyright in a work belongs initially to the author of the work (including, in the case of a work made for hire, the employer or other person for whom the work was prepared). The copyright claimant is either the author of the work or a person or organization to whom the copyright initially belonging to the author has been transferred.

Transfer: The statute provides that, if the copyright claimant is not the author, the application for registration must contain "a brief statement of how the claimant obtained ownership of the copyright." If any copyright claimant named in space 4 is not an author named in space 2, give a brief statement explaining how the claimant(s) obtained ownership of the copyright. Examples: "By written contract"; "Transfer of all rights by author"; "Assignment"; "By will." Do not attach transfer documents or other attachments or riders.

SPACE 5: Previous Registration

General Instructions: The questions in space 5 are intended to show whether an earlier registration has been made for this work and, if so, whether there is any basis for a new registration. As a general rule, only one basic copyright registration can be made for the same version of a particular work.

Same Version: If this version is substantially the same as the work covered by a previous registration, a second registration is not generally possible

unless: (1) the work has been registered in unpublished form and a second registration is now being sought to cover this first published edition; or (2) someone other than the author is identified as copyright claimant in the earlier registration, and the author is now seeking registration in his or her own name. If either of these two exceptions applies, check the appropriate box and give the earlier registration number and date. Otherwise, do not submit Form TX. Instead, write the Copyright Office for information about supplementary registration or recordation of transfers of copyright ownership.

Changed Version: If the work has been changed and you are now seeking registration to cover the additions or revisions, check the last box in space 5, give the earlier registration number and date, and complete both parts of space 6 in accordance with the instructions below.

Previous Registration Number and Date: If more than one previous registration has been made for the work, give the number and date of the latest registration.

SPACE 6: Derivative Work or Compilation

General Instructions: Complete space 6 if this work is a "changed version," "compilation," or "derivative work" and if it incorporates one or more earlier works that have already been published or registered for copyright or that have fallen into the public domain. A "compilation" is defined as "a work formed by the collection and assembling of preexisting materials or of data that are selected, coordinated, or arranged in such a way that the resulting work as a whole constitutes an original work of authorship." A "derivative work" is "a work based on one or more preexisting works." Examples of derivative works include translations, fictionalizations, abridgments, condensations, or "any other form in which a work may be recast, transformed, or adapted." Derivative works also include works "consisting of editorial revisions, annotations, or other modifications" if these changes, as a whole, represent an original work of authorship.

Preexisting Material (space 6a): For derivative works, complete this space *and* space 6b. In space 6a identify the preexisting work that has been recast, transformed, or adapted. The preexisting work may be material that has been previously published, previously registered, or that is in the public domain. An example of preexisting material might be: "Russian version of Goncharov's 'Oblomov.'"

Material Added to This Work (space 6b): Give a brief, general statement of the new material covered by the copyright claim for which registration is sought. *Derivative work* examples include: "Foreword, editing, critical annotations"; "Translation"; "Chapters 11–17." If the work is a *compilation*, describe both the compilation itself and the material that has been compiled. Example: "Compilation of certain 1917 speeches by Woodrow Wilson." A work may be both a derivative work and a compilation, in which case a sample statement might be: "Compilation and additional new material."

SPACE 7,8,9: Fee, Correspondence, Certification, Return Address

Deposit Account: If you maintain a Deposit Account in the Copyright Office, identify it in space 7a. Otherwise leave the space blank and send the fee with your application and deposit.

Correspondence (space 7b): Give the name, address, area code, telephone number, fax number, and email address (if available) of the person to be consulted if correspondence about this application becomes necessary.

Certification (space 8): The application cannot be accepted unless it bears the date and the *handwritten signature* of the author or other copyright claimant, or of the owner of exclusive right(s), or of the duly authorized agent of author, claimant, or owner of exclusive right(s).

Address for Return of Certificate (space 9): The address box must be completed legibly because the certificate will be returned in a window envelope.

Copyright Office fees are subject to change. For current fees, check the Copyright Office website at *www.copyright.gov*, write the Copyright Office, or call (202) 707-3000.

Privacy Act Notice: Sections 408-410 of title 17 of the *United States Code* authorize the Copyright Office to collect the personally identifying information requested on this form in order to process the application for copyright registration. By providing this information you are agreeing to routine uses of the information that include publication to give legal notice of your copyright claim as required by 17 U.S.C. §705. It will appear in the Office's online catalog. If you do not provide the information requested, registration may be refused or delayed, and you may not be entitled to certain relief, remedies, and benefits under the copyright law.

Ⓒ Form TX
For a Nondramatic Literary Work
UNITED STATES COPYRIGHT OFFICE

REGISTRATION NUMBER

_____

TX   TXU
EFFECTIVE DATE OF REGISTRATION

_____
Month   Day   Year

DO NOT WRITE ABOVE THIS LINE. IF YOU NEED MORE SPACE, USE A SEPARATE CONTINUATION SHEET.

1

TITLE OF THIS WORK ▼

PREVIOUS OR ALTERNATIVE TITLES ▼

PUBLICATION AS A CONTRIBUTION If this work was published as a contribution to a periodical, serial, or collection, give information about the collective work in which the contribution appeared.   **Title of Collective Work ▼**

If published in a periodical or serial give: **Volume ▼**   **Number ▼**   **Issue Date ▼**   **On Pages ▼**

2 **a**

NAME OF AUTHOR ▼

DATES OF BIRTH AND DEATH
Year Born ▼   Year Died ▼

Was this contribution to the work a "work made for hire"?
☐ Yes
☐ No

AUTHOR'S NATIONALITY OR DOMICILE
Name of Country
OR ⎨ Citizen of _____
      ⎩ Domiciled in _____

WAS THIS AUTHOR'S CONTRIBUTION TO THE WORK
Anonymous?   ☐ Yes ☐ No
Pseudonymous? ☐ Yes ☐ No

If the answer to either of these questions is "Yes," see detailed instructions.

NATURE OF AUTHORSHIP Briefly describe nature of material created by this author in which copyright is claimed. ▼

NOTE
Under the law, the "author" of a "work made for hire" is generally the employer, not the employee (see instructions). For any part of this work that was "made for hire" check "Yes" in the space provided, give the employer (or other person for whom the work was prepared) as "Author" of that part, and leave the space for dates of birth and death blank.

b

NAME OF AUTHOR ▼

DATES OF BIRTH AND DEATH
Year Born ▼   Year Died ▼

Was this contribution to the work a "work made for hire"?
☐ Yes
☐ No

AUTHOR'S NATIONALITY OR DOMICILE
Name of Country
OR ⎨ Citizen of _____
      ⎩ Domiciled in _____

WAS THIS AUTHOR'S CONTRIBUTION TO THE WORK
Anonymous?   ☐ Yes ☐ No
Pseudonymous? ☐ Yes ☐ No

If the answer to either of these questions is "Yes," see detailed instructions.

NATURE OF AUTHORSHIP Briefly describe nature of material created by this author in which copyright is claimed. ▼

c

NAME OF AUTHOR ▼

DATES OF BIRTH AND DEATH
Year Born ▼   Year Died ▼

Was this contribution to the work a "work made for hire"?
☐ Yes
☐ No

AUTHOR'S NATIONALITY OR DOMICILE
Name of Country
OR ⎨ Citizen of _____
      ⎩ Domiciled in _____

WAS THIS AUTHOR'S CONTRIBUTION TO THE WORK
Anonymous?   ☐ Yes ☐ No
Pseudonymous? ☐ Yes ☐ No

If the answer to either of these questions is "Yes," see detailed instructions.

NATURE OF AUTHORSHIP Briefly describe nature of material created by this author in which copyright is claimed. ▼

3 **a**

YEAR IN WHICH CREATION OF THIS WORK WAS COMPLETED This information must be given in all cases. _____ Year

b **DATE AND NATION OF FIRST PUBLICATION OF THIS PARTICULAR WORK**
Complete this information ONLY if this work has been published.   Month _____ Day _____ Year _____
_____ Nation

4

See instructions before completing this space.

COPYRIGHT CLAIMANT(S) Name and address must be given even if the claimant is the same as the author given in space 2. ▼

TRANSFER If the claimant(s) named here in space 4 is (are) different from the author(s) named in space 2, give a brief statement of how the claimant(s) obtained ownership of the copyright. ▼

DO NOT WRITE HERE / OFFICE USE ONLY
APPLICATION RECEIVED
_____
ONE DEPOSIT RECEIVED
_____
TWO DEPOSITS RECEIVED
_____
FUNDS RECEIVED

MORE ON BACK ▶   • Complete all applicable spaces (numbers 5-9) on the reverse side of this page.
                     • See detailed instructions.   • Sign the form at line 8.

DO NOT WRITE HERE
Page 1 of _____ pages

EXAMINED BY	FORM TX
CHECKED BY	
☐ CORRESPONDENCE Yes	FOR COPYRIGHT OFFICE USE ONLY

DO NOT WRITE ABOVE THIS LINE. IF YOU NEED MORE SPACE, USE A SEPARATE CONTINUATION SHEET.

PREVIOUS REGISTRATION Has registration for this work, or for an earlier version of this work, already been made in the Copyright Office?

☐ Yes ☐ No If your answer is "Yes," why is another registration being sought? (Check appropriate box.) ▼

a. ☐ This is the first published edition of a work previously registered in unpublished form.

b. ☐ This is the first application submitted by this author as copyright claimant.

c. ☐ This is a changed version of the work, as shown by space 6 on this application.

If your answer is "Yes," give: **Previous Registration Number** ▶   **Year of Registration** ▶

5

DERIVATIVE WORK OR COMPILATION
Preexisting Material Identify any preexisting work or works that this work is based on or incorporates. ▼

a

6

Material Added to This Work Give a brief, general statement of the material that has been added to this work and in which copyright is claimed. ▼

See instructions before completing this space.

b

DEPOSIT ACCOUNT If the registration fee is to be charged to a deposit account established in the Copyright Office, give name and number of account.
Name ▼   **Account Number** ▼

a

7

CORRESPONDENCE Give name and address to which correspondence about this application should be sent.   Name/Address/Apt/City/State/Zip ▼

b

Area code and daytime telephone number ▶   Fax number ▶

Email ▶

CERTIFICATION* I, the undersigned, hereby certify that I am the

Check only one ▶ {
☐ author
☐ other copyright claimant
☐ owner of exclusive right(s)
☐ authorized agent of _____
Name of author or other copyright claimant, or owner of exclusive right(s) ▲
}

of the work identified in this application and that the statements made by me in this application are correct to the best of my knowledge.

8

Typed or printed name and date ▼ If this application gives a date of publication in space 3, do not sign and submit it before that date.

_____ Date ▶ _____

Handwritten signature ▼

9

Certificate will be mailed in window envelope to this address:	Name ▼	YOU MUST: • Complete all necessary spaces • Sign your application in space 8
	Number/Street/Apt ▼	**SEND ALL 3 ELEMENTS IN THE SAME PACKAGE:** 1. Application form 2. Nonrefundable filing fee in check or money order payable to Register of Copyrights 3. Deposit material
	City/State/Zip ▼	**MAIL TO:** Library of Congress Copyright Office-TX 101 Independence Avenue SE Washington, DC 20559

*17 U.S.C. §506(e): Any person who knowingly makes a false representation of a material fact in the application for copyright registration provided for by section 409, or in any written statement filed in connection with the application, shall be fined not more than $2,500.

Form TX–Full Reviewed: 07/2012 Printed on recycled paper   U.S. Government Printing Office: 2012-xxx-xxx/xx,xxx

Form PA

Detach and read these instructions before completing this form.
Make sure all applicable spaces have been filled in before you return this form.

BASIC INFORMATION

When to Use This Form: Use Form PA for registration of published or unpublished works of the performing arts. This class includes works prepared for the purpose of being "performed" directly before an audience or indirectly "by means of any device or process." Works of the performing arts include: (1) musical works, including any accompanying words; (2) dramatic works, including any accompanying music; (3) pantomimes and choreographic works; and (4) motion pictures and other audiovisual works.

Deposit to Accompany Application: An application for copyright registration must be accompanied by a deposit consisting of copies or phonorecords representing the entire work for which registration is made. The following are the general deposit requirements as set forth in the statute:

Unpublished Work: Deposit one complete copy (or phonorecord).

Published Work: Deposit two complete copies (or one phonorecord) of the best edition.

Work First Published Outside the United States: Deposit one complete copy (or phonorecord) of the first foreign edition.

Contribution to a Collective Work: Deposit one complete copy (or phonorecord) of the best edition of the collective work.

Motion Pictures: Deposit *both* of the following: (1) a separate written description of the contents of the motion picture; and (2) for a published work, one complete copy of the best edition of the motion picture; or, for an unpublished work, one complete copy of the motion picture or identifying material. Identifying material may be either an audiorecording of the entire soundtrack or one frame enlargement or similar visual print from each 10-minute segment.

The Copyright Notice: Before March 1, 1989, the use of copyright notice was mandatory on all published works, and any work first published before that date should have carried a notice. For works first published on and after March 1, 1989, use of the copyright notice is optional. For more information about copyright notice, see Circular 3, *Copyright Notice.*

For Further Information: To speak to a Copyright Office staff member, call (202) 707-3000 or 1-877-476-0778 (toll free). Recorded information is available 24 hours a day. Order forms and other publications from the address in space 9 or call (202) 707-9100. Access and download circulars, certain forms, and other information from the Copyright Office website at *www.copyright.gov.*

PRIVACY ACT ADVISORY STATEMENT Required by the Privacy Act of 1974 (P.L. 93-579)
   The authority for requesting this information is title 17 U.S.C. §409 and §410. Furnishing the requested information is voluntary. But if the information is not furnished, it may be necessary to delay or refuse registration and you may not be entitled to certain relief, remedies, and benefits provided in chapters 4 and 5 of title 17 U.S.C.
   The principal uses of the requested information are the establishment and maintenance of a public record and the examination of the application for compliance with the registration requirements of the copyright code.
   Other routine uses include public inspection and copying, preparation of public indexes, preparation of public catalogs of copyright registrations, and preparation of search reports upon request.
NOTE: No other advisory statement will be given in connection with this application. Please keep this statement and refer to it if we communicate with you regarding this application.

LINE-BY-LINE INSTRUCTIONS

Please type or print using black ink. The form is used to produce the certificate.

1 SPACE 1: Title

Title of This Work: Every work submitted for copyright registration must be given a title to identify that particular work. If the copies or phonorecords of the work bear a title (or an identifying phrase that could serve as a title), transcribe that wording *completely* and *exactly* on the application. Indexing of the registration and future identification of the work will depend on the information you give here. If the work you are registering is an entire "collective work" (such as a collection of plays or songs), give the overall title of the collection. If you are registering one or more individual contributions to a collective work, give the title of each contribution, followed by the title of the collection. For an unpublished collection, you may give the titles of the individual works after the collection title.

Previous or Alternative Titles: Complete this space if there are any additional titles for the work under which someone searching for the registration might be likely to look, or under which a document pertaining to the work might be recorded.

Nature of This Work: Briefly describe the general nature or character of the work being registered for copyright. Examples: "Music"; "Song Lyrics"; "Words and Music"; "Drama"; "Musical Play"; "Choreography"; "Pantomime"; "Motion Picture"; "Audiovisual Work."

2 SPACE 2: Author(s)

General Instructions: After reading these instructions, decide who are the "authors" of this work for copyright purposes. Then, unless the work is a "collective work," give the requested information about every "author" who contributed any appreciable amount of copyrightable matter to this version of the work. If you need further space, request additional Continuation Sheets. In the case of a collective work such as a songbook or a collection of plays, give information about the author of the collective work as a whole.

Name of Author: The fullest form of the author's name should be given. Unless the work was "made for hire," the individual who actually created the work is its "author." In the case of a work made for hire, the statute provides that "the employer or other person for whom the work was prepared is considered the author."

What Is a "Work Made for Hire"? A "work made for hire" is defined as (1) "a work prepared by an employee within the scope of his or her employment"; or (2) "a work specially ordered or commissioned for use as a contribution to a collective work, as a part of a motion picture or other audiovisual work, as a translation, as a supplementary work, as a compilation, as an instructional text, as a test, as answer material for a test, or as an atlas, if the parties expressly agree in a written instrument signed by them that the work shall be considered a work made for hire." If you have checked "Yes" to indicate that the work was "made for hire," you must give the full legal name of the employer (or other person for whom the work was prepared). You may also include the name of the employee along with the name of the employer (for example: "Elster Music Co., employer for hire of John Ferguson").

"Anonymous" or "Pseudonymous" Work: An author's contribution to a work is "anonymous" if that author is not identified on the copies or phonorecords of the work. An author's contribution to a work is "pseudonymous" if that author is identified on the copies or phonorecords under a fictitious name. If the work is "anonymous" you may (1) leave the line blank; (2) state "anonymous" on the line; or (3) reveal the author's identity. If the work is "pseudonymous" you may (1) leave the line blank; (2) give the pseudonym and identify it as such (example: "Huntley Haverstock, pseudonym"); or (3) reveal the author's name, making clear which is the real name and which is the pseudonym (for example: "Judith Barton, whose pseudonym is Madeline Elster"). However, the citizenship or domicile of the author *must* be given in all cases.

Dates of Birth and Death: If the author is dead, the statute requires that the year of death be included in the application unless the work is anonymous or pseudonymous. The author's birth date is optional but is useful as a form of identification. Leave this space blank if the author's contribution was a "work made for hire."

Author's Nationality or Domicile: Give the country of which the author is a citizen, or the country in which the author is domiciled. Nationality or domicile *must* be given in all cases.

Nature of Authorship: Give a brief general statement of the nature of this particular author's contribution to the work. Examples: "Words"; "Coauthor of Music"; "Words and Music"; "Arrangement"; "Coauthor of Book and Lyrics"; "Dramatization"; "Screen Play"; "Compilation and English Translation"; "Editorial Revisions."

SPACE 3: Creation and Publication

General Instructions: Do not confuse "creation" with "publication." Every application for copyright registration must state "the year in which creation of the work was completed." Give the date and nation of first publication only if the work has been published.

Creation: Under the statute, a work is "created" when it is fixed in a copy or phonorecord for the first time. Where a work has been prepared over a period of time, the part of the work existing in fixed form on a particular date constitutes the created work on that date. The date you give here should be the year in which the author completed the particular version for which registration is now being sought, even if other versions exist or if further changes or additions are planned.

Publication: The statute defines "publication" as "the distribution of copies or phonorecords of a work to the public by sale or other transfer of ownership, or by rental, lease, or lending"; a work is also "published" if there has been an "offering to distribute copies or phonorecords to a group of persons for purposes of further distribution, public performance, or public display." Give the full date (month, day, year) when, and the country where, publication first occurred. If first publication took place simultaneously in the United States and other countries, it is sufficient to state "U.S.A."

SPACE 4: Claimant(s)

Name(s) and Address(es) of Copyright Claimant(s): Give the name(s) and address(es) of the copyright claimant(s) in this work even if the claimant is the same as the author. Copyright in a work belongs initially to the author of the work (including, in the case of a work made for hire, the employer or other person for whom the work was prepared). The copyright claimant is either the author of the work or a person or organization to whom the copyright initially belonging to the author has been transferred.

Transfer: The statute provides that, if the copyright claimant is not the author, the application for registration must contain "a brief statement of how the claimant obtained ownership of the copyright." If any copyright claimant named in space 4 is not an author named in space 2, give a brief statement explaining how the claimant(s) obtained ownership of the copyright. Examples: "By written contract"; "Transfer of all rights by author"; "Assignment"; "By will." Do not attach transfer documents or other attachments or riders.

SPACE 5: Previous Registration

General Instructions: The questions in space 5 are intended to show whether an earlier registration has been made for this work and, if so, whether there is any basis for a new registration. As a general rule, only one basic copyright registration can be made for the same version of a particular work.

Same Version: If this version is substantially the same as the work covered by a previous registration, a second registration is not generally possible unless (1) the work has been registered in unpublished form and a second registration is now being sought to cover this first published edition; or (2) someone other than the author is identified as copyright claimant in the earlier registration, and the author is now seeking registration in his or her own name. If either of these two exceptions applies, check the appropriate box and give the earlier registration number and date. Otherwise, do not submit Form PA; instead, contact the Copyright Office

for information about supplementary registration or recordation of transfers of copyright ownership.

Changed Version: If the work has been changed and you are now seeking registration to cover the additions or revisions, check the last box in space 5, give the earlier registration number and date, and complete both parts of space 6 in accordance with the instructions below.

Previous Registration Number and Date: If more than one previous registration has been made for the work, give the number and date of the latest registration.

SPACE 6: Derivative Work or Compilation

General Instructions: Complete space 6 if this work is a "changed version," "compilation," or "derivative work," and if it incorporates one or more earlier works that have already been published or registered for copyright or that have fallen into the public domain. A "compilation" is defined as "a work formed by the collection and assembling of preexisting materials or of data that are selected, coordinated, or arranged in such a way that the resulting work as a whole constitutes an original work of authorship." A "derivative work" is "a work based on one or more preexisting works." Examples of derivative works include musical arrangements, dramatizations, translations, abridgments, condensations, motion picture versions, or "any other form in which a work may be recast, transformed, or adapted." Derivative works also include works "consisting of editorial revisions, annotations, or other modifications" if these changes, as a whole, represent an original work of authorship.

Preexisting Material (space 6a): Complete this space *and* space 6b for derivative works. In this space identify the preexisting work that has been recast, transformed, or adapted. For example, the preexisting material might be: "French version of Hugo's 'Le Roi s'amuse.'" Do not complete this space for compilations.

Material Added to This Work (space 6b): Give a brief general statement of the *additional* new material covered by the copyright claim for which registration is sought. In the case of a derivative work, identify this new material. Examples: "Arrangement for piano and orchestra"; "Dramatization for television"; "New film version"; "Revisions throughout; Act III completely new." If the work is a compilation, give a brief general statement describing both the material that has been compiled *and* the compilation itself. Example: "Compilation of 19th Century Military Songs."

SPACE 7, 8, 9: Fee, Correspondence, Certification, Return Address

Deposit Account: If you maintain a Deposit Account in the Copyright Office, identify it in space 7a. Otherwise, leave the space blank and send the fee with your application and deposit.

Correspondence (space 7b): Give the name, address, area code, telephone number, fax number, and email address of the person to be consulted if correspondence about this application becomes necessary.

Certification (space 8): The application cannot be accepted unless it bears the date and the **handwritten signature** of the author or other copyright claimant, owner of exclusive right(s), or of the duly authorized agent of the author, claimant, or owner of exclusive right(s).

Address for Return of Certificate (space 9): The address box must be completed legibly since the certificate will be returned in a window envelope.

How to Register a Recorded Work: If the musical or dramatic work that you are registering has been recorded (as a tape, disk, or cassette), you may choose either copyright application Form PA (Performing Arts) or Form SR (Sound Recordings), depending on the purpose of the registration.

Use Form PA to register the underlying musical composition or dramatic work. Form SR has been developed specifically to register a "sound recording" as defined by the Copyright Act—a work resulting from the "fixation of a series of sounds," separate and distinct from the underlying musical or dramatic work. Form SR should be used when the copyright claim is limited to the sound recording itself. (In one instance, Form SR may also be used to file for a copyright registration for both kinds of works—see [4] below.) Therefore:

(1) **File Form PA** if you are seeking to register the musical or dramatic work, not the "sound recording," even though what you deposit for copyright purposes may be in the form of a phonorecord.

(2) **File Form PA** if you are seeking to register the audio portion of an audiovisual work, such as a motion picture soundtrack; these are considered integral parts of the audiovisual work.

(3) **File Form SR** if you are seeking to register the "sound recording" itself, that is, the work that results from the fixation of a series of musical, spoken, or other sounds, but not the underlying musical or dramatic work.

(4) **File Form SR** if you are the copyright claimant for both the underlying musical or dramatic work and the sound recording, *and* you prefer to register both on the same form.

(5) **File both forms PA and SR** if the copyright claimant for the underlying work and sound recording differ, or you prefer to have separate registration for them.

"Copies" and "Phonorecords": To register for copyright, you are required to deposit "copies" or "phonorecords." These are defined as follows:

Musical compositions may be embodied (fixed) in "copies," objects from which a work can be read or visually perceived, directly or with the aid of a machine or device, such as manuscripts, books, sheet music, film, and videotape. They may also be fixed in "phonorecords," objects embodying fixations of sounds, such as tapes and phonograph disks, commonly known as phonograph records. For example, a song (the work to be registered) can be reproduced in sheet music ("copies") or phonograph records ("phonorecords"), or both.

Copyright Office fees are subject to change. For current fees, check the Copyright Office website at www.copyright.gov, write the Copyright Office, or call (202) 707-3000.

Privacy Act Notice: Sections 408-410 of title 17 of the *United States Code* authorize the Copyright Office to collect the personally identifying information requested on this form in order to process the application for copyright registration. By providing this information you are agreeing to routine uses of the information that include publication to give legal notice of your copyright claim as required by 17 U.S.C. §705. It will appear in the Office's online catalog. If you do not provide the information requested, registration may be refused or delayed, and you may not be entitled to certain relief, remedies, and benefits under the copyright law.

Form PA
For a Work of Performing Arts
UNITED STATES COPYRIGHT OFFICE

REGISTRATION NUMBER

PA	PAU

EFFECTIVE DATE OF REGISTRATION

Month	Day	Year

DO NOT WRITE ABOVE THIS LINE. IF YOU NEED MORE SPACE, USE A SEPARATE CONTINUATION SHEET.

1

TITLE OF THIS WORK ▼

PREVIOUS OR ALTERNATIVE TITLES ▼

NATURE OF THIS WORK ▼ See instructions

2 **a**

NAME OF AUTHOR ▼

DATES OF BIRTH AND DEATH
Year Born ▼   Year Died ▼

Was this contribution to the work a "work made for hire"?
☐ Yes
☐ No

AUTHOR'S NATIONALITY OR DOMICILE
Name of Country
OR { Citizen of _____
Domiciled in _____

WAS THIS AUTHOR'S CONTRIBUTION TO THE WORK
Anonymous? ☐ Yes ☐ No
Pseudonymous? ☐ Yes ☐ No
If the answer to either of these questions is "Yes," see detailed instructions.

NATURE OF AUTHORSHIP Briefly describe nature of material created by this author in which copyright is claimed. ▼

NOTE
Under the law, the "author" of a "work made for hire" is generally the employer, not the employee (see instructions). For any part of this work that was "made for hire" check "Yes" in the space provided, give the employer (or other person for whom the work was prepared) as "Author" of that part, and leave the space for dates of birth and death blank.

b

NAME OF AUTHOR ▼

DATES OF BIRTH AND DEATH
Year Born ▼   Year Died ▼

Was this contribution to the work a "work made for hire"?
☐ Yes
☐ No

AUTHOR'S NATIONALITY OR DOMICILE
Name of Country
OR { Citizen of _____
Domiciled in _____

WAS THIS AUTHOR'S CONTRIBUTION TO THE WORK
Anonymous? ☐ Yes ☐ No
Pseudonymous? ☐ Yes ☐ No
If the answer to either of these questions is "Yes," see detailed instructions.

NATURE OF AUTHORSHIP Briefly describe nature of material created by this author in which copyright is claimed. ▼

c

NAME OF AUTHOR ▼

DATES OF BIRTH AND DEATH
Year Born ▼   Year Died ▼

Was this contribution to the work a "work made for hire"?
☐ Yes
☐ No

AUTHOR'S NATIONALITY OR DOMICILE
Name of Country
OR { Citizen of _____
Domiciled in _____

WAS THIS AUTHOR'S CONTRIBUTION TO THE WORK
Anonymous? ☐ Yes ☐ No
Pseudonymous? ☐ Yes ☐ No
If the answer to either of these questions is "Yes," see detailed instructions.

NATURE OF AUTHORSHIP Briefly describe nature of material created by this author in which copyright is claimed. ▼

3 **a**

YEAR IN WHICH CREATION OF THIS WORK WAS COMPLETED This information must be given in all cases.
_____ Year

b DATE AND NATION OF FIRST PUBLICATION OF THIS PARTICULAR WORK
Complete this information ONLY if this work has been published.
Month _____ Day _____ Year _____
_____ Nation

4

See instructions before completing this space.

COPYRIGHT CLAIMANT(S) Name and address must be given even if the claimant is the same as the author given in space 2. ▼

TRANSFER If the claimant(s) named here in space 4 is (are) different from the author(s) named in space 2, give a brief statement of how the claimant(s) obtained ownership of the copyright. ▼

APPLICATION RECEIVED

ONE DEPOSIT RECEIVED

TWO DEPOSITS RECEIVED

FUNDS RECEIVED

DO NOT WRITE HERE OFFICE USE ONLY

MORE ON BACK ▶   · Complete all applicable spaces (numbers 5-9) on the reverse side of this page.
· See detailed instructions.   · Sign the form at line 8.

DO NOT WRITE HERE
Page 1 of _____ pages

EXAMINED BY	FORM PA
CHECKED BY	
☐ CORRESPONDENCE Yes	FOR COPYRIGHT OFFICE USE ONLY

DO NOT WRITE ABOVE THIS LINE. IF YOU NEED MORE SPACE, USE A SEPARATE CONTINUATION SHEET.

PREVIOUS REGISTRATION Has registration for this work, or for an earlier version of this work, already been made in the Copyright Office?

☐ Yes ☐ No If your answer is "Yes," why is another registration being sought? (Check appropriate box.) ▼ If your answer is No, do **not** check box A, B, or C.

a. ☐ This is the first published edition of a work previously registered in unpublished form.

b. ☐ This is the first application submitted by this author as copyright claimant.

c. ☐ This is a changed version of the work, as shown by space 6 on this application.

If your answer is "Yes," give **Previous Registration Number** ▼   **Year of Registration** ▼

5

DERIVATIVE WORK OR COMPILATION Complete both space 6a and 6b for a derivative work; complete only 6b for a compilation.

Preexisting Material Identify any preexisting work or works that this work is based on or incorporates. ▼

a 6

See instructions before completing this space.

Material Added to This Work Give a brief, general statement of the material that has been added to this work and in which copyright is claimed. ▼

b

DEPOSIT ACCOUNT If the registration fee is to be charged to a Deposit Account established in the Copyright Office, give name and number of Account.

Name ▼   **Account Number** ▼

a 7

CORRESPONDENCE Give name and address to which correspondence about this application should be sent. Name/Address/Apt/City/State/Zip ▼

b

Area code and daytime telephone number   (   )   Fax number   (   )

Email

CERTIFICATION* I, the undersigned, hereby certify that I am the

Check only one ▶ ☐ author
☐ other copyright claimant
☐ owner of exclusive right(s)
☐ authorized agent of _____

Name of author or other copyright claimant, or owner of exclusive right(s) ▲

of the work identified in this application and that the statements made by me in this application are correct to the best of my knowledge.

8

Typed or printed name and date ▼ If this application gives a date of publication in space 3, do not sign and submit it before that date.

Date_____

Handwritten signature (X) ▼

☞   X _____

Certificate will be mailed in window envelope to this address:	Name ▼	**YOU MUST:** • Complete all necessary spaces • Sign your application in space 8
	Number/Street/Apt ▼	**SEND ALL 3 ELEMENTS IN THE SAME PACKAGE:** 1. Application form 2. Nonrefundable filing fee in check or money order payable to Register of Copyrights 3. Deposit material
	City/State/Zip ▼	**MAIL TO:** Library of Congress Copyright Office-PAD 101 Independence Avenue SE Washington, DC 20559-6230

9

*17 U.S.C. §506(e): Any person who knowingly makes a false representation of a material fact in the application for copyright registration provided for by section 409, or in any written statement filed in connection with the application, shall be fined not more than $2,500.

Form PA–Full   Reviewed: 09/2015   Printed on recycled paper

U.S. Government Publishing Office: 2015-xxx-xxx/xx,xxx

Form VA

Detach and read these instructions before completing this form.
Make sure all applicable spaces have been filled in before you return this form.

BASIC INFORMATION

When to Use This Form: Use Form VA for copyright registration of published or unpublished works of the visual arts. This category consists of "pictorial, graphic, or sculptural works," including two-dimensional and three-dimensional works of fine, graphic, and applied art; photographs; prints and art reproductions; and maps, globes, charts, technical drawings, diagrams, and models.

What Does Copyright Protect? Copyright in a work of the visual arts protects those pictorial, graphic, or sculptural elements that, either alone or in combination, represent an "original work of authorship." The statute declares: "In no case does copyright protection for an original work of authorship extend to any idea, procedure, process, system, method of operation, concept, principle, or discovery, regardless of the form in which it is described, explained, illustrated, or embodied in such work."

Works of Artistic Craftsmanship and Designs: You may register "works of artistic craftsmanship" on Form VA, but the statute makes clear that protection extends to "their form" and not to "their mechanical or utilitarian aspects." The "design of a useful article" is considered copyrightable "only if, and only to the extent that, such design incorporates pictorial, graphic, or sculptural features that can be identified separately from, and are capable of existing independently of, the utilitarian aspects of the article."

Labels and Advertisements: Works prepared for use in connection with the sale or advertisement of goods and services may be registered if they contain "original work of authorship." Use Form VA if the copyrightable material in the work you are registering is mainly pictorial or graphic; use Form TX if it consists mainly of text. **Note:** Words and short phrases such as names, titles, and slogans cannot be protected by copyright, and the same is true of standard symbols, emblems, and other commonly used graphic designs that are in the public domain. When used commercially, material of that sort can sometimes be protected under state laws of unfair competition or under the federal trademark laws. For information about trademark registration, call the U.S. Patent and Trademark Office, at 1-800-786-9199 (toll free) or go to *www.uspto.gov*.

Architectural Works: Copyright protection extends to the design of buildings created for the use of human beings. Architectural works created on or after December 1, 1990, or that on December 1, 1990, were unconstructed and embodied only in unpublished plans or drawings are eligible. Request Circular 41, *Copyright Claims in Architectural Works*, for more information. Architectural works and technical drawings cannot be registered on the same application.

Deposit to Accompany Application: An application for copyright registration must be accompanied by a deposit consisting of copies representing the entire work for which registration is to be made.

Unpublished Work: Deposit one complete copy.

Published Work: Deposit two complete copies of the best edition.

Work First Published Outside the United States: Deposit one complete copy of the first foreign edition.

Contribution to a Collective Work: Deposit one complete copy of the best edition of the collective work.

The Copyright Notice: Before March 1, 1989, the use of copyright notice was mandatory on all published works, and any work first published before that date should have carried a notice. For works first published on and after March 1, 1989, use of the copyright notice is optional. For more information about copyright notice, see Circular 3, *Copyright Notice*.

For Further Information: To speak to a Copyright Office staff member, call (202) 707-3000 or 1-877-476-0778 (toll free). Recorded information is available 24 hours a day. Order forms and other publications from the address in space 9 or call (202) 707-9100 or 1-877-476-0778 (toll free). Access and download circulars, forms, and other information from the Copyright Office website at *www.copyright.gov*.

LINE-BY-LINE INSTRUCTIONS

Please type or print using black ink. The form is used to produce the certificate.

SPACE 1: Title

Title of This Work: Every work submitted for copyright registration must be given a title to identify that particular work. If the copies of the work bear a title (or an identifying phrase that could serve as a title), transcribe that wording *completely* and *exactly* on the application. Indexing of the registration and future identification of the work will depend on the information you give here. For an architectural work that has been constructed, add the date of construction after the title; if unconstructed at this time, add "not yet constructed."

Publication as a Contribution: If the work being registered is a contribution to a periodical, serial, or collection, give the title of the contribution in the "Title of This Work" space. Then, in the line headed "Publication as a Contribution," give information about the collective work in which the contribution appeared.

Nature of This Work: Briefly describe the general nature or character of the pictorial, graphic, or sculptural work being registered for copyright. Examples: "Oil Painting"; "Charcoal Drawing"; "Etching"; "Sculpture"; "Map"; "Photograph"; "Scale Model"; "Lithographic Print"; "Jewelry Design"; "Fabric Design."

Previous or Alternative Titles: Complete this space if there are any additional titles for the work under which someone searching for the registration might be likely to look, or under which a document pertaining to the work might be recorded.

SPACE 2: Author(s)

General Instruction: After reading these instructions, decide who are the "authors" of this work for copyright purposes. Then, unless the work is a "collective work," give the requested information about every "author" who contributed any appreciable amount of copyrightable matter to this version of the work. If you need further space, request Continuation Sheets (Form CON). In the case of a collective work, such as a catalog of paintings or collection of cartoons by various authors, give information about the author of the collective work as a whole.

Name of Author: The fullest form of the author's name should be given. Unless the work was "made for hire," the individual who actually created the work is its "author." In the case of a work made for hire, the statute provides that "the employer or other person for whom the work was prepared is considered the author."

What Is a "Work Made for Hire"? A "work made for hire" is defined as: (1) "a work prepared by an employee within the scope of his or her employment"; or (2) "a work specially ordered or commissioned for use as a contribution to a collective work, as a part of a motion picture or other audiovisual work, as a translation, as a supplementary work, as a compilation, as an instructional text, as a test, as answer material for a test, or as an atlas, if the parties expressly agree in a written instrument signed by them that the work shall be considered a work made for hire." If you have checked "Yes" to indicate that the work was "made for hire," you must give the full legal name of the employer (or other person for whom the work was prepared). You may also include the name of the employee along with the name of the employer (for example: "Elster Publishing Co., employer for hire of John Ferguson").

"Anonymous" or "Pseudonymous" Work: An author's contribution to a work is "anonymous" if that author is not identified on the copies or phonorecords of the work. An author's contribution to a work is "pseudonymous" if that author is identified on the copies or phonorecords under a fictitious name. If the work is "anonymous" you may: (1) leave the line blank; or (2) state "anonymous" on the line; or (3) reveal the author's identity. If the work is "pseudonymous" you may: (1) leave the line blank; or (2) give the pseudonym and identify it as such (for example: "Huntley Haverstock, pseudonym"); or (3) reveal the author's name, making clear which is the real name and which is the pseudonym (for example: "Henry Leek, whose pseudonym is Priam Farrel"). However, the citizenship or domicile of the author *must* be given in all cases.

Dates of Birth and Death: If the author is dead, the statute requires that the year of death be included in the application unless the work is anonymous or pseudonymous. The author's birth date is optional but is useful as a form of identification. Leave this space blank if the author's contribution was a "work made for hire."

Author's Nationality or Domicile: Give the country of which the author is a citizen or the country in which the author is domiciled. Nationality or domicile *must* be given in all cases.

Nature of Authorship: Categories of pictorial, graphic, and sculptural authorship are listed below. Check the box(es) that best describe(s) each author's contribution to the work.

3-Dimensional sculptures: Fine art sculptures, toys, dolls, scale models, and sculptural designs applied to useful articles.

2-Dimensional artwork: Watercolor and oil paintings; pen and ink drawings; logo illustrations; greeting cards; collages; stencils; patterns; computer graphics; graphics appearing in screen displays; artwork appearing on posters, calendars, games, commercial prints and labels, and packaging; artwork applied to useful articles; designs reproduced on textiles, lace, and other fabrics and on wallpaper, carpeting, floor tile, wrapping paper, and clothing.

Reproductions of works of art: Reproductions of preexisting artwork made by, for example, lithography, photoengraving, or etching.

Maps: Cartographic representations of an area, such as state and county maps, atlases, marine charts, relief maps, and globes.

Photographs: Pictorial photographic prints and slides and holograms.

Jewelry designs: 3-dimensional designs applied to rings, pendants, earrings, necklaces, and the like.

Technical drawings: Diagrams illustrating scientific or technical information in linear form, such as architectural blueprints or mechanical drawings.

Text: Textual material that accompanies pictorial, graphic, or sculptural works, such as comic strips, game rules, commercial prints or labels, and maps.

Architectural works: Designs of buildings, including the overall form as well as the arrangement and composition of spaces and elements of the design.

NOTE: You must apply for registration for the underlying architectural plans on a separate Form VA. Check the box "Technical drawing."

SPACE 3: Creation and Publication

General Instructions: Do not confuse "creation" with "publication." Every application for copyright registration must state "the year in which creation of the work was completed." Give the date and nation of first publication only if the work has been published.

Creation: Under the statute, a work is "created" when it is fixed in a copy or phonorecord for the first time. If a work has been prepared over a period of time, the part of the work existing in fixed form on a particular date constitutes the created work on that date. The date you give here should be the year in which the author completed the particular version for which registration is now being sought, even if other versions exist or if further changes or additions are planned.

Publication: The statute defines "publication" as "the distribution of copies or phonorecords of a work to the public by sale or other transfer of ownership, or by rental, lease, or lending"; a work is also "published" if there has been an "offering to distribute copies or phonorecords to a group of persons for purposes of further distribution, public performance, or public display." Give the full date (month, day, year) when, and the country where, publication first occurred. If first publication took place simultaneously in the United States and other countries, it is sufficient to state "U.S.A."

SPACE 4: Claimant(s)

Name(s) and Address(es) of Copyright Claimant(s): Give the name(s) and address(es) of the copyright claimant(s) in this work even if the claimant is the same as the author. Copyright in a work belongs initially to the author of the work, including, in the case of a work made for hire, the employer or other person for whom the work was prepared. The copyright claimant is either the author of the work or a person or organization to whom the copyright initially belonging to the author has been transferred.

Transfer: The statute provides that, if the copyright claimant is not the author, the application for registration must contain "a brief statement of how the claimant obtained ownership of the copyright." If any copyright claimant named in space 4 is not an author named in space 2, give a brief statement explaining how the claimant(s) obtained ownership of the copyright. Examples: "By written contract"; "Transfer of all rights by author"; "Assignment"; "By will." Do not attach transfer documents or other attachments or riders.

SPACE 5: Previous Registration

General Instructions: The questions in space 5 are intended to find out whether an earlier registration has been made for this work and, if so, whether there is any basis for a new registration. As a rule, only one basic copyright registration can be made for the same version of a particular work.

Same Version: If this version is substantially the same as the work covered by a previous registration, a second registration is not generally possible unless: (1) the work has been registered in unpublished form and a second registration is now being sought to cover this first published edition; or (2) someone other than the author is identified as a copyright claimant in the earlier registration, and the author is now seeking registration in his or her own name. If either of these two exceptions applies, check the appropriate box and give the earlier registration number and date. Otherwise, do not submit Form VA. Instead, write the Copyright Office for information about supplementary registration or recordation of transfers of copyright ownership.

Changed Version: If the work has been changed and you are now seeking registration to cover the additions or revisions, check the last box in space 5, give the earlier registration number and date, and complete both parts of space 6 in accordance with the instruction below.

Previous Registration Number and Date: If more than one previous registration has been made for the work, give the number and date of the latest registration.

SPACE 6: Derivative Work or Compilation

General Instructions: Complete space 6 if this work is a "changed version," "compilation," or "derivative work," and if it incorporates one or more earlier works that have already been published or registered for copyright, or that have fallen into the public domain. A "compilation" is defined as "a work formed by the collection and assembling of preexisting materials or of data that are selected, coordinated, or arranged in such a way that the resulting work as a whole constitutes an original work of authorship." A "derivative work" is "a work based on one or more preexisting works." Examples of derivative works include reproductions of works of art, sculptures based on drawings, lithographs based on paintings, maps based on previously published sources, or "any other form in which a work may be recast, transformed, or adapted." Derivative works also include works "consisting of editorial revisions, annotations, or other modifications" if these changes, as a whole, represent an original work of authorship.

Preexisting Material (space 6a): Complete this space *and* space 6b for derivative works. In this space identify the preexisting work that has been recast, transformed, or adapted. Examples of preexisting material might be "Grunewald Altarpiece" or "19th century quilt design." Do not complete this space for compilations.

Material Added to This Work (space 6b): Give a brief, general statement of the *additional* new material covered by the copyright claim for which registration is sought. In the case of a derivative work, identify this new material. Examples: "Adaptation of design and additional artistic work"; "Reproduction of painting by photolithography"; "Additional cartographic material"; "Compilation of photographs." If the work is a compilation, give a brief, general statement describing both the material that has been compiled *and* the compilation itself. Example: "Compilation of 19th century political cartoons."

SPACE 7, 8, 9: Fee, Correspondence, Certification, Return Address

Deposit Account: If you maintain a deposit account in the Copyright Office, identify it in space 7a. Otherwise, leave the space blank and send the fee with your application and deposit.

Correspondence (space 7b): Give the name, address, area code, telephone number, email address, and fax number (if available) of the person to be consulted if correspondence about this application becomes necessary.

Certification (space 8): The application cannot be accepted unless it bears the date and the *handwritten signature* of the author or other copyright claimant, or of the owner of exclusive right(s), or of the duly authorized agent of the author, claimant, or owner of exclusive right(s).

Address for Return of Certificate (space 9): The address box must be completed legibly since the certificate will be returned in a window envelope.

PRIVACY ACT ADVISORY STATEMENT Required by the Privacy Act of 1974 (P.L. 93 - 579)
The authority for requesting this information is title 17 U.S.C. §409 and §410. Furnishing the requested information is voluntary. But if the information is not furnished, it may be necessary to delay or refuse registration and you may not be entitled to certain relief, remedies, and benefits provided in chapters 4 and 5 of title 17 U.S.C.

The principal uses of the requested information are the establishment and maintenance of a public record and the examination of the application for compliance with the registration requirements of the copyright code.

Other routine uses include public inspection and copying, preparation of public indexes, preparation of public catalogs of copyright registrations, and preparation of search reports upon request.

NOTE: No other advisory statement will be given in connection with this application. Please keep this statement and refer to it if we communicate with you regarding this application.

Copyright Office fees are subject to change. For current fees, check the Copyright Office website at www.copyright.gov, write the Copyright Office, or call (202) 707-3000 or 1-877-476-0778 (toll free).

Form VA
For a Work of the Visual Arts
UNITED STATES COPYRIGHT OFFICE

REGISTRATION NUMBER

VA   VAU

EFFECTIVE DATE OF REGISTRATION

Month   Day   Year

DO NOT WRITE ABOVE THIS LINE. IF YOU NEED MORE SPACE, USE A SEPARATE CONTINUATION SHEET.

1

TITLE OF THIS WORK ▼

NATURE OF THIS WORK ▼ See instructions

PREVIOUS OR ALTERNATIVE TITLES ▼

PUBLICATION AS A CONTRIBUTION If this work was published as a contribution to a periodical, serial, or collection, give information about the collective work in which the contribution appeared. **Title of Collective Work ▼**

If published in a periodical or serial give: **Volume ▼**   **Number ▼**   **Issue Date ▼**   **On Pages ▼**

2 **a**

NAME OF AUTHOR ▼

DATES OF BIRTH AND DEATH
Year Born ▼   Year Died ▼

NOTE

Under the law, the "author" of a "work made for hire" is generally the employer, not the employee (see instructions). For any part of this work that was "made for hire," check "Yes" in the space provided, give the employer (or other person for whom the work was prepared) as "Author" of that part, and leave the space for dates of birth and death blank.

WAS THIS CONTRIBUTION TO THE WORK A "WORK MADE FOR HIRE"?
☐ Yes
☐ No

AUTHOR'S NATIONALITY OR DOMICILE
Name of Country
OR {
Citizen of _____
Domiciled in _____

WAS THIS AUTHOR'S CONTRIBUTION TO THE WORK
Anonymous? ☐ Yes ☐ No
Pseudonymous? ☐ Yes ☐ No
If the answer to either of these questions is "Yes," see detailed instructions.

NATURE OF AUTHORSHIP Check appropriate box(es). **See instructions**
☐ 3-Dimensional sculpture   ☐ Map   ☐ Technical drawing
☐ 2-Dimensional artwork   ☐ Photograph   ☐ Text
☐ Reproduction of work of art   ☐ Jewelry design   ☐ Architectural work

b

NAME OF AUTHOR ▼

DATES OF BIRTH AND DEATH
Year Born ▼   Year Died ▼

WAS THIS CONTRIBUTION TO THE WORK A "WORK MADE FOR HIRE"?
☐ Yes
☐ No

AUTHOR'S NATIONALITY OR DOMICILE
Name of Country
OR {
Citizen of _____
Domiciled in _____

WAS THIS AUTHOR'S CONTRIBUTION TO THE WORK
Anonymous? ☐ Yes ☐ No
Pseudonymous? ☐ Yes ☐ No
If the answer to either of these questions is "Yes," see detailed instructions.

NATURE OF AUTHORSHIP Check appropriate box(es). **See instructions**
☐ 3-Dimensional sculpture   ☐ Map   ☐ Technical drawing
☐ 2-Dimensional artwork   ☐ Photograph   ☐ Text
☐ Reproduction of work of art   ☐ Jewelry design   ☐ Architectural work

3 **a**

YEAR IN WHICH CREATION OF THIS WORK WAS COMPLETED
Year ▶
This information must be given in all cases.

b
DATE AND NATION OF FIRST PUBLICATION OF THIS PARTICULAR WORK
Complete this information ONLY if this work has been published.
Month ▶ _____ Day ▶ _____ Year ▶ _____
Nation ▶ _____

4

See instructions before completing this space.

COPYRIGHT CLAIMANT(S) Name and address must be given even if the claimant is the same as the author given in space 2. ▼

TRANSFER If the claimant(s) named here in space 4 is (are) different from the author(s) named in space 2, give a brief statement of how the claimant(s) obtained ownership of the copyright. ▼

APPLICATION RECEIVED

ONE DEPOSIT RECEIVED

TWO DEPOSITS RECEIVED

FUNDS RECEIVED

DO NOT WRITE HERE
OFFICE USE ONLY

MORE ON BACK ▶ • Complete all applicable spaces (numbers 5-9) on the reverse side of this page.
• See detailed instructions.   • Sign the form at line 8.

DO NOT WRITE HERE
Page 1 of _____ pages

EXAMINED BY	FORM VA
CHECKED BY	
CORRESPONDENCE ☐ Yes	FOR COPYRIGHT OFFICE USE ONLY

DO NOT WRITE ABOVE THIS LINE. IF YOU NEED MORE SPACE, USE A SEPARATE CONTINUATION SHEET.

PREVIOUS REGISTRATION Has registration for this work, or for an earlier version of this work, already been made in the Copyright Office?
☐ Yes   ☐ No   If your answer is "Yes," why is another registration being sought? (Check appropriate box.) ▼
a. ☐ This is the first published edition of a work previously registered in unpublished form.
b. ☐ This is the first application submitted by this author as copyright claimant.
c. ☐ This is a changed version of the work, as shown by space 6 on this application.
If your answer is "Yes," give: **Previous Registration Number** ▼   **Year of Registration** ▼

5

DERIVATIVE WORK OR COMPILATION Complete both space 6a and 6b for a derivative work; complete only 6b for a compilation.
a. **Preexisting Material** Identify any preexisting work or works that this work is based on or incorporates. ▼

a **6**

See instructions before completing this space.

b. **Material Added to This Work** Give a brief, general statement of the material that has been added to this work and in which copyright is claimed. ▼

b

DEPOSIT ACCOUNT If the registration fee is to be charged to a Deposit Account established in the Copyright Office, give name and number of Account.
Name ▼   **Account Number** ▼

a **7**

CORRESPONDENCE Give name and address to which correspondence about this application should be sent. Name/Address/Apt/City/State/Zip ▼

b

Area code and daytime telephone number   (   )   Fax number   (   )

Email

CERTIFICATION* I, the undersigned, hereby certify that I am the
check only one ▶
☐ author
☐ other copyright claimant
☐ owner of exclusive right(s)
☐ authorized agent of _____
      Name of author or other copyright claimant, or owner of exclusive right(s) ▲
of the work identified in this application and that the statements made by me in this application are correct to the best of my knowledge.

8

Typed or printed name and date ▼ If this application gives a date of publication in space 3, do not sign and submit it before that date.

_____   Date _____

Handwritten signature (X) ▼

X _____

Certificate will be mailed in window envelope to this address:	Name ▼	YOU MUST: · Complete all necessary spaces · Sign your application in space 8
	Number/Street/Apt ▼	SEND ALL 3 ELEMENTS IN THE SAME PACKAGE: 1. Application form 2. Nonrefundable filing fee in check or money order payable to Register of Copyrights 3. Deposit material
	City/State/Zip ▼	MAIL TO: Library of Congress Copyright Office-VA 101 Independence Avenue SE Washington, DC 20559

9

*17 U.S.C. §506(e): Any person who knowingly makes a false representation of a material fact in the application for copyright registration provided for by section 409, or in any written statement filed in connection with the application, shall be fined not more than $2,500.

Form VA–Full Rev: 12/2018 Printed on recycled paper

Form SR

Detach and read these instructions before completing this form.
Make sure all applicable spaces have been filled in before you return this form.

BASIC INFORMATION

When to Use This Form: Use Form SR for registration of published or unpublished sound recordings. Form SR should be used when the copyright claim is limited to the sound recording itself, and it may also be used where the same copyright claimant is seeking simultaneous registration of the underlying musical, dramatic, or literary work embodied in the phonorecord.

With one exception, "sound recordings" are works that result from the fixation of a series of musical, spoken, or other sounds. The exception is for the audio portions of audiovisual works, such as a motion picture soundtrack or an audio cassette accompanying a filmstrip. These are considered a part of the audiovisual work as a whole.

Deposit to Accompany Application: An application for copyright registration must be accompanied by a deposit consisting of phonorecords representing the entire work for which registration is to be made.

Unpublished Work: Deposit one complete phonorecord.

Published Work: Deposit two complete phonorecords of the best edition, together with "any printed or other visually perceptible material" published with the phonorecords.

Work First Published Outside the United States: Deposit one complete phonorecord of the first foreign edition.

Contribution to a Collective Work: Deposit one complete phonorecord of the best edition of the collective work.

The Copyright Notice: Before March 1, 1989, the use of copyright notice was mandatory on all published works, and any work first published before that date should have carried a notice. For works first published on and after March 1, 1989, use of the copyright notice is optional. For more information about copyright notice, see Circular 3, *Copyright Notices.*

For Further Information: To speak to a Copyright Office staff member, call (202) 707-3000 or 1-877-476-0778. Recorded information is available 24 hours a day. Order forms and other publications from Library of Congress, Copyright Office-COPUBS, 101 Independence Avenue SE, Washington, DC 20559 or call (202) 707-9100 or 1-877-476-0778 (toll free). Access and download circulars and other information from the Copyright Office website at *www.copyright.gov.*

LINE-BY-LINE INSTRUCTIONS

Please type or print neatly using black ink. The form is used to produce the certificate.

1 SPACE 1: Title

Title of This Work: Every work submitted for copyright registration must be given a title to identify that particular work. If the phonorecords or any accompanying printed material bears a title (or an identifying phrase that could serve as a title), transcribe that wording completely and exactly on the application. Indexing of the registration and future identification of the work may depend on the information you give here.

Previous, Alternative, or Contents Titles: Complete this space if there are any previous or alternative titles for the work under which someone searching for the registration might be likely to look, or under which a document pertaining to the work might be recorded. You may also give the individual contents titles, if any, in this space or you may use a Continuation Sheet (Form CON). Circle the term that describes the titles given.

2 SPACE 2: Author(s)

General Instructions: After reading these instructions, decide who are the "authors" of this work for copyright purposes. Then, unless the work is a "collective work," give the requested information about every "author" who contributed any appreciable amount of copyrightable matter to this version of the work. If you need further space, use additional Continuation Sheets. In the case of a collective work such as a collection of previously published or registered sound recordings, give information about the author of the collective work as a whole. If you are submitting this Form SR to cover the recorded musical, dramatic, or literary work as well as the sound recording itself, it is important for space 2 to include full information about the various authors of all of the material covered by the copyright claim, making clear the nature of each author's contribution.

Name of Author: The fullest form of the author's name should be given. Unless the work was "made for hire," the individual who actually created the work is its "author." In the case of a work made for hire, the statute provides that "the employer or other person for whom the work was prepared is considered the author."

What Is a "Work Made for Hire"? A "work made for hire" is defined as: (1) "a work prepared by an employee within the scope of his or her employment"; or (2) "a

work specially ordered or commissioned for use as a contribution to a collective work, as a part of a motion picture or other audiovisual work, as a translation, as a supplementary work, as a compilation, as an instructional text, as a test, as answer material for a test, or as an atlas, if the parties expressly agree in a written instrument signed by them that the work shall be considered a work made for hire." If you have checked "Yes" to indicate that the work was "made for hire," you must give the full legal name of the employer (or other person for whom the work was prepared). You may also include the name of the employee along with the name of the employer (for example: "Elster Record Co., employer for hire of John Ferguson").

"Anonymous" or "Pseudonymous" Work: An author's contribution to a work is "anonymous" if that author is not identified on the copies or phonorecords of the work. An author's contribution to a work is "pseudonymous" if that author is identified on the copies or phonorecords under a fictitious name. If the work is "anonymous" you may: (1) leave the line blank; or (2) state "anonymous" on the line; or (3) reveal the author's identity. If the work is "pseudonymous" you may: (1) leave the line blank; or (2) give the pseudonym and identify it as such (for example: "Huntley Haverstock, pseudonym"); or (3) reveal the author's name, making clear which is the real name and which is the pseudonym (for example: "Judith Barton, whose pseudonym is Madeline Elster"). However, the citizenship or domicile of the author *must* be given in all cases.

Dates of Birth and Death: If the author is dead, the statute requires that the year of death be included in the application unless the work is anonymous or pseudonymous. The author's birth date is optional, but is useful as a form of identification. Leave this space blank if the author's contribution was a "work made for hire."

Author's Nationality or Domicile: Give the country in which the author is a citizen, or the country in which the author is domiciled. Nationality or domicile *must* be given in all cases.

Nature of Authorship: Sound recording authorship is the performance, sound production, or both, that is fixed in the recording deposited for registration. Describe this authorship in space 2 as "sound recording." If the claim also covers the underlying work(s), include the appropriate authorship terms for each author, for example, "words," "music," "arrangement of music," or "text."

Generally, for the claim to cover both the sound recording and the underlying work(s), every author should have contributed to both the sound recording *and* the underlying work(s). If the claim includes artwork or photographs, include an appropriate term in the statement of authorship.

3 SPACE 3: Creation and Publication

General Instructions: Do not confuse "creation" with "publication." Every application for copyright registration must state "the year in which creation of the work was completed." Give the date and nation of first publication only if the work has been published.

Creation: Under the statute, a work is "created" when it is fixed in a copy or phonorecord for the first time. If a work has been prepared over a period of time, the part of the work existing in fixed form on a particular date constitutes the created work on that date. The date you give here should be the year in which the author completed the particular version for which registration is now being sought, even if other versions exist or if further changes or additions are planned.

Publication: The statute defines "publication" as "the distribution of copies or phonorecords of a work to the public by sale or other transfer of ownership, or by rental, lease, or lending"; a work is also "published" if there has been an "offering to distribute copies or phonorecords to a group of persons for purposes of further distribution, public performance, or public display." Give the full date (month, date, year) when, and the country where, publication first occurred. If first publication took place simultaneously in the United States and other countries, it is sufficient to state "U.S.A."

4 SPACE 4: Claimant(s)

Name(s) and Address(es) of Copyright Claimant(s): Give the name(s) and address(es) of the copyright claimant(s) in the work even if the claimant is the same as the author. Copyright in a work belongs initially to the author of the work (including, in the case of a work made for hire, the employer or other person for whom the work was prepared). The copyright claimant is either the author of the work or a person or organization to whom the copyright initially belonging to the author has been transferred.

Transfer: The statute provides that, if the copyright claimant is not the author, the application for registration must contain "a brief statement of how the claimant obtained ownership of the copyright." If any copyright claimant named in space 4a is not an author named in space 2, give a brief statement explaining how the claimant(s) obtained ownership of the copyright. Examples: "By written contract"; "Transfer of all rights by author"; "Assignment"; "By will." Do not attach transfer documents or other attachments or riders.

5 SPACE 5: Previous Registration

General Instructions: The questions in space 5 are intended to show whether an earlier registration has been made for this work and, if so, whether there is any basis for a new registration. As a rule, only one basic copyright registration can be made for the same version of a particular work.

Same Version: If this version is substantially the same as the work covered by a previous registration, a second registration is not generally possible unless: (1) the work has been registered in unpublished form and a second registration is now being sought to cover this first published edition; or (2) someone other than the author is identified as copyright claimant in the earlier registration and the author is now seeking registration in his or her own name. If either of these two exceptions applies, check the appropriate box and give the earlier registration number and date. Otherwise, do not submit Form SR. Instead, write the Copyright Office for information about supplementary registration or recordation of transfers of copyright ownership.

Changed Version: If the work has been changed and you are now seeking registration to cover the additions or revisions, check the last box in space 5, give the earlier registration number and date, and complete both parts of space 6 in accordance with the instructions below.

Previous Registration Number and Date: If more than one previous registration has been made for the work, give the number and date of the latest registration.

6 SPACE 6: Derivative Work or Compilation

General Instructions: Complete space 6 if this work is a "changed version," "compilation," or "derivative work," and if it incorporates one or more earlier works that have already been published or registered for copyright, or that have fallen into the public domain, or sound recordings that were fixed before February 15, 1972. A "compilation" is defined as "a work formed by the collection and assembling of preexisting materials or of data that are selected, coordinated, or arranged in such a way that the resulting work as a whole constitutes an original work of authorship." A "derivative work" is "a work based on one or more preexisting works." Examples of derivative works include recordings reissued with substantial editorial revisions or abridgments of the recorded sounds, and recordings republished with new recorded material, or "any other form in which a work may be recast, transformed, or adapted." Derivative works also include works "consisting of editorial revisions, annotations, or other modifications" if these changes, as a whole, represent an original work of authorship.

Preexisting Material (space 6a): Complete this space and space 6b for derivative works. In this space identify the preexisting work that has been recast, transformed, or adapted. The preexisting work may be material that has been previously published, previously registered, or that is in the public domain. For example, the preexisting material might be: "1970 recording by Sperryville Symphony of Bach Double Concerto."

Material Added to This Work (space 6b): Give a brief, general statement of the additional new material covered by the copyright claim for which registration is sought. In the case of a derivative work, identify this new material. Examples: "Recorded performances on bands 1 and 3"; "Remixed sounds from original multitrack sound sources"; "New words, arrangement, and additional sounds." If the work is a compilation, give a brief, general statement describing both the material that has been compiled and the compilation itself. Example: "Compilation of 1938 recordings by various swing bands."

7,8,9 SPACE 7, 8, 9: Fee, Correspondence, Certification, Return Address

Deposit Account: If you maintain a deposit account in the Copyright Office, identify it in space 7a. Otherwise, leave the space blank and send the filing fee with your application and deposit. (See space 8 on form.) **Note:** Copyright Office fees are subject to change. For current fees, check the Copyright Office website at www.copyright.gov, write the Copyright Office, or call (202) 707-3000 or 1-877-476-0778 (toll free).

Correspondence (space 7b): Give the name, address, area code, telephone number, fax number, and email address (if available) of the person to be consulted if correspondence about this application becomes necessary.

Certification (space 8): This application cannot be accepted unless it bears the date and the *handwritten signature* of the author or other copyright claimant, or of the owner of exclusive right(s), or of the duly authorized agent of the author, claimant, or owner of exclusive right(s).

Address for Return of Certificate (space 9): The address box must be completed legibly since the certificate will be returned in a window envelope.

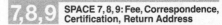

MORE INFORMATION

"Works": "Works" are the basic subject matter of copyright; they are what authors create and copyright protects. The statute draws a sharp distinction between the "work" and "any material object in which the work is embodied."

"Copies" and "Phonorecords": These are the two types of material objects in which "works" are embodied. In general, "copies" are objects from which a work can be read or visually perceived, directly or with the aid of a machine or device, such as manuscripts, books, sheet music, film, and videotape. "Phonorecords" are objects embodying fixations of sounds, such as audio tapes and phonograph disks. For example, a song (the "work") can be reproduced in sheet music ("copies") or phonograph disks ("phonorecords"), or both.

"Sound Recordings": These are "works," not "copies" or "phonorecords." "Sound recordings" are "works that result from the fixation of a series of musical, spoken, or other sounds, but not including the sounds accompanying a motion picture or other audiovisual work." Example: When a record company issues a new release, the release will typically involve two distinct "works": the "musical work" that has been recorded, and the "sound recording" as a separate work in itself. The material objects that the record company sends out are "phonorecords": physical reproductions of both the "musical work" and the "sound recording."

Should You File More Than One Application? If your work consists of a recorded musical, dramatic, or literary work and if both that "work" and the sound recording as a separate "work" are eligible for registration, the application form you should file depends on the following:

File Only Form SR if: The copyright claimant is the same for both the musical, dramatic, or literary work and for the sound recording, and you are seeking a single registration to cover both of these "works."

File Only Form PA (or Form TX) if: You are seeking to register only the musical, dramatic, or literary work, not the sound recording. Form PA is appropriate for works of the performing arts; Form TX is for nondramatic literary works.

Separate Applications Should Be Filed on Form PA (or Form TX) and on Form SR if: (1) The copyright claimant for the musical, dramatic, or literary work is different from the copyright claimant for the sound recording; or (2) you prefer to have separate registrations for the musical, dramatic, or literary work and for the sound recording.

Copyright Office fees are subject to change. For current fees, check the Copyright Office website at *www.copyright.gov*, write the Copyright Office, or call (202) 707-3000 or 1-877-476-0778 (toll free).

Form SR
For a Sound Recording
UNITED STATES COPYRIGHT OFFICE

REGISTRATION NUMBER

SR   SRU

EFFECTIVE DATE OF REGISTRATION

Month   Day   Year

DO NOT WRITE ABOVE THIS LINE. IF YOU NEED MORE SPACE, USE A SEPARATE CONTINUATION SHEET.

1 TITLE OF THIS WORK ▼

PREVIOUS, ALTERNATIVE, OR CONTENTS TITLES (CIRCLE ONE) ▼

2 NAME OF AUTHOR ▼

DATES OF BIRTH AND DEATH
Year Born ▼   Year Died ▼

a Was this contribution to the work a "work made for hire"?
☐ Yes
☐ No

AUTHOR'S NATIONALITY OR DOMICILE
Name of Country
OR { Citizen of ▶ _____
Domiciled in ▶ _____

WAS THIS AUTHOR'S CONTRIBUTION TO THE WORK
Anonymous? ☐ Yes ☐ No
Pseudonymous? ☐ Yes ☐ No
If the answer to either of these questions is "Yes," see detailed instructions.

NATURE OF AUTHORSHIP Briefly describe nature of material created by this author in which copyright is claimed. ▼

NOTE
Under the law, the "author" of a "work made for hire" is generally the employer, not the employee (see instructions). For any part of this work that was "made for hire," check "Yes" in the space provided, give the employer (or other person for whom the work was prepared) as "Author" of that part, and leave the space for dates of birth and death blank.

b NAME OF AUTHOR ▼

DATES OF BIRTH AND DEATH
Year Born ▼   Year Died ▼

Was this contribution to the work a "work made for hire"?
☐ Yes
☐ No

AUTHOR'S NATIONALITY OR DOMICILE
Name of Country
OR { Citizen of ▶ _____
Domiciled in ▶ _____

WAS THIS AUTHOR'S CONTRIBUTION TO THE WORK
Anonymous? ☐ Yes ☐ No
Pseudonymous? ☐ Yes ☐ No
If the answer to either of these questions is "Yes," see detailed instructions.

NATURE OF AUTHORSHIP Briefly describe nature of material created by this author in which copyright is claimed. ▼

c NAME OF AUTHOR ▼

DATES OF BIRTH AND DEATH
Year Born ▼   Year Died ▼

Was this contribution to the work a "work made for hire"?
☐ Yes
☐ No

AUTHOR'S NATIONALITY OR DOMICILE
Name of Country
OR { Citizen of ▶ _____
Domiciled in ▶ _____

WAS THIS AUTHOR'S CONTRIBUTION TO THE WORK
Anonymous? ☐ Yes ☐ No
Pseudonymous? ☐ Yes ☐ No
If the answer to either of these questions is "Yes," see detailed instructions.

NATURE OF AUTHORSHIP Briefly describe nature of material created by this author in which copyright is claimed. ▼

3 **a** YEAR IN WHICH CREATION OF THIS WORK WAS COMPLETED
Year ▶ _____
This information must be given in all cases.

b DATE AND NATION OF FIRST PUBLICATION OF THIS PARTICULAR WORK
Complete this information ONLY if this work has been published.
Month ▶ _____ Day ▶ _____ Year ▶ _____
Nation ▶ _____

4 **a** COPYRIGHT CLAIMANT(S) Name and address must be given even if the claimant is the same as the author given in space 2. ▼

APPLICATION RECEIVED

ONE DEPOSIT RECEIVED

TWO DEPOSITS RECEIVED

FUNDS RECEIVED

b See instructions before completing this space.
TRANSFER If the claimant(s) named here in space 4 is (are) different from the author(s) named in space 2, give a brief statement of how the claimant(s) obtained ownership of the copyright. ▼

DO NOT WRITE HERE
OFFICE USE ONLY

MORE ON BACK ▶ • Complete all applicable spaces (numbers 5-9) on the reverse side of this page.
• See detailed instructions. • Sign the form at line 8.

DO NOT WRITE HERE
Page 1 of _____ pages

EXAMINED BY	FORM SR
CHECKED BY	
CORRESPONDENCE ☐ Yes	FOR COPYRIGHT OFFICE USE ONLY

DO NOT WRITE ABOVE THIS LINE. IF YOU NEED MORE SPACE, USE A SEPARATE CONTINUATION SHEET.

PREVIOUS REGISTRATION Has registration for this work, or for an earlier version of this work, already been made in the Copyright Office?

☐ Yes ☐ No If your answer is "Yes," why is another registration being sought? (Check appropriate box) ▼

a. ☐ This work was previously registered in unpublished form and now has been published for the first time.

b. ☐ This is the first application submitted by this author as copyright claimant.

c. ☐ This is a changed version of the work, as shown by space 6 on this application.

If your answer is "Yes," give: **Previous Registration Number ▼**   **Year of Registration ▼**

5

DERIVATIVE WORK OR COMPILATION

Preexisting Material Identify any preexisting work or works that this work is based on or incorporates. ▼

a

Material Added to This Work Give a brief, general statement of the material that has been added to this work and in which copyright is claimed. ▼

b

6

See instructions
before completing
this space.

DEPOSIT ACCOUNT If the registration fee is to be charged to a deposit account established in the Copyright Office, give name and number of account.

a   Name ▼   Account Number ▼

7

b CORRESPONDENCE Give name and address to which correspondence about this application should be sent. Name/Address/Apt/City/State/Zip ▼

Area code and daytime telephone number   (   )   Fax number   (   )

Email

CERTIFICATION* I, the undersigned, hereby certify that I am the

Check only one ▼

☐ author

☐ other copyright claimant

☐ owner of exclusive right(s)

☐ authorized agent of _____

Name of author or other copyright claimant, or owner of exclusive right(s) ▲

of the work identified in this application and that the statements made by me in this application are correct to the best of my knowledge.

Typed or printed name and date ▼ If this application gives a date of publication in space 3, do not sign and submit it before that date.

_____   Date _____

Handwritten signature ▼

8

Certificate will be mailed in window envelope to this address:	Name ▼
	Number/Street/Apt ▼
	City/State/Zip ▼

YOU MUST:
• Complete all necessary spaces
• Sign your application in space 8
**SEND ALL 3 ELEMENTS
IN THE SAME PACKAGE:**
1. Application form
2. Nonrefundable filing fee in check or money order payable to Register of Copyrights
3. Deposit material
MAIL TO:
Library of Congress
Copyright Office-SR
101 Independence Avenue SE
Washington, DC 20559

9

*17 U.S.C. §506(e): Any person who knowingly makes a false representation of a material fact in the application for copyright registration provided for by section 409, or in any written statement filed in connection with the application, shall be fined not more than $2,500.

Form SR-Full   Rev: 12/2016   Printed on recycled paper   U.S. Government Printing Office: 2016-xxx-xxx/xx,xxx

Trademark/Service Mark Application, Principle Register, with Declarations

Identify the Mark: _____ Class No. (If Known): _____

Applicant Name: _____

Applicant Address: _____

Applicant Entity: (Check One and Supply Requested Information)

_ Individual—Citizenship (Country): _____

_ Partnership—Partnership Domicile (State and Country): _____

   Names and Citizenship (Country) of General Partners: _____

_ Corporation—State (Country, if Appropriate) of Incorporation: _____

_ Other (Specify Nature of Entity and Domicile): _____

To the Assistant Secretary and Commissioner of Patents and Trademarks:

Applicant requests registration of the above identified trademark/service mark shown in the accompanying drawing in the United States Patent and Trademark Office on the Principal Register established by the Act of July 5, 1946 (15 U.S.C. 1051 et seq., as amended) for the following goods/services:

_____

_____

Basis for Application: (Check One or More, but Not Both the First and Second Boxes, and Supply Requested Information)

_ Applicant is using the mark in commerce on or in connection with the above identified goods/services. (15 U.S.C. 105(a), as amended.) Three specimens showing the mark as used in commerce are submitted with this application.

• Date of first use of the mark anywhere: _____

• Date of first use of the mark in commerce which the U.S. Congress may regulate:

_____

• Specify the type of commerce (e.g., Interstate, between the United States and a Specified Foreign Country):

_____

• Specify manner or mode of use of mark on or in connection with the goods/services (e.g., Trademark Is Applied to Labels, Service Mark Is Used in Advertisements):

_____

_ Applicant has bona fide intention to use the mark in commerce on or in connection with the above identified goods/services. (15 U.S.C. 105(b), as amended.)

• Specify intended manner or mode of use of mark on or in connection with the goods or services: (e.g., Trademark Will Be Applied to Labels, Service Mark Will Be Used in Advertisements):

_____

_ Applicant has bona fide intention to use the mark in commerce on or in connection with the above identified goods/services, and asserts a claim of priority based upon a foreign application in accordance with 15 U.S.C. 1126(d), as amended.
Country of foreign filing: _____
Date of foreign filing: _____

_ Applicant has a bona fide intention to use the mark in commerce on or in connection with the above identified goods/ services and, accompanying this application, submits a certification or certified copy of a foreign registration in accordance with 15 U.S.C. 1126(e), as amended.
Country of registration: _____
Registration number: _____

Declaration

The undersigned being hereby warned that willful false statements and the like so made are punishable by fine or imprisonment, or both, under 18 U.S.C. 1001, and that such willful false statements may jeopardize the validity of the application or any resulting registration, declares that he/she is properly authorized to execute this application on behalf of the applicant; he/she believes the applicant to be the owner of the trademark/ service mark sought to be registered or, if the application is being filed under 15 U.S.C. 105(b), he/she believes applicant to be entitled to use such mark in commerce; to the best of his/her knowledge and belief no other person, firm, corporation, or association has the right to use the above identified mark in commerce, either in the identical form thereof or in such near resemblance thereto as to be likely, when used on or in connection with the goods/services of such other person; to cause confusion, or to cause mistake, or to deceive; and that all statements made of his/her own knowledge are true and all statements made on information and belief are believed to be true.

_____   _____

Signature   Date

_____   _____

Print or Type Name and Position   Telephone

PTO/AIA/01 (06-12)
Approved for use through 01/31/2014. OMB 0651-0032
U.S. Patent and Trademark Office; U.S. DEPARTMENT OF COMMERCE
Under the Paperwork Reduction Act of 1995, no persons are required to respond to a collection of information unless it displays a valid OMB control number.

DECLARATION (37 CFR 1.63) FOR UTILITY OR DESIGN APPLICATION USING AN APPLICATION DATA SHEET (37 CFR 1.76)

Title of Invention	

As the below named inventor, I hereby declare that:

This declaration is directed to:

☐ The attached application, or

☐ United States application or PCT international application number _____

filed on _____.

The above-identified application was made or authorized to be made by me.

I believe that I am the original inventor or an original joint inventor of a claimed invention in the application.

I hereby acknowledge that any willful false statement made in this declaration is punishable under 18 U.S.C. 1001 by fine or imprisonment of not more than five (5) years, or both.

WARNING:

Petitioner/applicant is cautioned to avoid submitting personal information in documents filed in a patent application that may contribute to identity theft. Personal information such as social security numbers, bank account numbers, or credit card numbers (other than a check or credit card authorization form PTO-2038 submitted for payment purposes) is never required by the USPTO to support a petition or an application. If this type of personal information is included in documents submitted to the USPTO, petitioners/applicants should consider redacting such personal information from the documents before submitting them to the USPTO. Petitioner/applicant is advised that the record of a patent application is available to the public after publication of the application (unless a non-publication request in compliance with 37 CFR 1.213(a) is made in the application) or issuance of a patent. Furthermore, the record from an abandoned application may also be available to the public if the application is referenced in a published application or an issued patent (see 37 CFR 1.14). Checks and credit card authorization forms PTO-2038 submitted for payment purposes are not retained in the application file and therefore are not publicly available.

LEGAL NAME OF INVENTOR

Inventor: _____ Date (Optional) :_____

Signature: _____

Note: An application data sheet (PTO/SB/14 or equivalent), including naming the entire inventive entity, must accompany this form or must have been previously filed. Use an additional PTO/AIA/01 form for each additional inventor.

This collection of information is required by 35 U.S.C. 115 and 37 CFR 1.63. The information is required to obtain or retain a benefit by the public which is to file (and by the USPTO to process) an application. Confidentiality is governed by 35 U.S.C. 122 and 37 CFR 1.11 and 1.14. This collection is estimated to take 1 minute to complete, including gathering, preparing, and submitting the completed application form to the USPTO. Time will vary depending upon the individual case. Any comments on the amount of time you require to complete this form and/or suggestions for reducing this burden, should be sent to the Chief Information Officer, U.S. Patent and Trademark Office, U.S. Department of Commerce, P.O. Box 1450, Alexandria, VA 22313-1450. DO NOT SEND FEES OR COMPLETED FORMS TO THIS ADDRESS. **SEND TO: Commissioner for Patents, P.O. Box 1450, Alexandria, VA 22313-1450.**
If you need assistance in completing the form, call 1-800-PTO-9199 and select option 2.

Doc Code: Oath
Document Description: Oath or declaration filed

PTO/AIA/08 (11-1!
Approved for use through 4/30/2017. OMB 0651-003:
U.S. Patent and Trademark Office; U.S. DEPARTMENT OF COMMERCE
Under the Paperwork Reduction Act of 1995, no persons are required to respond to a collection of information unless it contains a valid OMB control number.

DECLARATION FOR UTILITY OR DESIGN PATENT APPLICATION (37 CFR 1.63)	Attorney Docket Number	
	First Named Inventor	
	COMPLETE IF KNOWN	
	Application Number	
☐ Declaration Submitted With Initial Filing OR ☐ Declaration Submitted After Initial Filing (surcharge (37 CFR 1.16(f)) required)	Filing Date	
	Art Unit	
	Examiner Name	

(Title of the Invention)

As a below named inventor, I hereby declare that:

This declaration is directed to:

☐ The attached application,

OR

☐ United States Application Number or PCT International application number _____

filed on_____.

The above-identified application was made or authorized to be made by me.

I believe I am the original inventor or an original joint inventor of a claimed invention in the application.

I hereby acknowledge that any willful false statement made in this declaration is punishable under 18 U.S.C. 1001 by fine or imprisonment of not more than five (5) years, or both.

Direct all correspondence to:	The address associated with Customer Number: ☐		OR ☐	Correspondence address below
Name				
Address				
City		State		Zip
Country		Telephone		Email

[Page 1 of 2]

This collection of information is required by 35 U.S.C. 115 and 37 CFR 1.63. The information is required to obtain or retain a benefit by the public which is to file (and by the USPTO to process) an application. Confidentiality is governed by 35 U.S.C. 122 and 37 CFR 1.11 and 1.14. This collection is estimated to take 21 minutes to complete, including gathering, preparing, and submitting the completed application form to the USPTO. Time will vary depending upon the individual case. Any comments on the amount of time you require to complete this form and/or suggestions for reducing this burden, should be sent to the Chief Information Officer, U.S. Patent and Trademark Office, U.S. Department of Commerce, P.O. Box 1450, Alexandria, VA 22313-1450. DO NOT SEND FEES OR COMPLETED FORMS TO THIS ADDRESS. **SEND TO: Commissioner for Patents, P.O. Box 1450, Alexandria, VA 22313-1450.**

If you need assistance in completing the form, call 1-800-PTO-9199 and select option 2.

PTO/AIA/08 (11-15)
Approved for use through 4/30/2017. OMB 0651-0032
U.S. Patent and Trademark Office; U.S. DEPARTMENT OF COMMERCE
Under the Paperwork Reduction Act of 1995, no persons are required to respond to a collection of information unless it contains a valid OMB control number.

DECLARATION — Utility or Design Patent Application

WARNING:

Petitioner/applicant is cautioned to avoid submitting personal information in documents filed in a patent application that may contribute to identity theft. Personal information such as social security numbers, bank account numbers, or credit card numbers (other than a check or credit card authorization form PTO-2038 submitted for payment purposes) is never required by the USPTO to support a petition or an application. If this type of personal information is included in documents submitted to the USPTO, petitioners/applicants should consider redacting such personal information from the documents before submitting them to the USPTO. Petitioner/applicant is advised that the record of a patent application is available to the public after publication of the application (unless a non-publication request in compliance with 37 CFR 1.213(a) is made in the application) or issuance of a patent. Furthermore, the record from an abandoned application may also be available to the public if the application is referenced in a published application or an issued patent (see 37 CFR 1.14). Checks and credit card authorization forms PTO-2038 submitted for payment purposes are not retained in the application file and therefore are not publicly available. Petitioner/applicant is advised that documents which form the record of a patent application (such as the PTO/SB/01) are placed into the Privacy Act system of records DEPARTMENT OF COMMERCE, COMMERCE-PAT-7, System name: *Patent Application Files* . Documents not retained in an application file (such as the PTO-2038) are placed into the Privacy Act system of COMMERCE/PAT-TM-10, System name: *Deposit Accounts and Electronic Funds Transfer Profiles.*

LEGAL NAME OF SOLE OR FIRST INVENTOR:
(*E.g.,* Given Name (first and middle if any) and Family Name or Surname)

Inventor's Signature		Date (Optional)	

Residence: City	State	Country	

Mailing Address

City	State	Zip	Country

☐ Additional inventors are being named on the _____ Supplemental sheet(s) PTO/AIA/10 attached hereto

[Page 2 of 2]

PTO/AIA/14 (11-15)
Approved for use through 04/30/2017. OMB 0651-0032
U.S. Patent and Trademark Office; U.S. DEPARTMENT OF COMMERCE
Under the Paperwork Reduction Act of 1995, no persons are required to respond to a collection of information unless it contains a valid OMB control number.

Application Data Sheet 37 CFR 1.76	Attorney Docket Number	
	Application Number	

Title of Invention	

The application data sheet is part of the provisional or nonprovisional application for which it is being submitted. The following form contains the bibliographic data arranged in a format specified by the United States Patent and Trademark Office as outlined in 37 CFR 1.76.
This document may be completed electronically and submitted to the Office in electronic format using the Electronic Filing System (EFS) or the document may be printed and included in a paper filed application.

Secrecy Order 37 CFR 5.2:

☐ Portions or all of the application associated with this Application Data Sheet may fall under a Secrecy Order pursuant to 37 CFR 5.2 (Paper filers only. Applications that fall under Secrecy Order may not be filed electronically.)

Inventor Information:

Inventor	1		Remove
Legal Name			

Prefix	Given Name	Middle Name	Family Name	Suffix
▼				▼

Residence Information (Select One) ● US Residency ○ Non US Residency ○ Active US Military Service		
City	State/Province	Country of Residence

Mailing Address of Inventor:

Address 1	
Address 2	
City	State/Province
Postal Code	Country i

All Inventors Must Be Listed - Additional Inventor Information blocks may be generated within this form by selecting the **Add** button. | Add |

Correspondence Information:

Enter either Customer Number or complete the Correspondence Information section below.
For further information see 37 CFR 1.33(a).

☐ An Address is being provided for the correspondence Information of this application.

Customer Number	
Email Address		Add Email	Remove Email

Application Information:

Title of the Invention		
Attorney Docket Number		Small Entity Status Claimed ☐
Application Type		▼
Subject Matter		▼
Total Number of Drawing Sheets (if any)		Suggested Figure for Publication (if any)

EFS Web 2.2.12

PTO/AIA/14 (11-15)
Approved for use through 04/30/2017. OMB 0651-0032
U.S. Patent and Trademark Office; U.S. DEPARTMENT OF COMMERCE
Under the Paperwork Reduction Act of 1995, no persons are required to respond to a collection of information unless it contains a valid OMB control number.

| **Application Data Sheet 37 CFR 1.76** | Attorney Docket Number | |
| | Application Number | |

| Title of Invention | |

Filing By Reference:

Only complete this section when filing an application by reference under 35 U.S.C. 111(c) and 37 CFR 1.57(a). Do not complete this section if application papers including a specification and any drawings are being filed. Any domestic benefit or foreign priority information must be provided in the appropriate section(s) below (i.e., "Domestic Benefit/National Stage Information" and "Foreign Priority Information").

For the purposes of a filing date under 37 CFR 1.53(b), the description and any drawings of the present application are replaced by this reference to the previously filed application, subject to conditions and requirements of 37 CFR 1.57(a).

Application number of the previously filed application	Filing date (YYYY-MM-DD)	Intellectual Property Authority or Country

Publication Information:

☐ Request Early Publication (Fee required at time of Request 37 CFR 1.219)

☐ **Request Not to Publish.** I hereby request that the attached application not be published under 35 U.S.C. 122(b) and certify that the invention disclosed in the attached application **has not and will not** be the subject of an application filed in another country, or under a multilateral international agreement, that requires publication at eighteen months after filing.

Representative Information:

Representative information should be provided for all practitioners having a power of attorney in the application. Providing this information in the Application Data Sheet does not constitute a power of attorney in the application (see 37 CFR 1.32).
Either enter Customer Number or complete the Representative Name section below. If both sections are completed the customer Number will be used for the Representative Information during processing.

Please Select One:	● Customer Number	○ US Patent Practitioner	○ Limited Recognition (37 CFR 11.9)
Customer Number			

Domestic Benefit/National Stage Information:

This section allows for the applicant to either claim benefit under 35 U.S.C. 119(e), 120, 121, 365(c), or 386(c) or indicate National Stage entry from a PCT application. Providing benefit claim information in the Application Data Sheet constitutes the specific reference required by 35 U.S.C. 119(e) or 120, and 37 CFR 1.78.
When referring to the current application, please leave the "Application Number" field blank.

Prior Application Status	▼		Remove
Application Number	Continuity Type	Prior Application Number	Filing or 371(c) Date (YYYY-MM-DD)
	▼		

Additional Domestic Benefit/National Stage Data may be generated within this form by selecting the **Add** button. | Add |

PTO/AIA/14 (11-15)
Approved for use through 04/30/2017. OMB 0651-0032
U.S. Patent and Trademark Office; U.S. DEPARTMENT OF COMMERCE
Under the Paperwork Reduction Act of 1995, no persons are required to respond to a collection of information unless it contains a valid OMB control number.

Application Data Sheet 37 CFR 1.76	Attorney Docket Number	
	Application Number	

Title of Invention	

Foreign Priority Information:

This section allows for the applicant to claim priority to a foreign application. Providing this information in the application data sheet constitutes the claim for priority as required by 35 U.S.C. 119(b) and 37 CFR 1.55. When priority is claimed to a foreign application that is eligible for retrieval under the priority document exchange program (PDX)[i] the information will be used by the Office to automatically attempt retrieval pursuant to 37 CFR 1.55(i)(1) and (2). Under the PDX program, applicant bears the ultimate responsibility for ensuring that a copy of the foreign application is received by the Office from the participating foreign intellectual property office, or a certified copy of the foreign priority application is filed, within the time period specified in 37 CFR 1.55(g)(1).

Remove

Application Number	Country[i]	Filing Date (YYYY-MM-DD)	Access Code (if applicable)

Additional Foreign Priority Data may be generated within this form by selecting the **Add** button.

Add

Statement under 37 CFR 1.55 or 1.78 for AIA (First Inventor to File) Transition Applications

☐ This application (1) claims priority to or the benefit of an application filed before March 16, 2013 and (2) also contains, or contained at any time, a claim to a claimed invention that has an effective filing date on or after March 16, 2013.
NOTE: By providing this statement under 37 CFR 1.55 or 1.78, this application, with a filing date on or after March 16, 2013, will be examined under the first inventor to file provisions of the AIA.

PTO/AIA/14 (11-15)
Approved for use through 04/30/2017. OMB 0651-0032
U.S. Patent and Trademark Office; U.S. DEPARTMENT OF COMMERCE
Under the Paperwork Reduction Act of 1995, no persons are required to respond to a collection of information unless it contains a valid OMB control number.

| **Application Data Sheet 37 CFR 1.76** | Attorney Docket Number | |
| | Application Number | |

| Title of Invention | |

Authorization or Opt-Out of Authorization to Permit Access:

When this Application Data Sheet is properly signed and filed with the application, applicant has provided written authority to permit a participating foreign intellectual property (IP) office access to the instant application-as-filed (see paragraph A in subsection 1 below) and the European Patent Office (EPO) access to any search results from the instant application (see paragraph B in subsection 1 below).

Should applicant choose not to provide an authorization identified in subsection 1 below, applicant **must opt-out** of the authorization by checking the corresponding box A or B or both in subsection 2 below.

NOTE: This section of the Application Data Sheet is **ONLY** reviewed and processed with the **INITIAL** filing of an application. After the initial filing of an application, an Application Data Sheet cannot be used to provide or rescind authorization for access by a foreign IP office(s). Instead, Form PTO/SB/39 or PTO/SB/69 must be used as appropriate.

1. Authorization to Permit Access by a Foreign Intellectual Property Office(s)

A. Priority Document Exchange (PDX) - Unless box A in subsection 2 (opt-out of authorization) is checked, the undersigned hereby **grants the USPTO authority** to provide the European Patent Office (EPO), the Japan Patent Office (JPO), the Korean Intellectual Property Office (KIPO), the State Intellectual Property Office of the People's Republic of China (SIPO), the World Intellectual Property Organization (WIPO), and any other foreign intellectual property office participating with the USPTO in a bilateral or multilateral priority document exchange agreement in which a foreign application claiming priority to the instant patent application is filed, access to: (1) the instant patent application-as-filed and its related bibliographic data, (2) any foreign or domestic application to which priority or benefit is claimed by the instant application and its related bibliographic data, and (3) the date of filing of this Authorization. See 37 CFR 1.14(h)(1).

B. Search Results from U.S. Application to EPO - Unless box B in subsection 2 (opt-out of authorization) is checked, the undersigned hereby **grants the USPTO authority** to provide the EPO access to the bibliographic data and search results from the instant patent application when a European patent application claiming priority to the instant patent application is filed. See 37 CFR 1.14(h)(2).

The applicant is reminded that the EPO's Rule 141(1) EPC (European Patent Convention) requires applicants to submit a copy of search results from the instant application without delay in a European patent application that claims priority to the instant application.

2. Opt-Out of Authorizations to Permit Access by a Foreign Intellectual Property Office(s)

☐   A. Applicant **DOES NOT** authorize the USPTO to permit a participating foreign IP office access to the instant application-as-filed. If this box is checked, the USPTO will not be providing a participating foreign IP office with any documents and information identified in subsection 1A above.

☐   B. Applicant **DOES NOT** authorize the USPTO to transmit to the EPO any search results from the instant patent application. If this box is checked, the USPTO will not be providing the EPO with search results from the instant application.

NOTE: Once the application has published or is otherwise publicly available, the USPTO may provide access to the application in accordance with 37 CFR 1.14.

PTO/AIA/14 (11-15)
Approved for use through 04/30/2017. OMB 0651-0032
U.S. Patent and Trademark Office; U.S. DEPARTMENT OF COMMERCE
Under the Paperwork Reduction Act of 1995, no persons are required to respond to a collection of information unless it contains a valid OMB control number.

Application Data Sheet 37 CFR 1.76	Attorney Docket Number	
	Application Number	
Title of Invention		

Applicant Information:

Providing assignment information in this section does not substitute for compliance with any requirement of part 3 of Title 37 of CFR to have an assignment recorded by the Office.

Applicant 1   [Remove]

If the applicant is the inventor (or the remaining joint inventor or inventors under 37 CFR 1.45), this section should not be completed. The information to be provided in this section is the name and address of the legal representative who is the applicant under 37 CFR 1.43; or the name and address of the assignee, person to whom the inventor is under an obligation to assign the invention, or person who otherwise shows sufficient proprietary interest in the matter who is the applicant under 37 CFR 1.46. If the applicant is an applicant under 37 CFR 1.46 (assignee, person to whom the inventor is obligated to assign, or person who otherwise shows sufficient proprietary interest) together with one or more joint inventors, then the joint inventor or inventors who are also the applicant should be identified in this section.

[Clear]

| ○ Assignee | ○ Legal Representative under 35 U.S.C. 117 | ○ Joint Inventor |
| ○ Person to whom the inventor is obligated to assign. | | ○ Person who shows sufficient proprietary interest |

If applicant is the legal representative, indicate the authority to file the patent application, the inventor is:

[▼]

Name of the Deceased or Legally Incapacitated Inventor: [   ]

If the Applicant is an Organization check here. ☐

| Prefix | **Given Name** | Middle Name | **Family Name** | Suffix |
| ▼ | | | | ▼ |

Mailing Address Information For Applicant:

Address 1	
Address 2	
City		**State/Province**	
Country		Postal Code	
Phone Number		Fax Number	
Email Address			

Additional Applicant Data may be generated within this form by selecting the Add button. [Add]

Assignee Information including Non-Applicant Assignee Information:

Providing assignment information in this section does not substitute for compliance with any requirement of part 3 of Title 37 of CFR to have an assignment recorded by the Office.

PTO/AIA/14 (11-15)
Approved for use through 04/30/2017. OMB 0651-0032
U.S. Patent and Trademark Office; U.S. DEPARTMENT OF COMMERCE
Under the Paperwork Reduction Act of 1995, no persons are required to respond to a collection of information unless it contains a valid OMB control number.

| Application Data Sheet 37 CFR 1.76 | Attorney Docket Number | |
| | Application Number | |

| Title of Invention | |

Assignee 1

Complete this section if assignee information, including non-applicant assignee information, is desired to be included on the patent application publication. An assignee-applicant identified in the "Applicant Information" section will appear on the patent application publication as an applicant. For an assignee-applicant, complete this section only if identification as an assignee is also desired on the patent application publication.

Remove

If the Assignee or Non-Applicant Assignee is an Organization check here. ☐

Prefix	Given Name	Middle Name	Family Name	Suffix
▼				▼

Mailing Address Information For Assignee including Non-Applicant Assignee:

Address 1	
Address 2	

City		State/Province	
Country i		Postal Code	
Phone Number		Fax Number	
Email Address	

Additional Assignee or Non-Applicant Assignee Data may be generated within this form by selecting the Add button.   Add

Signature:
Remove

NOTE: This Application Data Sheet must be signed in accordance with 37 CFR 1.33(b). **However, if this Application Data Sheet is submitted with the INITIAL filing of the application and either box A or B is not checked in subsection 2 of the "Authorization or Opt-Out of Authorization to Permit Access" section, then this form must also be signed in accordance with 37 CFR 1.14(c).**
   This Application Data Sheet **must** be signed by a patent practitioner if one or more of the applicants is a **juristic entity** (e.g., corporation or association). If the applicant is two or more joint inventors, this form must be signed by a patent practitioner, **all** joint inventors who are the applicant, or one or more joint inventor-applicants who have been given power of attorney (e.g., see USPTO Form PTO/AIA/81) on behalf of **all** joint inventor-applicants.
   See 37 CFR 1.4(d) for the manner of making signatures and certifications.

Signature		Date (YYYY-MM-DD)	
First Name		Last Name		Registration Number	

Additional Signature may be generated within this form by selecting the Add button.   Add

PTO/AIA/14 (11-15)
Approved for use through 04/30/2017. OMB 0651-0032
U.S. Patent and Trademark Office; U.S. DEPARTMENT OF COMMERCE
Under the Paperwork Reduction Act of 1995, no persons are required to respond to a collection of information unless it contains a valid OMB control number.

Application Data Sheet 37 CFR 1.76	Attorney Docket Number	
	Application Number	
Title of Invention		

This collection of information is required by 37 CFR 1.76. The information is required to obtain or retain a benefit by the public which is to file (and by the USPTO to process) an application. Confidentiality is governed by 35 U.S.C. 122 and 37 CFR 1.14. This collection is estimated to take 23 minutes to complete, including gathering, preparing, and submitting the completed application data sheet form to the USPTO. Time will vary depending upon the individual case. Any comments on the amount of time you require to complete this form and/or suggestions for reducing this burden, should be sent to the Chief Information Officer, U.S. Patent and Trademark Office, U.S. Department of Commerce, P.O. Box 1450, Alexandria, VA 22313-1450. DO NOT SEND FEES OR COMPLETED FORMS TO THIS ADDRESS. **SEND TO: Commissioner for Patents, P.O. Box 1450, Alexandria, VA 22313-1450.**

PTO/AIA/15 (03-13)
Approved for use through 01/31/2014. OMB 0651-0032
U.S. Patent and Trademark Office; U.S. DEPARTMENT OF COMMERCE
Under the Paperwork Reduction Act of 1995 no persons are required to respond to a collection of information unless it displays a valid OMB control number

UTILITY
PATENT APPLICATION
TRANSMITTAL

(Only for new nonprovisional applications under 37 CFR 1.53(b))

Attorney Docket No.	
First Named Inventor	
Title	
Express Mail Label No.	

APPLICATION ELEMENTS
See MPEP chapter 600 concerning utility patent application contents.

ADDRESS TO:

Commissioner for Patents
P.O. Box 1450
Alexandria, VA 22313-1450

1. ☐ **Fee Transmittal Form**
   (PTO/SB/17 or equivalent)

2. ☐ **Applicant asserts small entity status.**
   See 37 CFR 1.27

3. ☐ **Applicant certifies micro entity status.** See 37 CFR 1.29.
   Applicant must attach form PTO/SB/15A or B or equivalent.

4. ☐ **Specification**   [*Total Pages* _____]
   Both the claims and abstract must start on a new page.
   (*See MPEP § 608.01(a) for information on the preferred arrangement*)

5. ☐ **Drawing(s)** (35 U.S.C. 113)   [*Total Sheets* _____]

6. **Inventor's Oath or Declaration**   [*Total Pages* _____]
   (*including substitute statements under 37 CFR 1.64 and assignments serving as an oath or declaration under 37 CFR 1.63(e)*)

   a. ☐   Newly executed (original or copy)

   b. ☐   A copy from a prior application (37 CFR 1.63(d))

7. ☐ **Application Data Sheet**   * *See note below.*
   See 37 CFR 1.76 (PTO/AIA/14 or equivalent)

8. ☐ **CD-ROM or CD-R**
   in duplicate, large table, or Computer Program (*Appendix*)

   ☐   Landscape Table on CD

9. **Nucleotide and/or Amino Acid Sequence Submission**
   (*if applicable, items a. – c. are required*)

   a. ☐   Computer Readable Form (CRF)

   b. ☐   Specification Sequence Listing on:

   i. ☐   CD-ROM or CD-R (2 copies); or

   ii. ☐   Paper

   c. ☐   Statements verifying identity of above copies

ACCOMPANYING APPLICATION PAPERS

10. ☐   **Assignment Papers**
    (cover sheet & document(s))
    Name of Assignee _____

    _____

11. ☐   **37 CFR 3.73(c) Statement**   ☐ **Power of Attorney**

12. ☐   **English Translation Document**
    (*if applicable*)

13. ☐   **Information Disclosure Statement**
    (PTO/SB/08 or PTO-1449)

    ☐   Copies of citations attached

14. ☐   **Preliminary Amendment**

15. ☐   **Return Receipt Postcard**
    (*MPEP § 503*) (*Should be specifically itemized*)

16. ☐   **Certified Copy of Priority Document(s)**
    (*if foreign priority is claimed*)

17. ☐   **Nonpublication Request**
    Under 35 U.S.C. 122(b)(2)(B)(i). Applicant must attach form PTO/SB/35 or equivalent.

18. ☐   **Other:** _____

    _____

    _____

    _____

*Note: (1) Benefit claims under 37 CFR 1.78 and foreign priority claims under 1.55 **must** be included in an Application Data Sheet (ADS).
(2) For applications filed under 35 U.S.C. 111, the application must contain an ADS specifying the applicant if the applicant is an assignee, person to whom the inventor is under an obligation to assign, or person who otherwise shows sufficient proprietary interest in the matter. See 37 CFR 1.46(b).

19. CORRESPONDENCE ADDRESS

☐   The address associated with Customer Number: _____   **OR**   ☐   Correspondence address below

Name	
Address	

City		State		Zip Code	
Country		Telephone		Email	

Signature			Date	
Name (Print/Type)			Registration No. (Attorney/Agent)	

This collection of information is required by 37 CFR 1.53(b). The information is required to obtain or retain a benefit by the public which is to file (and by the USPTO to process) an application. Confidentiality is governed by 35 U.S.C. 122 and 37 CFR 1.11 and 1.14. This collection is estimated to take 12 minutes to complete, including gathering, preparing, and submitting the completed application form to the USPTO. Time will vary depending upon the individual case. Any comments on the amount of time you require to complete this form and/or suggestions for reducing this burden, should be sent to the Chief Information Officer, U.S. Patent and Trademark Office, U.S. Department of Commerce, P.O. Box 1450, Alexandria, VA 22313-1450. DO NOT SEND FEES OR COMPLETED FORMS TO THIS ADDRESS. **SEND TO: Commissioner for Patents, P.O. Box 1450, Alexandria, VA 22313-1450.**
If you need assistance in completing the form, call 1-800-PTO-9199 and select option 2.

PTO/AIA/31 (03-14)
Approved for use through 07/31/2016. OMB 0651-0031
U.S. Patent and Trademark Office; U.S. DEPARTMENT OF COMMERCE
Under the Paperwork Reduction Act of 1995, no persons are required to respond to a collection of information unless it displays a valid OMB control number.

NOTICE OF APPEAL FROM THE EXAMINER TO THE PATENT TRIAL AND APPEAL BOARD

	Docket Number (Optional)

I hereby certify that this correspondence is being facsimile transmitted to the USPTO, EFS-Web transmitted to the USPTO, or deposited with the United States Postal Service with sufficient postage in an envelope addressed to "Commissioner for Patents, P.O. Box 1450, Alexandria, on Alexandria, VA 22313-1450" [37 CFR 1.8(a)] on _____.	In re Application of	
	Application Number	Filed
	For	
Signature _____		
Typed or printed name _____	Art Unit	Examiner

Applicant hereby **appeals** to the Patent Trial and Appeal Board from the last decision of the examiner.

The fee for this Notice of Appeal is (37 CFR 41.20(b)(1)) $ _____

[ ] Applicant asserts small entity status. See 37 CFR 1.27. Therefore, the fee shown above is reduced
by 50%, and the resulting fee is: $ _____

[ ] Applicant certifies micro entity status. See 37 CFR 1.29. Therefore, the fee shown above is reduced
by 75%, and the resulting fee is: $ _____
Form PTO/SB/15A or B or equivalent must either be enclosed or have been submitted previously.

[ ] A check in the amount of the fee is enclosed.

[ ] Payment by credit card. Form PTO-2038 is attached.

[ ] The Director is hereby authorized to charge any fees which may be required, or credit any overpayment
to Deposit Account No. _____.

[ ] Payment made via EFS-Web.

[ ] A petition for an extension of time under 37 CFR 1.136(a) (PTO/AIA/22 or equivalent) is enclosed.
For extensions of time in reexamination proceedings, see 37 CFR 1.550.

**WARNING: Information on this form may become public. Credit card information should not be included
on this form. Provide credit card information and authorization on PTO-2038.**

I am the

[ ] applicant   [ ] attorney or agent of record   [ ] attorney or agent acting under 37 CFR 1.34
                          Registration number _____   Registration number _____

Signature _____

Typed or printed name _____

Telephone Number _____

Date _____

NOTE: This form must be signed in accordance with 37 CFR 1.33. See 37 CFR 1.4 for signature requirements and certifications. Submit multiple
forms if more than one signature is required, see below*.

[ ] * Total of _____ forms are submitted.

This collection of information is required by 37 CFR 41.20(b)(1) and 41.31. The information is required to obtain or retain a benefit by the public which is to file (and
by the USPTO to process) an application. Confidentiality is governed by 35 U.S.C. 122 and 37 CFR 1.11, 1.14 and 41.6. This collection is estimated to take 12 minutes
to complete, including gathering, preparing, and submitting the completed application form to the USPTO. Time will vary depending upon the individual case. Any
comments on the amount of time you require to complete this form and/or suggestions for reducing this burden, should be sent to the Chief Information Officer,
U.S. Patent and Trademark Office, U.S. Department of Commerce, P.O. Box 1450, Alexandria, VA 22313-1450. DO NOT SEND FEES OR COMPLETED FORMS TO THIS
ADDRESS. **SEND TO: Commissioner for Patents, P.O. Box 1450, Alexandria, VA 22313-1450.**

If you need assistance in completing the form, call 1-800-PTO-9199 and select option 2.

PTO/AIA/32 (03-13)
Approved for use through 03/31/2013. OMB 0651-0031
U.S. Patent and Trademark Office; U.S. DEPARTMENT OF COMMERCE
Under the Paperwork Reduction Act of 1995, no persons are required to respond to a collection of information unless it displays a valid OMB control number.

REQUEST FOR ORAL HEARING BEFORE **THE PATENT TRIAL AND APPEAL BOARD**	Docket Number (Optional)	
I hereby certify that this correspondence is being facsimile transmitted to the USPTO, EFS-Web transmitted to the USPTO, or deposited with the United States Postal Service with sufficient postage in an envelope addressed to "Commissioner for Patents, P.O. Box 1450, Alexandria, VA 22313-1450" [37 CFR 1.8(a)]	In re Application of	
on _____ .	Application Number	Filed
	For	
Signature _____	Art Unit	Examiner
Typed or printed name _____		

Applicant hereby **requests an oral hearing** before the Patent Trial and Appeal Board in the appeal of the above-identified application.

The fee for this Request for Oral Hearing is (37 CFR 41.20(b)(3)) $ _____

☐ Applicant asserts small entity status. See 37 CFR 1.27. Therefore, the fee shown above is reduced
  by 50%, and the resulting fee is: $ _____

☐ Applicant certifies micro entity status. See 37 CFR 1.29. Therefore, the fee shown above is reduced
  by 75%, and the resulting fee is: $ _____
  Form PTO/SB/15A or B or equivalent must either be enclosed or have been submitted previously

☐ A check in the amount of the fee is enclosed.

☐ Payment by credit card. Form PTO-2038 is attached.

☐ The Director has already been authorized to charge fees in this application to a Deposit Account.

☐ The Director is hereby authorized to charge any fees which may be required, or credit any overpayment
  to Deposit Account No. _____ .

☐ Payment made via EFS-Web.

☐ A petition for an extension of time under 37 CFR 1.136(b) (PTO/SB/23 or equivalent) is enclosed.
  For extensions of time in reexamination proceedings, see 37 CFR 1.550.

  **WARNING: Information on this form may become public. Credit card information should not be included
  on this form. Provide credit card information and authorization on PTO-2038.**

I am the

☐ applicant   ☐ attorney or agent of record   ☐ attorney or agent acting under 37 CFR 1.34
                       Registration number _____   Registration number _____

Signature _____

Typed or printed name _____

Telephone Number _____

Date _____

NOTE: This form must be signed in accordance with 37 CFR 1.33. See 37 CFR 1.4 for signature requirements and certifications. Submit multiple forms if more than one signature is required, see below*.

☐ * Total of _____ forms are submitted.

This collection of information is required by 37 CFR 41.20(b)(3). The information is required to obtain or retain a benefit by the public which is to file (and by the USPTO to process) an application. Confidentiality is governed by 35 U.S.C. 122 and 37 CFR 1.11, 1.14 and 41.6. This collection is estimated to take 12 minutes to complete, including gathering, preparing, and submitting the completed application form to the USPTO. Time will vary depending upon the individual case. Any comments on the amount of time you require to complete this form and/or suggestions for reducing this burden, should be sent to the Chief Information Officer, U.S. Patent and Trademark Office, U.S. Department of Commerce, P.O. Box 1450, Alexandria, VA 22313-1450. DO NOT SEND FEES OR COMPLETED FORMS TO THIS ADDRESS. **SEND TO: Commissioner for Patents, P.O. Box 1450, Alexandria, VA 22313-1450.**

If you need assistance in completing the form, call 1-800-PTO-9199 and select option 2.

PCT

REQUEST

The undersigned requests that the present
international application be processed
according to the Patent Cooperation Treaty.

For receiving Office use only
International Application No.
International Filing Date
Name of receiving Office and "PCT International Application"

Applicant's or agent's file reference
(if desired) (12 characters maximum)

Box No. I   TITLE OF INVENTION

Box No. II   APPLICANT   ☐ This person is also inventor

Name and address: *(Family name followed by given name; for a legal entity, full official designation. The address must include postal code and name of country. The country of the address indicated in this Box is the applicant's State (that is, country) of residence if no State of residence is indicated below.)*

Telephone No.

Facsimile No.

Applicant's registration No. with the Office

E-mail authorization: Marking one of the check-boxes below authorizes the receiving Office, the International Searching Authority, the International Bureau and the International Preliminary Examining Authority to use the e-mail address indicated in this Box to send, notifications issued in respect of this international application to that e-mail address if those offices are willing to do so.
☐ as advance copies followed by paper notifications; or   ☐ exclusively in electronic form (no paper notifications will be sent).
E-mail address:

State *(that is, country)* of nationality: State *(that is, country)* of residence:

This person is applicant
for the purposes of: ☐ all designated States   ☐ the States indicated in the Supplemental Box

Box No. III   FURTHER APPLICANT(S) AND/OR (FURTHER) INVENTOR(S)

☐ Further applicants and/or (further) inventors are indicated on a continuation sheet.

Box No. IV   AGENT OR COMMON REPRESENTATIVE; OR ADDRESS FOR CORRESPONDENCE

The person identified below is hereby/has been appointed to act on behalf of the applicant(s) before the competent International Authorities as: ☐ agent   ☐ common representative

Name and address: *(Family name followed by given name; for a legal entity, full official designation. The address must include postal code and name of country.)*

Telephone No.

Facsimile No.

Agent's registration No. with the Office

E-mail authorization: Marking one of the check-boxes below authorizes the receiving Office, the International Searching Authority, the International Bureau and the International Preliminary Examining Authority to use the e-mail address indicated in this Box to send, notifications issued in respect of this international application to that e-mail address if those offices are willing to do so.
☐ as advance copies followed by paper notifications; or   ☐ exclusively in electronic form (no paper notifications will be sent).
E-mail address:

☐ **Address for correspondence:** Mark this check-box where no agent or common representative is/has been appointed and the space above is used instead to indicate a special address to which correspondence should be sent.

Form PCT/RO/101 (first sheet) (July 2015)   *See Notes to the request form*

Sheet No. . . . .

Box No. III   FURTHER APPLICANT(S) AND/OR (FURTHER) INVENTOR(S)

If none of the following sub-boxes is used, this sheet should not be included in the request.

Name and address: *(Family name followed by given name; for a legal entity, full official designation. The address must include postal code and name of country. The country of the address indicated in this Box is the applicant's State (that is, country) of residence if no State of residence is indicated below.)*	This person is: ☐ applicant only ☐ applicant and inventor ☐ inventor only *(If this check-box is marked, do not fill in below.)*
	Applicant's registration No. with the Office

State *(that is, country)* of nationality:	State *(that is, country)* of residence:

This person is applicant for the purposes of: ☐ all designated States	☐ the States indicated in the Supplemental Box

Name and address: *(Family name followed by given name; for a legal entity, full official designation. The address must include postal code and name of country. The country of the address indicated in this Box is the applicant's State (that is, country) of residence if no State of residence is indicated below.)*	This person is: ☐ applicant only ☐ applicant and inventor ☐ inventor only *(If this check-box is marked, do not fill in below.)*
	Applicant's registration No. with the Office

State *(that is, country)* of nationality:	State *(that is, country)* of residence:

This person is applicant for the purposes of: ☐ all designated States	☐ the States indicated in the Supplemental Box

Name and address: *(Family name followed by given name; for a legal entity, full official designation. The address must include postal code and name of country. The country of the address indicated in this Box is the applicant's State (that is, country) of residence if no State of residence is indicated below.)*	This person is: ☐ applicant only ☐ applicant and inventor ☐ inventor only *(If this check-box is marked, do not fill in below.)*
	Applicant's registration No. with the Office

State *(that is, country)* of nationality:	State *(that is, country)* of residence:

This person is applicant for the purposes of: ☐ all designated States	☐ the States indicated in the Supplemental Box

Name and address: *(Family name followed by given name; for a legal entity, full official designation. The address must include postal code and name of country. The country of the address indicated in this Box is the applicant's State (that is, country) of residence if no State of residence is indicated below.)*	This person is: ☐ applicant only ☐ applicant and inventor ☐ inventor only *(If this check-box is marked, do not fill in below.)*
	Applicant's registration No. with the Office

State *(that is, country)* of nationality:	State *(that is, country)* of residence:

This person is applicant for the purposes of: ☐ all designated States	☐ the States indicated in the Supplemental Box

☐   Further applicants and/or (further) inventors are indicated on another continuation sheet.

Form PCT/RO/101 (continuation sheet) (July 2015)   *See Notes to the request form*

Sheet No. . . . .

Supplemental Box	*If the Supplemental Box is not used, this sheet should not be included in the request.*

1.   *If, in any of the Boxes, except Boxes Nos. VIII(i) to (v) for which a special continuation box is provided, **the space is insufficient** to furnish all the information: in such case, write "Continuation of Box No...." (indicate the number of the Box) and furnish the information in the same manner as required according to the captions of the Box in which the space was insufficient, in particular:*

(i)   *if more than one person is to be indicated as applicant and/or inventor and no "continuation sheet" is available: in such case, write "Continuation of Box No. III" and indicate for each additional person the same type of information as required in Box No. III. The country of the address indicated in this Box is the applicant's State (that is, country) of residence if no State of residence is indicated below;*

(ii)   *if, in Box No. II or in any of the sub-boxes of Box No. III, the indication **"the States indicated in the Supplemental Box"** is checked: in such case, write "Continuation of Box No. II" or "Continuation of Box No. III" or "Continuation of Boxes No. II and No. III" (as the case may be), indicate the name of the applicant(s) involved and, next to (each) such name, the State(s) (and/or, where applicable, ARIPO, Eurasian, European or OAPI patent) for the purposes of which the named person is applicant;*

(iii)   *if, in Box No. II or in any of the sub-boxes of Box No. III, **the inventor or the inventor/applicant is not inventor for the purposes of all designated States**: in such case, write "Continuation of Box No. II" or "Continuation of Box No. III" or "Continuation of Boxes No. II and No. III" (as the case may be), indicate the name of the inventor(s) and, next to (each) such name, the State(s) (and/or, where applicable, ARIPO, Eurasian, European or OAPI patent) for the purposes of which the named person is inventor;*

(iv)   *if, in addition to the agent(s) indicated in Box No. IV, there are **further agents**: in such case, write "Continuation of Box No. IV" and indicate for each further agent the same type of information as required in Box No. IV;*

(v)   *if, in Box No. VI, there are **more than three earlier applications whose priority is claimed**: in such case, write "Continuation of Box No. VI" and indicate for each additional earlier application the same type of information as required in Box No. VI.*

2.   *If the applicant intends to make an indication of the wish that the international application be treated, in certain designated States, as an application for a patent of addition, certificate of addition, inventor's certificate of addition or utility certificate of addition: in such case, write the name or two-letter code of each designated State concerned and the indication "**patent of addition,**" "**certificate of addition,**" "**inventor's certificate of addition**" or "**utility certificate of addition,**" the number of the parent application or parent patent or other parent grant and the date of grant of the parent patent or other parent grant or the date of filing of the parent application (Rules 4.11(a)(i) and 49bis.1(a) or (b)).*

3.   *If the applicant intends to make an indication of the wish that the international application be treated, in the United States of America, as a continuation or continuation-in-part of an earlier application: in such case, write "United States of America" or "US" and the indication "**continuation**" or "**continuation-in-part**" and the number and the filing date of the parent application (Rules 4.11(a)(ii) and 49bis.1(d)).*

Sheet No. . . . .

Box No. V   DESIGNATIONS

The filing of this request **constitutes under Rule 4.9(a) the designation** of all Contracting States bound by the PCT on the international filing date, for the grant of every kind of protection available and, where applicable, for the grant of both regional and national patents.

However,

☐   DE Germany **is not designated** for any kind of national protection

☐   JP Japan **is not designated** for any kind of national protection

☐   KR Republic of Korea **is not designated** for any kind of national protection

(The check-boxes above may only be used to exclude (irrevocably) the designations concerned if, at the time of filing or subsequently under Rule 26bis.1, the international application contains in Box No. VI a priority claim to an earlier national application filed in the particular State concerned, in order to avoid the ceasing of the effect, under the national law, of this earlier national application.)

Box No. VI   PRIORITY CLAIM AND DOCUMENT

The priority of the following earlier application(s) is hereby claimed:

Filing date of earlier application *(day/month/year)*	Number of earlier application	Where earlier application is:		
		national application: country or Member of WTO	regional application: regional Office	international application: receiving Office
item (1)				
item (2)				
item (3)				

☐   Further priority claims are indicated in the Supplemental Box.

Furnishing the priority document(s):

☐   The **receiving Office** is requested to prepare and transmit to the International Bureau a certified copy of the earlier application(s) *(only if the earlier application(s) was filed with the receiving Office which, for the purposes of this international application, is the receiving Office)* identified above as:

☐ all items   ☐ item (1)   ☐ item (2)   ☐ item (3)   ☐ other, see Supplemental Box

☐   The **International Bureau** is requested to obtain from a digital library a certified copy of the earlier application(s) identified above, using, where applicable, the access code(s) indicated below *(if the earlier application(s) is available to it from a digital library)*:

☐ item (1)   ☐ item (2)   ☐ item (3)   ☐ other, see Supplemental Box
access code _____   access code _____   access code _____

Restore the right of priority: the receiving Office is requested to restore the right of priority for the earlier application(s) identified above or in the Supplemental Box as item(s) (_____). *(See also the Notes to Box No. VI; further information **must** be provided to support a request to restore the right of priority.)*

Incorporation by reference: where an element of the international application referred to in Article 11(1)(iii)(d) or (e) or a part of the description, claims or drawings referred to in Rule 20.5(a) is not otherwise contained in this international application but is completely contained in an earlier application whose priority is claimed on the date on which one or more elements referred to in Article 11(1)(iii) were first received by the receiving Office, that element or part is, subject to confirmation under Rule 20.6, incorporated by reference in this international application for the purposes of Rule 20.6.

Box No. VII   INTERNATIONAL SEARCHING AUTHORITY

Choice of International Searching Authority (ISA) *(if more than one International Searching Authority is competent to carry out the international search, indicate the Authority chosen; the two-letter code may be used)*:

ISA/ _____

Sheet No. . . . .

Continuation of Box No. VII	USE OF RESULTS OF EARLIER SEARCH, REFERENCE TO THAT SEARCH

☐ The ISA indicated in Box No. VII is requested to take into account the results of the earlier search(es) indicated below (*see also Notes to Box VII; use of results of more than one earlier search*).

Filing date *(day/month/year)*   Application Number   Country *(or regional Office)*

☐ **Statement (Rule 4.12(ii))**: this international application is the same, or substantially the same, as the application in respect of which the earlier search was carried out except, where applicable, that it is filed in a different language.

☐ **Availability of documents**: the following documents are available to the ISA in a form and manner acceptable to it and therefore do not need to be submitted by the applicant to the ISA (Rule 12*bis*.1(f)):

  ☐ a copy of the results of the earlier search,*
  ☐ a copy of the earlier application,
  ☐ a translation of the earlier application into a language which is accepted by the ISA,
  ☐ a translation of the results of the earlier search into a language which is accepted by the ISA,
  ☐ a copy of any document cited in the results of the earlier search. *(If known, please indicate below the document(s) available to the ISA):*

☐ **Transmit copy of results of earlier search and other documents** *(where the earlier search was not carried out by the ISA indicated above but by the same Office as that which is acting as the receiving Office)*: the **receiving Office** is requested to prepare and transmit to the ISA (Rule 12*bis*.1(c)):

  ☐ a copy of the results of the earlier search,*
  ☐ a copy of the earlier application,
  ☐ a copy of any document cited in the results of the earlier search.

* Where the results of the earlier search are neither available from a digital library nor transmitted by the receiving Office, the applicant is required to submit them to the receiving Office (Rule 12*bis*.1(a)) (*See item 11. in the check-list and also Notes to Box No. VII*).

Filing date *(day/month/year)*   Application Number   Country *(or regional Office)*

☐ **Statement (Rule 4.12(ii))**: this international application is the same, or substantially the same, as the application in respect of which the earlier search was carried out except, where applicable, that it is filed in a different language.

☐ **Availability of documents**: the following documents are available to the ISA in a form and manner acceptable to it and therefore do not need to be submitted by the applicant to the ISA (Rule 12*bis*.1(f)):

  ☐ a copy of the results of the earlier search,*
  ☐ a copy of the earlier application,
  ☐ a translation of the earlier application into a language which is accepted by the ISA,
  ☐ a translation of the results of the earlier search into a language which is accepted by the ISA,
  ☐ a copy of any document cited in the results of the earlier search. *(If known, please indicate below the document(s) available to the ISA):*

☐ **Transmit copy of results of earlier search and other documents** *(where the earlier search was not carried out by the ISA indicated above but by the same Office as that which is acting as the receiving Office)*: the **receiving Office** is requested to prepare and transmit to the ISA (Rule 12*bis*.1(c)):

  ☐ a copy of the results of the earlier search,*
  ☐ a copy of the earlier application,
  ☐ a copy of any document cited in the results of the earlier search.

* Where the results of the earlier search are neither available from a digital library nor transmitted by the receiving Office, the applicant is required to submit them to the receiving Office (Rule 12*bis*.1(a)) (*See item 11. in the check-list and also Notes to Box No. VII*).

☐ Further earlier searches are indicated on a continuation sheet.

Box No. VIII   DECLARATIONS

The following **declarations** are contained in Boxes Nos. VIII (i) to (v) *(mark the applicable check-boxes below and indicate in the right column the number of each type of declaration)*:   Number of declarations

☐ Box No. VIII (i)   Declaration as to the identity of the inventor   :

☐ Box No. VIII (ii)   Declaration as to the applicant's entitlement, as at the international filing date, to apply for and be granted a patent   :

☐ Box No. VIII (iii)   Declaration as to the applicant's entitlement, as at the international filing date, to claim the priority of the earlier application   :

☐ Box No. VIII (iv)   Declaration of inventorship (only for the purposes of the designation of the United States of America)   :

☐ Box No. VIII (v)   Declaration as to non-prejudicial disclosures or exceptions to lack of novelty   :

Form PCT/RO/101 (third sheet) (July 2015)   *See Notes to the request form*

Sheet No. . . . .

Box No. VIII (i)   DECLARATION: IDENTITY OF THE INVENTOR

The declaration must conform to the standardized wording provided for in Section 211; see Notes to Boxes Nos. VIII, VIII (i) to (v) (in general) and the specific Notes to Box No.VIII (i). If this Box is not used, this sheet should not be included in the request.

Declaration as to the identity of the inventor (Rules 4.17(i) and 51*bis*.1(a)(i)):

☐ This declaration is continued on the following sheet, "Continuation of Box No. VIII (i)".

Sheet No. . . . .

Box No. VIII (ii)   DECLARATION: ENTITLEMENT TO APPLY FOR AND BE GRANTED A PATENT

The declaration must conform to the standardized wording provided for in Section 212; see Notes to Boxes Nos. VIII, VIII (i) to (v) (in general) and the specific Notes to Box No. VIII (ii). If this Box is not used, this sheet should not be included in the request.

Declaration as to the applicant's entitlement, as at the international filing date, to apply for and be granted a patent (Rules 4.17(ii) and 51*bis*.1(a)(ii)), in a case where the declaration under Rule 4.17(iv) is not appropriate:

☐   This declaration is continued on the following sheet, "Continuation of Box No. VIII (ii)".

Form PCT/RO/101 (declaration sheet (ii)) (July 2015)   *See Notes to the request form*

Sheet No. . . . .

Box No. VIII (iii) DECLARATION: ENTITLEMENT TO CLAIM PRIORITY	

The declaration must conform to the standardized wording provided for in Section 213; see Notes to Boxes Nos. VIII, VIII (i) to (v) (in general) and the specific Notes to Box No.VIII (iii). If this Box is not used, this sheet should not be included in the request.

Declaration as to the applicant's entitlement, as at the international filing date, to claim the priority of the earlier application specified below, where the applicant is not the applicant who filed the earlier application or where the applicant's name has changed since the filing of the earlier application (Rules 4.17(iii) and 51*bis*.1(a)(iii)):

☐ This declaration is continued on the following sheet, "Continuation of Box No. VIII (iii)".

Sheet No. . . . .

Box No. VIII (iv)   DECLARATION: INVENTORSHIP (only for the purposes of the designation of the United States of America)

The declaration must conform to the following standardized wording provided for in Section 214; see Notes to Boxes Nos. VIII, VIII (i) to (v) (in general) and the specific Notes to Box No.VIII (iv). If this Box is not used, this sheet should not be included in the request.

Declaration of inventorship (Rules 4.17(iv) and 51*bis*.1(a)(iv))
for the purposes of the designation of the United States of America:

I hereby declare that I believe I am the original inventor or an original joint inventor of a claimed invention in the application.

This declaration is directed to the international application of which it forms a part (if filing declaration with application).

This declaration is directed to international application No. PCT/. . . . . (if furnishing declaration pursuant to Rule 26*ter*).

I hereby declare that the above-identified international application was made or authorized to be made by me.

I hereby acknowledge that any willful false statement made in this declaration is punishable under 18 U.S.C. 1001 by fine or imprisonment of not more than five (5) years, or both.

Name: . . . .

Residence: . . . .
(city and either US state, if applicable, or country)

Mailing Address: . . . .

. . . .

. . . .

 Inventor's Signature: . . . .   Date: . . . .
(The signature must be that of the inventor, not that of the agent)

Name: . . . .

Residence: . . . .
(city and either US state, if applicable, or country)

Mailing Address: . . . .

. . . .

. . . .

Inventor's Signature: . . . .   Date: . . . .
(The signature must be that of the inventor, not that of the agent)

Name: . . . .

Residence: . . . .
(city and either US state, if applicable, or country)

Mailing Address: . . . .

. . . .

. . . .

Inventor's Signature: . . . .   Date: . . . .
(The signature must be that of the inventor, not that of the agent)

☐   This declaration is continued on the following sheet, "Continuation of Box No. VIII (iv)".

Form PCT/RO/101 (declaration sheet (iv)) (July 2015)   *See Notes to the request form*

Sheet No. ....

Box No. VIII (v)   DECLARATION: NON-PREJUDICIAL DISCLOSURES OR EXCEPTIONS TO LACK OF NOVELTY

The declaration must conform to the standardized wording provided for in Section 215; see Notes to Boxes Nos. VIII, VIII (i) to (v) (in general) and the specific Notes to Box No. VIII (v). If this Box is not used, this sheet should not be included in the request.

Declaration as to non-prejudicial disclosures or exceptions to lack of novelty (Rules 4.17(v) and 51*bis*.1(a)(v)):

☐   This declaration is continued on the following sheet, "Continuation of Box No. VIII (v)".

Form PCT/RO/101 (declaration sheet (v)) (July 2015)   *See Notes to the request form*

Sheet No.   . . . .

Continuation of Box No. VIII (i) to (v)   DECLARATION

*If the space is insufficient in any of Boxes Nos. VIII (i) to (v) to furnish all the information, including in the case where **more than two inventors are to be named** in Box No. VIII (iv), in such case, write "Continuation of Box No. VIII ... " (indicate the item number of the Box) and furnish the information in the same manner as required for the purposes of the Box in which the space was insufficient. If additional space is needed in respect of two or more declarations, a separate continuation box must be used for each such declaration. If this Box is not used, this sheet should not be included in the request.*

Sheet No. . . . .

Box No. IX	CHECK LIST for PAPER filings – this sheet is only to be used when filing an international application on **PAPER**		

This international application contains the following:	Number of sheets	This international application is **accompanied by** the following item(s) (*mark the applicable check-boxes below and indicate in right column the number of each item*):	Number of items
(a) request form PCT/RO/101 (including any declarations and supplemental sheets). . . . . :		1. ☐ fee calculation sheet . . . . :	
		2. ☐ original separate power of attorney . . . . :	
		3. ☐ original general power of attorney . . . . :	
(b) description (excluding any sequence listing part of the description, see (f), below). . . . . :		4. ☐ copy of general power of attorney; reference number: . . . . :	
		5. ☐ priority document(s) identified in Box No. VI as item(s) . . . . :	
		6. ☐ Translation of international application into (*language*): . . . . :	
(c) claims . . . . :		7. ☐ separate indications concerning deposited microorganism or other biological material . . . . :	
(d) abstract . . . . :		8. ☐ (*only where item (f) is marked in the left column*) copy in electronic form (Annex C/ST.25 text file) on	
(e) drawings (if any) . . . . :		physical data carrier(s) of the sequence listing, not forming part of the international application, which is **furnished only**	
(f) sequence listing part of the description (if any) . . . . :		**for the purposes of international search** under Rule 13*ter* (*type and number of physical data carriers*) . . . . :	
		9. ☐ (*only where item (f) (in the left column) and item 8 (above) are marked*) a statement confirming that "the information recorded in electronic form submitted under Rule 13*ter* is identical to the sequence listing as contained in the international application" as filed on paper . . . . :	
Total number of sheets : 0		10. ☐ copy of results of earlier search(es) (Rule 12*bis*.1(a)) . . :	
		11. ☐ other (*specify*): . . . . :	
Figure of the drawings which should accompany the abstract:		**Language of filing** of the international application:	

Box No. X	SIGNATURE OF APPLICANT, AGENT OR COMMON REPRESENTATIVE
Next to each signature, indicate the name of the person signing and the capacity in which the person signs (if such capacity is not obvious from reading the request).	

━━━━━ For receiving Office use only ━━━━━

1. Date of actual receipt of the purported international application:	2. Drawings:
3. Corrected date of actual receipt due to later but timely received papers or drawings completing the purported international application:	☐ received:
4. Date of timely receipt of the required corrections under PCT Article 11(2):	☐ not received:
5. International Searching Authority (if two or more are competent): ISA /	6. ☐ Transmittal of search copy delayed until search fee is paid

━━━━━ For International Bureau use only ━━━━━

Date of receipt of the record copy
by the International Bureau:

Sheet No. ....

Box No. IX   CHECK LIST for EFS-Web filings - this sheet is only to be used when filing an international application with RO/US via **EFS-Web**

This international application **contains** the following:	Number of sheets
(a) request form PCT/RO/101 (including any declarations and supplemental sheets) .... :	
(b) description (excluding any sequence listing part of the description, see (f), below) ..... :	
(c) claims .... :	
(d) abstract .... :	
(e) drawings (if any) .... :	
(f) sequence listing part of the description in the form of an **image file** (e.g. PDF) .... :	

Total number of sheets (including the sequence listing part of the description if **filed as an image file**) .... :   0

(g) sequence listing part of the description

☐ filed in the form of an **Annex C/ST.25 text file**

☐ WILL BE filed separately on physical data carrier(s), on the same day and in the form of an **Annex C/ST.25 text file**

Indicate type and number of physical data carrier(s) ....

Figure of the drawings which should accompany the abstract:

This international application is **accompanied by** the following item(s) *(mark the applicable check-boxes below and indicate in right column the number of each item):*   Number of items

1. ☐ fee calculation sheet .... :
2. ☐ original separate power of attorney .... :
3. ☐ original general power of attorney .... :
4. ☐ copy of general power of attorney; reference number: .... :
5. ☐ priority document(s) identified in Box No. VI as item(s) .... :
6. ☐ Translation of international application into *(language):* .... :
7. ☐ separate indications concerning deposited microorganism or other biological material .... :
8. ☐ *(only where item (f) is marked in the left column)* copy of the sequence listing in electronic form (Annex C/ST.25 text file) not forming part of the international application but **furnished only for the purposes of international search** under Rule 13*ter* .... :
9. ☐ *(only where item (f) (in the left column) and item 8 (above) are marked)* a statement confirming that "the information recorded in electronic form submitted under Rule 13*ter* is identical to the sequence listing as contained in the international application" as filed via EFS-Web: ...... :
10. ☐ copy of results of earlier search(es) (Rule 12*bis*.1(a)) .. :
11. ☐ other *(specify):* .... :

Language of filing of the international application:

Box No. X   SIGNATURE OF APPLICANT, AGENT OR COMMON REPRESENTATIVE
Next to each signature, indicate the name of the person signing and the capacity in which the person signs (if such capacity is not obvious from reading the request).

── For receiving Office use only ──

1. Date of actual receipt of the purported international application:

3. Corrected date of actual receipt due to later but timely received papers or drawings completing the purported international application:

4. Date of timely receipt of the required corrections under PCT Article 11(2):

5. International Searching Authority (if two or more are competent):   ISA /

2. Drawings:

☐ received:

☐ not received:

6. ☐ Transmittal of search copy delayed until search fee is paid

── For International Bureau use only ──

Date of receipt of the record copy by the International Bureau:

NOTES TO THE REQUEST FORM (PCT/RO/101)

These Notes are intended to facilitate the filling in of the request form. For more detailed information, see the *PCT Applicant's Guide*, a WIPO publication, which is available, together with other PCT related documents, at WIPO's website: http://www.wipo.int/pct/en/. The Notes are based on the requirements of the Patent Cooperation Treaty (PCT), the Regulations and the Administrative Instructions under the PCT. In case of any discrepancy between these Notes and those requirements, the latter are applicable.

In the request form and these Notes, "Article", "Rule" and "Section" refer to the provisions of the PCT, the PCT Regulations and the PCT Administrative Instructions, respectively.

The request form should be typed or printed; check-boxes may be marked by hand with black ink (Rule 11.9(a) and (b)).

The request form and these Notes may be downloaded from WIPO's website at the address given above.

WHERE TO FILE
THE INTERNATIONAL APPLICATION

The international application (request, description, claims, abstract and drawings, if any) must be filed with a competent receiving Office (Article 11(1)(i)) – that is, subject to any applicable prescriptions concerning national security, at the choice of the applicant, either:

(i) the receiving Office of, or acting for, a PCT Contracting State of which the applicant or, if there are two or more applicants, is a resident or national (Rule 19.1(a)(i) or (ii) or (b)), or

(ii) the International Bureau of WIPO in Geneva, Switzerland, if the applicant or, if there are two or more applicants, at least one of the applicants is a resident or national of any PCT Contracting State (Rule 19.1(a)(iii)).

CONFIRMATION COPY
OF THE REQUEST FORM

Where the international application was initially filed by facsimile with a receiving Office that accepts such filings (see the *PCT Applicant's Guide*, Annex C) this should be indicated on the first sheet of the form by the annotation "CONFIRMATION COPY" followed by the date of the facsimile transmission.

APPLICANT'S OR AGENT'S FILE REFERENCE

A **File Reference** may be indicated, if desired. It should not exceed 12 characters. Characters in excess of 12 may be disregarded by the receiving Office or any International Authority (Rule 11.6(f) and Section 109).

BOX No. I

Title of Invention (Rules 4.3 and 5.1(a)): The title must be short (preferably two to seven words when in English or translated into English) and precise. It must be identical with the title heading the description.

BOXES Nos. II AND III

General: At least one of the applicants named must be a resident or national of a PCT Contracting State for which the receiving Office acts (Articles 9 and 11(1)(i) and Rules 18 and 19). If the international application is filed with the International Bureau under Rule 19.1(a)(iii), at least one of the applicants must be a resident or national of any PCT Contracting State.

Indication Whether a Person is Applicant and/or Inventor (Rules 4.5(a) and 4.6(a) and (b)):

Check-box "This person is also inventor" (Box No. II): Mark this check-box if the applicant named is also the inventor or one of the inventors; do not mark this check-box if the applicant is a legal entity.

Check-box "applicant and inventor" (Box No. III): Mark this check-box if the person named is both applicant and inventor; do not mark this check-box if the person is a legal entity.

Check-box "applicant only" (Box No. III): Mark this check-box if the person named is a legal entity or if the person named is not also inventor.

Check-box "inventor only" (Box No. III): Mark this check-box if the person named is inventor but not also applicant. This would be the case, for example, where the inventor is deceased or has assigned the invention and the assignee is the applicant for all designated States. Do not mark this check-box if the person is a legal entity.

In Box No. III, one of the three check-boxes must always be marked for each person named.

A person must not be named more than once in Boxes Nos. II and III, even where that person is both applicant and inventor.

Different Applicants for Different Designated States (Rules 4.5(d), 18.3 and 19.2): It is possible to indicate different applicants for the purposes of different designated States. At least one of all the applicants named must be a national or resident of a PCT Contracting State for which the receiving Office acts, irrespective of the designated State(s) for the purposes of which that applicant is named.

For the indication of the designated States for which a person is applicant, mark the applicable check-box (only one for each person). If the person is not an applicant for all designated States, the check-box "the States indicated in the Supplemental Box" must be marked, and the name of the person must be repeated in the Supplemental Box with an indication of the States for which that person is applicant (see item 1(ii) in that Box).

Naming of Inventor (Rule 4.1(a)(iv) and (c)(i)): It is strongly recommended to always name the inventor since such information is generally required in the national phase. For details, see the *PCT Applicant's Guide*, Annex B.

Different Inventors for Different Designated States (Rule 4.6(c)): Different persons may be indicated as inventors for different designated States (for example, where, in this respect, the requirements of the national laws of the designated States are not the same); in such a case, the Supplemental Box must be used (see item 1(iii) in that Box). In the absence of any indication, it will be assumed that the inventor(s) named is (are) inventor(s) for all designated States.

Names and Addresses (Rule 4.4): The family name (preferably in capital letters) must be indicated before the given name(s). Titles and academic degrees must be omitted. Names of legal entities must be indicated by their full official designations.

page 2

The address must be indicated in such a way that it allows prompt postal delivery; it must consist of all the relevant administrative units (up to and including the indication of the house number, if any), the postal code (if any), and the name of the country.

Only one address may be indicated per person. For the indication of a special "address for correspondence", see the notes to Box No. IV.

Telephone, Facsimile Numbers and/or E-mail Addresses should be indicated for the persons named in Boxes Nos. II and IV in order to allow rapid communication with them (see Rule 4.4(c)). Any telephone or facsimile number should include the applicable country and area codes. A single e-mail address only should be indicated.

Unless one of the applicable check-boxes is marked, any e-mail address supplied will be used only for the types of communication which might be made by telephone. If one of the applicable check-boxes is marked, the receiving Office, the International Searching Authority, the International Bureau and the International Preliminary Examining Authority may send notifications in respect of the international application to the applicant, avoiding processing or postal delays. Note that not all Offices will send such notifications by e-mail, (for details about each Office's procedure see the *PCT Applicant's Guide*, Annex B). If the first check-box is marked, any such e-mail notification will always be followed by the official notification on paper. Only that paper copy of the notification is considered the legal copy of the notification and only the date of mailing of that paper copy will commence any time limit within the meaning of Rule 80. If the second check-box is marked, the applicant requests the discontinuation of the sending of paper copies of notifications and acknowledges that the date of mailing indicated on the electronic copy will commence any time limit within the meaning of Rule 80.

Note that it is the applicant's responsibility to keep any e-mail address details up-to-date and to ensure that incoming e-mails are not blocked for any reason on the recipient's side. Changes to the e-mail address indicated in the request should be requested to be recorded, preferably directly at the International Bureau, under Rule 92*bis*. Where the e-mail authorization is given both in respect of the applicant and in respect of an agent or common representative, the International Bureau will send e-mail communications only to the appointed agent or common representative.

Applicant's Registration Number with the Office (Rule 4.5(e)): Where the applicant is registered with the national or regional Office acting as receiving Office, the request may indicate the number or other indication under which the applicant is so registered.

Nationality (Rules 4.5(a) and (b) and 18.1): For each applicant, the nationality must be indicated by the name or two-letter code of the State (that is, country) of which the person is a national. A legal entity constituted according to the national law of a State is considered a national of that State. The indication of the nationality is not required where a person is inventor only.

Residence (Rules 4.5(a) and (c) and 18.1): For each applicant, the residence must be indicated by the name or two-letter code of the State (that is, country) of which the person is a resident. If the State of residence is not indicated, it will be assumed to be the same as the State indicated in the address. Possession of a real and effective industrial or commercial establishment in a State is considered residence in that State. The indication of the residence is not required where a person is inventor only.

Names of States (Section 115): For the indication of names of States, the two-letter codes appearing in WIPO Standard ST.3 and in the *PCT Applicant's Guide*, Annex K, may be used.

BOX No. IV

Who Can Act as Agent? (Article 49 and Rule 83.1*bis*): For each of the receiving Offices, information as to who can act as agent is given in the *PCT Applicant's Guide*, Annex C.

Agent or Common Representative (Rules 4.7, 4.8, 90.1 and 90.2 and Section 108): Mark the applicable check-box in order to indicate whether the person named is (or has been) appointed as "agent" or "common representative" (the "common representative" must be one of the applicants). For the manner in which name(s), address(es) (including names of States), telephone, facsimile numbers and/or e-mail addresses must be indicated, see the notes to Boxes Nos. II and III. Where several agents are listed, the agent to whom correspondence should be addressed is to be listed first. If there are two or more applicants but no common agent is appointed to represent all of them, one of the applicants who is a national or resident of a PCT Contracting State may be appointed by the other applicants as their common representative. If this is not done, the applicant first named in the request who is entitled to file an international application with the receiving Office concerned will be considered to be the common representative.

Manner of Appointment of Agent or Common Representative (Rules 90.4 and 90.5 and Section 106): The appointment of an agent or a common representative may be effected by designating the agent or common representative in Box No. IV and by the applicant signing the request or a separate power of attorney. Where there are two or more applicants, the appointment of a common agent or common representative must be effected by each applicant signing, at his choice, the request or a separate power of attorney. If the separate power of attorney is not signed, or if the required separate power of attorney is missing, or if the indication of the name or address of the appointed person does not comply with Rule 4.4, the power of attorney will be considered non-existent unless the defect is corrected. However, the receiving Office may waive the requirement that a separate power of attorney be submitted to it (for details about each receiving Office, see the *PCT Applicant's Guide*, Annex C).

Where a general power of attorney has been filed and is referred to in the request, a copy thereof must be attached to the request. Any applicant who did not sign the general power of attorney must sign either the request or a separate power of attorney, unless the receiving Office has waived the requirement that a separate power of attorney be submitted to it (for details, see the *PCT Applicant's Guide*, Annex C).

Agent's Registration Number with the Office (Rule 4.7(b)): Where the agent is registered with the national or regional Office that is acting as receiving Office, the request may indicate the number or other indication under which the agent is so registered.

Address for Correspondence (Rule 4.4(d) and Section 108): Where an agent is appointed, any correspondence intended for the applicant will be sent to the address indicated for that agent (or for the first-mentioned agent, if more than one is appointed). Where one of two or more applicants is appointed as common representative, the address indicated for that applicant in Box No. IV will be used.

Where no agent or common representative is appointed, any correspondence will be sent to the address, indicated in Box No. II or III, of the applicant (if only one person is named as applicant) or of the applicant who is considered to be common representative (if there are two or more persons named as applicants). However, if the applicant wishes correspondence to be sent to a different address in such a case, that address must be indicated in Box No. IV instead of the designation of an agent or common representative. In this case, and only in this case, the last check-box of Box No. IV must be marked (that is, the last check-box must not be marked if either of the check-boxes "agent" or "common representative" has been marked).

Notes to the request form (PCT/RO/101) (page 2) (July 2015)

page 3

Telephone, Facsimile Numbers and/or E-mail Addresses
See Notes to Boxes Nos II and III.

BOX No. V

Designations (Regional and national patents) (Rule 4.9): Upon filing of the request, the applicant will obtain an automatic and all-inclusive coverage of all designations available under the PCT on the international filing date, in respect of every kind of protection available and, where applicable, in respect of both regional and national patents. If the applicant wishes the international application to be treated, in a certain designated or elected State, as an application not for a patent but for another kind of protection available under the national law of the designated or elected State concerned, the applicant will have to indicate his choice directly to the designated or elected Office when performing the acts, referred to in Articles 22 or 39(1), for entry into the national phase. For details about various kinds of protection available in designated or elected States, see the *PCT Applicant's Guide*, Annex B.

However, for the reasons explained below, it is possible to indicate, by marking the applicable check-box(es), that DE Germany, JP Japan and/or KR Republic of Korea are not designated for any kind of national protection. Each of those States has notified the International Bureau that Rule 4.9(b) applies to it since its national law provides that the filing of an international application which contains the designation of that State and claims the priority, **at the time of filing** or subsequently under Rule 26*bis*.1, of an earlier national application (for DE: for the same kind of protection) having effect in that State shall have the result that the earlier national application ceases, where applicable, after the expiration of certain time limits, to have effect with the same consequences as the withdrawal of the earlier national application. The designation of DE Germany for the purposes of a EP European patent is not affected by what is said above. For details see the *PCT Applicant's Guide*, in the relevant Annex B.

Only the three States mentioned above may be excluded from the all-inclusive coverage of all designations in Box No. V. For any other PCT Contracting State which the applicant wishes to exclude from the all-inclusive coverage of all designations, the applicant should submit a separate notice of withdrawal of the designation concerned under Rule 90*bis*.2. **Important: Should a notice of withdrawal be filed, that notice will have to be signed by the applicant or, if there are two or more applicants, by all of them (Rule 90*bis*.5), or by an agent or a common representative whose appointment has been effected by each applicant signing, at his choice, the request, the demand or a separate power of attorney (Rule 90.4(a)).**

BOX No. VI

Priority Claim(s) (Rule 4.10): If the priority of an earlier application is claimed, the declaration containing the priority claim must be made in the request.

The request must indicate the *date* on which the earlier application from which priority is claimed was filed and the *number* it was assigned. Note that that date must fall within the period of 12 months preceding the international filing date.

Where the earlier application is a national application, the *country* party to the Paris Convention for the Protection of Industrial Property, or the *Member* of the World Trade Organization that is not a party to that Convention, in which that earlier application was filed must be indicated. Where the earlier application is a regional application, the *regional Office* concerned must be indicated. Where the earlier application is an international application, the *receiving Office* with which that earlier application was filed must be indicated.

Where the earlier application is a regional application (see however below), or an international application, the priority claim may also, if the applicant so wishes, indicate one or more countries party to the Paris Convention for which that earlier

application was filed (Rule 4.10(b)(i)); such an indication is not, however, mandatory. Where the earlier application is a regional application and at least one of the countries party to the regional patent treaty is neither party to the Paris Convention nor a Member of the World Trade Organization, at least one country party to the Paris Convention or one Member of the World Trade Organization for which that earlier application was filed must be indicated (Rule 4.10(b)(ii)) in the Supplemental Box.

As to the possibility of correcting or adding a priority claim, see Rule 26*bis*.1 and the *PCT Applicant's Guide*, International Phase.

Restoration of the Right of Priority (Rules 4.1(c)(v) and 26*bis*.3): The procedure for restoration of the right of priority is not applicable to a receiving Office which has provided notice to the International Bureau under Rule 26*bis*.3(j) of the incompatibility of Rule 26*bis*.3(a) to (i) with the national law applied by that Office. Where the international application is filed on a date which is later than the date on which the priority period (see Rule 2.4) expired but within the period of two months from that date, the applicant may request the receiving Office to restore the right of priority (Rule 26*bis*.3). Such a request must be filed with the receiving Office within two months from the date on which the priority period expired; it may be included in the request (Rule 4.1(c)(v)) by identifying the priority claim(s) in Box No. VI. If, in Box No. VI, a priority claim is identified in respect of which a request to restore the right of priority is made, in such case, a separate document should be submitted entitled "Statement for Restoration of the Right of Priority". This separate document should indicate, for each earlier application concerned, the filing date, the earlier application number and the name or two-letter code of the country, Member of WTO, regional Office or receiving Office. Then, for each earlier application concerned, the applicant should state the reasons for the failure to file the international application within the priority period (Rules 26*bis*.3(a) and 26*bis*.3(b)(ii)). Note that such a request may be subjected by the receiving Office to the payment to it of a fee, payable within the time limit referred to above (Rule 26*bis*.3(e)). According to Rule 26*bis*.3(d), the time limit for payment of the fee may be extended, at the option of the receiving Office, for a period of up to two months from the expiration of the time limit applicable under Rule 26*bis*.3(e). Note further that the receiving Office may require the furnishing, within a reasonable time limit, of a declaration or other evidence in support of the statement of reasons; preferably, such declaration or other evidence should already be submitted to the receiving Office together with the request for restoration (Rule 26*bis*.3(b) and (f)). The receiving Office shall restore the right of priority if it finds that a criterion for restoration applied by the Office is satisfied (Rule 26*bis*.3(a)). For information on which criteria a receiving Office applies see the *PCT Applicant's Guide*, Annex C.

Incorporation by Reference (Rules 4.18 and 20): The procedure for incorporation by reference is not applicable to a receiving Office which has provided notice to the International Bureau under Rule 20.8(a) of the incompatibility of Rules 20.3(a)(ii) and (b)(ii), 20.5(a)(ii) and (d), and 20.6 with the national law applied by that Office. Where the receiving Office finds that any of the requirements of Article 11(1)(iii)(d) and (e) are not or appear not to be fulfilled, it will invite the applicant to either furnish the required correction or confirm that the element concerned referred to in Article 11(1)(iii)(d) or (e) is incorporated by reference under Rule 4.18. Where the applicant furnishes the required correction under Article 11(2), the international filing date will be the date on which the receiving Office receives the required correction (see Rule 20.3(a)(ii) and (b)(i)), provided that all other requirements of Article 11(1) are fulfilled. However, where the applicant confirms the incorporation by reference of an element referred to in Article 11(1)(iii)(d) or (e) which is completely contained in an earlier application the priority of which is claimed in the international application, that element will be considered to have been contained in the purported international application on the date on which one or more elements referred to in

page 4

Article 11(1)(iii) were first received by the receiving Office, and the international filing date will be the date on which all Article 11(1) requirements are fulfilled (see Rule 20.3(a)(ii) and (b)(ii)).

Where the applicant furnishes a missing part to the receiving Office after the date on which all of the requirements of Article 11(1) were fulfilled but within the applicable time limit under Rule 20.7, that part will be included in the international application and the international filing date will be corrected to the date on which the receiving Office received that part (see Rule 20.5(c)). In such a case, the applicant will be given the opportunity to request the receiving Office to disregard the missing part concerned, in which case the missing part would be considered not to have been furnished and the correction of the international filing date not to have been made (see Rule 20.5(e)). However, where the applicant confirms the incorporation by reference of a part of the description, claims or drawings under Rule 4.18 and the receiving Office finds that all the requirements of Rules 4.18 and 20.6(a) are complied with, that part will be considered to have been contained in the purported international application on the date on which one or more elements referred to in Article 11(1)(iii) were first received by the receiving Office, and the international filing date will be the date on which all of the requirements of Article 11(1) are fulfilled (see Rule 20.5).

Furnishing the priority document(s) (Rule 17.1): A certified copy of each earlier application the priority of which is claimed (priority document) must be submitted by the applicant, irrespective of whether that earlier application is a national, regional or international application. The priority document must be submitted to the receiving Office or to the International Bureau before the expiration of 16 months from the (earliest) priority date or, where an early start of the national phase is requested, not later than at the time such request is made. Any priority document received by the International Bureau after the expiration of the 16-month time limit but before the date of international publication shall be considered to have been received on the last day of that time limit (Rule 17.1(a)).

Where the priority document was issued by the receiving Office, the applicant may, instead of submitting the priority document, request the receiving Office (not later than 16 months after the priority date) to prepare and transmit the priority document to the International Bureau (Rule 4.1(c)(ii)). Such requests may be made by marking the applicable check-boxes in Box No. VI. Note that where such a request is made, the applicant must, where applicable, pay to the receiving Office the *fee for priority document*, otherwise, the request will be considered not to have been made (see Rule 17.1(b)).

Where the priority document is available from an Office that participates in the WIPO Digital Access Service for Priority Documents (DAS) (http://www.wipo.int/patentscope/en/priority_documents/offices.html), the applicant may use DAS to provide the priority document to the International Bureau. Once the applicant requests the depositing Office to provide a copy of the priority document to DAS (see *PCT Applicant's Guide*, Annex B of the DAS depositing Office for further indications of the procedure to be followed), the applicant will receive an access code. The applicant should then mark the applicable check-boxes in Box No. VI, and indicate the access code for each specific priority document. (For a transitional period, until all DAS accessing offices are using the system described above, the old system will continue to work, where the check-box to request retrieval from DAS can be selected without indicating the access code, as long as the applicant allows access to the priority document for the International Bureau using the access control list in the DAS applicant portal.)

Information concerning whether and which priority documents are available to the International Bureau from a digital library is published in the *Official Notices (PCT Gazette)* pursuant to Section 715(c) and the *PCT Applicant's Guide*, Annex B(IB).

Dates (Section 110): Dates must be indicated by the Arabic number of the day, the name of the month and the Arabic number of the year – in that order; after, below or above such indication, the date should be repeated in parentheses, using two-digit Arabic numerals each for the number of the day and for the number of the month followed by the number of the year in four digits, in that order and separated by periods, slants or hyphens, for example, "26 October 2012 (26.10.2012)", "26 October 2012 (26/10/2012)" or "26 October 2012 (26-10-2012)".

BOX No. VII

Choice of International Searching Authority (ISA) (Rules 4.1(b)(iv) and 4.14*bis*): If two or more International Searching Authorities are competent for carrying out the international search in relation to the international application – depending on the language in which that application is filed and the receiving Office with which it is filed – the name of the competent Authority chosen by the applicant must be indicated in the space provided, either by its full name or two-letter code.

Request to Use Results of Earlier Search; Reference to that Search (Rules 4.12, 12*bis*, 16.3 and 41.1). The applicant may request the ISA to take into account, in carrying out the international search, the results of an earlier search carried out either by that Authority, by another ISA or by a national Office (Rule 4.12). Where the applicant has made such a request and complied with the requirements under Rule 12*bis*, the ISA shall, to the extent possible, take into account the results of the earlier search. If, on the other hand, the earlier search was carried out by another ISA or by another national or regional Office, the ISA may, but is not obliged to, take the results of the earlier search into account (Rule 41.1). Where the ISA takes into account the results of an earlier search, it shall (partially) refund the search fee to the extent and under the conditions provided for in the agreement under Article 16(3)(b) (see, for each ISA, the *PCT Applicant's Guide*, Annex D).

Any request to take into account the results of an earlier search should identify: the filing date and number of the application in respect of which the earlier search was carried out and the Authority or Office which carried out the earlier search (Rules 4.1(b)(ii) and 4.12(i)).

The applicant shall submit to the receiving Office, together with the international application at the time of filing, a copy of the results of the earlier search (Rule 12*bis*.1(a)), except:

– where the earlier search was carried out by the same Office as that which is acting as the receiving Office, the applicant may, instead of submitting copies of the required documents, request the receiving Office to transmit copies of those documents to the ISA by marking the appropriate check-box (Rule 12*bis*.1(c));

– where the earlier search was carried out by the same Authority or Office as that which is acting as ISA, no copy or translation of any document (i.e. of the results of the earlier search or of the earlier application or of any document cited in the earlier search, where applicable) is required to be submitted (Rule 12*bis*.1(d));

– where a copy or translation of the earlier search is available to the ISA in a form and manner acceptable to it, and if so indicated in the request form by the applicant by marking the appropriate check-box, no copy or translation of any document is required to be submitted to the ISA (Rule 12*bis*.1(f));

– where the request form contains a statement under Rule 4.12(ii) that the international application is the same, or substantially the same, as an application in respect of which the earlier search was carried out, or that the international application is the same, or substantially the same, as that earlier application, except that it is filed in a different language, no copy of the earlier application or its translation is required to be transmitted to the ISA (Rules 4.12(ii) and 12*bis*.1(e)).

Use of Results of more than one Earlier Search: Where the ISA is requested to use the results of more than one earlier search, the check-boxes in Box No. VII should be marked, as applicable, for each earlier search. Where *more than two results of previous searches are indicated*, please mark the relevant check-box, and furnish duplicates of this page, marked "continuation sheet for Box No. VII" and attached to the request form.

BOX No. VIII

Declarations Containing Standardized Wording (Rules 4.1(c)(iii) and 4.17): At the option of the applicant, the request may, for the purposes of the national law applicable in one or more designated States, contain one or more of the following declarations:

(i)   declaration as to the identity of the inventor;

(ii) declaration as to the applicant's entitlement, as at the international filing date, to apply for and be granted a patent;

(iii) declaration as to the applicant's entitlement, as at the international filing date, to claim the priority of the earlier application;

(iv) declaration of inventorship (only for the purposes of the designation of the United States of America);

(v)   declaration as to non-prejudicial disclosures or exceptions to lack of novelty;

which must conform to the standardized wording provided for in Sections 211 to 215, respectively, and which must be set forth in Boxes Nos. VIII (i) to (v), as detailed below. Where any such declarations are included, the appropriate check-boxes in Box No. VIII should be marked and the number of each type of declaration should be indicated in the right-hand column. As to the possibility of correcting or adding a declaration, see Rule 26*ter*, Section 216 and the *PCT Applicant's Guide*, International Phase.

If the circumstances of a particular case are such that the standardized wordings are not applicable, the applicant should not attempt to make use of the declarations provided for in Rule 4.17 but rather will have to comply with the national requirements concerned upon entry into the national phase.

The fact that a declaration is made under Rule 4.17 does not of itself establish the matters declared; the effect of those matters in the designated States concerned will be determined by the designated Offices in accordance with the applicable national law.

Even if the wording of a declaration does not conform to the standardized wording provided for in the Administrative Instructions pursuant to Rule 4.17, any designated Office may accept that declaration for the purposes of the applicable national law, but is not required to do so.

Details as to National Law Requirements: For information on the declarations required by each designated Office, see the *PCT Applicant's Guide*, in the relevant National Chapter.

Effect in Designated Offices (Rule 51*bis*.2): Where the applicant submits any of the declarations provided for in Rule 4.17(i) to (iv) containing the required standardized wording (either with the international application, or to the International Bureau within the relevant time limit under Rule 26*ter*, or directly to the designated Office during the national phase), the designated Office may not, in the national phase, require further documents or evidence on the matter to which the declaration relates, unless that designated Office may reasonably doubt the veracity of the declaration concerned.

Incompatibility of Certain Items of Rule 51*bis*.2(a) with National Laws (Rule 51*bis*.2(c)): Certain designated Offices have informed the International Bureau that the applicable national law is not compatible in respect of certain declarations provided in Rule 4.17(i), (ii) and (iii). Those designated

Offices are therefore entitled to require further documents or evidence on the matters to which those declarations relate. For regularly updated information on such Offices, see the WIPO website: http://www.wipo.int/pct/en/texts/reservations/res_incomp.html.

BOXES Nos. VIII (i) TO (v)
(IN GENERAL)

Different Declaration Boxes: There are six different declaration boxes in the pre-printed request form – one box for each of the five different types of declarations provided for in Rule 4.17 (Box No. VIII (i) to Box No. VIII (v)) and a continuation sheet (Continuation of Box No. VIII (i) to (v)) to be used in case any single declaration does not fit in the corresponding box. The title of each type of declaration which is found in the standardized wording provided for in the Administrative Instructions is pre-printed on the appropriate sheet of the request.

Separate Sheet for Each Declaration: Each declaration must start on a separate sheet of the request form in the appropriate Declaration Box.

Titles, Items, Item Numbers, Dotted Lines, Words in Parentheses and Words in Brackets: The prescribed standardized wording of the declarations includes titles, various items, item numbers, dotted lines, words in parentheses and words in brackets. Except for Box No. VIII (iv) which contains the pre-printed standardized wording, only those items which are applicable should be included in a declaration where necessary to support the statements in that declaration (that is, omit those items which do not apply) and item numbers need not be included. Dotted lines indicate where information is required to be inserted. Words in parentheses are instructions to applicants as to the information which may be included in the declaration depending upon the factual circumstances. Words in brackets are optional and should appear in the declaration without the brackets if they apply; if they do not apply, they should be omitted together with the corresponding brackets.

Naming of Several Persons: More than one person may be named in a single declaration. In the alternative, with one exception, a separate declaration may be made for each person. With respect to the declaration of inventorship set forth in Box No. VIII (iv), which is applicable only for the purposes of the designation of the United States of America, all inventors must be indicated in a single declaration (see Notes to Box No. VIII (iv), below). The wording of declarations to be set forth in Boxes Nos. VIII (i), (ii), (iii) and (v) may be adapted from the singular to the plural as necessary.

BOX No. VIII (i)

Declaration as to the Identity of the Inventor (Rule 4.17(i) and Section 211): The declaration must be worded as follows:

"Declaration as to the identity of the inventor (Rules 4.17(i) and 51*bis*.1(a)(i)):

in relation to [this] international application [No. PCT/...],

... *(name)* of ... *(address)* is the inventor of the subject matter for which protection is sought by way of [the] [this] international application"

Such a declaration is not necessary in respect of any inventor who is indicated as such (either as inventor only or applicant and inventor) in Box No. II or No. III in accordance with Rule 4.5 or 4.6. However, where the inventor is indicated as applicant in Box No. II or No. III in accordance with Rule 4.5, a declaration as to the applicant's entitlement to apply for and be granted a patent (Rule 4.17(ii)) may be appropriate. Where indications regarding the inventor in accordance with Rule 4.5 or 4.6 are not included in Box No. II or No. III, this declaration may be combined with the prescribed wording of the declaration as to the applicant's entitlement to apply for and be granted a patent (Rule 4.17(ii)). For details on such a combined declaration, see Notes to Box No. VIII (ii), below. For details as to the declaration of inventorship for the purposes of the designation of the United States of America, see Notes to Box No. VIII (iv), below.

BOX No. VIII (ii)

Declaration as to the Applicant's Entitlement to Apply for and Be Granted a Patent (Rule 4.17(ii) and Section 212): The declaration must be worded as follows, with such inclusion, omission, repetition and re-ordering of the matters listed as items (i) to (viii) as is necessary to explain the applicant's entitlement:

"Declaration as to the applicant's entitlement, as at the international filing date, to apply for and be granted a patent (Rules 4.17(ii) and 51*bis*.1(a)(ii)), in a case where the declaration under Rule 4.17(iv) is not appropriate:

in relation to [this] international application [No. PCT/...],

... *(name)* is entitled to apply for and be granted a patent by virtue of the following:

(i)   ... *(name)* of ... *(address)* is the inventor of the subject matter for which protection is sought by way of [the] [this] international application

(ii) ... *(name)* [is] [was] entitled as employer of the inventor, ... *(inventor's name)*

(iii) an agreement between ... *(name)* and ... *(name)*, dated ...

(iv) an assignment from ... *(name)* to ... *(name)*, dated ...

(v)   consent from ... *(name)* in favor of ... *(name)*, dated ...

(vi) a court order issued by ... *(name of court)*, effecting a transfer from ... *(name)* to ... *(name)*, dated ...

(vii) transfer of entitlement from ... *(name)* to ... *(name)* by way of ... *(specify kind of transfer)*, dated ...

(viii) the applicant's name changed from ... *(name)* on ... *(date)*"

Items (i) to (viii) may be incorporated as is necessary to explain the applicant's entitlement. *This declaration is only applicable to those events which have occurred prior to the international filing date.* The possible kinds of transfer of entitlement in item (vii) include merger, acquisition, inheritance, donation, etc. Where there has been a succession of transfers from the inventor, the order in which transfers are listed should follow the actual succession of transfers, and items may be included more than once, as necessary to explain the applicant's entitlement. Where the inventor is not indicated in Box No. II or No. III, this declaration may be presented as a combined declaration explaining the applicant's entitlement to apply for and be granted a patent and identifying the inventor. In such a case, the introductory phrase of the declaration must be as follows:

"Combined declaration as to the applicant's entitlement, as at the international filing date, to apply for and be granted a patent (Rules 4.17(ii) and 51*bis*.1(a)(ii)) and as to the identity of the inventor (Rules 4.17(i) and 51*bis*.1(a)(i)), in a case where the declaration under Rule 4.17(iv) is not appropriate:"

The remainder of the combined declaration must be worded as indicated in the preceeding paragraphs.

For details as to the declaration as to the identity of the inventor, see the Notes to Box No. VIII (i), above.

BOX No. VIII (iii)

Declaration as to the Applicant's Entitlement to Claim Priority of the Earlier Application (Rule 4.17(iii) and Section 213): The declaration must be worded as follows,

with such inclusion, omission, repetition and re-ordering of the matters listed as items (i) to (viii) as is necessary to explain the applicant's entitlement:

"Declaration as to the applicant's entitlement, as at the international filing date, to claim the priority of the earlier application specified below, where the applicant is not the applicant who filed the earlier application or where the applicant's name has changed since the filing of the earlier application (Rules 4.17(iii) and 51*bis*.1(a)(iii)):

in relation to [this] international application [No. PCT/...],

... *(name)* is entitled to claim priority of earlier application No. ... by virtue of the following:

(i)   the applicant is the inventor of the subject matter for which protection was sought by way of the earlier application

(ii)   ... *(name)* [is] [was] entitled as employer of the inventor, ... *(inventor's name)*

(iii) an agreement between ... *(name)* and ... *(name)*, dated ...

(iv)   an assignment from ... *(name)* to ... *(name)*, dated ...

(v)   consent from ... *(name)* in favor of ... *(name)*, dated ...

(vi)   a court order, issued by ... *(name of court)*, effecting a transfer from ... *(name)* to ... *(name)*, dated ...

(vii) transfer of entitlement from ... *(name)* to ... *(name)* by way of ... *(specify kind of transfer)*, dated ...

(viii) the applicant's name changed from ... *(name)* to ... *(name)* on ... *(date)*"

Items (i) to (viii) may be incorporated as is necessary to explain the applicant's entitlement. *This declaration is only applicable to those events which have occurred prior to the international filing date.* In addition, this declaration is only applicable where the person or name of the applicant is different from that of the applicant who filed the earlier application from which priority is claimed. For example, this declaration may be applicable where only one applicant out of five is different from the applicants indicated in respect of an earlier application. The possible kinds of transfer of entitlement in item (vii) include merger, acquisition, inheritance, donation, etc. Where there has been a succession of transfers from the applicant in respect of the earlier application, the order in which transfers are listed should follow the actual succession of transfers, and items may be included more than once, as necessary to explain the applicant's entitlement.

BOX No. VIII (iv)

Declaration of Inventorship (Rule 4.17(iv) and Section 214): The standardized wording for the declaration is pre-printed in Box No. VIII (iv).

The name, residence and address must be included for each inventor. If the name and address of an inventor is not written in the Latin alphabet, the name and address must be indicated in the Latin alphabet. All inventors must sign and date the declaration even if they do not all sign the same copy of the declaration (Section 214(b)).

If there are more than three inventors, those other inventors must be indicated on the "Continuation of Box No. VIII (i) to (v)" sheet. The continuation sheet should be entitled "Continuation of Box No. VIII (iv)," must indicate the name, residence and address for those other inventors, and at least the name and address in the Latin alphabet. In such a case, the "complete declaration" includes Box No. VIII (iv) and the continuation sheet. All inventors must sign and date a complete declaration even if they do not all sign the same copy of the complete declaration, and a copy of each separately signed complete declaration must be submitted (Section 214(b)).

Where the declaration was not included in the request, but **is furnished later**, the PCT application number MUST be indicated within the text of Box No. VIII (iv).

BOX No. VIII (v)

Declaration as to Non-prejudicial Disclosures or Exceptions to Lack of Novelty (Rule 4.17(v) and Section 215): The declaration must be worded as follows, with such inclusion, omission, repetition and re-ordering of the matters listed as items (i) to (iv) as is necessary:

"Declaration as to non-prejudicial disclosures or exceptions to lack of novelty (Rules 4.17(v) and 51*bis*.1(a)(v)):

in relation to [this] international application [No. PCT/...],

... *(name)* declares that the subject matter claimed in [the] [this] international application was disclosed as follows:

   (i)   kind of disclosure *(include as applicable)*:
        (a) international exhibition
        (b) publication
        (c) abuse
        (d) other: ... *(specify)*
  (ii) date of disclosure: ...
 (iii) title of disclosure *(if applicable)*: ...
 (iv) place of disclosure *(if applicable)*: ...."

Either (a), (b), (c) or (d) of item (i) should always be included in the declaration. Item (ii) should also always be included in the declaration. Items (iii) and (iv) may be incorporated depending upon the circumstances.

BOX No. IX

Sheets Constituting the International Application: The number of sheets of the various parts of the international application must be indicated in the check list using Arabic numerals. Sheets containing any of the Boxes Nos. VIII(i) to (v) (declaration sheets) must be counted as part of the request. It is noted that any tables, including those related to a sequence listing, should be an integral part of the description and the pages containing such tables will be counted as sheets of the international application. There is no longer any provision for submission of those tables separately or a reduced fee for such a submission.

Nucleotide and/or amino acid sequences: Paper Filings: Where the international application is filed on paper (using the sheet "last sheet - paper") and contains disclosure of one or more nucleotide and/or amino acid sequences, a sequence listing must be presented as a separate part of the description ("sequence listing part of description") in accordance with the standard contained in Annex C of the Administrative Instructions, that is, in compliance with WIPO Standard ST.25. The number of pages of the sequence listing must be indicated under item (f) in Box No. IX and included in the total number of sheets. Furthermore, where the sequence listing is filed on paper, a copy of the sequence listing in the form of an Annex C/ST.25 text file saved on physical data carrier(s) (together with the required statement) should accompany the international application, if so required by the ISA but **only** for the purposes of international search under Rule 13*ter*. In such cases therefore, check-boxes Nos. 8 and 9 must be marked in Box No. IX. In addition, the type and number of carriers such as diskettes, CD-ROMs, CD-Rs or other data carriers accepted by the ISA, should be indicated in item 8.

For EFS-Web filing with RO/US

Nucleotide and/or amino acid sequences: Electronic Filings via EFS-Web with RO/US: There exist two alternative last sheets of the request form which contain two distinct

Boxes No. IX. The sheet "last sheet – paper", described earlier, should be used if the applicant intends to file the international application on paper. The sheet "last sheet – EFS" should **only** be used if the request form is filed online with the receiving Office of the United States of America via EFS-Web.

(a) EFS-Web and text file: Where the international application is filed via EFS-Web (using the sheet "last sheet - EFS") and contains disclosure of one or more nucleotide and/or amino acid sequences, a sequence listing must be presented as a separate part of the description ("sequence listing part of description") in accordance with the standard contained in Annex C of the Administrative Instructions, that is, in compliance with WIPO Standard ST.25. The sequence listing should **preferably** be furnished as an Annex C/ST.25 text file; in such cases, the first check-box of check-box (g) in Box No. IX should be marked. When furnished in this manner, the number of sheets of the sequence listing is **not** included in the total number of sheets making up the international application. Whenever the sequence listing is furnished as an Annex C/ST.25 text file, there is no need to file another copy of the text file for search purposes under Rule 13*ter* since the text file submitted will be used for both disclosure of the international application and for search purposes.

(b) EFS-Web and image file: If the sequence listing is filed online via EFS-Web as an image file (e.g. PDF file) rather than the recommended text file, the corresponding boxes in check-box (f) in Box No. IX should be marked. The number of sheets of the sequence listing **must** be included in the total number of sheets making up the international application. Where the sequence listing is filed in image format, a copy of the sequence listing in the form of an Annex C/ST.25 text file (together with the required statement) should accompany the international application, if so required by the ISA but **only** for the purposes of international search under Rule 13*ter*. In such cases, check-boxes Nos. 8 and 9 must be marked in Box No. IX.

(c) EFS-Web and physical data carriers: The receiving Office of the United States of America has two distinct limitations on the size of the sequence listing file it can accept via EFS-Web. If the text file containing the sequence listing is larger than 100MB, or if the image file (e.g. PDF file) containing the sequence listing is larger than 25MB, the applicant must file the sequence listings as an Annex C/ST.25 text file on physical data carrier(s). The receiving Office does not accept the filing of image (e.g. PDF file) on physical data carrier(s). In such cases, the data carrier(s) must be furnished on the same day that the international application is filed online. This may be furnished via "Express Mail Post Office to Addressee" with a date-in by the United States Postal Service the same date as the online filing date, or via commercial delivery services or by hand, provided that it reaches the receiving Office on the same day as the international application filed online. In such cases, the corresponding check-boxes in check-box (g) in Box No. IX must be marked. The number and type of carrier(s) should be indicated in check-box (g). Whenever the sequence listing is furnished as an Annex C/ST.25 text file, there is no need to file another copy of the text file for search purposes under Rule 13*ter* since the text file submitted will be used for both disclosure of the international application and for search purposes.

Items Accompanying the International Application: Where the international application is accompanied by certain items, the applicable check-boxes must be marked, any applicable indication must be made on the dotted line after the applicable item, and the number of such items should be indicated at the end of the relevant line; detailed explanations are provided below only in respect of those items which so require.

Check-box No. 4: Mark this check-box where a copy of a general power of attorney is filed with the international application; where the general power of attorney has been deposited with the receiving Office, and that Office has accorded to it a reference number, that number may be indicated.

Check-box No. 6: Mark this check-box where a translation of the international application for the purposes of international search (Rule 12.3) is filed together with the international application and indicate the language of that translation.

Check-box No. 7: Mark this check-box where a filled-in Form PCT/RO/134 or any separate sheet containing indications concerning deposited microorganisms and/or other biological material is filed with the international application. If Form PCT/RO/134 or any sheet containing the said indications is included as one of the sheets of the description (as required by certain designated States (see the *PCT Applicant's Guide*, Annex L)), do not mark this check-box (for further information, see Rule 13*bis* and Section 209).

Check-boxes Nos. 8 and 9: Where the sequence listing part of the description is submitted on paper, a copy of the sequence listing in the form of an Annex C/ST.25 text file (together with the required statement) should accompany the international application, if so required by the ISA, but **only** for the purposes of international search under Rule 13*ter*. In this case, check-boxes Nos. 8 and 9, must be marked in Box No. IX.

Language of Filing of the International Application (Rules 12.1(a) and 20.4(c) and (d)): With regard to the language in which the international application is filed, for the purposes of according an international filing date, it is, subject to the following sentence, sufficient that the description and the claims are in the language, or one of the languages, accepted by the receiving Office for the filing of international applications; that language should be indicated in that check-box (as regards the language of the abstract and any text matter in the drawings, see Rule 26.3*ter*(a) and (b); as regards the language of the request, see Rules 12.1(c) and 26.3*ter*(c) and (d)). Note that where the international application is filed with the United States Patent and Trademark Office as receiving Office, all elements of the international application (request, description, claims, abstract, text matter of drawings) must, for the purposes of according an international filing date, be in English except that the free text in any sequence listing part of the description, complying with the standard set out in Annex C of the Administrative Instructions, may be in a language other than English.

BOX No. X

Signature (Rules 4.1(d), 4.15, 26.2*bis*(a), 51*bis*.1(a)(vi) and 90): The signature must be that of the applicant; if there are several applicants, all must sign. However, if the signature of one or more of the applicants is missing, the receiving Office will not invite the applicant to furnish the missing signature(s) provided that at least one of the applicants signed the request.

Important: Should a notice of withdrawal be filed at any time during the international phase, that notice will have to be signed by the applicant or, if there are two or more applicants by all of them (Rule 90*bis*.5), or by an agent or a common representative whose appointment has been effected by each applicant signing, at his choice, the request, the demand, a separate power of attorney (Rule 90.4(a)) or a general power of attorney (Rule 90.5(a)).

Furthermore, for the purposes of the national phase processing, each designated Office will be entitled to require the applicant to furnish the confirmation of the international application by the signature of any applicant for the designated State concerned, who has not signed the request.

Where the signature on the request is not that of the applicant but that of the agent, or the common representative, a separate power of attorney appointing the agent or the common representative, respectively, or a copy of a general

power of attorney already in the possession of the receiving Office, must be furnished. The power of attorney must be signed by the applicant, or if there is more than one applicant, by at least one of them. If the power is not filed with the request, the receiving Office will invite the applicant to furnish it, unless it has waived the requirement for a separate power of attorney (for details about each receiving Office, see the *PCT Applicant's Guide*, Annex C).

SUPPLEMENTAL BOX

The cases in which the Supplemental Box may be used and the manner of making indications in it are explained in the left column of that Box.

Items 2 and 3: Even if an indication is made in respect of items 2 and 3 under Rule 49*bis*.1(a), (b) or (d), the applicant will be required to make an indication to this effect upon entry into the national phase before the designated offices concerned.

If the applicant wishes to specify that the international application be treated in any designated State as an application for a utility model, see Notes to Box No. V.

GENERAL REMARKS

Language of Correspondence (Rule 92.2 and Section 104): Any letter from the applicant to the receiving Office must be in the language of filing of the international application provided that, where the international application is to be published in the language of a translation required under Rule 12.3, such letter should be in the language of that translation; however, the receiving Office may authorize the use of another language.

Any letter from the applicant to the International Bureau must be in the same language as the international application if that language is English or French; otherwise, it must be in English or French, at the choice of the applicant.

Any letter from the applicant to the ISA must be in the same language as the international application, provided that, where a translation of the international application for the purposes of international search has been transmitted under Rule 23.1(b), such letter is in the language of that translation. However, the ISA may authorize the use of another language.

Arrangement of Elements and Numbering of Sheets of the International Application (Rule 11.7 and Section 207): The elements of the international application must be placed in the following order: the request, the description (excluding the sequence listing part, if any), the claim(s), the abstract, the drawings (if any), the sequence listing part of the description (if any).

All sheets of the description (excluding the sequence listing part), claims and abstract must be numbered in consecutive Arabic numerals, which must be placed at the top or bottom of the sheet, in the middle, but not in the margin which must remain blank. The number of each sheet of the drawings must consist of two Arabic numerals separated by an oblique stroke, the first being the sheet number and the second being the total number of sheets of drawings (for example, 1/3, 2/3, 3/3). For numbering of the sheets of the sequence listing part of the description, see Section 207.

Indication of the Applicant's or Agent's File Reference on the sheets of the description (excluding the sequence listing part, if any), claim(s), abstract, drawings and sequence listing part of the description (Rule 11.6(f)): The file reference indicated on the request may also be indicated in the left-hand corner of the top margin, within 1.5 cm from the top of any sheet of the international application.

This sheet is not part of and does not count as a sheet of the international application.

PCT

FEE CALCULATION SHEET

Annex to the Request

For receiving Office use only

International Application No.

Applicant's or agent's
file reference

Date stamp of the receiving Office

Applicant

CALCULATION OF PRESCRIBED FEES

(Applicants may be entitled to a reduction of certain fees as indicated in the PCT Fee Tables
(http://www.wipo.int/pct/en/fees.pdf))

1. TRANSMITTAL FEE: .... [T]

2. SEARCH FEE: .... [S]

   International search to be carried out by: _____

3. INTERNATIONAL FILING FEE

   Enter total number of sheets indicated in Box No IX: _____

   [i1] Fixed amount for the first 30 sheets . . . . [i1]

   [i2] _____ x _____ = [i2]
        number of sheets   fee per sheet
        in excess of 30

   Add amounts entered at i1 and i2 and enter total at I: .... [I]

   (Applicants from certain States are entitled to a reduction of 90% of the international filing fee (see
   http://www.wipo.int/pct/en/fees/fee_reduction.pdf). Where the applicant is (or all applicants are) so entitled,
   the total to be entered at I is 10% of the international filing fee.)

4. FEE FOR PRIORITY DOCUMENT *(if applicable)*: .... [P]

5. FEE FOR RESTORATION OF THE RIGHT OF PRIORITY *(if*
   applicable): .... [RP]

6. FEE FOR EARLIER SEARCH DOCUMENTS *(if applicable)*: .... [ES]

7. TOTAL FEES PAYABLE . . . .

   Add amounts entered at T, S, I, P, RP and ES,
   and enter total in the TOTAL box

   TOTAL

MODE OF PAYMENT *(Not all modes of payment may be available at all receiving Offices)*

☐ credit card *(details should*
not be included on this sheet)   ☐ authorization to charge deposit
or current account (see below)   ☐ bank transfer   ☐ cash

☐ postal money order   ☐ check   ☐ revenue stamps   ☐ other *(specify)*:

AUTHORIZATION TO CHARGE (OR CREDIT) DEPOSIT OR CURRENT ACCOUNT
(This mode of payment may not be available at all receiving Offices)

Receiving Office: RO/ _____

Deposit or Current Account No.: _____

☐ Authorization to charge the total fees indicated above.

☐ *(This check-box may be marked only if the conditions for deposit or current*
accounts of the receiving Office so permit) Authorization to charge any
deficiency or credit any overpayment in the total fees indicated above.

☐ Authorization to charge the fee for priority document.

Date: _____

Name: _____

Signature: _____

Form PCT/RO/101 (Annex) (July 2015)

See Notes to the fee calculation sheet

NOTES TO THE FEE CALCULATION SHEET
(ANNEX TO FORM PCT/RO/101)

The purpose of the fee calculation sheet is to help the applicant to identify the prescribed fees and to calculate the amounts to be paid. It is strongly recommended that the applicant complete the sheet by entering the appropriate amounts in the boxes provided and submit the fee calculation sheet at the time of filing the international application. This will help the receiving Office to verify the calculations and to identify any error in them.

Information about the applicable fees payable can be obtained from the receiving Office and the International Bureau at http://www.wipo.int/pct/en/fees.pdf. The amounts of the international filing and search fees may change due to currency fluctuations. Applicants are advised to check what are the latest applicable amounts. All fees, must be paid within one month from the date of receipt of the international application.

CALCULATION OF PRESCRIBED FEES

Box T: Transmittal Fee for the benefit of the receiving Office (Rule 14.1): The amount of the transmittal fee, if any, is fixed by the receiving Office. It must be paid within one month from the date of receipt of the international application by the receiving Office. Information about this fee is contained in the *PCT Applicant's Guide*, Annex C.

Box S: Search Fee for the benefit of the International Searching Authority (ISA) (Rule 16.1): The amount of the search fee is fixed by the ISA. It must be paid within one month from the date of receipt of the international application by the receiving Office. Information about this fee is contained in the *PCT Applicant's Guide*, Annex D.

Where two or more ISAs are competent, the applicant must indicate his choice in the space provided for this purpose and pay the amount of the international search fee fixed by the ISA chosen. Information on the competent ISA and whether the applicant has a choice between two or more ISAs is contained in the *PCT Applicant's Guide*, Annex C.

Box I: International Filing Fee: The amount of the international filing fee depends on the number of sheets of the international application indicated in Box No. IX of the request as explained below.

That number is the **Total number of sheets** indicated in Box No. IX of the request, which includes the actual number of sheets of the sequence listing part of the description, if the listing is filed on paper and not as an Annex C/ST.25 text file.

For EFS-Web filing with RO/US

Nucleotide and/or amino acid sequences: via EFS-Web: Where the international application is filed via EFS-Web and contains a sequence listing filed in an Annex C/ST.25 text file, even when, due to the size of the text file, the sequence listing has to be submitted on a data carrier, no fee is due for filing the sequence listing.

Where the sequences listing is an image file (e.g. PDF) the actual number of sheets that make up this part of the description must be included.

The international filing fee must be paid within one month from the date of receipt of the international application by the receiving Office.

Reductions: Applicants may be entitled to reductions to certain fees, which are indicated in the PCT Fee Tables (http://www.wipo.int/pct/en/fees.pdf) and the relevant Annex C of the *PCT Applicants Guide*. If reduced fees apply, the reduced amount should be indicated in the fee calculation sheet. These include reductions that apply where the international application is filed in electronic form and/or if the

applicant is a natural person from certain States. These two types of fees reduction are fully explained below.

Reduction of the International Filing Fee Where the International Application Is Filed in Electronic Form: Where the international application is filed in electronic form, the total amount of the international filing fee is reduced depending on the electronic formats used. The international filing fee is reduced by: 100 Swiss francs (or the equivalent in the currency in which the international filing fee is paid to the receiving Office) in respect of international applications where the request is not in character coded format (see PCT Schedule of Fees, item 4(b)); 200 Swiss francs (or the equivalent in the currency in which the international filing fee is paid to the receiving Office) where the request is in character coded format (see PCT Schedule of Fees, item 4(c)); and 300 Swiss francs (or the equivalent in the currency in which the international filing fee is paid to the receiving Office) where the request, description, claims and abstract are all in character coded format (see PCT Schedule of Fees, item 4(d)). For further details, see the *PCT Applicant's Guide*, International Phase and Annex C, as well as information published in the *Official Notices (PCT Gazette)* and the *PCT Newsletter*. Since international applications filed in electronic form will contain the Request Form and Fee Calculation Sheet in such electronic form, no provision is made for this fee reduction in the Fee Calculation Sheet annexed to Form PCT/RO/101.

Reduction of the International Filing Fee for Applicants from Certain States: An applicant who is a natural person and who is a national of and resides in a State that is listed as being a State whose per capita gross domestic product is below US$ 25,000 (according to the most recent ten year average per capita gross domestic product figures at constant 2005 US$ values published by the United Nations), and whose nationals and residents who are natural persons have filed less than 10 international applications per year (per million population) or less than 50 international applications per year (in absolute numbers) according to the most recent 5-year average yearly filing figures published by the International Bureau; or an applicant, whether a natural person or not, who is a national of and resides in a State that is listed as being classified by the United Nations as a least developed country, is entitled, in accordance with the Schedule of Fees, to a reduction of 90% of certain PCT fees including the international filing fee. If there are several applicants, each must satisfy the above-mentioned criteria. The reduction of the international filing fee will be automatically available to any applicant (or applicants) who is (or are) so entitled on the basis of the indications of name, nationality and residence given in Boxes Nos. II and III of the request.

The fee reduction is available even if one or more of the applicants are not from PCT Contracting States, provided that each of them is a national and resident of a State that meets the above-mentioned requirements and that at least one of the applicants is a national or resident of a PCT Contracting State and thus is entitled to file an international application.

page 2

Information about PCT Contracting States whose nationals and residents are entitled to a reduction of 90% of certain PCT fees, including the international filing fee, is contained in the *PCT Applicant's Guide*, Annex C and on the WIPO website (see http://www.wipo.int/pct/en/), and is also published and regularly updated in the *Official Notices (PCT Gazette)* and the *PCT Newsletter*.

Calculation of the International Filing Fee in Case of Fee Reduction: Where the applicant is (or all applicants are) entitled to a reduction of the international filing fee, the total to be entered in box I is 10% of the international filing fee (see below).

Box P: Fee for Priority Document (Rule 17.1(b)): Where the applicant has requested, by marking the applicable check-box in Box No. VI of the request, that the receiving Office prepare and transmit to the International Bureau a certified copy of the earlier application the priority of which is claimed, the amount of the fee prescribed by the receiving Office for such service may be entered (for information, see the *PCT Applicant's Guide*, Annex C).

If that fee is not paid at the latest before the expiration of 16 months from the priority date, the receiving Office may consider the request under Rule 17.1(b) as not having been made.

Box RP: Fee for the restoration of the right of priority (Rule 26*bis*.3(d)): Where the applicant has requested within the applicable time limit under Rule 26*bis*.3(e) that the receiving Office restore the right of priority in connection with any earlier application the priority of which is claimed in the international application, the amount of the fee prescribed by the receiving Office for such service may be entered (for information, see the *PCT Applicant's Guide*, Annex C).

Box ES: Fee for earlier search documents (Rule 12*bis*.1(c)): Where the applicant has requested, by marking the appropriate check-box in Box No. VII of the request, that the receiving Office prepare and transmit to the ISA copies of the documents in connection with an earlier search, the results of which are requested by the applicant to be taken into consideration by the ISA (such a request may only be filed if the earlier search was carried out by the same Office as that which is acting as the receiving Office (Rule 12*bis*.1(c))), the amount of the fee prescribed by the receiving Office for such service may be entered (for information, see the *PCT Applicant's Guide*, Annex C).

Total Box: The total of the amounts entered in boxes T, S, I, P, RP and ES should be entered in this box. If the applicant so wishes, the currency, or currencies, in which the fees are paid may be indicated next to or in the total box.

MODE OF PAYMENT

In order to help the receiving Office identify the mode of payment of the prescribed fees, it is recommended that the applicable check-box(es) be marked. Credit card details should not be included on the fee calculation sheet. They should be furnished separately and by secure means acceptable to the receiving Office.

AUTHORIZATION TO CHARGE (OR CREDIT) DEPOSIT OR CURRENT ACCOUNT

The receiving Office will not charge (or credit) fees to deposit or current accounts unless the deposit or current account authorization is signed and indicates the deposit or current account number.

PATENT COOPERATION TREATY

PCT

LIST OF DOCUMENTS FILED WITH THE
INTERNATIONAL BUREAU
AS RECEIVING OFFICE

To:

The International Bureau of WIPO
PCT Receiving Office Section
34, chemin des Colombettes
1211 Geneva 20
Switzerland

Facsimile No. +41 22 910 06 10

Applicant's or agent's file reference		

International application No. *(if known)*	International filing date *(day/month/year)* *(if known)*	(Earliest) Priority date *(day/month/year)*

Applicant

Title of invention

The applicant hereby requests the International Bureau to acknowledge to the following person *(include full name, address, facsimile No. and telephone No.)*:

the receipt by the following means:

☐ mail *(surface, air mail, registered)*   ☐ delivery service   ☐ facsimile transmission   ☐ hand delivery

of the documents/elements listed below:

☐ PCT request (including declaration sheets)   (pages)

☐ description (excluding sequence listing and/or tables relating thereto) (pages)

☐ claims   (pages)

☐ abstract   (pages)

☐ drawings   (pages)

☐ sequence listing and/or tables relating thereto   (pages)

☐ fee calculation sheet

☐ separate authorization to charge deposit account

☐ cheque *(indicate currency and amount)*

☐ cash *(in person only) (indicate amount)*

☐ power of attorney *(general power, copy of general power, separate power) (indicate kind and number)*

☐ priority document *(if more than one, indicate number)*

☐ separate indications concerning deposited microorganism or other biological material (pages)

☐ sequence listing and/or tables relating thereto in electronic form *(indicate type and number of carriers)*

☐ statement accompanying sequence listing and/or tables relating thereto in electronic form *(if more than one, indicate number)*

☐ accompanying letter

☐ other *(specify)*:

Form PCT/RO/198 (RO/IB) (16 September 2012)

PATENT COOPERATION TREATY

PCT

ACKNOWLEDGEMENT OF RECEIPT OF
DOCUMENTS FILED WITH THE
INTERNATIONAL BUREAU
AS RECEIVING OFFICE

To:

Date of mailing *(day/month/year)*	Facsimile No.:
Applicant's or agent's file reference	**IMPORTANT COMMUNICATION**
International application No.	Date of receipt/International filing date *(day/month/year)*

Applicant

Title of invention

1. The International Bureau has received the documents/elements listed below on: _____
   by the following means:

   ☐ mail *(surface, air mail, registered)*   ☐ delivery service   ☐ facsimile transmission   ☐ hand delivery

   ☐ PCT request (including declaration sheets)   (pages)
   ☐ description (excluding sequence listing and/or tables relating thereto)   (pages)
   ☐ claims   (pages)
   ☐ abstract   (pages)
   ☐ drawings   (pages)
   ☐ sequence listing and/or tables relating thereto   (pages)
   ☐ fee calculation sheet
   ☐ separate authorization to charge deposit account
   ☐ cheque
   ☐ cash *(in person only)*
   ☐ power of attorney *(general power, copy of general power, separate power) (indicate kind and number)*
   ☐ priority document *(if more than one, indicate number)*
   ☐ separate indications concerning deposited microorganism or other biological material (pages)
   ☐ sequence listing and/or tables relating thereto in electronic form *(indicate type and number of carriers)*
   ☐ statement accompanying sequence listing and/or tables relating thereto in electronic form *(if more than one, indicate number)*
   ☐ accompanying letter
   ☐ form PCT/RO198 (RO/IB)
   ☐ other *(specify)*:

   The applicant's attention is drawn to the fact that **these papers have not yet been checked by this receiving Office** in respect of their compliance with the requirements of Article 11(1), that is, whether these papers meet the requirements necessary for the according of an international filing date. As soon as these papers have been checked, the applicant will be informed accordingly.

2. Additional observations *(if necessary)*:

Name and mailing address of the receiving Office: International Bureau of WIPO PCT Receiving Office Section 34, chemin des Colombettes, 1211 Geneva 20, Switzerland Facsimile No. +41 22 910 06 10	Authorized officer Telephone No. +41 22 338 92 22

Form PCT/RO/199 (RO/IB) (16 September 2012)

PTO-1382 (Rev. 01-2017)
Approved for use through 08/31/2019. OMB 0651-0021
U.S. Patent and Trademark Office; U.S. DEPARTMENT OF COMMERCE
Under the Paperwork Reduction Act of 1995, no persons are required to respond to a collection of information unless it displays a valid OMB control number.

TRANSMITTAL LETTER TO THE UNITED STATES RECEIVING OFFICE (RO/US)

Priority Mail Express Mailing Label No.:	Date of Deposit:
File Reference No.:	International Application No. (If known):
Customer Number[1]:	Earliest Priority Date Claimed (dd/mm/yyyy):
Title of Invention:	
Applicant:	

[1] Customer Number will allow access to the application in Private PAIR but cannot be used to establish or change the correspondence address.

☐ This is a new International Application

SCREENING DISCLOSURE INFORMATION:

In order to assist in screening the accompanying international application for purposes of determining whether a license for foreign transmittal should and could be granted and for other purposes, the following information is supplied. (check all boxes as apply):

☐ The invention disclosed was **not** made in the United States of America.

☐ There is no prior U.S. application relating to this invention.

☐ The following prior U.S. application(s) contain subject matter which is related to the invention disclosed in the attached international application. *(NOTE: priority to these applications may or may not be claimed on the Request (form PCT/RO/101) and this listing does not constitute a claim for priority.)*

application no.		filed on
application no.		filed on

☐ The present international application contains additional subject matter not found in the prior U.S. application(s) identified above. The additional subject matter is found on pages_____

and ☐ DOES NOT ALTER ☐ MIGHT BE CONSIDERED TO ALTER the general nature of the invention in a manner which would require the U.S. application to have been made available for inspection by the appropriate defense agencies under 35 U.S.C. 181 and 37 C.F.R. 5.15.

Itemized list of contents & entity status

Sheets of Request form:	Check no.:
Sheets of description (excluding sequence listing):	Return receipt postcard:
Sheets of claims:	Power of attorney:
Sheets of abstract:	Certified copy of priority document (specify):
Sheets of drawings:	PTO/SB15A or B or equivalent:
Sheets (paper or pdf) of sequence listing:	Other (specify):
Sequence listing text file: ☐ CD or diskette ☐ via EFS-Web	

☐ Applicant asserts small entity status. See 37 CFR 1.27. If this written assertion is made by the applicant, all applicants must sign (37 C.F.R. §1.42)

☐ Applicant certifies micro entity status. See 37 CFR 1.29. Applicant must attach form PTO/SB/15A or B or equivalent.

The person signing this form is:	☐ Applicant	
	☐ Attorney/Agent Registration No. _____	Name of person signing
	☐ Common Representative	Signature

This collection of information is required by 37 CFR 1.10 and 1.412. The information is required to obtain or retain a benefit by the public, which is to file (and by the USPTO to process) an application. Confidentiality is governed by 35 U.S.C. 122 and 37 CFR 1.11 and 1.14. This collection is estimated to take 15 minutes to complete, including gathering information, preparing, and submitting the completed form to the USPTO. Time will vary depending upon the individual case. Any comments on the amount of time you require to complete this form and/or suggestions for reducing this burden, should be sent to the Chief Information Officer, U.S. Patent and Trademark Office, U.S. Department of Commerce, P.O. Box 1450, Alexandria, VA 22313-1450. DO NOT SEND FEES OR COMPLETED FORMS TO THIS ADDRESS.

SEND TO: Mail Stop PCT, Commissioner for Patents, P.O. Box 1450, Alexandria, VA 22313-1450.

Form **PTO-1595** (Rev. 6-12)
OMB No. 0651-0027 (exp. 04/30/2018)

U.S. DEPARTMENT OF COMMERCE
United States Patent and Trademark Office

RECORDATION FORM COVER SHEET
PATENTS ONLY

To the Director of the U.S. Patent and Trademark Office: Please record the attached documents or the new address(es) below.

1. Name of conveying party(ies)

Additional name(s) of conveying party(ies) attached? ☐ Yes ☐ No

2. Name and address of receiving party(ies)

Name: _____

Internal Address: _____

_____

Street Address: _____

_____

City: _____

State: _____

Country:_____ Zip:_____

Additional name(s) & address(es) attached? ☐ Yes ☐ No

3. Nature of conveyance/Execution Date(s):

Execution Date(s)_____

☐ Assignment   ☐ Merger
☐ Security Agreement ☐ Change of Name
☐ Joint Research Agreement
☐ Government Interest Assignment
☐ Executive Order 9424, Confirmatory License
☐ Other_____

4. Application or patent number(s):   ☐ This document serves as an Oath/Declaration (37 CFR 1.63).

A. Patent Application No.(s)   B. Patent No.(s)

Additional numbers attached? ☐ Yes ☐ No

5. Name and address to whom correspondence concerning document should be mailed:

Name:_____

Internal Address:_____

_____

Street Address:_____

_____

City: _____

State:_____ Zip:_____

Phone Number:_____

Docket Number:_____

Email Address:_____

6. Total number of applications and patents involved:_____

7. Total fee (37 CFR 1.21(h) & 3.41) $_____

☐ Authorized to be charged to deposit account
☐ Enclosed
☐ None required (government interest not affecting title)

8. Payment Information

Deposit Account Number _____

Authorized User Name_____

9. Signature:

_____   _____
Signature   Date

_____
Name of Person Signing

Total number of pages including cover sheet, attachments, and documents: ☐

Documents to be recorded (including cover sheet) should be faxed to (571) 273-0140, or mailed to:
Mail Stop Assignment Recordation Services, Director of the USPTO, P.O.Box 1450, Alexandria, V.A. 22313-1450

Guidelines for Completing Patents Cover Sheets (PTO-1595)

Cover Sheet information must be submitted with each document to be recorded. If the document to be recorded concerns both patents and trademarks separate patent and trademark cover sheets, including any attached pages for continuing information, must accompany the document. All pages of the cover sheet should be numbered consecutively, for example, if both a patent and trademark cover sheet is used, and information is continued on one additional page for both patents and trademarks, the pages of the cover sheet would be numbered from 1 to 4.

Item 1. Name of Conveying Party(ies).
Enter the full name of the party(ies) conveying the interest. If there is insufficient space, enter a check mark in the "Yes" box to indicate that additional information is attached. The name of the additional conveying party(ies) should be placed on an attached page clearly identified as a continuation of the information Item 1. Enter a check mark in the "No" box, if no information is contained on an attached page. If the document to be recorded is a joint research agreement, enter the name(s) of the party(ies) other than the owner of the patent or patent application as the conveying party(ies).

Item 2. Name and Address of Receiving Party(ies).
Enter the name and full address of the first party receiving the interest. If there is more than one party receiving the interest, enter a check mark in the "Yes" box to indicate that additional information is attached. Enter a check mark in the "No" box, if no information is contained on an attached page. If the document to be recorded is a joint research agreement, enter the name(s) of the patent or patent application owner(s) as the receiving party.

Item 3. Nature of Conveyance/Execution Date(s).
Enter the execution date(s) of the document. It is preferable to use the name of the month, or an abbreviation of that name, in order that confusion over dates is minimized. Place a check mark in the appropriate box describing the nature of the conveying document. If the "Other" box is checked, specify the nature of the conveyance.

Item 4. Application Number(s) or Patent Number(s).
Indicate the application number(s), and/or patent number(s) against which the document is to be recorded. National application numbers must include both the series code and a six-digit number (e.g., 07/123,456), and international application numbers must be complete (e.g., PCT/US91/12345).
Enter a check mark in the appropriate box: "Yes" or "No " if additional numbers appear on attached pages. Be sure to identify numbers included on attached pages as the continuation of Item 4. Also enter a check mark if this Assignment is being filed as an Oath/Declaration (37 CFR 1.63).

Item 5. Name and Address of Party to whom correspondence concerning the document should be mailed. Enter the name and full address of the party to whom correspondence is to be mailed.

Item 6. Total Applications and Patents involved.
Enter the total number of applications and patents identified for recordation. Be sure to include all applications and patents identified on the cover sheet and on additional pages.

Block 7. Total Fee Enclosed.
Enter the total fee enclosed or authorized to be charged. A fee is required for each application and patent against which the document is recorded.

Item 8. Payment Information.
Enter the deposit account number and authorized user name to authorize charges.

Item 9. Signature.
Enter the name of the person submitting the document. The submitter must sign and date the cover sheet. Enter the total number of pages including the cover sheet, attachments, and document.

This collection of information is required by 35 USC 261 and 262 and 15 USC 1057 and 1060. The information is used by the public to submit (and by the USPTO to process) patent and trademark assignment requests. After the USPTO records the information, the records for patent and trademarks, assignments, and other associated documents can be inspected by the public. To view documents recorded under secrecy orders or documents recorded due to the interest of the federal government, a written authorization must be submitted. This collection is estimated to take 30 minutes to complete, including gathering, preparing, and submitting the form to the USPTO. Any comments on the amount of time you require to complete this form and/or suggestions for reducing this burden, should be sent to the Manager of the Assignment Division, USPTO, P.O. Box 1450, Alexandria, VA 22313-1450. DO NOT SEND FEES OR COMPLETED FORMS TO THIS ADDRESS. SEND TO: Mail Stop Assignment Recordation Services, Director of the USPTO, P.O. Box 1450, Alexandria, VA 22313-1450.

PTO/SB/08a (07-09)
Approved for use through 07/31/2016. OMB 0651-0031
U.S. Patent and Trademark Office; U.S. DEPARTMENT OF COMMERCE
Under the Paperwork Reduction Act of 1995, no persons are required to respond to a collection of information unless it contains a valid OMB control number.

Substitute for form 1449/PTO

INFORMATION DISCLOSURE STATEMENT BY APPLICANT

(Use as many sheets as necessary)

Complete if Known	
Application Number	
Filing Date	
First Named Inventor	
Art Unit	
Examiner Name	
Attorney Docket Number	

Sheet _____ of _____

U. S. PATENT DOCUMENTS

Examiner Initials*	Cite No.[1]	Document Number Number-Kind Code[2] *(if known)*	Publication Date MM-DD-YYYY	Name of Patentee or Applicant of Cited Document	Pages, Columns, Lines, Where Relevant Passages or Relevant Figures Appear
		US-			
		US-			
		US-			
		US-			
		US-			
		US-			
		US-			
		US-			
		US-			
		US-			
		US-			
		US-			
		US-			
		US-			
		US-			
		US-			
		US-			
		US-			

FOREIGN PATENT DOCUMENTS

Examiner Initials*	Cite No.[1]	Foreign Patent Document Country Code[3] Number[4] Kind Code[5] *(if known)*	Publication Date MM-DD-YYYY	Name of Patentee or Applicant of Cited Document	Pages, Columns, Lines, Where Relevant Passages Or Relevant Figures Appear	T[6]

Examiner Signature		Date Considered	

*EXAMINER: Initial if reference considered, whether or not citation is in conformance with MPEP 609. Draw line through citation if not in conformance and not considered. Include copy of this form with next communication to applicant. [1] Applicant's unique citation designation number (optional). [2] See Kinds Codes of USPTO Patent Documents at www.uspto.gov or MPEP 901.04. [3] Enter Office that issued the document, by the two-letter code (WIPO Standard ST.3). [4] For Japanese patent documents, the indication of the year of the reign of the Emperor must precede the serial number of the patent document. [5] Kind of document by the appropriate symbols as indicated on the document under WIPO Standard ST.16 if possible. [6] Applicant is to place a check mark here if English language Translation is attached.

This collection of information is required by 37 CFR 1.97 and 1.98. The information is required to obtain or retain a benefit by the public which is to file (and by the USPTO to process) an application. Confidentiality is governed by 35 U.S.C. 122 and 37 CFR 1.14. This collection is estimated to take 2 hours to complete, including gathering, preparing, and submitting the completed application form to the USPTO. Time will vary depending upon the individual case. Any comments on the amount of time you require to complete this form and/or suggestions for reducing this burden, should be sent to the Chief Information Officer, U.S. Patent and Trademark Office, P.O. Box 1450, Alexandria, VA 22313-1450. DO NOT SEND FEES OR COMPLETED FORMS TO THIS ADDRESS. **SEND TO: Commissioner for Patents, P.O. Box 1450, Alexandria, VA 22313-1450.**
If you need assistance in completing the form, call 1-800-PTO-9199 (1-800-786-9199) and select option 2.

PTO/SB/08b (07-09)
Approved for use through 07/31/2016. OMB 0651-0031
U.S. Patent and Trademark Office; U.S. DEPARTMENT OF COMMERCE
Under the Paperwork Reduction Act of 1995, no persons are required to respond to a collection of information unless it contains a valid OMB control number.

Substitute for form 1449/PTO

INFORMATION DISCLOSURE STATEMENT BY APPLICANT

(Use as many sheets as necessary)

	Complete if Known
Application Number	
Filing Date	
First Named Inventor	
Art Unit	
Examiner Name	

Sheet [ ] of [ ]   Attorney Docket Number

NON PATENT LITERATURE DOCUMENTS

Examiner Initials*	Cite No.[1]	Include name of the author (in CAPITAL LETTERS), title of the article (when appropriate), title of the item (book, magazine, journal, serial, symposium, catalog, etc.), date, page(s), volume-issue number(s), publisher, city and/or country where published.	T[2]

Examiner Signature		Date Considered	

*EXAMINER: Initial if reference considered, whether or not citation is in conformance with MPEP 609. Draw line through citation if not in conformance and not considered. Include copy of this form with next communication to applicant.

1 Applicant's unique citation designation number (optional). 2 Applicant is to place a check mark here if English language Translation is attached. This collection of information is required by 37 CFR 1.98. The information is required to obtain or retain a benefit by the public which is to file (and by the USPTO to process) an application. Confidentiality is governed by 35 U.S.C. 122 and 37 CFR 1.14. This collection is estimated to take 2 hours to complete, including gathering, preparing, and submitting the completed application form to the USPTO. Time will vary depending upon the individual case. Any comments on the amount of time you require to complete this form and/or suggestions for reducing this burden, should be sent to the Chief Information Officer, U.S. Patent and Trademark Office, P.O. Box 1450, Alexandria, VA 22313-1450. DO NOT SEND FEES OR COMPLETED FORMS TO THIS ADDRESS. **SEND TO: Commissioner for Patents, P.O. Box 1450, Alexandria, VA 22313-1450.**

If you need assistance in completing the form, call 1-800-PTO-9199 (1-800-786-9199) and select option 2.

PTO/SB/16 (03-13)
Approved for use through 01/31/2014. OMB 0651-0032
U.S. Patent and Trademark Office; U.S. DEPARTMENT OF COMMERCE
Under the Paperwork Reduction Act of 1995 no persons are required to respond to a collection of information unless it displays a valid OMB control number

PROVISIONAL APPLICATION FOR PATENT COVER SHEET – Page 1 of 2

This is a request for filing a PROVISIONAL APPLICATION FOR PATENT under 37 CFR 1.53(c).

Express Mail Label No. _____

INVENTOR(S)

Given Name (first and middle [if any])	Family Name or Surname	Residence (City and either State or Foreign Country)

Additional inventors are being named on the _____ separately numbered sheets attached hereto.

TITLE OF THE INVENTION (500 characters max):

Direct all correspondence to: **CORRESPONDENCE ADDRESS**

☐ The address corresponding to Customer Number: _____

OR

☐ Firm or Individual Name

Address

City	State	Zip
Country	Telephone	Email

ENCLOSED APPLICATION PARTS (*check all that apply*)

☐ Application Data Sheet. See 37 CFR 1.76.   ☐ CD(s), Number of CDs _____

☐ Drawing(s) *Number of Sheets* _____   ☐ Other (specify) _____

☐ Specification (e.g., description of the invention) *Number of Pages* _____

Fees Due: Filing Fee of $260 ($130 for small entity) ($65 for micro entity). If the specification and drawings exceed 100 sheets of paper, an application size fee is also due, which is $400 ($200 for small entity) ($100 for micro entity) for each additional 50 sheets or fraction thereof. See 35 U.S.C. 41(a)(1)(G) and 37 CFR 1.16(s).

METHOD OF PAYMENT OF THE FILING FEE AND APPLICATION SIZE FEE FOR THIS PROVISIONAL APPLICATION FOR PATENT

☐ Applicant asserts small entity status. See 37 CFR 1.27.

☐ Applicant certifies micro entity status. See 37 CFR 1.29.
Applicant must attach form PTO/SB/15A or B or equivalent.

☐ A check or money order made payable to the *Director of the United States Patent and Trademark Office* is enclosed to cover the filing fee and application size fee (if applicable).   **TOTAL FEE AMOUNT ($)**

☐ Payment by credit card. Form PTO-2038 is attached.

☐ The Director is hereby authorized to charge the filing fee and application size fee (if applicable) or credit any overpayment to Deposit Account Number: _____.

USE ONLY FOR FILING A PROVISIONAL APPLICATION FOR PATENT

This collection of information is required by 37 CFR 1.51. The information is required to obtain or retain a benefit by the public which is to file (and by the USPTO to process) an application. Confidentiality is governed by 35 U.S.C. 122 and 37 CFR 1.11 and 1.14. This collection is estimated to take 10 hours to complete, including gathering, preparing, and submitting the completed application form to the USPTO. Time will vary depending upon the individual case. Any comments on the amount of time you require to complete this form and/or suggestions for reducing this burden, should be sent to the Chief Information Officer, U.S. Patent and Trademark Office, U.S. Department of Commerce, P.O. Box 1450, Alexandria, VA 22313-1450. DO NOT SEND FEES OR COMPLETED FORMS TO THIS ADDRESS. **SEND TO: Commissioner for Patents, P.O. Box 1450, Alexandria, VA 22313-1450.**
If you need assistance in completing the form, call 1-800-PTO-9199 and select option 2.

PTO/SB/16 (03-13)
Approved for use through 01/31/2014. OMB 0651-0032
U.S. Patent and Trademark Office; U.S. DEPARTMENT OF COMMERCE
Under the Paperwork Reduction Act of 1995 no persons are required to respond to a collection of information unless it displays a valid OMB control number

PROVISIONAL APPLICATION FOR PATENT COVER SHEET – Page 2 of 2

The invention was made by an agency of the United States Government or under a contract with an agency of the United States Government.

☐ No.

☐ Yes, the invention was made by an agency of the U.S. Government. The U.S. Government agency name is: _____

_____

☐ Yes, the invention was made under a contract with an agency of the U.S. Government. The name of the U.S. Government agency and Government contract number are: _____

_____

WARNING:

Petitioner/applicant is cautioned to avoid submitting personal information in documents filed in a patent application that may contribute to identity theft. Personal information such as social security numbers, bank account numbers, or credit card numbers (other than a check or credit card authorization form PTO-2038 submitted for payment purposes) is never required by the USPTO to support a petition or an application. If this type of personal information is included in documents submitted to the USPTO, petitioners/applicants should consider redacting such personal information from the documents before submitting them to the USPTO. Petitioner/applicant is advised that the record of a patent application is available to the public after publication of the application (unless a non-publication request in compliance with 37 CFR 1.213(a) is made in the application) or issuance of a patent. Furthermore, the record from an abandoned application may also be available to the public if the application is referenced in a published application or an issued patent (see 37 CFR 1.14). Checks and credit card authorization forms PTO-2038 submitted for payment purposes are not retained in the application file and therefore are not publicly available.

SIGNATURE _____   DATE _____

TYPED OR PRINTED NAME _____   REGISTRATION NO. _____
(*if appropriate*)

TELEPHONE _____   DOCKET NUMBER _____

PTO/SB/17 (03-13)
Approved for use through 04/30/2017. OMB 0651-0032
U.S. Patent and Trademark Office; U.S. DEPARTMENT OF COMMERCE
Under the Paperwork Reduction Act of 1995 no persons are required to respond to a collection of information unless it displays a valid OMB control number

FEE TRANSMITTAL

	Complete if known
Application Number	
Filing Date	

☐ Applicant asserts small entity status. See 37 CFR 1.27.

☐ Applicant certifies micro entity status. See 37 CFR 1.29.
Form PTO/SB/15A or B or equivalent must either be enclosed or have been submitted previously.

First Named Inventor	
Examiner Name	
Art Unit	

| TOTAL AMOUNT OF PAYMENT | ($) | Practitioner Docket No. | |

METHOD OF PAYMENT (check all that apply)

☐ Check ☐ Credit Card ☐ Money Order ☐ None ☐ Other (please identify): _____

☐ Deposit Account Deposit Account Number: _____ Deposit Account Name: _____

For the above-identified deposit account, the Director is hereby authorized to (check all that apply):

☐ Charge fee(s) indicated below   ☐ Charge fee(s) indicated below, **except for the filing fee**

☐ Charge any additional fee(s) or underpayment of fee(s)   ☐ Credit any overpayment of fee(s)
under 37 CFR 1.16 and 1.17

WARNING: Information on this form may become public. Credit card information should not be included on this form. Provide credit card information and authorization on PTO-2038.

FEE CALCULATION

1. BASIC FILING, SEARCH, AND EXAMINATION FEES (U = undiscounted fee; S = small entity fee; M = micro entity fee)

	FILING FEES			SEARCH FEES			EXAMINATION FEES			
Application Type	U ($)	S ($)	M ($)	U ($)	S ($)	M ($)	U ($)	S ($)	M ($)	Fees Paid ($)
Utility	280	140*	70	600	300	150	720	360	180	_____
Design	180	90	45	120	60	30	460	230	115	_____
Plant	180	90	45	380	190	95	580	290	145	_____
Reissue	280	140	70	600	300	150	2,160	1,080	540	_____
Provisional	260	130	65	0	0	0	0	0	0	_____

* The $140 small entity status filing fee for a utility application is further reduced to $70 for a small entity status applicant who files the application via EFS-Web.

2. EXCESS CLAIM FEES

Fee Description	**Undiscounted Fee ($)**	**Small Entity Fee ($)**	**Micro Entity Fee ($)**
Each claim over 20 (including Reissues)	80	40	20
Each independent claim over 3 (including Reissues)	420	210	105
Multiple dependent claims	780	390	195

Total Claims		**Extra Claims**	**Fee ($)**		**Fee Paid ($)**	
_____	-20 or HP =	_____	x _____	= _____		

HP = highest number of total claims paid for, if greater than 20.

Multiple Dependent Claims	
Fee ($)	**Fee Paid ($)**
_____	_____

Indep. Claims		**Extra Claims**	**Fee ($)**		**Fee Paid ($)**
_____	-3 or HP =	_____	x _____	= _____	

HP = highest number of independent claims paid for, if greater than 3.

3. APPLICATION SIZE FEE

If the specification and drawings exceed 100 sheets of paper (excluding electronically filed sequence or computer listings under 37 CFR 1.52(e)), the application size fee due is $400 ($200 for small entity) ($100 for micro entity) for each additional 50 sheets or fraction thereof. See 35 U.S.C. 41(a)(1)(G) and 37 CFR 1.16(s).

Total Sheets	**Extra Sheets**	**Number of each additional 50 or fraction thereof**	**Fee ($)**	**Fee Paid ($)**
_____ - 100 =	_____ / 50 =	_____ (round **up** to a whole number) x	_____	= _____

4. OTHER FEE(S)

	Fees Paid ($)
Non-English specification, $130 fee (no small or micro entity discount)	_____
Non-electronic filing fee under 37 CFR 1.16(t) for a utility application, $400 fee ($200 small or micro entity)	_____
Other (e.g., late filing surcharge): _____	_____

SUBMITTED BY

Signature		Registration No. (Attorney/Agent)		Telephone	
Name (Print/Type)				Date	

This collection of information is required by 37 CFR 1.136. The information is required to obtain or retain a benefit by the public which is to file (and by the USPTO to process) an application. Confidentiality is governed by 35 U.S.C. 122 and 37 CFR 1.14. This collection is estimated to take 30 minutes to complete, including gathering, preparing, and submitting the completed application form to the USPTO. Time will vary depending upon the individual case. Any comments on the amount of time you require to complete this form and/or suggestions for reducing this burden, should be sent to the Chief Information Officer, U.S. Patent and Trademark Office, U.S. Department of Commerce, P.O. Box 1450, Alexandria, VA 22313-1450. DO NOT SEND FEES OR COMPLETED FORMS TO THIS ADDRESS. **SEND TO: Commissioner for Patents, P.O. Box 1450, Alexandria, VA 22313-1450.**

If you need assistance in completing the form, call 1-800-PTO-9199 and select option 2.

PTO/AIA/22 (03-13)
Approved for use through 7/31/2016. OMB 0651-0031
U.S. Patent and Trademark Office; U.S. DEPARTMENT OF COMMERCE
Under the Paperwork Reduction Act of 1995, no persons are required to respond to a collection of information unless it displays a valid OMB control number.

	Docket Number (Optional)
PETITION FOR EXTENSION OF TIME UNDER 37 CFR 1.136(a)	

Application Number	Filed

For

Art Unit	Examiner

This is a request under the provisions of 37 CFR 1.136(a) to extend the period for filing a reply in the above-identified application.

The requested extension and fee are as follows (check time period desired and enter the appropriate fee below):

		Fee	Small Entity Fee	Micro Entity Fee	
☐	One month (37 CFR 1.17(a)(1))	$200	$100	$50	$ _____
☐	Two months (37 CFR 1.17(a)(2))	$600	$300	$150	$ _____
☐	Three months (37 CFR 1.17(a)(3))	$1,400	$700	$350	$ _____
☐	Four months (37 CFR 1.17(a)(4))	$2,200	$1,100	$550	$ _____
☐	Five months (37 CFR 1.17(a)(5))	$3,000	$1,500	$750	$ _____

☐ Applicant asserts small entity status. See 37 CFR 1.27.

☐ Applicant certifies micro entity status. See 37 CFR 1.29.
Form PTO/SB/15A or B or equivalent must either be enclosed or have been submitted previously.

☐ A check in the amount of the fee is enclosed.

☐ Payment by credit card. Form PTO-2038 is attached.

☐ The Director has already been authorized to charge fees in this application to a Deposit Account.

☐ The Director is hereby authorized to charge any fees which may be required, or credit any overpayment, to

Deposit Account Number _____.

☐ Payment made via EFS-Web.

WARNING: Information on this form may become public. Credit card information should not be included on this form. Provide credit card information and authorization on PTO-2038.

I am the

☐ applicant.

☐ attorney or agent of record. Registration number _____.

☐ attorney or agent acting under 37 CFR 1.34. Registration number _____.

_____	_____
Signature	Date
_____	_____
Typed or printed name	Telephone Number

NOTE: This form must be signed in accordance with 37 CFR 1.33. See 37 CFR 1.4 for signature requirements and certifications. Submit multiple forms if more than one signature is required, see below*.

☐ * Total of _____ forms are submitted.

This collection of information is required by 37 CFR 1.136(a). The information is required to obtain or retain a benefit by the public, which is to file (and by the USPTO to process) an application. Confidentiality is governed by 35 U.S.C. 122 and 37 CFR 1.11 and 1.14. This collection is estimated to take 6 minutes to complete, including gathering, preparing, and submitting the completed application form to the USPTO. Time will vary depending upon the individual case. Any comments on the amount of time you require to complete this form and/or suggestions for reducing this burden should be sent to the Chief Information Officer, U.S. Patent and Trademark Office, U.S. Department of Commerce, P.O. Box 1450, Alexandria, VA 22313-1450. DO NOT SEND FEES OR COMPLETED FORMS TO THIS ADDRESS. SEND TO: Mail Stop PCT, Commissioner for Patents, P.O. Box 1450, Alexandria, VA 22313-1450.

PTO/SB/25a (02-14)
Approved for use through 7/31/2016. OMB 0651-0031
U.S. Patent and Trademark Office; U.S. DEPARTMENT OF COMMERCE
Under the Paperwork Reduction Act of 1995, no persons are required to respond to a collection of information unless it displays a valid OMB control number.

TERMINAL DISCLAIMER IN A PATENT OR PROCEEDING IN VIEW OF AN APPLICATION	Docket Number (Optional)

Application/Control Number:

Filing Date:

First Named Inventor:

Title:

Patent No.:

The patentee, _____, owner of _____ percent interest in the instant patent hereby disclaims, except as provided below, the terminal part of the statutory term of the instant patent which would extend beyond the expiration date of the full statutory term of any patent granted on pending **reference** application No. _____, filed _____, as the term of any patent granted on said **reference** application may be shortened by any terminal disclaimer filed prior to the grant of any patent on the pending **reference** application. The patentee hereby agrees that the instant patent shall be enforceable only for and during such period that the instant patent and any patent granted on the **reference** application are commonly owned. This agreement runs with the instant patent and is binding upon the grantee, its successors or assigns.

In making the above disclaimer, the patentee does not disclaim the terminal part of the instant patent that would extend to the expiration date of the full statutory term of any patent granted on said **reference** application, "as the term of any patent granted on said **reference** application may be shortened by any terminal disclaimer filed prior to the grant of any patent on the pending **reference** application," in the event that any such patent granted on the pending **reference** application: expires for failure to pay a maintenance fee; is held unenforceable; is found invalid by a court of competent jurisdiction; is statutorily disclaimed in whole or terminally disclaimed under 37 CFR 1.321; has all claims canceled by a reexamination certificate; is reissued; or is in any manner terminated prior to the expiration of its full statutory term as shortened by any terminal disclaimer filed prior to its grant.

I. Check either box 1, 2, or 3 below, as appropriate, if there is an assignment:

1. ☐ The current ownership was established by the filing of a statement under 37 CFR 3.73 during prosecution of the application that issued as the instant patent.

2. ☐ The instant patent was issued from an application filed on or after September 16, 2012, and the current patent owner was the applicant under 37 CFR 1.46.

3. ☐ A statement under 37 CFR 3.73 is attached herewith. Form PTO/SB/96 or PTO/AIA/96, as appropriate, may be used.

II. Authorization for Terminal Disclaimer - Check either box 1 or 2 below, if appropriate:

I hereby acknowledge that any willful false statements made are punishable under 18 U.S.C. 1001 by fine or imprisonment of not more than five (5) years, or both.

1. ☐ For submissions on behalf of a business/organization (e.g., corporation, partnership, university, government agency, etc.), the undersigned is empowered to act on behalf of the business/organization.

2. ☐ The undersigned is an attorney or agent of record. Reg. No. _____

_____	_____
Signature	Date

_____	_____
Typed or printed name	Telephone number

☐ The terminal disclaimer fee under 37 CFR 1.20(d) is included.

NOTE: Submit multiple forms if more than one signature is required, see below.*

WARNING: Information on this form may become public. Credit card information should not be included on this form. Provide credit card information and authorization on PTO-2038.

☐ *Total of _____ forms are submitted.

This collection of information is required by 37 CFR 1.321. The information is required to obtain or retain a benefit by the public, which is to file (and by the USPTO to process) an application. Confidentiality is governed by 35 U.S.C. 122 and 37 CFR 1.11 and 1.14. This collection is estimated to take 12 minutes to complete, including gathering, preparing, and submitting the completed application form to the USPTO. Time will vary depending upon the individual case. Any comments on the amount of time you require to complete this form and/or suggestions for reducing this burden should be sent to the Chief Information Officer, U.S. Patent and Trademark Office, U.S. Department of Commerce, P.O. Box 1450, Alexandria, VA 22313-1450. DO NOT SEND FEES OR COMPLETED FORMS TO THIS ADDRESS. **SEND TO: Commissioner for Patents, P.O. Box 1450, Alexandria, VA 22313-1450.**

If you need assistance in completing the form, call 1-800-PTO-9199 and select option 2.

PTO/SB/26a (02-14)
Approved for use through 7/31/2016. OMB 0651-0031
U.S. Patent and Trademark Office; U.S. DEPARTMENT OF COMMERCE
Under the Paperwork Reduction Act of 1995, no persons are required to respond to a collection of information unless it displays a valid OMB control number.

TERMINAL DISCLAIMER IN A PATENT OR PROCEEDING IN VIEW OF ANOTHER PATENT

Docket Number (Optional)

Application/Control Number:

Filing Date:

First Named Inventor:

Title:

Patent No.:

The patentee, _____ , owner of _____ percent interest in the instant patent hereby disclaims, except as provided below, the terminal part of the statutory term of the instant patent which would extend beyond the expiration date of the full statutory term of patent No. _____ (the "**reference** patent"), as the term of said **reference** patent is presently shortened by any terminal disclaimer. The patentee hereby agrees that the instant patent shall be enforceable only for and during such period that the instant patent and the **reference** patent are commonly owned. This agreement runs with the instant patent and is binding upon the grantee, its successors or assigns.

In making the above disclaimer, the patentee does not disclaim the terminal part of the instant patent that would extend to the expiration date of the full statutory term of the **reference** patent, "as the term of said **reference** patent is presently shortened by any terminal disclaimer," in the event that said **reference** patent later: expires for failure to pay a maintenance fee; is held unenforceable; is found invalid by a court of competent jurisdiction; is statutorily disclaimed in whole or terminally disclaimed under 37 CFR 1.321; has all claims canceled by a reexamination certificate; is reissued; or is in any manner terminated prior to the expiration of its full statutory term as shortened by any terminal disclaimer.

I. Check either box 1, 2, or 3 below, as appropriate, if there is an assignment:

1. ☐ The current ownership was established by the filing of a statement under 37 CFR 3.73 during prosecution of the application that issued as the instant patent.

2. ☐ The instant patent was issued from an application filed on or after September 16, 2012, and the current patent owner was the applicant under 37 CFR 1.46.

3. ☐ A statement under 37 CFR 3.73 is attached herewith. Form PTO/SB/96 or PTO/AIA/96, as appropriate, may be used.

II. Authorization for Terminal Disclaimer - Check either box 1 or 2 below, if appropriate:

I hereby acknowledge that any willful false statements made are punishable under 18 U.S.C. 1001 by fine or imprisonment of not more than five (5) years, or both.

1. ☐ For submissions on behalf of a business/organization (e.g., corporation, partnership, university, government agency, etc.), the undersigned is empowered to act on behalf of the business/organization.

2. ☐ The undersigned is an attorney or agent of record. Reg. No. _____

_____   _____
Signature   Date

_____   _____
Typed or printed name   Telephone number

☐ The terminal disclaimer fee under 37 CFR 1.20(d) is included.

NOTE: Submit multiple forms if more than one signature is required, see below.*

WARNING: Information on this form may become public. Credit card information should not be included on this form. Provide credit card information and authorization on PTO-2038.

☐ *Total of _____ forms are submitted.

This collection of information is required by 37 CFR 1.321. The information is required to obtain or retain a benefit by the public, which is to file (and by the USPTO to process) an application. Confidentiality is governed by 35 U.S.C. 122 and 37 CFR 1.11 and 1.14. This collection is estimated to take 12 minutes to complete, including gathering, preparing, and submitting the completed application form to the USPTO. Time will vary depending upon the individual case. Any comments on the amount of time you require to complete this form and/or suggestions for reducing this burden should be sent to the Chief Information Officer, U.S. Patent and Trademark Office, U.S. Department of Commerce, P.O. Box 1450, Alexandria, VA 22313-1450. DO NOT SEND FEES OR COMPLETED FORMS TO THIS ADDRESS. **SEND TO: Commissioner for Patents, P.O. Box 1450, Alexandria, VA 22313-1450.**

If you need assistance in completing the form, call 1-800-PTO-9199 and select option 2.

Doc code: RCEX
Doc description: Request for Continued Examination (RCE)

PTO/SB/30EFS (07-14)
Approved for use through 07/31/2016. OMB 0651-0031
U.S. Patent and Trademark Office; U.S. DEPARTMENT OF COMMERCE
Under the Paperwork Reduction Act of 1995, no persons are required to respond to a collection of information unless it contains a valid OMB control number.

REQUEST FOR CONTINUED EXAMINATION(RCE)TRANSMITTAL
(Submitted Only via EFS-Web)

Application Number		Filing Date		Docket Number (if applicable)		Art Unit	
First Named Inventor				Examiner Name			

This is a Request for Continued Examination (RCE) under 37 CFR 1.114 of the above-identified application.
Request for Continued Examination (RCE) practice under 37 CFR 1.114 does not apply to any utility or plant application filed prior to June 8, 1995, to any international application that does not comply with the requirements of 35 U.S.C. 371, or to any design application. The Instruction Sheet for this form is located at WWW.USPTO.GOV.

SUBMISSION REQUIRED UNDER 37 CFR 1.114

Note: If the RCE is proper, any previously filed unentered amendments and amendments enclosed with the RCE will be entered in the order in which they were filed unless applicant instructs otherwise. If applicant does not wish to have any previously filed unentered amendment(s) entered, applicant must request non-entry of such amendment(s).

☐ Previously submitted. If a final Office action is outstanding, any amendments filed after the final Office action may be considered as a submission even if this box is not checked.

  ☐ Consider the arguments in the Appeal Brief or Reply Brief previously filed on _____

  ☐ Other _____

☐ Enclosed

  ☐ Amendment/Reply

  ☐ Information Disclosure Statement (IDS)

  ☐ Affidavit(s)/ Declaration(s)

  ☐ Other _____

MISCELLANEOUS

☐ Suspension of action on the above-identified application is requested under 37 CFR 1.103(c) for a period of months _____
(Period of suspension shall not exceed 3 months; Fee under 37 CFR 1.17(i) required)

☐ Other _____

FEES

The RCE fee under 37 CFR 1.17(e) is required by 37 CFR 1.114 when the RCE is filed.
☐ The Director is hereby authorized to charge any underpayment of fees, or credit any overpayments, to Deposit Account No _____

SIGNATURE OF APPLICANT, ATTORNEY, OR AGENT REQUIRED

☒ Patent Practitioner Signature

☐ Applicant Signature

EFS - Web 2.1.15

Doc code: RCEX
Doc description: Request for Continued Examination (RCE)

PTO/SB/30EFS (07-14)
Approved for use through 07/31/2016. OMB 0651-0031
U.S. Patent and Trademark Office; U.S. DEPARTMENT OF COMMERCE
Under the Paperwork Reduction Act of 1995, no persons are required to respond to a collection of information unless it contains a valid OMB control number.

Signature of Registered U.S. Patent Practitioner			
Signature		Date (YYYY-MM-DD)	
Name		Registration Number	

This collection of information is required by 37 CFR 1.114. The information is required to obtain or retain a benefit by the public which is to file (and by the USPTO to process) an application. Confidentiality is governed by 35 U.S.C. 122 and 37 CFR 1.11 and 1.14. This collection is estimated to take 12 minutes to complete, including gathering, preparing, and submitting the completed application form to the USPTO. Time will vary depending upon the individual case. Any comments on the amount of time you require to complete this form and/or suggestions for reducing this burden, should be sent to the Chief Information Officer, U.S. Patent and Trademark Office, U.S. Department of Commerce, P.O. Box 1450, Alexandria, VA 22313-1450.

If you need assistance in completing the form, call 1-800-PTO-9199 and select option 2.

EFS - Web 2.1.15

PTO/SB/92 (07-16)
Approved for use through 07/31/2016. OMB 0651-0031
U.S. Patent and Trademark Office; U.S. DEPARTMENT OF COMMERCE
Under the Paperwork Reduction Act of 1995, no persons are required to respond to a collection of information unless it displays a valid OMB control number.

Certificate of Mailing or Transmission under 37 CFR 1.8

I hereby certify that this correspondence is being:

1. ☐ Deposited with the United States Postal Service with sufficient postage as first class mail in an envelope addressed to:

Commissioner for Patents
P.O. Box 1450
Alexandria, VA 22313-1450

on _____ ,
     Date

2. ☐ Facsimile transmitted to the United States Patent and Trademark Office, or

OR

3. ☐ EFS-Web transmitted to the USPTO.

_____   _____
            Signature   Date

_____   _____
    Typed or printed name   Telephone number

Note: Each paper must have its own certificate of mailing or transmission, or this certificate must identify each submitted paper:

_____

_____

_____

_____

This collection of information is required by 37 CFR 1.8. The information is required to obtain or retain a benefit by the public, which is to file (and by the USPTO to process) an application. Confidentiality is governed by 35 U.S.C. 122 and 37 CFR 1.11 and 1.14. This collection is estimated to take 1.8 minutes to complete, including gathering, preparing, and submitting the completed application form to the USPTO. Time will vary depending upon the individual case. Any comments on the amount of time you require to complete this form and/or suggestions for reducing this burden should be sent to the Chief Information Officer, U.S. Patent and Trademark Office, U.S. Department of Commerce, P.O. Box 1450, Alexandria, VA 22313-1450. DO NOT SEND FEES OR COMPLETED FORMS TO THIS ADDRESS. **SEND TO: Commissioner for Patents, P.O. Box 1450, Alexandria, VA 22313-1450.**
If you need assistance in completing the form, call 1-800-PTO-9199 and select option 2.

PTO/SB/125A (11-08)
Approved for use through 01/18/2018. OMB 0651-0035
U.S. Patent and Trademark Office, U.S. DEPARTMENT OF COMMERCE
Under the Paperwork Reduction Act of 1995, no persons are required to respond to a collection of information unless it displays a valid OMB control number.

Request for Customer Number	Address to: Mail Stop CN Commissioner for Patents P.O. Box 1450 Alexandria, VA 22313-1450

☐ Although the Requester acknowledges that Internet communications are not secure, the Requester hereby authorizes the USPTO to send the assigned customer number by e-mail to the email address listed below.

To the Commissioner for Patents:
Please assign a Customer Number to the address indicated below:

Firm *or* Individual Name	
Address	

City		State		Zip	
Country					
Telephone		Email			

Please associate the following practitioner registration number(s) with the Customer Number assigned to the address cited above.

☐ Additional practitioner registration numbers are listed on supplemental sheet(s) attached hereto.

Request Submitted by:

Firm Name (if applicable)	
Signature	
Name of person submitting request		Date	
Registration Number, if applicable		Telephone Number	

This collection of information is required by 37 CFR 1.33. The information is required to obtain or retain a benefit by the public which is to file (and by the USPTO to process) an application. Confidentiality is governed by 35 U.S.C. 122 and 37 CFR 1.11 and 1.14. This collection is estimated to take 12 minutes to complete, including gathering, preparing, and submitting the completed application form to the USPTO. Time will vary depending upon the individual case. Any comments on the amount of time you require to complete this form and/or suggestions for reducing this burden should be sent to the Chief Information Officer, U.S. Patent and Trademark Office, U.S. Department of Commerce, P.O. Box 1450, Alexandria, VA 22313-1450. DO NOT SEND FEES OR COMPLETED FORMS TO THIS ADDRESS. **SEND TO: Mail Stop CN, Commissioner for Patents, P.O. Box 1450, Alexandria, VA 22313-1450.**

If you need assistance in completing the form, call 1-800-PTO-9199 (1-800-786-9199) and select option 2.

PTO/SB/125A (11-08)
Approved for use through 01/18/2018. OMB 0651-0035
U.S. Patent and Trademark Office, U.S. DEPARTMENT OF COMMERCE
Under the Paperwork Reduction Act of 1995, no persons are required to respond to a collection of information unless it displays a valid OMB control number.

Request for Customer Number	Practitioner Registration Number Supplement Sheet		
	Page	of	Pages

Please associate the following practitioner registration number(s) with the Customer Number assigned to the Address cited on Request for Customer Number form attached.

Firm Name	
Date	

☐ Additional supplemental sheets(s) attached hereto

This collection of information is required by 37 CFR 1.33. The information is required to obtain or retain a benefit by the public which is to file (and by the USPTO to process) an application. Confidentiality is governed by 35 U.S.C. 122 and 37 CFR 1.11 and 1.14. This collection is estimated to take 12 minutes to complete, including gathering, preparing, and submitting the completed application form to the USPTO. Time will vary depending upon the individual case. Any comments on the amount of time you require to complete this form and/or suggestions for reducing this burden, should be sent to the Chief Information Officer, U.S. Patent and Trademark Office, U.S. Department of Commerce, P.O. Box 1450, Alexandria, VA 22313-1450. DO NOT SEND FEES OR COMPLETED FORMS TO THIS ADDRESS. **SEND TO: Mail Stop CN, Commissioner for Patents, P.O. Box 1450, Alexandria, VA 22313-1450.**

If you need assistance in completing the form, call 1-800-PTO-9199 (1-800-786-9199) and select option 2.

Doc code : PET.OP.AGE
Description : Petition to make special based on Age/Health

PTO/SB/130 (07
Approved for use through 01/31/2013. OMB 0651- 0
U.S. Patent and Trademark Office; U.S. DEPARTMENT OF COMMEF
Under the Paperwork Reduction Act of 1995, no persons are required to respond to a collection of information unless it contains a valid OMB control num

**PETITION TO MAKE SPECIAL BASED ON AGE FOR ADVANCEMENT OF EXAMINATION
UNDER 37 CFR 1.102(c)(1)**

Application Information

Application Number		Confirmation Number		Filing Date	
Attorney Docket Number (optional)		Art Unit		Examiner	
First Named Inventor					
Title of Invention					

Attention: Office of Petitions
An application may be made special for advancement of examination upon filing of a petition showing that the applicant is
years of age, or more. No fee is required with such a petition. See 37 CFR 1.102(c)(1) and MPEP 708.02 (IV).

APPLICANT HEREBY PETITIONS TO MAKE SPECIAL FOR ADVANCEMENT OF EXAMINATION IN THIS APPLICATIO
UNDER 37 CFR 1.102(c)(1) AND MPEP 708.02 (IV) ON THE BASIS OF THE APPLICANT'S AGE.

A grantable petition requires one of the following items:
(1) Statement by one named inventor in the application that he/she is 65 years of age, or more; or
(2) Certification by a registered attorney/agent having evidence such as a birth certificate, passport, driver's license, etc.
showing one named inventor in the application is 65 years of age, or more.

Name of Inventor who is 65 years of age, or older

Given Name	Middle Name	Family Name	Suffix

A signature of the applicant or representative is required in accordance with 37 CFR 1.33 and 10.18.
Please see 37 CFR 1.4(d) for the format of the signature.

Select (1) or (2) :

◉ (1) I am an inventor in this application and I am 65 years of age, or more.

○ (2) I am an attorney or agent registered to practice before the Patent and Trademark Office, and I certify that I am in possession of
evidence, and will retain such in the application file record, showing that the inventor listed above is 65 years of age, or more.

Signature		Date (YYYY-MM-DD)	
Name			

CHAPTER 14

Infringement of Patents

A US patent grants for a term of twenty years from the date on which the application for patent was filed "the right to exclude others from making, using, offering for sale, or selling the invention throughout the United States or importing the invention into the United States." Under the General Agreement on Tariffs and Trade (GATT) legislation, the term of a US patent was changed from seventeen years from its issuance to twenty years from its US filing date. If the invention is a process, the patent laws also grant the right to exclude others from making, using, offering for sale, or selling throughout the United States or importing into the United States, products made by the patented process. Any violation of these federal rights constitutes patent infringement. If a patent is infringed, the patentee may sue for relief in the appropriate federal court. The patentee may ask the court for an injunction to prevent the continuation of the infringement and may also ask the court for an award of damages because of the infringement. In such an infringement suit, the defendant may raise the question of the validity of the patent, which is then decided by the court. The defendant may also claim that what is being done does not constitute infringement.

An understanding of which acts constitute patent infringement is important in determining the protection a patent provides for your invention. Naturally, once your patent issues, you should ensure that you are cognizant of others who may be infringing. Keep in mind that your patent is not self-enforcing and that you have to monitor the market for infringing activities and take action to stop them.

THE CATEGORIES OF PATENT INFRINGEMENT

The specific acts that constitute patent infringement are defined by statute (subsections (a) through (g) of 35 U.S.C. § 271) and may be through the "direct" actions of an infringer or through actions which cause another to infringe (i.e., contributory or inducement of infringement).

Direct infringement occurs when, without authority, the infringer makes, uses, offers to sell, or sells any patented invention within the United States or imports into the United States any patented invention during the term of the patent. Infringement occurs even if only one of the proscribed activities is performed. But, one of the prohibited acts must actually occur—the mere threat of future activities does not constitute infringement. Direct infringement occurs when the infringer has made an operable embodiment of the patented invention.

Certain activities, which may appear to be infringements, are permitted. For example, it is not an infringement if someone makes or uses a patented invention solely for experimental purposes that do not advance any significant business interest. This so-called "experimental use" exception is a narrow one. If someone manufactures or uses the patented invention for experimental tests in preparation for commercial exploitation, this is considered an infringement.

In addition, if a patented product is purchased from the patentee, or one with authority to sell the patented product (i.e., a licensee of the patent owner), the purchaser may use and resell that product in the United States free of any risk of infringement. The purchaser may also make repairs on the patented product and replace worn-out parts, but he or she cannot completely reconstruct an entirely new product when the original product, viewed as a whole, has become spent. Although the rule is straightforward, its application is less so because it is not always clear how much repair is allowed before an item is deemed to be reconstructed.

Liability for patent infringement due to indirect infringement applies to those who actively induce or contribute to the infringement of a patent. Active inducement is often described as aiding and abetting another's direct infringement. Contributory infringement is the selling of a component, material, or apparatus that constitutes a material part of a patented invention, where the seller knows that the component, material, or apparatus is "especially made or especially adapted for use in an infringement of such patent, and not a staple article or commodity of commerce suitable for substantial noninfringing use."

A wide range of actions may be found to induce or contribute to another's infringement. To prove inducement of infringement, you need to show that the infringers knew or should have known that his or her actions would cause infringement by another. To prove contributory infringement, you need only show that the infringer sold a material part of a patented invention with knowledge that such part is especially made or adapted for infringement and has no substantial noninfringing use. Protection against inducement of infringement and contributory infringement may be very important for the owners of method patents, because it is usually impractical to sue the large numbers of individual purchasers who are using products to practice the patented method. Nevertheless, both active inducement and contributory infringement are predicated on direct infringement of the patent at issue for, without such direct infringement, there can be neither contributory infringement nor inducement of infringement.

GENERAL PRINCIPLES OF AN INFRINGEMENT ANALYSIS

If you believe that another is infringing your patent, you should first find out as much as possible about the infringing process or product. Once you have gathered this information, use the following guidelines to assess whether the product or process actually infringes the claims of your patent.

It is important to note that, although a patent may comprise a description, examples, drawings, an abstract, and claims, only the claims of a patent can be infringed. To determine whether a product or process infringes, you must, therefore, compare the allegedly infringing product or process to your patent claims. This is ordinarily done in two separate steps. The first step is to construe or interpret the scope of the claims: What do the claims, as they are written, actually cover? The second step is to compare the properly construed claims with the accused composition, device, or method to determine whether it contains all the elements recited in the claims and therefore infringes the patent claims. If the accused composition, device, or method meets all the limitations of a claim, it infringes. Although many patents contain more than one claim, if the accused composition, device, or process infringes only a single claim, it still infringes the patent.

In determining the meanings of the words of a patent claim to construe or interpret its scope, first consider the language of the claim itself. A determination of what a patent claim actually covers is often complex and rarely is uncontroverted. For example, the language of the claim must be construed in light of the other claims, the specification, the prior art, and the prosecution history of the patent. Express representations to the patent examiner regarding the meanings of the terms used in the claim will also affect the claim scope.

Claims are construed as they would be by people skilled in the relevant art, but a patent applicant can define his or her terms as he or she so chooses—even in a manner contrary to their ordinary meanings. Words must, of course, be used consistently in both the claims and the specification. Further, the terms of a claim will be given their ordinary meaning, unless it appears that the inventor used them differently.

Claims are generally not limited to any specific or preferred embodiment or example disclosed in the patent. Accordingly, it is improper to read a limitation from the patent specification into a claim, unless the limitation is actually required. It is, however, entirely proper to consult the patent specification to determine the correct meaning of a claim term that is in dispute.

It is presumed that two claims that differ in wording have different meanings and scopes; this is known as the "doctrine of claim differentiation." Under this settled rule, specific limitations set forth in narrow claims cannot be read into broader claims. Moreover, a claim must be given the same meaning for purposes of both validity and infringement analyses. In areas of complex technology, an evaluation of how a court may construe patent claims may require an in-depth analysis by an experienced patent attorney.

After the claims have been properly construed, they are compared with the suspected infringing composition, device, or process. Literal infringement requires that every limitation of the claim must be literally present in the accused device. For example, if an invention claims a computer system comprising a modem, monitor, and keyboard, it would not be infringed by a system containing only a monitor and a keyboard, but no modem. The infringement analysis is rarely this simple, as it is complicated by the manner in which the claims are written and the legal concepts applied to determine infringement.

For example, an element in a claim may be expressed as a means or step for performing a specified function without the recital of structure. So-called means-plus-function claims are an exception to the general rule regarding literal infringement as those claims literally cover not only the relevant structure, material, or acts described in the specification to perform the specified function, but also their equivalents. Therefore, certain products may be found to literally infringe means-plus-function claims even though they contain components not specifically claimed.

INFRINGEMENT UNDER THE DOCTRINE OF EQUIVALENTS

Even though you may conclude that a device or process is not within the literal scope of a patent claim it may, under certain circumstances, infringe under the "doctrine of equivalents." This doctrine was created to extend liability to infringers who misappropriate the benefits of an invention while avoiding the literal language of patent claims. The US Supreme Court has recognized that to permit infringers to subordinate substance to form, and thereby deprive inventors of the full benefits of their inventions, would discourage the disclosure of inventions through patents, and thereby frustrate one of the primary purposes of the patent system.

Thus, an accused product, although outside the literal scope of the claim, may still infringe under the doctrine of equivalents if that product substantially performs the same function in the same way to obtain the same overall result as the claimed invention. This three-pronged test (i.e., function/way/result) is applied to the claimed invention as a whole, not to the individual limitations of the claim. Still, the rule further requires that all claim limitations, or their substantial equivalents, must be found in the accused device. Thus, the doctrine of equivalents does not really expand the scope of the patent claims, but, rather, the doctrine expands the right to exclude to equivalents of what is claimed.

The courts have not articulated any specific test that must be followed to show that a substitute for a claim limitation in the accused product is the substantial equivalent of the limitation recited in the claim. Thus, the function/way/result analysis is an acceptable way but not the only way to show equivalence. A determination of equivalency is made in view of the patent, the state of the relevant technology at the time the invention in question was made (i.e., the prior art), and the particular facts of a given case.

The purpose and function of a particular element and the qualities it has when combined with other elements are proper considerations when determining infringement under the doctrine of equivalents. An important factor is whether those reasonably skilled in the art would know that the accused element is interchangeable with the limitation in the patent claim. Proof of equivalence can be made in many forms, such as expert testimony, treatises, disclosures in the prior art, technological demonstrations, and tests. While a substantial equivalent for each claim limitation must be found in the accused product, a one-to-one correspondence between the claim limitations and the elements of the accused product is not necessary under the doctrine of equivalents. Other things being equal, a pioneering invention is entitled to a broad range of equivalents, and a modest advance in a crowded art is only entitled to a narrow range of equivalents.

The doctrine of equivalents serves important public policies by encouraging the disclosure of inventions in patents and protecting research and development investments. But, when the reach of a patent is extended too far under this doctrine, two different public policies are frustrated. First, the public has the right to fair notice of where the boundaries of a claimed invention lie so that others can avoid infringing the patent. Second, the important policy of encouraging others to advance technology by successfully designing around patents is frustrated when the boundaries of a patent claim cannot be determined or are drawn too broadly under the doctrine of equivalents. In recognition of these polices, the doctrine of equivalents cannot be used to ensnare an accused device already disclosed in the prior art and cannot be used to recapture claim coverage clearly given up during prosecution before the USPTO.

The converse principle to the doctrine of equivalents is the "reverse doctrine of equivalents." The reverse doctrine of equivalents provides that an accused product or process does not infringe, even though it is covered by the literal language of a patent claim, if the product or process has been so drastically changed in principle that it performs the same or similar function in a substantially different way. Put another way, this doctrine prevents a finding of infringement when the accused device is so dissimilar to those contemplated by the inventor that it would be inequitable to regard the accused device as being within the scope of the patent claims. The reverse doctrine of equivalents has been successfully employed to avert a finding of literal infringement, although only on rare occasions.

TAKING ACTION AGAINST INFRINGEMENT

Once you have determined that your patent is being infringed, contact an experienced patent attorney to pursue appropriate action against the infringement. Although it is not required that you obtain legal representation to enforce your patent, it is very difficult and surely unwise for one who is not a lawyer to handle the complexities of patent litigation. Patent litigation is expensive, and the legal fees to enforce a patent through litigation will, in even what may appear to be the simplest of cases, likely exceed $1 million. Some patent attorneys, although clearly not the majority, will handle patent infringement cases on a contingent fee basis.

Legal action for patent infringement is brought in the appropriate US district court. An action for infringement of a patent must be filed within six years of occurrence of the infringing activity. The patent owner can recover damages from the infringer as well as an injunction to stop future infringing activities.

Suits for infringement of patents follow the rules of procedure of the federal courts. From the decision of the district court, there is an appeal to the Court of Appeals for the Federal Circuit. The US Supreme Court may thereafter take a case by writ of certiorari. If the US government infringes a patent, the patentee has a remedy for damages in the US claims court. The government may use any patented invention without permission of the patentee, but the patentee is entitled to obtain compensation for the use by or for the government.

Fortunately, you may be able to enforce your patent and obtain compensation for its infringement without a lawsuit. Usually, the first step is to contact the infringer. Depending on your objectives, you can offer the infringer a license under the patent or some other business arrangement wherein you allow him or her to sell the accused product. However, you should consider, before sending a cease-and-desist letter, that if you charge someone with infringement, he or she may sue you to obtain a declaration that the patent was invalid or was not infringed. As a result of your threat of enforcement, you can be unwittingly brought into an expensive litigation.

WHAT IF YOUR ACTIVITIES INFRINGE A PATENT?

If you intend to make, sell, or import a new product or process, determine whether your intended activity is patented by someone else. Even though you can never be certain that what you intend to do is free from the patent protection of another party, you can minimize your risks by doing a little research.

There are private companies that, for a relatively inexpensive fee, will search the patent literature for patents that may relate to your product or process. Alternatively, you can, on your own, obtain information about whether products similar to yours are protected by patents through product literature (which often contains patent information) or the product itself (which is often marked with a patent number). Naturally, if you are copying the product or process of another, you should carefully assess whether it is patented. If you identify patents that are in force and may cover your product or process, obtain copies of the patents from the USPTO and perform the infringement analysis described above. Where questions of possible infringement arise and you still desire to proceed with the sale of the composition, device, or process, you should obtain competent legal advice so the risks of infringement, which can be substantial, are properly evaluated.

Be aware that the patent statute authorizes the court to award up to three times the amount of the actual damages caused by the infringement and to award attorney fees where the case is found to be "exceptional." When the court finds that infringement has been willful, exceptional circumstances may be found to exist and enhanced damages may be properly granted. It is, therefore, paramount that when you face an issue of infringement, you avoid a finding that your infringement has been willful.

Simply stated, your infringement will be found to have been willful if you acted in disregard for the patent. Your infringement is willful if you have no reasonable basis for believing you were not infringing. You must have had actual notice of the patent to be found guilty of willful infringement. There is a duty, from the time you become aware of a patent, to either cease the allegedly infringing activity or form a good faith belief of patent invalidity or noninfringement.

Willfulness is determined by the totality of the circumstances. Generally, infringement will not be found to have been willful if (1) you possess a good faith belief that the patent is invalid or the allegedly infringing device does not infringe, (2) you had reason to believe that the infringing act was covered by a license, or (3) you made a good faith attempt to alter the device or process to avoid infringement.

Although the presence or absence of a legal opinion is not necessarily determinative, the courts have often relied solely on the quality of a legal opinion to determine whether or not the infringement was willful. A comprehensive legal opinion will generally be considered by the court as strong evidence of a good faith belief that the infringing activity was permitted.

Questions of patent infringement are almost always complex and are rarely amenable to simple resolution. When faced with a question as to whether your activities may infringe a patent, or whether another is infringing a patent that you own, it is almost always prudent to consult an experienced patent attorney. Naturally, if your attorneys conclude that your activities will infringe a valid patent, you may attempt to seek a license under the patent. Obviously, seeking a license will bring your possible infringing activities to the attention of the patent owner. Moreover, a patent owner is under no obligation to grant you a license under his or her invention (see chapter 15 for a review of licensing).

PATENT MARKING

A patentee who makes or sells patented articles, or a person who does so for the patentee, is required to mark the articles with the word "patent" and the number of the patent. If the articles are not marked, the patentee may not recover damages from an infringer, unless the infringer was duly notified of the infringement and continued to infringe after the notice.

It is against the law to mark an article as patented when it is not, and the offender is subject to penalty. Some people mark articles sold with the terms "patent applied for" or "patent pending." These phrases have no legal effect, and only state that an application for patent has been filed in the USPTO. The protection afforded by a patent does not start until the actual grant of the patent. False use of these phrases, or their equivalent, is prohibited.

CHAPTER 15

Licensing Your Patents and Inventions

As explained earlier, intellectual property—patents, trademarks, copyrights—can be bought, sold, and exploited like other forms of personal and real property. For this reason, the exploitation of intellectual property, in particular patents, has become a significant element of the financial strategy of small and large businesses as well as opportunities for individual inventors to derive economic benefit from their inventions.

UNDERSTANDING THE VALUE OF LICENSING

Licensing is a form of intellectual property exploitation that allows an inventor or owner of the invention to capitalize on the financial earning power of patents, trademarks, and copyrights by making them available for use in exchange for some level of consideration. Licensing allows a patent owner to exploit the value of the patent without giving up ownership and control of the patent or having to work to bring the patent to commercialization. The owner, or licensor, generally collects lump-sum payments and/or running royalties without assuming any business risks.

The process of licensing begins with the inventor's or owner's understanding and evaluation of the intrinsic value of the patent or invention. This involves examining a number of factors to determine how much the patent and invention is worth and how to maximize the value. Does the invention represent a technological breakthrough? Has the invention been fully developed or commercialized? What are the real or perceived benefits of the invention? Is the invention adequately protected by patents or other intellectual property rights? These are some of the questions you must answer before you can determine the licensing potential of your invention.

Realize that an invention not protected by a patent will likely have little or no licensing potential. No one wants to pay for a license to an invention that the rest of the world can access freely. Likewise, prospective licensees may not have a strong interest in an invention that has limited marketability.

It is important that the inventor or patent owner size up the market in which the respective patent or invention would compete. As explained in chapter 1, you will need to assess the commercial potential and marketability of your invention before you can begin to measure its licensing value. This may require market studies and an analysis of your invention in comparison to similar products as well as unrelated alternatives. Look at other licensing agreements that you may have access to for determining customary royalties and conditions. When this analysis is complete, you are ready to examine licensing as a way to exploit your intellectual property. You may want to seek the assistance of a patent attorney or invention broker in preparing for and going through the licensing process.

LICENSING REQUIREMENTS AND CONSIDERATIONS

If someone else wants to legally make, use, sell, or import your patented invention, he or she would need a license from you. A license used in connection with patents essentially provides assurances that the person or entity practicing the patented invention will not be sued by the patent owner for infringement. In exchange for receiving a license, the licensee pays a royalty or lump-sum or both to the patent owner as the licensor.

A patent license is basically a contract and requires the essential elements of an offer, acceptance, and consideration. The license is a negotiated agreement that should always be in writing and signed by both the licensee and licensor.

The license agreement can be simple or complex depending on the terms and conditions required by the parties. A sample license agreement is provided at the end of this chapter; this form can be used for most simple patent licensing situations. Keep in mind, however, that each licensing agreement is a distinct transaction with terms that are negotiated and agreed to by the parties on a case-by-case basis.

There are several fundamental prerequisites to creating an effective patent license. First, the party granting the license must have ownership of the patent. Second, the license must specify what rights are being granted. The license should also indicate the consideration (e.g., royalties, lump-sum payments) that is being paid by the licensee to the patent owner. The patent license must also be free of instances of patent misuse and antitrust violations.

The ownership of an invention and any patent covering it originally lies with the inventor. The inventor can then assign his or her ownership of the invention and patent to another party or retain ownership and license the patent to another party. If the inventor retains ownership of the patent, nothing more is required to evidence this ownership because the patent itself will issue in the inventor's name. If the inventor transfers ownership, a written patent assignment should be executed by the inventor and recorded with the USPTO.

If the inventor decides to license rather than assign the patented invention, a written license agreement is needed. The license agreement should be executed by both the inventor, as patent owner, and the licensee. Patent licenses usually are not filed for recording with the USPTO.

The licensor grants permission to the licensee through a patent license to practice under the licensed patent within certain respects. The licensor can give or grant the licensee permission to make, use, sell, or import the patented invention. In granting a license, the licensor can do so on an "exclusive" or "nonexclusive" basis. Under an exclusive license, the licensor agrees to license the patented invention only to the licensee. The licensor also typically gives up his or her own right to practice the patented invention under an exclusive license. Thus, the patent owner, as licensor, must be keenly aware that the grant of an exclusive license will result in his or her inability to manufacture or sell the patented invention, unless such a right is expressly reserved by the licensor. In granting a license on a nonexclusive basis, the licensor remains free to grant licenses to others.

In addition to granting a license on an exclusive or nonexclusive basis, a licensor can also limit the license according to a specific activity known as "field of use" or "territory." For example, the patent license can be divided into the rights to make, to use, to sell, or to import. The license can grant the right to use, but not the right to make or sell. The field of use can also be divided. For example, an inventor of a patent on a drug can license the patent to one party to produce medicine for humans and to another party to produce medicine for animals. The inventor, as licensor, can also grant a patent license for a limited and specific geographic territory, such as by city, state, region, or country.

The licensor and licensee must also consider the duration of the patent license. The patent license can be for any period of time through the life of the patent. If the license does not specify the duration, the license is good for the term of the patent. In practical terms, duration is dependent on the life of the patent, the commercialization plans of the licensee, the market trends, and relative obsolescence of the patented technology. There are restrictions on the period for which royalties can be charged under a patent license. A patent license that provides for payment of royalties after the expiration of the patent would be in violation of the federal antitrust laws.

One of the paramount factors to a licensor in licensing his or her patent is the amount the licensor will be paid as consideration for the license grant. As mentioned earlier, payment to a licensor by a licensee in exchange for a license grant is typically in the form of a running royalty. A common question raised by most licensors in evaluating a patent license is "What royalty should be charged?" There is generally no magic rate of royalty. The amount of royalty is determined by many factors that may include the custom of the industry for which the patent or invention will be used; whether the licensee is getting an exclusive or nonexclusive license; whether the license includes other rights like trademarks, know-how, or technical assistance; whether the license limits the licensor's use of the patent or invention; and whether the size of the market for the invention and its pricing is sufficient to accommodate the royalty charged for the license.

Royalty payments are usually made on a "paid-up" basis or a "running-royalty" basis. A paid-up basis of payment for a license typically pays the licensor a one-time, lump-sum amount for an irrevocable license for the life of the patent. This is different from the running royalty basis of payment, where payments are made over time usually as a percentage of the net sales of products covered by the licensed patent. Payment by the running royalty basis can also include an up-front payment to the licensor, which may or may not be creditable against running royalties. Running royalties in patent licenses are usually structured as a percentage of defined net sales, net profits, or production output on a monthly, quarterly, semiannually, or other periodic basis.

It is also important that the licensor consider the following issues in structuring the royalty arrangement:

- the time and frequency of royalty payments;
- the requirement that the licensee keep accurate and complete accounting records;
- the right of the licensor to inspect the licensee's records;
- definition of the net sales or net profits against which the royalties are to be calculated; and
- the requirement that the licensee pay annual minimum royalties.

Many other terms and conditions can be included in the patent license, but the license must avoid provisions that violate the antitrust laws or constitute patent misuse. It has already been explained that a patent license cannot provide for royalty payments after the patent has expired. In addition, the patent license must avoid illegal price fixing between the licensor and licensee and tying arrangements, such as one where the licensee would be required to purchase unpatented products from the licensor to maintain the patent license; this is considered patent misuse.

Selecting the right licensee is essential to being successful in licensing your patented invention. Grant licenses only to reputable companies that are seriously committed to commercializing and marketing the invention. Being viewed as a leader in a particular market or industry, possessing an entrepreneurial spirit, being receptive to new ideas, and having the demonstrated ability to successfully launch new products are attributes to be considered in the selection of a licensee.

NEGOTIATING A PATENT LICENSE

Even if the inventor is able to successfully prepare and prosecute a patent application, it may be more difficult for an inventor who is inexperienced in the art of negotiation and lacking in legal and business acumen to handle a transaction to license the invention. While licensing is presented as a basic procedure in this chapter, it can in practice be difficult and complex. To the extent that your licensing deal takes on complex issues different from those outlined in this chapter, it is advisable that you hire a patent attorney to assist in the structuring and review of your license transaction. If you have a good patent and an invention that is extremely marketable, you will find that any cost invested in hiring an attorney to assist in the protection of your interest at the negotiation table will far outweigh the agony of negotiating a bad deal on your own.

You negotiate every day; you negotiate any time you deal with another person to obtain something that you want. You negotiate at work with supervisors, co-workers, customers, suppliers, government officials; at home with your spouse, parents, children, neighbors, and friends; and elsewhere with salespeople, auto dealers, merchants, and others. Being able to negotiate effectively is an important part of successfully licensing and profiting from your patented invention.

The ability to negotiate successfully requires creativity and good people skills. Negotiating also requires persistence, endurance, patience, organization, risk-taking, vision, and high ethical values. Nearly everyone can be an effective negotiator given the right preparation and knowledge of negotiating principles.

Three basic principles emerge from studying top negotiators. The first principle is "be soft on people, hard on ideas." This means that, as a negotiator, you should separate emotions from issues. This will help maintain a cooperative relationship between both parties. The second principle is "focus your attention on the major relevant issues and the desires and intentions behind the issues." The objective is to discover what each party really wants so that you can understand the actual needs of the parties and seek to create multiple options to help reach an agreement. The principle is to realize that there are many ways to reach a final agreement. The basis for successful negotiation is to be highly flexible and prolific in generating options.

Effective negotiation requires that the intentions of all the parties be acceptably satisfied. Initially, this element may seem ironic. How can everybody be satisfied? Somebody has to give while the other receives. According to traditional game theory, every gain by one party must equivalently correspond to a loss by the opposing party. While this outcome may apply to certain types of games, it has no place in successful negotiations.

Without planning and gathering information, you will be at a disadvantage in any negotiation. Nowhere is the saying "information is power" more significant than in the art of negotiation. All other things being equal, the negotiating party with the most knowledge and information about his or her opponent has the advantage.

Prepare for the license negotiations by establishing your opening, target, and bottom-line positions. Be ready to explain your positions and develop a good negotiating plan beforehand.

Start the negotiation process by establishing a positive climate. Be casual, friendly, and relaxed, and try to get the other party to do the same. Prepare an agenda and review the rules of the negotiation. Begin the negotiation by discussing and trying to reach agreement on minor issues. The major issues can be addressed later, when you and the other party have developed a rapport and a positive climate for negotiating. After both parties have outlined what they want out of the negotiations, begin generating options that will satisfy the interests of both parties.

Negotiate the patent license on the basis of some reasonable, customary, and objective standard apart from the emotional wills of the parties. Negotiating on the basis of standards that are fair and objective has several advantages, as it removes the battle for dominance that occurs in most negotiations where each party tries to force the other to back down from their position. This style of negotiating reduces the potential for escalating conflict. Even when the parties cannot agree on what the objective standards should be, you can agree to search for some objective standards that are fair to both parties. This agreement alone represents a commitment to fairness that will enhance the working relationship between parties. In turn, this relationship improves the chances for an agreement that meets the interests of both parties. Using objective standards helps ensure that neither party is shafted or taken advantage of.

This, too, helps in preserving a long-term working relationship, which is important to both parties.

In summary, step-by-step procedures for conducting and concluding successful negotiations include the following suggestions:

- Establish a cooperative climate, agreeing on ground rules, an agenda, and identifying mutual outcomes
- Identify the problems and restate them in positive and resolvable terms
- Establish criteria by identifying outside objective standards and individual expectations
- Generate multiple options and evaluate these options using established criteria; agree on the best option for each issue; then develop, enhance, and refine the best options
- Summarize specific areas of agreement to obtain closure
- Establish action plans and accountability to complete negotiations within the time allotted
- Summarize consequences and options if no agreement is reached
- Acknowledge others' participation in the negotiation and thank them for their contributions; reinforce the desire for a win-win situation and a long-term relationship

Patent License Agreement

1. Parties, Addresses, and Recitals

1.1 THIS PATENT LICENSE AGREEMENT is made as of this _____ day of _____, 20___ by and between _____ (hereinafter Licensor), at _____ (Licensor's Address)_____, and _____ (hereinafter Licensee) located at _____ (Licensee's Address)___. The parties agree as follows:

1.2 Licensor is owner of United States Patent No. _____, granted _____, covering the following invention: _____

1.3 Licensee desires a (nonexclusive/exclusive) license under said United States Patent No. _____.

2. Definitions

2.1 Licensed Patent means United States Patent No. _____, granted on _____.

2.2 Licensed Product means any product which is covered by any claim of the Licensed Patent or is made by a process or machine which, at the time of such making, is covered by any claim of the Licensed Patent.

2.3 Net Selling Price in respect to Licensed Products sold means invoice price, after deduction of regular trade and quantity discounts, freight, insurance, taxes, and agents' commissions where separately identified in the invoice. Where Licensed Products are not sold, but are otherwise disposed of, Net Selling Price for the purpose of computing royalties shall be the Net Selling Price at which products of similar kind and quality, sold in similar quantities, are currently being offered for sale by Licensee. Where such products are not currently being separately offered for sale by Licensee, the Net Selling Price of Licensed Products otherwise disposed of shall be Licensee's cost of manufacture, determined by Licensee's customary accounting procedures, increased by _____ percent (____%).

3. License Grant

3.1 Licensor grants to Licensee a (nonexclusive/exclusive) license to make, use, sell, or import Licensed Product and to practice under

(Continued)

the Licensed Product throughout the United States, its territories, and possessions.

3.2   The term of the license granted to Licensee hereunder shall be for the full life of the Licensed Patent.

4. Royalties, Reports, and Payments

4.1   Licensee shall pay royalties to Licensor on Licensed Products at the rate of _____ percent (_____%) of the Net Selling Price of all such Licensed Products sold or otherwise disposed of by Licensee.

4.2   Licensee shall make written reports to Licensor within thirty (30) days after the close of each calendar quarter stating in each such report the number, description, and aggregate Net Selling Price of Licensed Products sold or otherwise disposed of by Licensee during that calendar quarter.

Concurrently with the making of each report, Licensee will pay to Licensor any and all royalties due and payable to Licensor on the Licensed Products included in the report.

4.3   Licensee shall keep adequate and accurate records showing the Licensed Products sold or otherwise disposed of; such records are to be in sufficient detail to enable the royalties payable to Licensor to be determined. Licensee shall also permit his books and records to be examined from time to time to the extent necessary to verify the reports provided for a Section 4.2, such examination to be made at the expense of Licensor by an independent auditor appointed by Licensor, who shall report to Licensor only the amount of royalty payable for the period under audit.

5. Representations and Warranties; Limitations

5.1   Licensor and Licensee each represents that he has the legal right to enter into this Patent License Agreement and to carry out his obligations hereunder.

5.2   Nothing in this Patent License Agreement shall be construed as:

  i. A warranty or representation by either party as to the validity or scope of any LICENSED PATENT; or

(Continued)

ii. A warranty or representation that anything made, used, sold, or otherwise disposed of under any license granted in this Agreement is or will be free from infringement of patents of third persons; or

iii. A requirement that either party shall file any patent application, secure any patent, or maintain any patent in force; or

iv. An obligation to bring or prosecute actions or suits against third parties for infringement of any patent; or

v. An obligation to furnish any manufacturing or technical information, or any information concerning pending patent applications; or

vi. Conferring a right to use in advertising, publicity, or otherwise any trademark or trade name of the party from which a license is received under the Agreement; or

vii. Granting by implication, estoppel, or otherwise, any licenses or rights under patents other than the LICENSE PATENT.

5.3   Neither party makes any representations, extends any warranties of any kind, either express or implied, or assumes any responsibilities whatever with respect to use, sale, or other disposition by the other party or its vendees or transferees of products incorporating or made by use of inventions licensed under this Patent License Agreement.

6. Transferability of Rights and Obligations

6.1   The license or release granted in this Patent License Agreement by Licensor in respect to the Licensed Patent shall be binding upon any successor of the Licensor in ownership or control of the Licensed Patent.

6.2   The obligations of Licensee to make reports, pay royalties, and maintain records under this agreement shall run in favor of any person or legal entity which is a successor or assignee of Licensor in respect to Licensor's benefits under this Patent License Agreement.

6.3   The license granted to Licensee under this Patent License Agreement shall pass to any assigns for the benefit of creditors of the licensed party, and to any receiver of its assets, or to any person or

(Continued)

corporation succeeding to its entire business in Licensed Products as a result of sale, consolidation, reorganization, or otherwise, provided such assignee, receiver, person, or legal entity shall, promptly, accept in writing the provisions of this Agreement and agree to become in all respects bound thereby in the place and stead of the Licensee, but this Patent License Agreement and Licensee's obligations hereunder may not otherwise be transferred without the written consent of the Licensor.

7. Terms and Termination

7.1   Unless otherwise terminated as provided in Section 7.2, this agreement shall remain in effect until the date of expiration of the Licensed Patents and shall thereupon terminate.

7.2   Licensor may terminate this Patent License Agreement at any time in the event of a default by Licensee in the due observance or performance of any covenant, condition, or limitation of this Patent License Agreement required to be performed by Licensee, but only if Licensee has not remedied its default within thirty (30) days after receipt from Licensee of written notice of such default.

8. Notices; Applicable Law; Arbitration

8.1   Any notice, report, or payment provided for in this Agreement shall be deemed sufficiently given when sent by certified or registered mail addressed to the party for whom intended at the address given at the beginning of this Agreement or at such changed address as the party shall have specified by written notice.

8.2   This Agreement shall be construed, interpreted, and applied in accordance with the laws of the State of _____.

8.3   Any controversy or claim arising under or related to this Patent License Agreement shall be settled by binding arbitration in accordance with the Rules of the American Arbitration Association before a single arbitrator selected in accordance with those rules, and judgment upon the award rendered by the arbitrator may be entered in any court having jurisdiction thereof.

(Continued)

9. Entire Agreement

9.1   This Agreement contains the entire and only agreement between the parties and supersedes all preexisting Agreements between them respecting its subject matter. Any representation, promise, or condition in connection with such subject matter which is not incorporated in this Agreement shall not be binding upon either party. No modification, renewal, extension, waive, and (except as provided in Article VII hereof) no termination of this Agreement or any of its provisions shall be binding upon the party against whom enforcement of such modification, renewal, extension, waiver, or termination is sought, unless made in writing and signed on behalf of such party by one of its executive officers. As used herein, the word "termination" includes any and all means of bringing to an end prior to its expiration by its own terms this agreement, or any provision thereof, whether by release, discharge, abandonment, or otherwise.

IN WITNESS WHEREOF, each of the parties has caused this Agreement to be executed and duly sealed in duplicate originals by its duly authorized representative.

LICENSOR   **LICENSEE**

By: _____   By: _____

Date: _____   Date: _____

CHAPTER 16

Starting a Business to Market Your Invention

One approach to commercializing your ideas or inventions is to start your own business. You may want to do all or part of the manufacturing, distribution, and marketing yourself. This approach can be difficult and time-consuming, but it can also be the most rewarding. This chapter provides essential information for evaluating and implementing your skills and resources in starting your own business.

EVALUATING YOURSELF AS A BUSINESS OWNER

Entrepreneurship may not be for everyone. You may not have the characteristics of a true entrepreneur, and you may not want to invest the time and resources that a successful business requires. To be sure about entrepreneurship, study the characteristics of successful business owners to see if you have the right traits.

Studies have shown that entrepreneurs are generally people who have high initiative, are self-confident, set long-term goals, are able to solve problems, take appropriate risks, learn from mistakes, and use all available resources. They compete with themselves and believe that success or failure lies within their personal control and influence.

Answering some basic questions about your abilities and your business endeavors can provide reality testing for your ideas. You can order a copy of the pamphlet *Checklist for Going into Business* from the SBA. Answer the questions and discuss your answers with friends and family. Or, better yet, ask several people who know you well to think carefully about you and answer the checklist for you. Have you underestimated or overestimated your abilities? Sometimes an evaluation by a friend is more useful than a self-evaluation.

The SBA offers many publications and other sources of information that may be useful to you in starting a new business. The following pamphlets are available for a small fee by writing to the Small Business Administration, PO Box 15436, Fort Worth, TX 76119:

Title	Publication No.
Thinking About Going into Business	MA 2.025
Checklist for Going into Business	MA 2.016
Ideas into Dollars	SBB 91
Selecting the Legal Structure for Your Business	MA 6.004
Marketing for Small Business	SBB 89
Keeping Records in Small Business	MA 1.017

Before starting your own business, think about what resources are available to you. Will you start by keeping your job and "moonlighting" for a while? Do you have a small nest egg, inheritance, or retirement income to live on until you get the business going? Do you have a network of contacts and possible customers through your previous lines of work, or will you be starting from scratch? Answering these questions honestly and completely will help you assess the chances of success with a new business idea.

EXAMINING YOUR BUSINESS IDEA

Now that you have come up with an invention or business idea, consider the following questions: Are there customers for my product or service? How do I know there are customers? How will I find them? Who are my competitors? What will I charge for my product or service? How will I promote my product or service? Finding the answers to these questions is the challenging and sometimes tedious homework that will help you determine your chances for success, and whether you should look for another more marketable idea. Keep in mind that a person may be able to start and operate a business, particularly a part-time one, out of his or her home.

However, developing a professional image may be hard if you work out of your home. Projecting a businesslike image is an important part of building credibility with your customers and contributing to your own professional self-image. Design a logo or have one designed, and order business cards and stationery. Set regular business hours. Use an answering machine or answering service. If other members of the family also answer the phone, make sure they know what to say. Have a businesslike office or showroom if meeting customers face to face. Consider referring to the apartment number as "suite number" or rent a post office box. Work with a website developer to set up a professional online site for your business. Such practices might improve the chance of doing business with potential customers.

The first step in creating a business is to decide what your product or service is. What are you selling? Write a short, specific statement describing your product or service. Getting a clear idea of a business concept is one of the most difficult tasks in creating a business. The statement may change several times as you experiment with the market and test your skills. Describe the product or service to family, friends, potential customers, and fellow businesspeople. Is the description clear and brief? Can you say it with confidence and enthusiasm?

Answer the question "Who will buy my product or service?" to develop and test your business idea. Make a list of potential customers, such as individuals, groups, segments of the population, or other businesses, that need the product or service. Ask friends and colleagues for help in brainstorming potential customers, markets, and uses for your product or service.

Your business planning must also include an up-to-date analysis of the competition. Analysis of the competition is important to help you plan your market position—how you will fit into the marketplace. Will the product or service be cheaper or more expensive than that of the major competitors? Will it be more durable? What benefits can be built into the product or service that the competitors don't offer? In planning your business, look for a unique product or niche that will differentiate you from strong competitors or that will make the product or service more valuable than others in the market.

As a new business owner becoming more familiar with the competition, you will also be discovering where and how to find customers.

Whatever the type of business you want to open, you will need to do market research to determine if there are buyers for your idea, where they are, and how to find them. And in the process, you will also be gathering information on pricing and competition. The more you learn about the competition, the better you will be able to decide how to position yourself in the market.

Visit the local library to compile local and county statistics on the size and makeup of the market. While at the library, check out books on marketing research. Also, check the following resources that might have data about the product or service or the people who would use it:

- *Encyclopedia of Associations*, 17th Edition. Gale Research Company, Book Tower, Detroit, Michigan.
- *Ayer Directory of Publications*. Lists trade publications by subject matter. Contact the sales, marketing, or research departments for buying patterns among their readers.
- "Survey of Buying Power." *Sales, Marketing, Management* Magazine. July issue each year.
- *Thomas Register*. Lists companies by product and service line, organized geographically and alphabetically.
- *Directory of Business, Trade and Public Policy Organizations*. US Small Business Administration, Office of Advocacy.
- Publications of the Department of Commerce. Data User Series Division, Bureau of the Census, Washington, DC.
- *County Business Patterns*. US Department of Commerce, Bureau of the Census. Available for each state.

Newspaper ads and trade magazines are other good sources of market information. Check also with the Chamber of Commerce, the county office of economic development, the Census Bureau, and businesses and professional organizations to gather market and pricing data.

Finding money to finance your new business idea can be your biggest obstacle. Most banks and financial institutions will be unwilling to lend money for a new and untested idea. You will have to rely on your own funds to a large extent to start your new business, or you may perhaps turn to a venture capitalist.

Calculate how much money it would take to develop your idea for commercialization, to set up the new business, and to operate it for two to three years. This amount will likely be your minimum capital requirement. Then, see if you can meet these requirements from your personal savings or through access to credit. Consider loans from your credit union or employer's 401(k) savings plan as relatively easy sources of credit.

Prepare a professional business plan that describes your product or service, analyzes the potential markets and customers, reviews the competitive situation, and spells out your marketing strategy.

Form a network of friends and business associates, if necessary, and have them invest money and services in your new business in exchange for part ownership. Create a network of people with diverse professional skills to handle the various technical, legal, financial, and marketing issues for your new business.

Venture capitalists are typically willing to take on the risks of financing promising new ideas. They may, however, want control of the business and a large share of the profits. You can find sources for venture capitalists at your libraries and universities. For less than $100, you can obtain information on venture capitalists by calling the Venture Capital Hotline at (408) 625-0700. To seek venture capital, you will need to prepare a good business plan that explains your business idea, the funding requirements, and its market potential.

When the marketing research is completed, it will have identified potential customers; helped discover their habits, needs, preferences, and buying cycles; and provided insight on how to reach them to generate sales.

Promotion is an overall, long-range plan designed to inform potential customers about what is being sold. Advertising is usually thought of as the paid communication part of the promotion program.

Answer these questions to develop a total promotional campaign: (1) What image or message do I want to promote? (2) What are the best media and activities for reaching my potential customers? (3) How much time and money can I spend on the effort?

Develop a long-range, consistent program for building image and reaching customers. Your image should be reflected in your business card, logo, website, stationery, brochure, newsletter, telephone answering service, signs, paid ads, and promotional activities.

Several small ads may have more impact than one large, splashy ad. Conduct a campaign rather than having a one-shot ad or event. If hiring a public relations firm, look for one that gives personal attention and develops a total marketing plan, not just a couple of ads. The plan should include market research, a profile of the target audience, a clear description of the image you want to project, the written copy, and a list of media (including cost and scheduling calendars) that are best for your product or service. Most new small business owners will probably want to set aside a certain dollar amount per year or a percentage of past, current, or projected sales for paid advertising.

CHOOSING YOUR FORM OF BUSINESS ORGANIZATION

One of the most important decisions a business owner will make is whether to set up the business as a sole proprietorship, a partnership, or a corporation. Note, however, that as a small business owner you essentially risk it all, no matter what form of business organization you choose. Although most small businesses are sole proprietorships or partnerships, a comparison of the advantages and disadvantages of each type of organization should be made.

A sole proprietorship is the least costly way of starting a business. You can form a sole proprietorship by finding a location and opening the door for business. There are the usual fees for registering the business name and for legal work in changing zoning restrictions and obtaining necessary licenses. Attorney's fees for starting a sole proprietorship will be less than for the other forms because less document preparation is required.

Here are some advantages and disadvantages of the sole proprietorship:

Advantages
- Easiest to get started
- Greatest freedom of action
- Maximum authority
- Income tax advantages in very small firms
- Social Security advantage to owner

Disadvantages
- Unlimited liability
- Death or illness endanger business
- Growth limited to owner's energies
- Personal affairs easily mixed with business

A partnership can be formed by simply making an oral agreement between two or more people, although such informality is not recommended. Legal fees for drawing up a partnership agreement are higher than those for a sole proprietorship, but the fees may be lower than those for incorporating. Partners would be wise, however, to consult an attorney to have a partnership agreement drafted to help resolve future disputes.

Here are some advantages and disadvantages of the partnership form of business:

Advantages	Disadvantages
• Two heads better than one	• Difficult to transfer interest
• Additional sources of venture capital	• Death, withdrawal, or bankruptcy of one partner endangers business
• Better credit rating than corporation of similar size	• Personal liability for partnership obligations
	• Difficult to get rid of bad partner
	• Hazy line of authority

A special form of business organization is the limited partnership, which combines features of a general partnership and a corporation. With this form there must always be at least one general partner who remains personally liable for partnership liabilities. The limited partners are usually only liable up to the extent of their investment in the limited partnership. This exemption from personal liability normally continues as long as the limited partner does not participate in the management or control of the business. As many complex issues may arise with a limited partnership, it is recommended that legal counsel be obtained.

A corporation is the most complex form of business, and statutory requirements must be met to bring it into existence. A corporation is a separate legal entity that is established pursuant to state law. As a separate legal entity, a corporation can contract in its own name, hold property in its own name, and can sue and be sued in court in its own name.

The formation of a corporation requires the preparation of Articles of Incorporation, which are filed with the secretary of state in the locale where the corporation is being formed. The Articles of Incorporation usually include the name of the corporation, its location and registered agent, its purposes, the amount and classes of stocks, the first board of directors, and the names and addresses of the incorporators. Generally, once the Articles of Incorporation are filed and approved by the secretary of state, the corporation comes into existence.

You can incorporate without an attorney, but it may be unwise to do so. People may think a small family corporation does not need an attorney, but an attorney can save members of a family corporation from hard feelings and family squabbles. Attorney's fees can be expensive if organization problems are complex. The corporate form of business is usually the costliest to organize.

Here are some advantages and disadvantages of the corporate form of business:

Advantages
- Limited liability for stockholders (while true for big business, may not be for small business)
- Continuity
- Transfer of shares
- Easier to raise capital
- Possible to separate business functions into different corporations

Disadvantages
- Gives owner a false sense of security
- Heavier taxes
- Power limited by the charter
- Less freedom of activity
- Legal formalities
- More expensive to launch

A corporation is generally taxed as a separate entity, and shareholders are also taxed on corporate income paid to them as dividends. The election of Subchapter S status, however, allows an eligible corporation to escape the double taxation. The purpose of Subchapter S is to permit a "small business corporation" to elect to have its income taxed to the shareholders as if the corporation were a partnership. Subchapter S status overcomes the double taxation of corporate income, and permits the shareholders to have the benefit of offsetting business losses by the corporation against the income of the shareholders. An election for Subchapter S status requires that the corporation file Form 2553 with the Internal Revenue Service.

LAWS AFFECTING YOUR BUSINESS

Most localities have registration and licensing requirements that will apply to business owners. A license is a formal permission to practice a certain business activity, issued by a local, state, or federal government. The activities may be the type of business that requires a permit from the local authorities. There is often a small fee for licenses and permits (usually $15 to $25). A license may require an examination to certify that the recipient is qualified. The business name must usually be registered, and an appropriate tax number must be obtained. Separate business telephones and bank accounts are recommended. If there are employees, the business owner is responsible for withholding income and social security taxes. The business owner is also responsible for paying worker's compensation and unemployment insurance and complying with minimum wage and employee health laws.

If your operations are intrastate, you will be concerned primarily with state and local, rather than federal, licensing. Businesses frequently subject to state or local control are retail food establishments, nightclubs and taverns, barber shops, beauty shops, plumbing firms, and taxi companies. These are primarily service businesses and are subject to regulations for the protection of public health and morals. An attorney can help make sure that you have complied with all licensing and permit requirements. Depending on the type of business, you may have to comply with building and safety codes, too.

Think twice about the liabilities of operating without proper licenses and registrations. If you begin to advertise or make the news, you will probably hear from a local official. You will pay with embarrassment, time, and money if your business is not properly licensed.

If you find legal regulations, permits, and licenses confusing, make sure you find some way to get the information you need in order to operate legally. You can get help from your attorney, accountant, business partner, or even your local librarian. Complying with legal regulations is not an aspect of business operations that can be delayed until you "get around to it." Your business reputation and financial standing are at stake.

WORKING WITH PROFESSIONALS

Even the smallest and newest business needs help from at least two kinds of specialists, an attorney and an accountant. Depending on the type of business and your skills, from time to time, you may need the advice of professionals, such as a direct mail or marketing specialist, an insurance representative, a management consultant, a computer specialist, a realtor, or a public relations expert.

Several guidelines will hold true, no matter what type of expert you are dealing with. Interview professionals to see whether you will be comfortable working with them. Make sure they provide the service you need, agree on the working relationship, and state appropriate fees. Be completely honest about your business situation. Advice based on partial or incorrect information is no advice at all. If the business is having problems, don't be embarrassed. If the sales are down, give the experts all the available information and work as a team to solve the problem. If business is good, don't be afraid that professionals will steal ideas or expect a raise. Build a trusting, businesslike relationship. Expect the professionals to spend some time teaching and explaining complex concepts. But don't expect to be spoon-fed decisions or to delegate all decisions to them. Take a course at the local community college in recordkeeping and taxes or in public relations to develop more skill in your areas of inexperience. Keep appointments and pay bills promptly.

To find an attorney who is familiar with businesses of your size and type, ask for referrals from business colleagues, your accountants, the local Chamber of Commerce, your bankers, or some other trusted source. Some local bar associations run an attorney referral and information service. Some services provide only names, while others give information on experience and fees to help match needs to the attorney's background and charges.

An attorney can help decide which is the most advantageous business structure (sole proprietorship, partnership, or corporation). He or she can help with zoning, permit, or licensing problems; health inspection problems; unpaid bills, contracts, and agreements; patents, trademarks, and copyright protection; and some tax problems. Because there is always the possibility of a lawsuit, claim, or other legal action against your business, it is wise to have an attorney who is already familiar with the business before a crisis arises. An attorney experienced with your type of venture could also advise on laws, programs, and agencies—federal, state, or local—that help small businesses through loans, grants, procurement set-a-sides, counseling, and other means. He or she can tell you about unexpected legal opportunities and pitfalls that can affect the business.

In choosing an attorney, his or her experiences and fees should be related. One attorney may charge an hourly rate that, at first, looks cheaper than that of another. However, because of a lack of experience in some area, the less expensive attorney may charge a larger fee by the time the service is provided. Ask your attorney for a résumé and check with references. If you feel overwhelmed with the process, take a trusted friend to the initial meeting to help you keep on track as you interview the attorney about services and fees.

If a law firm is retained, be sure to understand who will work on the case and who will supervise the work. If junior attorneys handle the work, the fees should be lower. This arrangement is usually fine as long as an experienced attorney reviews the case periodically.

Tell the attorney that you expect to be informed of all developments and consulted before any decisions are made. You may also want to receive copies of all documents, letters, and memos written and received in the case or have a chance to read them in the attorney's office.

Ask the attorney to estimate the timetable and costs of the work. You may consider placing a periodic ceiling on fees, after which the attorney will call before proceeding to do work that would add to the bill. Always have a written retainer agreement describing what you and your attorney expect of each other.

Most businesses fail not for lack of good ideas or goodwill, but rather for lack of financial expertise and planning. Look for an accountant as you would an attorney. Get referrals from trusted friends, business associations, or professional organizations. Discuss fees in advance, and draw up a written agreement about how you will work together. Accountants (along with an attorney) can advise about initial business decisions, such as the form of the business. They can also help set up the books, draw up and analyze profit-and-loss statements, advise on financial decisions, and give advice on cash requirements for the startup phase. Accountants can make budget forecasts, help prepare financial information for a loan application, and handle tax matters.

Accounting firms offer a variety of services. If accounting is not an easy area for you as a business owner, the fees you pay will be well worth it. Most accounting firms maintain books of original entry, prepare bank reconciliation statements and post the general ledger, prepare balance sheets and income statements on a quarterly or semiannual basis, and design and implement various accounting and recordkeeping systems. They will also get federal and state withholding numbers, give instructions on where and when to file tax returns, prepare tax returns, and do general tax planning for the small businessperson.

As a business owner, your accountant is your key financial advisor. The accountant should alert you to potential danger areas, advise you on how to handle growth spurts, help you to best plan for times of slow business, and direct you on how to financially nurture and protect your business future.

MAINTAINING YOUR BUSINESS RECORDS

Keeping accurate and up-to-date business records is, for many people, the most difficult and uninteresting aspect of operating a small business. If this area of business management is one that you anticipate will be hard for you, plan now for how you will cope with it. Don't wait until tax time or until business transactions are totally confused. Take a course on recordkeeping at the local community college, ask a volunteer SCORE* (Service Corps of Retired Executives) representative from the SBA to help you in the beginning, or hire an accountant to give advice on setting up and maintaining a recordkeeping system.

Business records will be used to prepare tax returns, make business decisions, and apply for loans. Set aside a special time each day to update business records. Keeping up-to-date, accurate records will pay off in the long run with more deductions and fewer headaches.

If the business is small or related to an activity that is usually considered a hobby, it's even more important that good records be kept. The Internal Revenue Service may decide that the activity is only a hobby, and deductions for expenses or losses from income produced at home would not be allowed at tax time. So, as a business owner, keep records of all transactions, which include spending or earning money.

The business records should tell how much cash is owed, how much cash is due, and how much cash is on hand. A business owner should keep these basic records:

- A check register to record each check disbursed, the date of disbursement, the number of the check, to whom it was made out (the payee), the amount of money disbursed, and for what purpose.
- Cash receipts to show the amount of money received from whom, and for what.
- A sales journal to record each business transaction, the date of the transaction, for whom it was performed, the amount of the invoice, and the sales tax, if applicable. The journal may be divided to indicate labor and goods.
- A voucher register to record bills, money owed, the date of the bill, to whom it is owed, the amount owed, and for what service.
- A general journal as a means of adjusting some entries in the other four journals.

Business records should be set up to reflect the amount and type of activity in the particular business. There are a wide range of prepackaged recordkeeping systems. The pamphlet *Small Business Bibliography*, No. 15, from the SBA lists many such systems. The most useful system for a small business is usually based on what is called the "One-Write System." It captures information at the time the transaction takes place. One-Write Systems are efficient because they eliminate the need for re-copying the data and are compatible with electronic data processing if the business is computerized.

Even though the business may be small and just beginning, it is wise to consult an accountant to help decide which recordkeeping system is best for the business. Once it is set up, record the daily transactions in the general ledger and prepare financial statements for the business.

Establish a separate bank account for the business—even before the first sale. Then you will have a complete and distinct record of your income and expenditures for tax purposes, and you won't have to remember which expenses were business and which were personal.

Choosing a recordkeeping system you understand and will use is important. The records will help you see how well the business is doing, which is the first step toward responsible financial management.

LEARNING FROM EXPERIENCE AND NETWORKING

Successful business owners learn from experience—their own experiences and those of others. In a study of entrepreneurial personality characteristics, it was noted that successful entrepreneurs are disappointed but not discouraged by failure. They use failures as learning experiences and try to understand their role in causing the failure in order to avoid similar problems in the future. Furthermore, the study found that entrepreneurs seek and use feedback on their performance in order to take corrective action and improve.

As an entrepreneur, you can learn from experience in several ways. You can work closely and creatively with professional advisors, such as your attorney and accountant. As you continually review your business records, you will see mistakes, but you will also begin to develop skill in planning and managing.

You will continue to learn about all areas of business operations, constantly acquiring new ideas. Most community colleges have short, inexpensive, practical courses for business owners in topics such as "Financing Small Business," "Choosing a Small Business Computer," and "Starting and Operating a Home-Based Business."

Get to know other business owners with similar needs or problems. Talking with others can be a way to avoid repeating the mistakes they have made and to benefit from their experience. Local and national organizations offer memberships, social events, networking opportunities, newsletters, and seminars for small business owners. Advertise your product or service to other business owners through these organizations. They can also provide a way to learn about services you may need, such as accounting, public relations, or a responsible secretarial service.

These organizations may offer updates in such areas as taxes and zoning in their newsletters and workshops.

Whatever your current business problems, there is likely to be a solution. Somewhere there is information, a book, a person, an organization, or a government agency that can help. A word of warning though: Finding resources and building networks can be very time-consuming. Joining organizations can turn out to be expensive, especially if you are too busy to use their services and support once you join.

Use the following list or organize a search for useful resources, then pick and choose carefully what to read, join, buy, or attend.

- **Public Libraries:** Visit the local library and become familiar with its resources. In addition to books, many libraries offer free workshops, lend skill-building video or audio recordings, and are a place to pick up catalogues and brochures describing continuing education opportunities for business owners. Ask the librarian for current copies of zoning regulations. Become familiar with new books and resources in pertinent fields (computers, health care, crafts, etc.) as well as in business skills (advertising techniques, financing, etc.). Look for magazines such as *In Business, Black Enterprise, Venture,* or *The Journal of Small Business Management*. Reading selectively is free. Subscribing to too many magazines may be expensive.

- **Organizations:** A wide variety of local and national organizations have sprung up to serve the informational, lobbying, and networking needs of business entrepreneurs. Through meetings, services, or newsletters, groups such as the National Association of Women Business Owners, American Entrepreneurs Association, Business of Professional Women's Club, National Alliance of Home-Based Businesswomen, and the National Association for Cottage Industry offer members everything from camaraderie to valuable "perks," such as group rates on health insurance. David Gumpert's book, *The Insider's Guide to Small Business Resources*, provides addresses for many of these groups and other information on such resources.

- **Government Resources:** Contact the local or district office of the SBA to learn about their services and publications. The SBA also offers free or inexpensive workshops and counseling through SCORE[.]. As mentioned earlier, SCORE[.] is a volunteer program sponsored by the SBA through which retired executives who have management expertise are linked with owners and managers of small businesses or prospective entrepreneurs who need help.

- **Additional Government Resources:** The Department of Commerce, Bureau of the Census, Department of Defense (procurement), Department of Labor, Internal Revenue Service (ask for the free "Business Tax Kit"), FTC, and the GPO all have publications and services to inform and support small businesses. Local and state government offices may also provide services and assistance. Addresses are available in the telephone book under US Government, at the public library, at the SBA office, or online.

- **Community Colleges:** Most community colleges offer short, inexpensive, noncredit programs for entrepreneurs. The classes usually are convenient to business owners and are taught by experienced owners and managers.

If you are an owner of a small business, particularly if you operate from your home, you can overcome feelings of isolation and give and receive valuable information through networks and other resources. Being active in professional and trade associations will help you build a good marketing network for your business's service or product. Take the time and invest the money for memberships. Then, continually evaluate which organizations and resources best serve your business information and networking needs.

Appendix

35 UNITED STATES CODE
§101. Inventions patentable

Whoever invents or discovers any new and useful process, machine, manufacture, or composition of matter, or any new and useful improvement thereof, may obtain a patent therefor, subject to the conditions and requirements of this title.

§102. Conditions for patentability; novelty (Amended effective March 16, 2013)

(a) Novelty; Prior Art

A person shall be entitled to a patent unless—

1. the claimed invention was patented, described in a printed publication, or in public use, on sale, or otherwise available to the public before the effective filing date of the claimed invention; or
2. the claimed invention was described in a patent issued under section 151, or in an application for patent published or deemed published under section 122(b), in which the patent or application, as the case may be, names another inventor and was effectively filed before the effective filing date of the claimed invention.

(b) Exceptions

1. DISCLOSURES MADE 1 YEAR OR LESS BEFORE THE EFFECTIVE FILING DATE OF THE CLAIMED INVENTION

   A disclosure made 1 year or less before the effective filing date of a claimed invention shall not be prior art to the claimed invention under subsection (a)(1) if—

   A. the disclosure was made by the inventor or joint inventor or by another who obtained the subject matter disclosed directly or indirectly from the inventor or a joint inventor; or

   B. the subject matter disclosed had, before such disclosure, been publicly disclosed by the inventor or a joint inventor or another who obtained the subject matter disclosed directly or indirectly from the inventor or a joint inventor.

2. DISCLOSURES APPEARING IN APPLICATIONS AND PATENTS

   A disclosure shall not be prior art to a claimed invention under subsection (a)(2) if—

   A. the subject matter disclosed was obtained directly or indirectly from the inventor or a joint inventor;

   B. the subject matter disclosed had, before such subject matter was effectively filed under subsection (a)(2), been publicly disclosed by the inventor or a joint inventor or another who obtained the subject matter disclosed directly or indirectly from the inventor or a joint inventor; or

   C. the subject matter disclosed and the claimed invention, not later than the effective filing date of the claimed invention, were owned by the same person or subject to an obligation of assignment to the same person.

(c) Patents and Published Applications Effective as Prior Art

For purposes of determining whether a patent or application for patent is prior art to a claimed invention under subsection (a)(2), such patent or application shall be considered to have been effectively filed, with respect to any subject matter described in the patent or application—

1. if paragraph (2) does not apply, as of the actual filing date of the patent or the application for patent; or

2. if the patent or application for patent is entitled to claim a right of priority under section 119, 365(a), or 365(b), or to claim the benefit of an earlier filing date under section 120, 121, or 365(c), based upon 1 or more prior filed applications for patent, as of the filing date of the earliest such application that describes the subject matter.

§103. Conditions for patentability, nonobvious subject matter (Amended effective March 16, 2013)

A patent for a claimed invention may not be obtained, notwithstanding that the claimed invention is not identically disclosed as set forth in section 102, if the differences between the claimed invention and the prior art are such that the claimed invention as a whole would have been obvious before the effective filing date of the claimed invention to a person having ordinary skill in the art to which the claimed invention pertains. Patentability shall not be negatived by the manner in which the invention was made.

§112. Specification

This specification shall contain a written description of the invention, and of the manner and process of making and using it, in such full, clear, concise, and exact terms as to enable any person skilled in the art to which it pertains, or with which it is most nearly connected, to make and use the same, and shall set forth the best mode contemplated by the inventor of carrying out his invention.

The specification shall conclude with one or more claims particularly pointing out and distinctly claiming the subject matter which the applicant regards as his invention.

§ 271. Infringement of patent

(a) Except as otherwise provided in this title, whoever without authority makes, uses, offers to sell, or sells any patented invention within the United States or imports into the United States any patented invention during the term of the patent therefor, infringes the patent.

(b) Whoever actively induces infringement of a patent shall be liable as an infringer.

(c) Whoever offers to sell or sells within the United States or imports into the United State a component of a patented machine, manufacture, combination or composition, or a material or apparatus for use in practicing a patented process, constituting a material part of the invention, knowing the same to be especially made or especially adapted for use in an infringement of such patent, and not a staple article or commodity of commerce suitable for substantial noninfringing use, shall be liable as a contributory infringer.

(d) No patent owner otherwise entitled to relief for infringement or contributory infringement of a patent shall be denied relief or deemed guilty of misuse or illegal extension of the patent right by reason of his having done one or more of the following: (1) derived revenue from acts which if performed by another without his consent would constitute contributory infringement of the patent; (2) licensed or authorized another to perform acts which if performed without his consent would constitute contributory infringement of the patent; (3) sought to enforce his patent rights against infringement or contributory infringement; (4) refused to license or use any rights to the patent; or (5) conditioned the license of any rights to the patent or sale of the patented product on the acquisition of a license to rights in another patent or purchase of a separate product, unless, in view of the circumstances, the patent owner has market power in the relevant market for the patent or patented product on which the license or sale is conditioned.

(e) (1) It shall not be an act of infringement to make, use, offer to sell, or sell within the United States or imports into the United States a patented invention (other than a new animal drug or veterinary biological product (as those terms are used in the Federal Food, Drug, and Cosmetic Act and the Act of March

4, 1913) which is primarily manufactured using recombinant DNA, recombinant RNA, hybridoma technology, or other processes involving site specific genetic manipulation techniques) solely for uses reasonably related to the development and submission of information under a federal law which regulates the manufacture, use, or sale of drugs or veterinary biological products. . . .

(f) (1) Whoever without authority supplies or causes to be supplied in or from the United States all or a substantial portion of the components of a patented invention, where such components are uncombined in whole or in part, in such manner as to actively induce the combination of such components outside of the United States in a manner that would infringe the patent if such combination occurred within the United States, shall be liable as an infringer. (2) Whoever without authority supplies or causes to be supplied in or from the United States any component of a patented invention that is especially made or especially adapted for use in the invention and not a staple article or commodity of commerce suitable for substantial noninfringing use, where such component is uncombined in whole or in part, knowing that such component is so made or adapted and intending that such component will be combined outside of the United States in a manner that would infringe the patent if such combination occurred within the United States, shall be liable as an infringer.

(g) Whoever without authority imports into the United States or offers to sell, sells or uses within the United States a product which is made by a process patented in the United States shall be liable as an infringer, if the importation, offer to sell, sale, or use of the product occurs during the term of such process patent. In an action for infringement of a process patent, no remedy may be granted for infringement on account of the noncommercial use or retail sale of a product unless there is no adequate remedy under this title for infringement on account of the importation or other use, offer to sell, or sale of that product. A product which is made by a patented process will, for purposes of this title, not be considered to be so made after (1) it is materially changed by subsequent processes; or (2) it becomes a trivial and nonessential component of another product.

§ 284. Damages

Upon finding for the claimant the court shall award the claimant damages adequate to compensate for the infringement but in no event less than a reasonable royalty for the use made of the invention by the infringer, together with interest and costs as fixed by the court. When the damages are not found by a jury, the court shall assess them. In either event the court may increase the damages up to three times the amount found or assessed. The court may receive expert testimony as an aid to the determination of damages or of what royalty would be reasonable under the circumstances.

§ 285. Attorney fees

The court in exceptional cases may award reasonable attorney fees to the prevailing party.

US Patent Office fees[1]

Patent Application Filing Fees				
37 Code of Federal Regulations	Description	Fee	Small Entity Fee	Micro Entity Fee
1.16(a)	Basic filing fee—Utility (paper filing—also requires non-electronic filing fee under 1.16(t))	280.00	140.00	70.00
1.16(a)	Basic filing fee—Utility (electronic filing)	280.00	70.00	70.00
1.16(b)	Basic filing fee—Design	180.00	90.00	45.00
1.16(b)	Basic filing fee—Design (CPA)	180.00	90.00	45.00
1.16(c)	Basic filing fee—Plant	180.00	90.00	45.00
1.16(d)	Provisional application filing fee	260.00	130.00	65.00
1.16(e)	Basic filing fee—Reissue	280.00	140.00	70.00

---

1   These fees are also available at: www.uspto.gov/learning-and-resources/fees -and-payment/uspto-fee-schedule#PatentFees

1.16(e)	Basic filing fee—Reissue (CPA)	280.00	140.00	70.00
1.16(f)	Surcharge—Late filing fee, search fee, examination fee or oath or declaration, or application filed without at least one claim or by reference	140.00	70.00	35.00
1.16(g)	Surcharge—Late provisional filing fee or cover sheet	60.00	30.00	15.00
1.16(h)	Each independent claim in excess of three	420.00	210.00	105.00
1.16(h)	Each reissue independent claim in excess of three	420.00	210.00	105.00
1.16(i)	Each claim in excess of 20	80.00	40.00	20.00
1.16(i)	Each reissue claim in excess of 20	80.00	40.00	20.00
1.16(j)	Multiple dependent claim	780.00	390.00	195.00
1.16(s)	Utility Application Size Fee—for each additional 50 sheets that exceeds 100 sheets	400.00	200.00	100.00
1.16(s)	Design Application Size Fee—for each additional 50 sheets that exceeds 100 sheets	400.00	200.00	100.00
1.16(s)	Plant Application Size Fee—for each additional 50 sheets that exceeds 100 sheets	400.00	200.00	100.00
1.16(s)	Reissue Application Size Fee—for each additional 50 sheets that exceeds 100 sheets	400.00	200.00	100.00
1.16(s)	Provisional Application Size Fee—for each additional 50 sheets that exceeds 100 sheets	400.00	200.00	100.00
1.16(t)	Non-electronic filing fee — Utility (additional fee for applications filed in paper)	400.00	200.00	200.00
1.17(i)(1)	Non-English translation	140.00	70.00	35.00

Patent Search Fees				
37 Code of Federal Regulations	Description	Fee	Small Entity Fee	Micro Entity Fee
1.16(k)	Utility Search Fee	600.00	300.00	150.00
1.16(l)	Design Search Fee	120.00	60.00	30.00
1.16(m)	Plant Search Fee	380.00	190.00	95.00
1.16(n)	Reissue Search Fee	600.00	300.00	150.00

Patent Examination Fees				
37 Code of Federal Regulations	**Description**	**Fee**	**Small Entity Fee**	**Micro Entity Fee**
1.16(o)	Utility Examination Fee	720.00	360.00	180.00
1.16(p)	Design Examination Fee	460.00	230.00	115.00
1.16(q)	Plant Examination Fee	580.00	290.00	145.00
1.16(r)	Reissue Examination Fee	2,160.00	1,080.00	540.00

PCT Fees—National Stage				
37 Code of Federal Regulations	**Description**	**Fee**	**Small Entity Fee**	**Micro Entity Fee**
1.492(a)	Basic National Stage Fee	280.00	140.00	70.00
1.492(b)(1)	National Stage Search Fee—US was the ISA or IPEA and all claims satisfy PCT Article 33(1)-(4)	0.00	0.00	0.00
1.492(b)(2)	National Stage Search Fee—US was the ISA	120.00	60.00	30.00
1.492(b)(3)	National Stage Search Fee—search report prepared and provided to USPTO	480.00	240.00	120.00
1.492(b)(4)	National Stage Search Fee—all other situations	600.00	300.00	150.00
1.492(c)(1)	National Stage Examination Fee—US was the ISA or IPEA and all claims satisfy PCT Article 33(1)-(4)	0.00	0.00	0.00
1.492(c)(2)	National Stage Examination Fee—all other situations	720.00	360.00	180.00
1.492(d)	Each independent claim in excess of three	420.00	210.00	105.00
1.492(e)	Each claim in excess of 20	80.00	40.00	20.00
1.492(f)	Multiple dependent claim	780.00	390.00	195.00
1.492(h)	Search fee, examination fee or oath or declaration after the date of commencement of the national stage	140.00	70.00	35.00
1.492(i)	English translation after thirty months from priority date	140.00	70.00	35.00
1.492(j)	National Stage Application Size Fee—for each additional 50 sheets that exceeds 100 sheets	400.00	200.00	100.00

References

US Patent and Trademark Office Publications and Reference Materials

Manual of Patent Examining Procedure, US Government Printing Office, mpep.uspto.gov/RDMS/detail/manual/MPEP/e8r9/d0e18.xml

Patents and How to Get One: A Practical Handbook, US Dept. of Commerce, 2008

PCT Applicants Guide, www.wipo.int/pct/guide/en/gdvol1/pdf/gdvol1.pdf

Title 37—Code of Federal Regulations: Patents, Trademarks, and Copyrights, www.uspto.gov/web/offices/pac/mpep/consolidated_rules.pdf

United States Code Title 35 - Patents, www.uspto.gov/web/offices/pac/mpep/consolidated_laws.pdf

USPTO Fees, www.uspto.gov/web/offices/ac/qs/ope/fee092611.htm

USPTO Forms, www.uspto.gov/forms/index.jsp

USPTO Patent Process, www.uspto.gov/patents/process/index.jsp

USPTO PCT Process: www.uspto.gov/sites/default/files/patents/process/file/efs/guidance/indexing-pct-new-appl.pdf

WIPO PCT Filing guide: www.wipo.int/pct/en/filing/filing.html

Books

Brunsvold, Brian. *Drafting Patent Licensing Agreements*. 6th ed. Washington, DC: Bureau of National Affairs, 2008.

Faber, Robert C., and Landis, John L. *Landis on Mechanics of Patent Claim Drafting*. 4th ed. New York: Practicing Law Institute, 1997.

Hanellin, Elizabeth, Jacobs, Alan J. and Anne Marie Greene. *Patents Throughout the World*. New York: Clark Boardman Callaghan, 1989.

Klein, Bernard T. *Guide to American Directories*. 13th ed. B. Klein Publications, 1994.

McCarthy, J. T. *McCarthy's Desk Encyclopedia of Intellectual Property*. Washington, DC: Bureau of National Affairs, 1995.

Paige, Richard E. *Complete Guide to Making Money with Your Ideas and Inventions*. Mindsight Publishing, 1986.

Patent Licensing Transactions. New York: Matthew Bender, 2009.

Reese, Harvey. *How to License Your Million Dollar Idea*. New York: Wiley, 2002.

Thomas Register of American Manufacturers. New York: Thomas Publishing Co.

White, Robert A., and Caldwell, Rodney K., *Patent Litigation: Procedure and Tactics*. New York: Matthew Bender, 1971.

Wilson, Lee. *The Copyright Guide*. New York: Allworth Press, 1996.

Wilson, Lee. *The Trademark Guide*. New York: Allworth Press, 1996.

Resources for Inventors

Business Know-How
Phone: (631) 467-8883
www.businessknowhow.com

Intellectual Property Owners
1501 M Street, NW, Suite 1150
Washington, DC 20005
Phone: (202) 507-4500
www.ipo.org

Inventor's Digest Online
520 Elliot Street, Suite 200
Charlotte, NC 28202
Phone: (704) 369-7312
www.inventorsdigest.com

Minnesota Inventors Congress
500 Airport Road, Suite 211A
Redwood Falls, MN 56283
Phone: (800) 468-3681
www.minnesotainventorscongress.org

National Congress of Inventor Organizations
8306 Wilshire Boulevard, Suite 391
Beverly Hills, CA 90211
Phone: (800) 458-5624
www.nationalcongressofinventororganizations.org
www.inventionconvention.com

Pratt's Guide to Private Equity and Venture Capital Sources,
Thomson Reuters
Phone: (646) 223-4431
www.prattsguide.com

SCORE
www.score.org

Small Business Ideas and Resources for Entrepreneurs
Phone: (800) 234-0999
www.inc.com

Small Business Resources
www.smallbusinessresources.com

The United Inventors Association
1025 Connecticut Avenue, Suite 1000
Washington, DC 20036
www.uiausa.org

The US Small Business Administration
www.sba.gov

Additional Internet Resources for Inventors

www.delphion.com
www.edisonnation.com
www.inventions.org
www.lambertinvent.com
www.landis-ip.com
www.startupnation.com
www.thomsoninnovation.com

Index

Books from Allworth Press

The Art of Digital Branding (Revised Edition)
by Ian Cocoran (6 × 9, 272 pages, paperback, $19.95)

Brand Thinking and Other Noble Pursuits
by Debbie Millman (6 × 9, 336 pages, paperback, $19.95)

Business and Legal Forms for Graphic Designers
by Tad Crawford and Eva Doman Bruck (8½ × 11, paperback, 256 pages, $29.95)

The Copyright Guide (Fourth Edition)
by Lee Wilson (6 × 9, 288 pages, hardcover, $24.99)

Corporate Creativity
by Thomas Lockwood and Thomas Walton (6 × 9, 256 pages, paperback $24.95)

Design Thinking
by Thomas Lockwood (6 × 9, 304 pages, paperback, $24.95)

The Elements of Logo Design
by Alex W. White with Foreword by Jerry Kuyper (8 × 10, 224 pages, hardcover, $34.99)

Emotional Branding
by Marc Gobé with Foreword by Sergio Zyman (6 × 9, 352 pages, paperback, $19.95)

From Idea to Exit (Revised Edition)
by Jeffrey Weber (6 × 9, 272 pages, paperback, $19.95)

Infectious
by Achim Nowak (5½ × 8¼, 224 pages, paperback, $19.95)

Intentional Leadership
by Jane A. G. Kise (7 × 10, 224 pages, paperback, $19.95)

Legal Forms for Everyone (Sixth Edition)
by Carl Battle (8 × 11, 280 pages, paperback, $24.99)

Legal Guide for the Visual Artist (Fifth Edition)
by Tad Crawford (8½ × 11, 304 pages, paperback, $29.95)

Millennial Rules
by T. Scott Gross (6 × 9, 176 pages, paperback, $16.95)

The Pocket Small Business Owner's Guide to Building Your Business
by Kevin Devine (5¼ × 8¼, 256 pages, paperback, $14.95)

Rebuilding the Brand
by Clyde Fessler (6 × 9, 128 pages, paperback, $14.95)

The Trademark Guide (Third Edition)
by Lee Wilson (6 × 9, 256 pages, hardcover, $24.99)

To see our complete catalog or to order online, please visit *www.allworth.com*.